MILITARY POSTCARDS

1870 TO 1945

JACK H. SMITH

Cover Photos

Front

Top row:

Kaiser Wilhelm II: Portrait of a dedicated military leader. ***R3***

Edward VII as colonel in chief of the Household Cavalry. Gale and Polden. ***R3***

War and romance, a frequent combination. Visé. ***R2***

General John J. "Blackjack" Pershing. J. F. Bouchor portrait. ***R2***

Robert E. Lee, the South's leading general. Albertype. ***R2***

Second row:

A typical Civil War skirmish. Anonymous. ***R2***

German general von Mackensen; facsimile signature. B. L. ***R4***

French sentimental and patriotic card. Anonymous. ***R2***

Austrian commander in chief Hötzendorff; facsimile signature. B. L. ***R4***

Von Hindenburg, the German idol. Hermann Wolff. ***R3***

Bottom:

General Joffre. Visé. ***R4***

Back

Top row:

German general von Beseler. Anonymous. ***R3***

German general von Kluck. Anonymous. ***R3***

Enver Pascha, Turkish war minister. S. V. D. ***R4***

German general von Emmich. Anonymous. ***R3***

German general von Heeringen. Anonymous. ***R3***

Bottom row:

Lord Kitchener. J. Salmon. ***R2***

Franz Joseph, resplendent with medals. Anonymous. ***R3***

Cover design and interior layout: Anthony Jacobson
Edited by Jill Champion

Library of Congress Catalog Card Number 87-51422

ISBN 0-87069-502-9

10 9 8 7 6 5 4 3 2 1

Published by

Wallace-Homestead
A Capital Cities/ABC, Inc. Company

Wallace-Homestead Book Company
Post Office Box 5406
Greensboro, NC 27403
(919) 275-9809

To

Sherry

and

Shanna

The Two Women in My Life

Contents

Apologia

It has long been my contention that many, if not most, collectors of early political and military postcards are amateur historians of one sort or another. All one need do is ask to examine any of their collections to ascertain this fact. Almost from the onset, the examiner will be treated to a series of dissertations on this individual or that event.

Unfortunately, most books on postcards are little more than price lists punctuated with an occasional comment. Even those texts that are more detailed in their analyses devote precious little space to social, political, or military history; rather they incline toward descriptions of the cards themselves as if they existed in some sort of ageless, eraless vacuum.

This volume, along with my earlier one, *Royal Postcards,* is my own attempt to rectify that situation. The more scholarly may find fault with my methodology or disagree with several of my conclusions. Fine. I am more than willing to learn from my fellows. But I trust even they will concur with the judgment that a book along these lines is long overdue.

Jack H. Smith
September 1987

Preface

Since the middle of the 1960s, the time from which the true beginning of antique collecting may be rightfully traced, growth of the various areas of collectibles has been remarkable. During this period, antique shops, garage sales, and flea markets—not to mention Salvation Army and Goodwill Industry stores—were ransacked for furniture and bric-a-brac that reflected the nostalgia for the simpler (and to many, more substantial) days of yore. Solid oak fern tables once painted a frightening pink by those presumed to have urban polish and flair, along with pine wood chests of drawers coated with an equally repulsive stark white, were rescued in large numbers by folk who intended to strip and stain and varnish until the wood's natural beauty returned.

As with furniture, so with furnishings. Early objects of brass and all-wooden handmade items as well as early glassworks were purchased with passion and exhibited with pride. A generation two decades removed from the World Wars and as many years into an unbelievably prosperous era took full advantage of the rising salaries and decreasing work hours to search for and procure pleasure wherever it could be found. For many of that generation, this quest included acquiring relics from ages forever gone. Though modern dad would never experience the feel of reins attaching his fingers to a covered wagon, and contemporary mom no longer found it necessary to use a washboard (or a rock), both could appreciate the strength of the stock from which they sprang. Both wistfully attempted to surround themselves with reminders of a time when *hard work* and *craftsmanship* were not demeaning terms.

Perhaps no one may, with any degree of certainty, be able to posit the reason for this yearning for times past, or satisfactorily explain why it occurred in so many fields simultaneously. That it did and that it continues to do so is beyond doubt or question. Early baseball cards, comic books, thimbles, mechanical savings banks, Shirley Temple dolls, and an incredibly long list of other items testify both to the diversity and strength of the attraction. Even the well-established areas of numismatics and philately, which have had long and venerable histories, gained a phenomenal number of new adherents.

Of more significance to this book is the fact that the field of *deltiology*, or postcard collecting, also made tremendous strides at this time. Actually, for the postcard this was not a beginning, but rather a renewal of interest. During its "craze period" (1894–1914), card collecting was the greatest of hobbies, realizing the largest number of active participants of any recreational activity in human history. Since its first use in 1869–1870, the picture postcard's popularity as a communication device and as an attractive, informative collectible has continued unabated. Indeed, it was forever adding to its constituency in unchecked, balloon-like fashion until 1914. Greeting cards, advertising cards, cards devoted to famous people, holiday cards, view cards, and topical cards were among those being produced annually by the multiple billions.

World War I changed things, and the fascination dwindled, creating an ominous diminution of interest. This occurred, or so we are told, because of the cutoff of the supply of German inks and the unavailability of German printers to continue working for many postcard publishers outside their own country. After the war, a general malaise took hold—a lethargy not to be fully discarded until the seventh decade of this century. From that point until now, the influx of "new blood" into the deltiological community has amounted to a resurgence of both pleasing and alarming proportions. Further, it has witnessed the publishing of more books about postcard collecting than in all the preceding years placed together. Perhaps more significantly, monthly magazines, auction catalogs, weekly newspapers, and bulletins from a constantly enlarging number of postcard organizations have come into existence and increased deltiological information manyfold. Still, there are numerous areas where informational voids need to be filled.

Military cards, a category previously unmentioned, is a prime example. Unlike the other types of cards, which were all but killed by World War I, the military card—not surprisingly—experienced its greatest growth at this time, and it was produced in prodigious numbers by at least a half-dozen of the larger nations and a score of the smaller countries. Unfortunately, the written record on military postcards is sketchy at best, and although there are a number of excellent books and catalogs devoted to either a specific war or a set of military personalities, no effort has thus far appeared in the form of a general work to include the years covered by this volume. Therefore, my book does attempt, however successfully, to fill part of the chasm that currently exists regarding military postcards.

As I discovered when I composed an earlier work on royal postcards, there are some things one finds it necessary to do for oneself. For a number of years I waited for a book to be written on royal postcards before finally concluding that if I wanted such a volume, I would have to write it myself.

The same situation has occurred regarding military postcards, and I find myself taking the same course of action. While preparing this book, I was pleased and honored to have the assistance of the people identified in the acknowledgment section of this book. I especially wish to direct the reader's attention to Mr. Charles Burns. A true student of history, Mr. Burns' willingness to help manifested itself in his writing the article related to the various Balkan incidences. Also deserving of mention is Gary Destro, whose cards and books proved of inestimable value.

I do not wish to denigrate the efforts of the many others who aided me. All have some expertise in at least one area of this broad topic and I consider myself fortunate for having been able to solicit their counsel and borrow their cards as illustrations.

Finally, any errors that may be found are undoubtedly of my own making. I also beg the reader's indulgence for any omissions; they are certainly unintentional.

Acknowledgments

For me, one of the easiest and most pleasing parts of composing this book has been penning a recognition of those whose help was so instrumental in its formulation.

Among them are Mrs. Patricia Klein, to whom I am grateful for the loan of her postcards and the items about West Point she included; and Gorden Rosen, Larry Noder, Erv Felix, and Mrs. Thelma Kemp, each of whose assistance proved more than helpful.

Frank Hoak III is to be thanked for his free sharing of information. In this connection, I also wish to acknowledge my debt to Jim Sobery, Gary Destro, and Orville Sundermeyer. Mr. Sundermeyer's checklists proved especially helpful and I appreciate the use of them. A hand of thanks is also hereby extended to Mr. Jackson Taylor of Ferris Stamp and Coin Company for being a willing helper with his contribution of two Canadian postcard texts.

Mr. Charles Burns and Mr. Gary Destro are mentioned elsewhere for their contributions, but I will confess that I cannot acknowledge their helpfulness too highly or too much.

In this vein, I wish to recall both the efforts and the exertions of friend and fellow historian William F. Huber. More than any other single individual, it was through the conversations with him that I first devised the idea for this book. Bill and I had long since agreed that the fundamental problem with the way most history courses were conducted was that teachers stressed dates and events in a most impersonal way. We knew better and recognized the appeal of history when presented properly, which is to say, interestingly and intimately.

Finally, but firstly, I wish to acknowledge a personal debt to man's creator and sustainer. We all owe Him much more than can be repayed.

1
Introduction

Including a section on the value of military postcards and a rarity scale.

Wars, wars, and rumors of wars. Such has been man's estate since the Biblical account of Cain, who, in a moment of anger, misunderstanding, and jealousy, slew his brother Abel in the Garden of Eden. And although the terminology, the weapons, and the means of making war have changed, the rationale will always be the same, just as man will remain the same. Although "righteous indignation" may take the place of anger and disputes over sovereignty and territorial rights, there is no disguising the fact that in every conflict there is both an aggressor and a defender. Just exactly which party is which in any given situation might not always be an easy matter to resolve, but one issue remains certain: In the wars past, each combatant knew that justice and moral turpitude were on his side.

From the battles of antiquity, with their Dariuses and Alexanders and Caesars, through the conflicts of the Middle Ages and up to the present, man has ever sought to dominate his fellows. When the art of persuasion, the misuse of religion, or the force of custom has been ineffectual to this end, a standing army has always been ready at hand to punctuate the eventual escalation of temper, should one side be unwilling to heed the voice of reason from the other.

To judge from the many statues of military heroes, the countless campaign ribbons and medals for soldierly merit, the innumerable and abundantly well-received speeches in support of military endeavors, and the multiplicity of photographs of commanders and battles, it seems less than hazardous to assume that man sees a sort of glory in battle equaled nowhere else in human experience. Patriotism, self-sacrifice, and dedication to what is perceived to be an exalted cause permits him to transcend the realities of daily living and enter a world where only the brave dare tread. It is for this reason that war, unlike yesterday's designer offerings from the House of Paris, is never out of fashion.

To collectors of military postcards, this last revelation arrives as no great surprise. They know what the numbers tell—specifically, that the billions of postcards attest to war's popularity. Since their invention, these pieces of pasteboard have frequently been used as devices of communication in more ways than one, many sharing themes either dignifying or lamenting war.

The illustrated cards printed by both sides during the Franco-Prussian War of 1870–1871 were introduced within months of the postcard's birth. Subsequent wars witnessed an ever-increasing number and variety of specimens whose purposes were numerous indeed. Used as tools of propaganda, as illumination for the folks back home, or simply as a means of sending messages to relatives and loved ones, the postcard was speedily pressed into active service and dispatched over the face of the entire globe.

The statistics are overwhelming: During World War I alone it has been reported that the German postal service delivered 11 billion letters from soldiers; the French and British carried slightly less. When these figures are combined with the mail of all other combatants, the final tally is staggering. As even the most conservative of estimates would suggest, the ratio of postcards to letters sent must have been at least two to one. Clearly, all of them were not (strictly speaking) military postcards bearing war photos or drawings; many did, however, contain war-related messages along with special cancelations and stamps and are therefore retained by the present generation of dedicated collectors.

As postcard producers churned out more diverse sorts of cards for the conflicts raging during the late nineteenth and early twentieth centuries, the numbers of cards reached astounding proportions. Had all of them been retained, their sheer volume would have relegated them to the position of being the cheapest of postcards, sharing the same status as the common greeting card (which was also produced in incredible abundance). But most cards were not kept; rather, they were seen as mute testaments of a war that brought all too much death and disgrace in its wake, so they were pitched, discarded, and put out with the trash. Sadly, the lesson was not of lasting substance. When sufficient time elapsed for the memory to dim, yet another conflict would display its ugly countenance, affording a new generation the opportunity for glory and prestige. Out once more came the photographers and artists executing their continuing commissions to satisfy the lusts for honor, but also for the simple desire to remain apprised of the action. Then, inevitably, back to the dustbin or garbage heap went the cards after another "lasting peace" was realized.

Today, military postcards dating to the Second World War and earlier are rightfully regarded both as antiques and as priceless glimpses of the past. They show what history books can only tell—and in more commanding fashion. Military engagements (wars, if you will), which witness all too often the destruction of life and property, are actions contrary to civilized behavior and all precepts of a morally refined people. Postcards as first-hand history illustrate this message. In no uncertain way, their messages are vital and immediate ones, pertinent to our generation and to all those that may follow.

War is a costly business, some postcards seem to exclaim—too costly to be engaged in frivolously. Postcards show us the price of war in faces alternately reflecting victory and defeat, and intimating that both postures are at least a little fraudulent. War is not power, but loss of life; not broad smiles, but the anguish and disappointment of promises unfulfilled and maturity unrealized.

At last we are reminded that the only war worth fighting, the one between good and evil, requires neither guns nor bombs. It demands instead the highest order of morality to which man may aspire and recognition of the fact that all men are, under the skin and beneath any class and race distinctions, brothers whose lonely flight through space and eternity links them to a choice of destinies.

The Value of Military Postcards

I have not made the mistake of confusing popularity or desirability with value, although some people—collectors and dealers among them—may take issue with that approach, which differs from the "tried and true" methods of pricing according to popularity. Very little in the way of a defense will come from this corner, only that popularity and faddishness, unstable as they are, hold less appeal than knowing that the item one possesses is indeed rare.

Thus it should come as no surprise that a naval military postcard of World War I will be more greatly valued than one of the beautifully executed Harry Payne cards relating to the same conflict, even though the latter will undoubtedly always be more popular and, consequently, more in demand.

There is another factor that should be entered into the equation when value is discussed: the historical merit of a given postcard. It requires no genius to make the observation that a card of Adolf Hitler, fascinating a character study as the man is, is less useful as a historical tool for understanding the past than is a postcard that pictures Russian women and children building barricades to prevent themselves from being overrun by Nazis. Such an illustration helps illuminate a little-known fact about World War II, and in that way becomes instrumental in aiding the Western world to better understand the apparent Russian preoccupation with security and defense.

Now, or perhaps one should say *at last,* the world has arrived at the place where the picture postcard may take its bow and assume its position among the other cherished mementos of the past. Not as a memento only, but also as revealer of what is often called *the human condition.* For the astute and curious, military postcards are more than just real photos or pretty pieces of colored paper with their quaintness intact; they are reminders and recorders of a past shared by all humans. The times they depict may be different from our own, but postcards share a common denominator with all mankind: They deal with real people reacting in real ways to the very real situations of life. For this reason, if for none other, military postcards should always be reexamined for whatever useful information they may impart.

Picture postcards of times past should always be cherished as illustrated road maps that bridge the gap from then to now. Clearly, the rarer the view, the better the opportunity for exploring and for learning.

A final note: The general values given for the various types of military postcards are for material in very fine or better condition. Cards with tears, dirt, ink marks, bends, creases, and the like are only worth a fraction of the value given—a fact that should be borne in mind by both sellers and purchasers.

Rarity Scale

Readers of my book on royalty postcards are already familiar with my system for assigning prices based on rarity. I have retained that system for this volume, modifying it a bit to suit the different topics.

My rationale is an easy one to follow: I begin with the universally held assumption that some postcards were produced in greater numbers than others; from this position I proceed to the commonsense thesis that value should be attributed on the basis of *scarcity* rather than on that more elusive quality we call *popularity.* The benefits of this system to the collector are obvious and need little recapitulation. It is hoped that the simple, straightforward scale presented below may impose at least a little order on what is generally recognized as a fascinating area of postcard collecting.

Table 1-1. Rarity Scale

Code	Definition	Price range
R1	For cards commonly encountered.	$ .50 – $ 1.00
R2	Cards frequently seen, but which generate a modest amount of interest.	$ 1.00 – $ 5.00
R3	Cards originally printed in large numbers, but always in demand.	$ 5.00 – $10.00
R4	Seldom-seen cards that are often socially or politically significant.	$10.00 – $20.00
R5	Very rare specimens seldom offered for sale.	$20.00 – $50.00

2
The Franco-Prussian War

Part I: History and Chronology

A War of Humiliation for France

Few things in human experience are more difficult to endure than witnessing the demise of one's dreams. For the soldier, this acceptance entails the swallowing of that most distasteful of pills, *defeat.* To the French who suffered humiliation at the hands of Prussia in 1870–1871, the loss was even more keenly felt than is usual in such affairs. To the French, it meant their visions of empire and glory—of spreading French tastes and French culture—were to be squashed under the jackboot of what was, to their way of thinking, an ill-bred and ill-mannered member of the lowest order of Homo sapiens—a *German.*

Not only had the French soldier lost on the battlefields of Woerth and Sedan, he also had to stand helpless as his civilian counterparts in the city of Paris were starved through blockade to the point of consuming rats and, in some few instances, their citizen brothers. The final severance of dignity arrived in the form of a peace treaty demanding reparations from the vanquished in the amount of 1 billion dollars (5 milliards of francs).

Setting the Tone for Europe-to-Be

Because of that one campaign, the history of Europe—and consequently, of the world—was to be printed in different letters. For France, unlike the rest of the world, the results were more immediately calculable. Gone was the last emperor France was to know. Gone were any lingering beliefs that Germany could be trusted. Gone was Alsace-Lorraine. And agreed to be gone was the amount of 1 billion dollars, assigned to France—a victim without the resources to pay.

Never to be seen again was the stalwart countenance of 350,000 French soldiers—men lost in a war that offered neither thanks nor glory. Equally lamentable to their memories was the fact that the casualties they were able to inflict totaled slightly more than a third of their own numbers. Further, German deaths totaled only 28,600.

For Prussia, the picture was a different one composing a more pleasing mosaic. Gained was the defeat of that vaunted enemy with whom it shared a common border. Gained was an opportunity to display a military tactical genius such as Europe would not forget. Gained was the unification of Germany under the hegemony of its first kaiser (Caesar), a Prussian Junker.

And if, as a natural consequence of Prussia's victories over Austria-Hungary (1866) and France, a large portion of the world's population began to develop a fear and distrust of Germany, that "minor negative" was considered a small price for all the acclaim. Prince Bismarck revealed the Prussian mind set with his succinct, if indelicate, statement:

> The great questions of the day will not be settled by speeches and majority resolutions—that was the blunder of 1848 and 1849—but by blood and iron.

Considering the growth of munitions factories and the increasing size of the army, the "Iron Chancellor" was mentioning the two commodities militaristic Germany possessed in abundance.

The First Military Postcards

Because the postcard's birth had occurred only a few months earlier, the war was not afforded an outburst of pasteboard illustrations. In fact, only three types of postcards contemporary to the Franco-Prussian War are known to exist. It is to be appreciated that they represent each side. (It should also be gratefully acknowledged that a couple of publishers produced a few, now scarce, remembrance cards at a later date.)

The first card was offered for sale on September 29, 1870, by the German Army Corps Society. Designated for the wounded, the uncolored card was illustrated with the Red Cross symbol. Signed by the commander of Occupied France and authorized by German Occupation Headquarters in France, it was released barely more than two months (July 15, 1870) after the war was declared. Perhaps even more surprising, the missive was in circulation a mere three months after Germany initially introduced the postcard (June 1870).

The second group was a series of sketches drawn by M. Leon Besnardeau, a stationer at Sille-le-Guillaume. Their intended use, once the drawings had been reproduced on postcard stock, was for homeward correspondence from the French soldiers then in training at the camp at Conlie under Count Keratry. The printing was accomplished by the House of Oberthur de Rennes. The first series (November 1870) contained sketches of cannons, pyramids of shells, and stacked guns. Cards in the second series (early 1871) were outline drawings of cartridges, in the center of which the soldiers might include such information as military camp, battle units, and the like. Both series were instant successes and required printing in quantity.

A card postmarked July 16, 1870 (the third type) may be a one-of-a-kind specimen. Sent by A. Schwartz, a printer from Oldenburg, Germany, to his father-in-law in Magdeburg, the artistic piece of pasteboard depicts a soldier and cannon on the front and has a patriotic poem on the reverse.

Unmentioned thus far is a fourth postcard related to the war. The *Par Ballon Nom Monte,* or *balloon* cards, of 1870 were privately produced specimens whose purpose was to send messages out of Paris by air, which was the only means available since the city was in a state of siege by the Prussian Army. Although they are very rare and are in every way to be considered postcards, balloon cards were not included with the others since they were not dispatched through normal postal channels. Interestingly enough, had these cards been similarly transported 40 years later, they would have been classified as *airmail.*

Clearly, the Franco-Prussian War set the disquieting tone for European politics for years to come. Industrial expansion and technological achievement progressed alongside a continuing wave of preparedness and international mistrust. Picture postcards still in the nascent stages of their development during the seventh and eighth decades of the nineteenth century failed to record the illustrated evidences of these mind sets, but their publishers did print specimens of some of the more important characters and events of the war at a later date. For this reason, the chronology that follows may prove helpful to those fortunate enough to acquire some of these cards.

French Monetary Costs

$ 400,000,000	In actual expenses
$ 200,000,000	Repairing materials and helping victims
$1,000,000,000	War indemnity
$ 400,000,000	Interest on war indemnity

Chronology: Franco-Prussian War

Date	Event
1870	
July	Ems telegram.
July 19	France declares war on Prussia.
July 23	French emperor joins his army.
July 26	First battle at Niederbronn.
August 2	Battle at Saarbruch.
August 4	French defeated at Weissenburg.
August 6	Major German victory at Woerth.
August 14	French defeated at Courcelles.
August 18	Germans win battle of Mars-la-Tour Gravelotte.
August 18	French defeated at Gravelotte.
August 25	Germans occupy Challons.
September 1	Battle at Sedan.
September 2	Surrender of General MacMahon's army and of Napoleon III.
September 4	Revolution and siege of Paris.
October 7	Germans take Orléans.
October 31	Metz is taken by Germans; Bazaine's army surrenders.
November 9	Battle at Coulmiers.
November 28	Battle of Beaune-la-Rolande.
December 2–4	French defeated at Orléans.
December 23	Battle of Pont at Noyelles.
1871	
January 3	Battles at Bapaume.
January 11–12	Battle of Le Mans.
January 15–17	Defeat of Bourbaki near Belfort.
January 18	William I proclaimed emperor at Versailles.
January 19	Battle of St. Quentin.
January 19	Great sortie of 100,000 men from Paris repulsed.
January 28	Paris surrenders.
January 30	Bourbaki's army of 80,000 driven into Switzerland and "interned."
February 26	Preliminaries signed regarding Treaty of Peace, ceding Alsace and part of Lorraine, and agreeing to pay German Empire $1 billion indemnity.
March 1–3	German troops enter Paris and remain 48 hours.
May 10	Treaty of Frankfurt concluded.
May 18	Treaty ratified by the French Assembly.

Part II: Details of War

Military Leaders

French

Name	Position/Significance
General Bataille	
Marshal Bazaine	
General Bourbaki	Commander of Imperial Guard
Marshal Canrobert	
General d'Aurelle	
General de Failly	
General de l'Admirault	
General Abel Douay	
General Felix Douay	
General Dercrat	
General Frossard	
Marshal Lebeauf	Chief of staff to emperor
General Lecomte	
General Le Flo	
Marshal MacMahon	Defeated at Woerth, wounded and captured at Sedan.
General Micheler	
General Reille	
General Clement Thomas	
General Trochu	
General Vinoy	
General Wimpffer	Replaced MacMahon after the latter was wounded at Sedan.

German

Name	Position/Significance
Field Marshal Blücher	
General Boyer	
Prinz Friedrich Charles	Commander 2nd Army
Kronprinz Friedrich	Commander 3rd Army
General Kummer	
General Sternmetz	Chief of staff, 1st Army
Lt. Colonel von Broussart	
Helmut von Moltke	Chief of staff
Major General von Sperlong	Chief of staff, 1st Army
Colonel von Stiehie	Chief of staff, 2nd Army

(Also: Royal families of Saxony, Wurttemburg, and Bavaria represented.)

Part III: Postcards

Types and Categories of Cards

Type	Category
Army Corps Society card	R5
A. Schwartz card	R5
Cards drawn by Leon Besnardeau, 1st series	R5
Cards drawn by Leon Besnardeau, 2nd series	R5
Later cards of action in the field	R3
Later cards depicting military leaders or events	R3
Later cards with Franco-Prussian War connection	
Bismarck dictating peace terms to French delegates	R2
Bismarck with Napoleon III	R2
Wilhelm I being crowned emperor at Versailles	R2
Later cards of French ruins/destruction	R3
Later cards of heroes	R3
Later cards of men in the field, non-action-related	R3
Later cards for returning heroes	R3
Later cards for veterans	R3
Later cards of victory parades	R3
Monument cards	R2

Publishers

Name	Origin
Deyhle and Wagner	Germany
Albert Frisch	Germany
Th. Lehmstedt	Germany

Close-up of Le Mans monument at base. Anonymous. R2

Remembrance card to raise funds for servicemen's home. Anonymous. R3.

Monument to the French army of the Loire that defended Le Mans in January 1871. Anonymous. R2

Monument to the brave French and French allies defending Paris, 1871. Anonymous. R2

Multiple views of monuments at Worth, where French forces under General McMahan were defeated by Prussia, 1870. Th. Lemstedt. R2

Red Cross card for German war veterans; Wilhelm I inspecting troops. Albert Frisch. R3

Wilhelm I at Ems, 1870. Anonymous. R3

General Henri D'Orléans, Duc d'Aumale. Anonymous. R3

Chateau de Saint Cloud, residence of Marie Antoinette, Napoleon, Louis XVIII, Charles X, Louis Philippe, and Napoleon III. Burned by Prussia in October 1870. Anomymous. R3

Von Moltke; artist-drawn sketch. Stengel and Company. R3

Wilhelm I with Field Marshal Blücher. R3

Red Cross card for German veterans; troops being reviewed by Wilhelm I. Albert Frisch. R3

Victorious German troops entering Berlin. Red Cross card. R3

A 1910 postcard eulogizing von Moltke. Franz von Lenbach. R3

Prince Bismarck, a realistic portrait of the old war horse. Anonymous. R3

3
Wars of English Imperialism

Reconquest of the Sudan and the Boer War.

Part I: History and Chronology

Reconquest of the Sudan, 1896–1898

When British general Charles "Chinese" Gordon was murdered in 1885 by the followers of that Bedouin fanatic, the Mahdi, the outcry in England was one of prolonged anguish. A popular figure among the common folk of the empire—if considered somewhat headstrong and irregular by his superiors—Gordon had seemed to be the right man to dispatch to the Sudan once trouble erupted there. His orders were straightforward: Evacuate Khartoum. Had those in power known that he would stubbornly refuse to retreat from his position once his situation became hopeless, Gordon would never have been sent. Of so much worth, we are told, is hindsight.

Having served in the area some years previously, Gordon—a religiously devout, almost mystical man—had managed to ingratiate himself with a large section of the Sudan's indigenous population. The renegade Mahdi also used the force of *his* personality, but in a different manner. Claiming authority, if not outright descent, from a chain that reached all the way to Mohammed and Allah, he secured the services of thousands of converts, all of whom were disposed to believe that he had not misappropriated the lineage. The Mahdi's plan was a simple but ambitious one: to subdue for Allah—and presumably for himself—all the territory and peoples from Sudan to Egypt. With insufficient manpower and inadequate supplies, Gordon attempted to block the Mahdi's passage. This was the general's first mistake. His next one proved to be his last. Refusing to desert his loyal followers, certain they would be butchered if he did, Gordon gambled, justifying his action with the belief that England would send reinforcements. However, Britain's leaders never had any intention of starting a war (at least not in that part of Egypt or during that time) because of General Gordon's insubordination. Neither were they inclined to permit his martyrdom.

After some equivocation and delay, they dispatched a rescue expedition down the Nile, but it arrived two days too late. Moreover, it was to be 13 years more before retribution was exacted and England's honor reclaimed.

Kitchener of Khartoum

It is at this juncture that the central figure of this drama entered the picture. During the year of Gordon's death, young British army officer Horatio Herbert Kitchener was in the process of making a name for himself. A military man who was the son of a military man, Kitchener was nothing if not hungry for glory and power. Drilled along military lines as a child by an autocratic father whom he always sought to please, the future general had not only military discipline, but military reality ingrained in his thinking early in life. To be a success, he was told, it was necessary to be efficient, to be determined, and to be "in the right place at the right time." Kitchener never forgot, but continually made productive use of these lessons. Before his fortieth birthday he had fought in the Franco-Prussian War and the British conquest of Egypt, and he had even engaged the khalifa Abdullahi (successor to the Mahdi) in an action where a bullet wound in the neck and lower jaw nearly cost him his life.

During the Egyptian campaign, Kitchener made a few useful contacts and soon saw service as a trainer of the newly emerging Egyptian cavalry. He rose through the ranks, becoming commander in chief of the entire Egyptian army. By 1896 he was raised to the rank of general. Knowing the time was ripe for the reconquest of the Sudan, he chose that time to begin intensely training the Egyptians for the campaign.

An abstemious man regarding his own personal habits, Kitchener could be stringent and miserly in demanding military precision and economy from his subordinates. Every man under his command correctly classified him as a tightwad concerning everything but their energies. Uncaring about their thoughts or feelings, the man ever after called "Kitchener of Khartoum" relentlessly planned his forthcoming operations. Although he didn't know Gordon personally, Kitchener knew him by reputation and in his own not-so-peculiar way identified with him. Both men, as it turns out, were imperialists, determined to bring the "blessings" of British culture and civilization to an unrefined, if not actually un-Christian, world. Both men perceived their roles in this enterprise to be God-inspired; both were aloof and demanding; both were self-assured. For Kitchener, the rescuing of Gordon's honor was also the rescuing of his own and of those values which they both admired and for which they both fought.

The campaign battles themselves, filled as they were with suspense and intrigue, were not, as one might suppose, decided ahead of time. Although Kitchener had years to train the Egyptians, there was no escaping the fact that the war had to be fought and won on desert terrain all too familiar to the khalifa and his hordes. Add to this the knowledge that Kitchener's army was outnumbered four to one and his enemy was more mobile. Complicate matters a bit more with the news that Kitchener had less than 9000 (although dedicated) British soldiers, compared with 17,000 well-trained but essentially unbattle-tested Egyptians, and the complexion of the campaign assumes a different hue. Having neither the element of surprise nor the cover of fortifications in their favor, Kitchener's army rode out onto the sand.

Battle at Omdurman

Their destination was the city of Omdurman, which had been made the capital after the evacuation of Khartoum. The Anglo-Egyptian army acquitted itself well, engaging the enemy in strong numbers as it pushed forward. Less than ten miles outside the city, Kitchener rested his men before beginning the final bombardment of the protective forts surrounding Omdurman. The date was September 1, 1898. Early the next morning, a group of 10,000 dervishes hurled their bulk against the army sent to subdue them. Field artillery dropped them just as quickly and unceremoniously as if they were bowling pins. Foolishly undeterred, 20,000 more took their place in a headlong rush a mere two hours later. Within a matter of minutes, the second group took their place again, this time on the ground as corpses. Obviously, superior weapons accounted for part of this success; the remainder of it may be seen in the excellent military training of the British and Egyptian troops.

There remained but one major battle, and for it the khalifa had selected 20,000 of his best fighters, who now lay in hiding, preparing for a sneak attack. Anticipating that Kitchener's army would deploy itself into smaller groups as it approached Omdurman, the khalifa hoped to use the old Roman ploy of dividing and conquering. His calculations were correct; unfortunately, his tactics went awry. Not only did his men fail to attack in the prescribed manner and at the appropriate time; he was also unaware that in Kitchener he had met an enemy who could bring order out of chaos more quickly than any man in uniform.

The result was an utter rout, the numbers testifying to the competence of the Anglo-Egyptian army; 80,000 Sudanese troops were defeated by slightly more than a quarter of that number. The impressive numbers had an even more surprising breakdown: Of Kitchener's army, less than 50 men were killed, compared with 11,000 dervishes.

The Boer War, 1899–1902

In the poetic style used so frequently by writers of the early twentieth century, modern students of history find plausible reasons for the behaviors of their ancestors, and nowhere is this more evident than when the actions under scrutiny involve warfare. In seeking to assign responsibility for the conflict which was later to be called the *Boer War,* an oversized, colorfully illustrated and methodically outlined book titled *The War in South Africa* begins by drawing a series of parallels between certain individuals and the course of events. A period tome that does not enjoy the more balanced perspective of hindsight, *The War in South Africa* does, nonetheless, present the reader with some historically useful speculation such as that demonstrated in the following excerpt:

> When the political student looks into the causes of the war in South Africa, he will see constantly before him the faces of three famous men.... In Stephanus Johannes Paulus Krüger, President of the South African Republic, we see ... a spirit of independence and an irreconcilable hostility to a great power (Great Britain).... Then looms up the figure of the Right Honorable Cecil Rhodes, the energetic and adventurous representative of a large segment of the British people in South Africa who knew that there must be a supreme struggle for supremacy between the English and Dutch. Next stands the Right Honorable Joseph Chamberlain, the ruler of a colonial empire by virtue of his position as Secretary of State for the Colonies in Her Majesty's Government. Mr. Chamberlain has been the foremost in the new school of British statesmen thoroughly inbued with that imperial idea....

It seems that all three were men of vision; they were also men of competing ideologies. When men like these are prepared to lend their energies, their intellects, and the weight of their political power to a specified cause, it is a foregone conclusion that men of lesser standing will soon be required to relinquish their lives. For these souls, their ideals become banners proclaiming liberty, justice, equality, or whatever other catchword is popular at the time. Patriotism is the glue that holds the fabric of war together, and the world never appears to run short of it. In the case of the Boer War, there was evil enough and more to go around. A look back might prove instructive.

The Boers

The protracted era of colonization and territorial annexation that followed the explorations of the fifteenth and sixteenth centuries was, although greatly reduced in activity and restricted by remaining geography, still proceeding into the nineteenth and early twentieth centuries. One example of such activity involved the Dutch, who as early as 1652 began settling vast tracts of land in lower South Africa. A hardy people well-suited to endure the rigors of the South African topography and climate, the Dutch, or *Boers,* as they were later called, became mainly an agricultural people. Their unrefined, little-cultured lifestyle permitted them to think of existence in relatively basic terms, and from the first, they were slave owners. Their treatment of the African native was clearly less than humane and provided the substance of several critical accounts written by English missionaries who came to South Africa after England had gained sovereignty over a large part of the territory in 1814.

The British speedily put an end to the institution of slavery and, rather than stop at this point, went even further and adopted policies guaranteed to antagonize the indigenous Boers. English was adopted as the official language of the Cape. The migration of both poor and entrepreneurial-minded British subjects to the area was promoted, and various English practices, as well as Anglo law, were quickly put into effect.

Young Paul Krüger

Unable by temperament and linear rigidity of thought to endure these affronts, more than 16,000 of the early settlers migrated east and northeast, eventually founding the Transvaal State. Among those making this "Great Trek," which began in 1836 and continued intermittently for several years, was Paul Krüger, then a ten-year-old boy helping to guide his father's cattle. It is doubtful this future Boer president actually remembered much about the journey or the circumstances necessitating it, but there can be little doubt that during his growing years, "Oom Paul" (or "Uncle" Paul) was given liberal doses of anti-Anglo hostility.

Unwilling to acknowledge any authority but that of a God who granted them special consideration due to what they presumed was their biblically favored status, the Dutch once more became slave owners. Claiming a scriptural basis for their treatment of the native blacks, they fully believed the Zulu-Kaffirs of South Africa were the Amalekites of the Old Testament, and thus deserving to be smitten. Not to be overlooked, of course, is the fact that victorious wars against these tribesmen gained territory for the Boers to expand their influence and hegemony—results which they attributed to a heavenly dispensation (except, of course, when the Zulus were victors—which was often).

It was only a matter of time before the Boers collided once more with the British, who were a people equally certain that God had granted them specific prerogatives. Included among these were territorial expansion and a need to teach the blessings of English civilization to more backward folk. The friction began in 1877, when England annexed the Transvaal under the pretext that this was in accordance with Dutch wishes. In fact, there were a few Boers who had requested the action, and there were the facts of poverty, depression, and agressive Zulus that the Boers found increasingly difficult to deal with. So for three years, the reality of British occupation was endured.

South African Republic

Finally, primarily as a result of the Zulus' defeat by the British Army, the Boers rose in protest against English occupation and won three signal victories over it (Laing's Nek, Tingogo Heights, and Majuba Hill). Gladstone's government was only too pleased to return semi-independent status to the Dutch with certain provisos. More complete control (although the British claimed final authority rested with them) was granted in 1884 when the Transvaal State was changed to the South African Republic. This concession was viewed by Krüger as an agreement between sovereign powers; it also set the stage for the igniting of passions on both sides.

Considering this a poor enough territory, barely self-sustaining, the British would no doubt have been pleased eventually to turn absolute mastery of the region over to the Boers, had not gold been discovered there in 1885. Gold—it caused thoughts of wealth for the taking in the minds of men the world over, and caused thousands to travel to and set up residences in the South African Republic.

For a short period of time, the Boers cheerfully accepted the influx, grateful for the additional capital these outlanders produced from the mines. The celebration was short-lived, however, for whereas the money was welcome, the new ideas and demands for political autonomy by these strangers was ill tolerated. Indeed, the Boer government sought to discourage immigration to the area and promulgated a series of laws that proved to be most repressive, especially against their old enemy, England.

Foreigners were forbidden to have English taught to their children in the public schools, Catholics and Jews were prohibited from holding public office, all effective political power was denied any of the abovementioned, and all their business activities—even some of their social activities—were subject to restriction.

Appeals of the English portion of the population to their elected representative back home began to have an effect. Dispatches and proposals to the Boer government proved ineffectual, and Britain hesitated at this point to commit her energies to a place so far removed from any substantial portion of her military might. Complicating matters was an abortive attempt, apparently sponsored by Mr. Cecil Rhodes—diamond entrepreneur and prime minister of the Cape—to invade the

Transvaal in December 1895. The unfortunate debacle (afterward known as the Jameson Raid because of Dr. Jameson, its leader) was rapidly and effectively crushed by the Boers. The resentment it engendered led to Rhode's political retirement and exacerbated anti-Anglo feelings among those Boers who surmised that the attempt had approval from the highest echelon of the government in London.

This perceived insolence was met in time with insistence that Her Majesty's Government relinguish any and all control of the South African Republic. The dominos continued to fall; Britain's subsequent withdrawal from what she thought were insubordinate demands from an unauthorized inferior led the Dutch to cease further negotiation. Krüger next dictated policy to the British—withdraw all troops from the Boer border, remove those troops recently arrived in South Africa, and prohibit the landing of any of those soldiers in ships adjoining the region. The two days Krüger gave Britain to comply elicited a simple reply, "The conditions demanded by the government of the South African Republic are such as Her Majesty's government finds it impossible to discuss."

The War

As might have been expected, the British first met with a series of setbacks. Defeat preceded defeat as the native Boers waged successful guerilla warfare on familiar terrain. The British soldier, tactically speaking, was the same animal who had waged close-quarter formation-style battle against Napoleon. Fighting from behind rocks, ambushes against the enemy's rear, and the commando tactics that included the mobility afforded from living off the land were all alien concepts to the British soldier. Under such conditions, it is to be wondered why England did not suffer more reverses. Adding to the problems were supply lines always in danger of being interrupted, an enemy who fought in swiftly appearing and just as quickly disappearing small groups, and an inability on the part of the British high command to understand that the Boer fought with a sense of determination and desperation unequaled by his numerically superior British counterparts.

Lt. General Redvers Buller was replaced in short order by the much-admired war hero of the India campaign, Lord Frederick Roberts. To his credit, Roberts, a gentleman above all else, chose as his second-in-command General H. H. Kitchener—a man, as we have seen, who knew something about unorthodox means of waging war. Kitchener's assistance was to prove invaluable. Unfortunately, Kitchener himself had to relearn some of his own lessons as the result of a disastrous turn of events.

The battle of Paardeberg (February 1900) was a total rout as well as Kitchener's first battle defeat. British losses exceeded 1200, while Boer casualties did not reach 300. Ever a man who lived and learned, Kitchener examined the prevailing situation and implemented some necessary reforms. Returning to his demanding and exacting, if not innovative, self, he created his own group of commandos, the Bushveldt Carbineers. Next, he began burning Boer farmhouses and destroying all crops not appropriated for the use of the British Army. Realizing that although there were 60,000 Dutch fighters, only one-third of that number would be in the field of conflict at any given time (while the others planted and harvested), Kitchener knew he had to disrupt their chain of activities. He also knew no army could effectively wage war without the necessities to do so: primarily and fundamentally, shelter (farmhouses) and foodstuffs (crops).

Women, old men, and children—now left homeless—were herded into refugee camps, where thousands starved or died of diseases. It should be noted, however, that without these camps, virtually all of the dispossessed would have perished. Also, these tactics, while regrettable, set no precedent. From antiquity onward they have been used with greater or lesser success.

Kitchener, as a soldier, did what he thought best in order to win the war. One may legitimately wonder what he thought of British politicians who shortly after the conflict relinquished autonomy to the Boers. Strangely, he may not have been overly concerned, for it was some of the key Boer commanders who were among the first to offer assistance to the British during World War I.

Chronology: Boer War

Date	Event
1899	
May 31	Conference convenes at Bloemfontein between Lord Milner and President Krüger of Transvaal regarding Uitland complaints.
July 18	Transvaal Volksraad offers Uitlanders franchise after seven years of residence; in August, modified to five years if British agree to abandon suzerainty in Transvaal.
August	Britain refuses to relinquish suzerainty over Transvaal.
September 2	Transvaal government withdraws offer of franchise.
October 9	Krüger's government presents its humiliating demands to British; insists on compliance after two days.
October 12	Contingent of Boers lead incursion into the Natal.
October 20–21	Battles at Glencoe and Elandslaagte; no certain victor of either.
October 30	British defeated at Nicholson's Neck; within days, Ladysmith, Kimberley, and Mafeking are under siege.
November 23–28	Lord Methuen routs the Boers at Belmont and Enslin (Grospan); British casualty list high at Modder River.
December 10	General Gatacre defeated by Boers at Stormberg.
December 11	Lord Methuan defeated at Magersfontein.
December 15	General Buller utterly routed by Boers at Colenso.
December 16	Field marshal Roberts placed in command of campaign, with Lord Kitchener as his chief of staff.

1900

January 6	Boer assault on Ladysmith unsuccessful.
January 23–24	British seriously defeated at Spion Kon.
February 15	Lord Roberts relieves Kimberley.
February 27	General Cronje's army surrenders to British at Paardeberg.
March 13	Bioemfontein, capital of Orange Free State, is recaptured by Lord Roberts.
March 27	Death of Piet Jonbert, Boer commander in chief.
April	British force captured at Reddersburg in Orange Free State; Boers begin extensive use of guerilla warfare tactics.
May 17	Mafeking relieved.
May 28	Lord Roberts annexes Orange Free State, or Orange River Colony, by proclamation.
May 31	British occupy Johannesburg.
June 5	British enter Pretoria, capital of South African Republic; British force at Kumassi Ashantrland attacked by natives and finally relieved in July.
July 9	Surrender of Boer general Prinsloo.
September 1	Lord Roberts annexes South African Republic by proclamation.
October 25	Transvaal formally proclaimed part of British Empire as Vaal River Colony.
December 13	General Clements' army defeated by Boers under Delarey at Noortgedacht in the Transvaal.

1901

February	Boer commander Christian De Wet invades Cape Colony.
September 17	Boer general Botha defeats British near Utrecht (Transvaal).
September 26	Boers repulsed at Forts Stala and Prospect.

1902

January	Guerilla tactics and destruction of Boer farmhouses and crops implemented by Lord Kitchener (who succeeded Roberts) slowly taking effect; Boers losing by attrition (capture and battle losses).
April 12	Boer leaders assemble at Pretoria to discuss peace terms.
May 31	Boers sign surrender at Pretoria.

Part II: Details of War

Military Leaders

Boer War

Name	Position/Significance
Major Albrent	Commanded Orange Free State Artillery
General Louis Botha	Successor to Joubert
General Pret A. Cronje	Surrendered to Lord Roberts after ten days of fighting at Paardeberg, February 27, 1900
General J. H. Delarey	Next in command to Botha
Colonel de Villebois	Mareuil (origin uncertain)
General Christian R. de Wet	
General Petrus Jacobus Joubert	Vice president of South African Republic and commandant general of its forces; died March 3, 1900
General Jan Kock	
General Kolbe	
Colonel Maximoff	
General Lucas Meyer	Military advisor to President Krüger
General Pretorius	Wounded and captured by British
General Schalk-Berger	Commanded under Joubert
General Synman	

British

Name	Position/Significance
Lord Airlie	Colonel of the 12th Lancers
Colonel Edwin Alfred Hervey Alderson	Chief of Mounted Cavalry
Colonel Robert Stephenson Smyth Baden-Powell (later Major General)	
Brigadier General Geoffry Barton	
Colonel Barton	
Lord O. Beauclerk (Lt.)	17th Lancers
Lord Bentinck (Lt.)	9th Lancers
Major E. H. Bethell	Royal Engineers
Captain Cecil Boyle	Additional aide to General French; wrote *The Cavalry Rush to Kimberley*
Brigadier General Sir Edward Brabant	
Lt. General Sir Redvers Henry Buller	First British commander in chief in South Africa; later replaced by Roberts, who was replaced by Kitchener
Major Burnham	Famous American scout
Lt. General Sir William Frances Butler (was replaced by by General Buller)	
Lt. Colonel T. R. C. Carleton	Royal Irish Fusiliers
Major General Sir Frederick Carrington	
Lord Edward Cecil	
Major General Sir Herbert Charles Chermside	Commanded 14th Brigade
Lt. Winston Churchill	
Brigadier General Ralph Arthur Clements	
Lt. General Sir Cornelius Francis Clery	Commanded 2nd Division
Major General Sir Henry Edward Colvelle	
Colonel Dick Cunyngham	Gordon Highlanders

British Military Leaders, cont.

Name	Position/Significance
Brigadier General Horace Lockwood Smith Dorrien	
Major General the Earl of Dundonald	
Major Ésteban	Spain
General Sir Frederick William Edward Forestier-Walker	First Army Corps
Major General Sir John Denton Pinkstone French	Lt. general when war started; commanded cavalry division
Major General Sir William Forbes Gatacre	
Colonel James Henry Gordon	
Lt. Colonel Frederick Gordon	
Lt. Colonel Greene	Natal Carbineers
Brigadier General Sir Ian Standish Monterth Hamilton	
Brigadier General Sir Bruce Meade Hamilton	
Major General A. Fitzroy Hart	
Lt. Colonel Davidson Henderson	
Colonel Herchmer	Northwest Police
Major General Sir Henry John Thoroton Hildyard	
Captain Hiravka	Japan
Major General Sir Archibald Hunter	
Major General Sir Edward Thomas Henry Hutton	
Colonel Robert George Kekewich	A defender of Kimberley
Major General Sir Thomas Kelly-Kenny	Commanded 6th Division
Major General Lord Horatio Herbert Kitchener	Khartoum
Brigadier General Sir Charles Edmond Knox	
Brigadier General Sir William George Knox	
Major General Sir Neville Gerald Lythleton	
Major General Hector A. MacDonald	Successor to the late General Wauchope (who was killed at Magersfontein)
Colonel Bryan T. Mahon	
Brigadier General Sir John Grenfell Maxwell	
Lt. General Lord Paul Sanford Methuen	
Colonel Herbert Scott Gould Miles	
Sir Alfred Milner	
Lt. Colonel W. D. Other	Commander of Canadian troops
Colonel Thomas David Pilcher	
Colonel Herbert Charles Onslow Plumer	Of the Mounted Rifles
Major General Sir Reginald Pole-Carew	Succeeded General Gatacre
Major General Sir George Tindal Pretyman	
Colonel Elmhurst Rhodes (brother of Cecil Rhodes)	
Field Marshal Lord Frederick Sleigh Roberts (Lord Roberts)	
Major General Sir Henry Macleod Leslie Rundle	Commanded 8th Division
Colonel Settle	
Colonel Smith	Battery A, Royal Australian Artillery
Sir C. Smith	Commanded Australian troops
Lt. Colonel Steele	Strathcona Horse
Colonel Alexander Whitelaw Thorneycroft	Commanded Mounted Infantry
Lord E. Tolbat (Major)	11th Hussars
Major General Sir Charles Tucker	
Colonel S. Howard Vincent	
Lt. General Sir Charles Warren	Commanded 5th Division
Lt. General Sir George Stuart White	Defender of Ladysmith
Major General Sir Elliot Wood	
Colonel S. Wortley	King's Royal Rifles
Brigadier General James Herbert Yule	Symon's successor after his death

Military Attachés to the British Army

Name	Origin or Purpose
Major Gentilini	Italy
Colonel Stekovitch	Russia
Colonel Stocum	United States

Military Contingents and Groups

1st Grenadier Guards	Madres Lancers
1st Scots Guards	Medical Corps
2nd Queen's West Surrey Regiment	Montreal Infantry
9th Lancers (from India)	Mounted Rifles
10th Hussars	Natal Carbineers
13th Hussars	New South Wales Mount
19th Hussars	New Zealand Battery
93rd Gold Coast	Northwest Mounted Police (Canadian)
Constabulary	Quebec Infantry
Army Service Corps	Queensland Mounted Infantry
Australian Mounted Infantry	Rhodesian Horse
British Lancers	Rhodesian Scouts
Bushveldt Carbineers ("Breaker Morant")	Royal Artillery
Cameron Highlanders Gold Coast Constabulary	Royal Australian Artillery
Cameron Scottish Rifles	Royal Canadian Infantry
Canadian Rough Riders	Royal Dublin Fusiliers
Cape Colony Bicycle Corps	Royal Engineers
Coldstream Guards	Royal Horse Guards
Gordon Highlanders	Royal Irish Fusiliers
Household Cavalry	Royal Munster Fusiliers
Imperial Volunteers of the City of London	Scots Greys
King's Own Royal Lancaster	Shropshire Light Infantry
	South African Light Horse
	Strathcona Horse
	Yorkshire Light Infantry

War Wites and Campaigns (Boer War)

Battle of Amajuba	Madder River Battle
Battle of Farquhar's Farm (near Ladysmith)	Mafeking
Clandslaagte	Monte Cristo
Colenso	Najuba Hill
Diamond Hill	Orange River
Dronfield	Paardeberg
Dundee	Pieter's Hill
Jameson Raid	Siege of Ladysmith
Kimberley	Spion Kop
Krantz Kloof	Tugela
Laing's Nek	Wepener

Part III: Postcards

Types and Categories of Cards

Type	Category
Advertising cards	R4–R5
Aerial views of camps	R3
Allegorical representations surrounding images of Kitchener or Lord Roberts	R4–R5
Ambush-related	R4–R5
Ammunition and supply caches or depots	R3–R4
Anti-Boer cartoons	R5
Anti-British caricatures	R4–R5
Anti-British cartoons	R5
Armies in retreat	R4
Battle sites	
After battle	R3–R4
During siege	R4–R5
Boer ambulance train	R4
Boer burghers	
Enlisting	R4
In action or in the field	R4
Training	R4
Boer commanders	
In action	R5
Posed	R4–R5
Boer scouts	
Formal poses	R4
On the Veldt	R4–R5
Bomb shelters	R3–R4
Building campsites, bridges, breastworks, and so on	R4–R5
Burning Boer farms	R4
Camp post officers	R4
Caring for the wounded	R4
Cavalry-related	R4
Ferryboats in military use	R4–R5
Field artillery	R3–R4
Field hospitals	R4
Field kitchens	R4
Field library	R4
Field telegraphs	R4
Fighting from fixed positions	R4
Fond, romantic, or patriotic farewells	R4–R5
Funeral services	R5
Heliograph use	R4–R5
Hospital Ship *Marne* related	R4
Irish-American Corps–related	R5
Map cards	R3–R4
Military headquarters	R3–R4
Military leaders (British)	
Formal poses	R4–R5
In action	R5
In memorium	R4
Insets with scenes, maps, or other people	R4–R5
With other officers or soldiers	R5
Military trials and court martials	R5
Monuments and grave sites	R3–R4
Naval brigade (dressed like soldiers)	R4
Naval vessels	R3
Nursing-related	R4
O'Neil's Farm (location of conference between General Buller and General Botha)	R4–R5
Overviews of battle scenes	R4–R5
Peace-related cards	R4–R5
Postwar memorials and statues	R3–R4
POW cards	R5
Recreational activities of soldiers	R5
Red Cross cards	R4
Religious services	R4–R5
Resting in the field	R4–R5
Scouting and reconnoitering	R4–R5
Soldiers departing or arriving	R3–R4
Spy-related	R5
Transporting military supplies	R4
Transvaal telegram	R4
Transvaal Volksraad	R5
Troops being reviewed	R4
Troops on the march	R3–R4
Unfavorable caricatures of military leaders	R5

Types and Categories, cont.

Various regiments and contingents	R4
Victory parades	R4–R5
War balloons	R4
Weapons	
Immobile	R3–R4
In action	R4
Winston Churchill–related	R5
Woven silk cards, all types	R5
Wrecked trains	R4
The only card of U.S. origin relating to the Boer War was published by A. Selige. The obverse features insets of George Washington and Paul Krüger to the left and right, respectively. Beneath the insets is an appeal to the U.S. President to help stop the war against the South African Republic. The reverse of the card is preaddressed to the Honorable Theodore Roosevelt. To the left of the address is a plea to "Help the cause of the Boers." Very rare.	R5

Sets and Series

Bürger and Ottillie. Published a #6000 and a #6100 series titled *Der Boerenkrieg.* These light blue-colored artist-drawn sketches depict, among other things, the ineptness and cowardice of the British; insulting caricatures of British Royalty; and the fortitude of the Boers—many types that are comments of a social or military nature. The cards are of German manufacture and indicate all too well which side Germany applauded during the war.

Pictorial Postcard Company, Ltd. British postcard firm which produced several sets of numbered, artist-drawn cards. Included are cards of both British and Boer military commanders, British regiments, individuals of significance, nursing-related subjects, activities, and individual soldier types. The famous R. Caton-Woodville was the artist. These cards are quite scarce and decidedly historic.

Raphael Tuck. Produced several sets and series on the Boer War:

☆ *Empire Series #406–#417.* This 12-card set contains artist-drawn black-and-white portraits of British military commanders. Each drawing is within an oval that has crossed, colored flags to the top left. In gold lettering above the oval are the words *Souvenir of 1900.* The commander's name, also in gold, appears below the oval. Commanders pictured on the cards, along with their corresponding numbers, are as follows:

406	Field Marshal Lord Roberts
407	Lord Kitchener
408	Major General T. Kelly Kenny
409	Lt. Colonel Baden-Powell
410	General Sir F. Carrington
411	General Clements
412	General Clery
413	Colonel Plumer
414	Lt. General Sir G. White
415	General Sir Archibald Hunter
416	General Lyttleton
417	Major General J. D. P. French

☆ *Empire Series #418–#429.* Although similar to the earlier numbered series, this set has a few differences. A single flag (an embossed Union Jack) is pictured in color. In its center is a wreath containing the initials *VR.* A crown is above the wreath. The words *Souvenier 1900* are to the right above some flowered artwork. Beneath the flag is a black-and-white artist-drawn portrait of the various British commanders. Below is more artwork of leaves and the commander identification.

☆ Other Raphael Tuck series include the Empire series #240 and #260, which contain ships, regiments, and individuals under a Union Jack flag, and other patriotic symbols. Series #300 has various categories and scenes, including individual regiments and soldiers. Series #324–#336 is a set of "write-away" types, featuring some of the above motifs. Series #663–#665 is of peace commemoratives.

Miscellaneous Series. Related miscellaneous cards are as follows:

☆ *Faulkner.* Published at least six scenics (numbered alternately from 19 to the 40s).

☆ *Patriotic Pictorial Postcard Company.* Produced an unnumbered series of song cards.

☆ *Stewart and Woolf.* Produced cartoon cards related to espionage.

Publishers

A. Selige
Current Events
Ernst Rennert
Faulkner
G. Stewart
H. M. Guest
Joseph Eilen
Louis Van Neck
Meyer, Ltd.
Patriotic Pictorial Postcard Company
Picture Postcard Company
Raphael Tuck
Rotary
Scherer, Nabholz & Co.
Stewart and Woolf
W. and A. K. Johnston
Weiss-Reinschmidt
Wieck

Artists

A. F.
Eysler
Geldrop
Le Clerc
Mailick*
Orens*
Harry Payne*
Hector Talvart
Arthur Thiele*
R. Caton-Woodville*

* *most popular*

Colonel Plumer. *Raphael Tuck* Empire *series; #413. R4*

General Lyttleton. Raphael Tuck Empire *series; #416. R4*

Field Marshal Lord Roberts, V. C. Raphael Tuck Empire *series; #418. R4*

General Sir Archibald Hunter, K. C. B. Raphael Tuck Empire *series; #423. R4*

Boers attacking arriving British troops; German anti-British, propaganda. Bürger and Ottillie. R4

Map of South Africa with insets of President Krüger and General Joubert. Anonymous. R4

A Boer family prepared for defense. Anonymous. R4

General Viscount Kitchener. Raphael Tuck. R3

Boer leader Christian de Wet. Meyer Ltd. R4

Boers with a howitzer, ready for action. Anonymous. R4

Boer's reconnoitering activity. Anonymous. R4

Field Marshal von Waldersee—a hero's welcome. Peter Goh. R4

The "Gentle Giant," Francisco Madero. Curt Teich. R3

K. k. infantry regiment. Anonymous; #37. R4

K. u. k. infantry regiment. Anonymous; #75. R4

Japanese soldiers riding through a village that displays patriotic symbols. Anonymous. R4

Wilhelm II, Germany's warlord. Anonymous. R3

Wilhelm II and Hindenburg, propoganda, poster-type. Carl Schmidt. R3

Wilhelm II and Franz Joseph, propaganda card. W. Grieger. R3

A German sentimental card. R & K. R3

Von Hötzendorff, Austrian chief of staff. Red Cross card. R3

K. u. k. infantry regiment. Anonymous; #75. R4

King Ludwig III of Bavaria decorating his officers. Kilophot. R4

General Field Marshal von Hindenburg. F. H. & S. R3

Von Gallwitz. J. & S. M. R4

Von Vojna, Austrian General of Infantry. L & P. R4

Belgium's hero, Albert I. Anonymous. R4

French troops receiving a special Christmas blessing. A. Noyer. R3

"Christmas in the Field"; card sold for benefit of Austro-Hungarian army. Anonymous. R4

Crown Prince Karl of Austria-Hungary visiting troops at Russia-Poland front, 1915. Kilophot. R4

An American patriotic Christmas card. Illustrated Postal Card Company. R2

Military Silhouettes. G. Savigny. R3

A German iron cross with the four H's: Hohenzollern, Habsburg, Hindenburg, and Hötzendorf. Anonymous. R2

Arrival of French war prisoners at Luxembourg; special censor cancellation. Von Walter Müller. R4

Flags of the Allied nations. Anonymous. R2

"Helping a French Cavalryman Wounded at St. Quentin." Underwood and Underwood; W. C. A. 145 series, #27. R2

One of Austria's giant cannons; special cancellation. L & P. R4

Austrian soldier in a romantic setting. H. H. i. W. R3

Italian Bersagliere (rifle soldier). H. Guggenheim and Company. R3

Wounded Austrian soldier receiving blessings that involve both the monarchy and the Holy See. Anonymous. R4

"Defenders of the Empire, 1914–15." Raphael Tuck. R3

German kaiser and the crown prince discussing strategy. M. Munk. R3

Caricature of American soldier. Anonymous. R2

Christ on the field of battle. Hungarian card. R4

"Oh Lord, Be with Us." O. K. W. R3

Wilhelm II being hailed by his domestic and colonial armies. Anonymous. R4

The king at the Front, meeting a hospital matron. *Daily* Mail; #84. R3

General John J. Pershing. Anonymous. R2

German general von Kluck. M.L.M. R4

The kaiser observing the crown prince's army. P.F.B. R3

Admiral "Jacky" Fisher, head of admiralty at war's inception. Underwood and Underwood; W. C. A. 146 series, #70. R2

Von Hindenburg, Germany's symbol of stability. E. A. Seemann. R3

Von Hindenburg. G. Stalling. R3

Marshal Ferdinand Foch. Anonymous. R3

Austrian general Kövess von Kövessháza. G. G. W. R4

Austrian general von Muhr. G. G. W. R4

Field Marshal Peter Hofmann. Official card for Red Cross. R4

Austrian General Dankl. G. G. W. R4

Posed battle position. E. A. Schwerdtfeger. R3

Flag/insignia cards of German military. Central Office N.S.D.A.P. R3

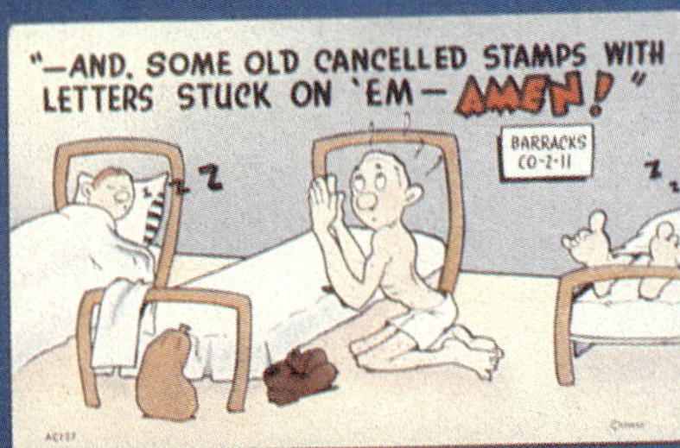

An often-spoken prayer. M.W.M. R1

A new twist on an old game. Army Comics Series T. Anonymous. R2

Drill sergeant intimidating one of his charges (all in the best military tradition, of course). Curt Teich. R1

Children as the Axis Powers walloping Britain in Africa, Asia, and Europe. Anonymous. R4

"We're Giving 'Em a Big WAC." Asheville Post Card Company. R2

Italian 39th Infantry Regiment; remembrance card of past military accomplishments. Italian card. Anonymous. R4

Heroism on the battlefield. Heinrich Hoffmann. R3

Total solidarity for Nazism, 1938. Official celebration card. R3

Children as military leaders planning strategy on maneuvers, pre-World War I. Anonymous. R4

History and Traditions of British Regiments, 10th Hussars, pre-World War I. Gale and Polden. R3

History and Traditions of British Regiments, 19th Hussars, pre-World War I. Gale and Polden. R3

"Through thick and thin," Austrian Cavalry, pre-World War I. B. K. W. I. R3

Portrait of Hitler by Willy Exner. Photo Hoffmann. R3

Capital of the Nazi movement commemorating November 9, 1923. August Lengauer. R3

General Tchang (Chiang) Kai-Tchek (Shek). G.P.D. R3

General Charles de Gaulle. G.P.D. R3

British Admiral Louis Mountbatten. G.P.D. R4

War bonds; poster-type. U.S. Treasury Department. R3

German appreciation for their leader. Brend'amour, Simbart & Company. R3

"100-Year Defeat of Napoleon—50-Year Celebration for Bavaria." Hans Pernat. R4

Wilhelm II as a German admiral, pre-World War I. Raphael Tuck "Oilette." R3

Count Bismarck, military leader and politician, pre-1900. Meissner & Buch. R4

"Drummer, Royal Scots Fusiliers." Millar and Lang. R2

Napoleon with Mary Louise, Museum at Versailles. A. Noyer. R2

Napoleon at the battle of Eylau, Louvre museum. R2

Napoleon at the coronation, Louvre museum. A. Noyer. R2

Battle of Lexington. A. C. Bosselman & Company. R2

General Montcalm congratulating his troops in 1758 at Fort Ticonderoga. Curt Teich. R2

Caricature satirizing military parades and military pomp in general; an interesting card. R3

"Corporal, U.S. Cavalry." Army and Navy Novelty Company (Curt Teich). R3

Otto von Bismarck. Anonymous. R4

George Washington; facsimile signature. Eastern National Park and Monument Association. R1

4
The Spanish-American War

Part I: History and Chronology

"Unremarkable" Cuba

Since October 1492, when Christopher Columbus initially laid claim to it, the island of Cuba has had a tumultuous history. From that first conquest to the barbarous unwritten policy of extermination and the subsequent series of revolts, what otherwise might have been an unremarkable nation became one continually drenched with the blood of innocents and aggressors alike. In all these activities it must be observed that Spain played the central role.

None of the earlier conflicts, however, had the impact of the one that engaged the energies of Cuba's northern neighbor. That set of battles—known collectively as the Spanish-American War—turned a crucial page in the military history of the United States of America.

Originally populated by natives variously described as generous, amiable, and mild-natured, Cuba was a land that witnessed the same fate as other territories invaded by Western Europeans. Dispossession of native sovereignty was followed in certain order by extermination of the indigenous inhabitants. One historian has put the case distinctly and dramatically: "There is little doubt," he says "that before 1560, the whole of this population had disappeared from the island." Unable to readily absorb and adapt to European culture, and unwilling to align themselves single file behind the concept of a God who accepted—indeed, who promoted—the use of savagery, the original Cubans consigned themselves to the underworld.

The story of the Cuban chieftain who would rather be burned on a spit than convert to Christianity is, whether true or not, quite revealing. "I'm afraid if I accept your religion," he said, "that I'll have to go to heaven and there meet other Christians." Often before rebellious Cubans were executed, their hands were cut off when they no longer brought gold or valuables to their Spanish overlords, and their feet were removed when their usefulness as slaves was thought to be completed.

Over the centuries, conditions clearly improved from these extremes, but unfortunately, not much. By the final decade of the nineteenth century, and after a repeated history of problems ranging from insurrectionary activity to a growing deficit, Spain found itself embroiled in a growing dilemma—she had to decide what to do with her ill-respected colony. Retaining it meant keeping an economic liability that was also a state of constant unrest. The decision, lamentable though it might have been, was not debatable. *Not* to maintain the Spanish Empire, regardless of the expense in dollars and military deployment, was unthinkable. Even the Cuban rebellion of 1895 failed to dissuade the Spanish in their determination to keep the colony. In fact, during that crisis, Spain reacted with a cruelty unimaginable in its scope—the starvation, deportation, and murder of civilians only added to the activity of the battle lines. America's sympathies were deeply stirred and the resulting dispatchment of aid included not only money, foodstuffs, and medical supplies, but also a growing number of U.S. male citizens who surreptitiously found their way into the insurgent armies.

From 1895 to 1898, the only movement toward resolution was in a negative direction. Unable to resolve its conflict, the plight of the fairest island in the Western ocean grew increasingly worse. Slowly and surely, Cuba was becoming a massive graveyard.

Then occurred the incident involving the battleship *Maine.*

American Involvement

The situation involving her southern neighbor elicited both sympathy and alarm throughout the United States. By 1898, prevailing conditions in Cuba included a policy of concentration whereby farmland on much of the island was purposely destroyed and the inhabitants—mainly women, children, and elderly men—were herded into overcrowded cities. It was reported that the death rate in these unsanitary fortresses exceeded 50 percent, mainly from starvation and disease. In a message to Congress, April 1989, President McKinley put the case succinctly:

> As the scarcity of food increased with the devastation of the depopulated areas of production, destitution and want became misery and starvation. Month by month the death rate increased in alarming rates. No practical relief was accorded the destitute. The overburdened towns, already suffering from the general death, could give no aid. The unfortunates, being for the most part women and children, or aged and helpless men enfeebled by disease and hunger, could not have tilled the soil without tools, seed or shelter, to provide for their own support. It was extermination. The only peace it could beget was that of the wilderness and the grave.

What many Americans found paradoxical was the fact that Spain was a civilized, God-fearing, God-promoting nation. This point was reinforced by Senator John Thurston of Nebraska after a visit to Cuba:

> Christ died 1900 years ago, and Spain is a Christian nation; she has set up more crosses in more lands beneath more skies, and under them has butchered more people than all the nations on earth combined.

The last pursuer of this policy was General Valeriano Weyler, dispatched from Spain in 1896 as captain-general in charge of crushing all signs of Cuban rebellion. If Weyler did not succeed, it was not through lack of effort. His distasteful methods led eventually to his resignation, but not before the assassination of Prime Minister Canovar on August 6, 1897, led to his replacement by the liberal Sagosta. What did not change was Spain's determination to prosecute the war to a satisfactory conclusion, regardless of the cost. Thus, the reforms instituted by General Blanco, although welcome, did not include Cuban autonomy or any real measure of political freedom. A strange sort of political paranoia was displayed by the Spanish when they accused the United States of aiding and abetting the insurgents because of the $50,000 Congress had appropriated to feed suffering Cubans. This was far from true, as the U.S. had spent nearly $2 million preventing expeditions to the island. Furthermore, those caught making any such attempt were brought before American courts. Still it was obvious that passions were sufficiently ignited on both sides to keep the fires of misunderstanding ablaze. Incident followed incident and accusation preceded accusation. The courses of action pursued by each nation were of the type that courted, if not guaranteed, diplomatic disaster. Not unpredictably, disaster occurred.

Remember the *Maine*

On February 15, 1898, the U.S. Battleship *Maine* was peacefully docked at Havana harbor when a mine explosion under her port side sent the vessel to the bottom of the harbor. Two officers and 266 men died either from the explosion or by drowning. The worst fears, suggested in the papers of William Randolph Hearst and Joseph Pulitzer and fanned by their invective-filled editorials, seemed to have become reality. Revisionist history suggests that the "accident" may have been engineered by certain individuals—with or without the complicity of key U.S. officials—for the purpose of beginning a war with Spain. (The results of a 1976 study commissioned by Admiral Hyman Rickover stated with certainty that the explosion could not possibly have been an external one.)

The evidence at that time was interpreted to support the popular belief that the explosion was anterior to the ship. For most Americans, the ultimate insult was delivered when the Spanish government declared that the accident was the result of carelessness by the *Maine*'s captain and a lack of discipline and order from her crew.

America's feeling—at least a large slice of it—was in agreement with the observation of Captain Robley D. Evans, commander of the battleship *Iowa*. Evans claimed that if he had his way about it, nothing but Spanish would be spoken in hell for the next five years.

The report issued by the board of inquiry came as no surprise; its statement that the ship was destroyed by the explosion of a submarine mine was enough to convince Congress that its $50 million appropriation for possible hostilities against Spain had been a wise action. When President McKinley issued his executive proclamation reciting the board's findings and demanding the withdrawal of all land and naval forces from Cuba, it was to be expected that the Spanish—not alien to displays of emotion themselves—sent the American ambassador his passport even before he could deliver the message. What everyone had expected, and too many had wanted, happened: War began.

U.S. War Expenditures

Mobilization of troops and troopships	$ 17,000,000
Additions to the Navy	20,000,000
Ordnance and arms	10,000,000
Commissary supplies	15,000,000
Pay for the Army and Navy	27,000,000
Ammunition	8,000,000
Ammunition for Navy at Santiago	4,000,000
Coal for warships	5,000,000
Cuban relief	2,000,000
Harbor defenses and mines	10,000,000
Total	$118,000,000

A Splendid Little War

First and foremost, the Spanish-American war was a series of naval engagements. From the bombing of the *Maine* to Dewey's impressive victory at Manila Bay to the various other "water battles," the conflict's major acts of hostility occurred ship-to-ship or ship-to-land.

For those who tend to think of war in terms of personal exploits, the story of Theodore Roosevelt and his Rough Riders fulfills their expectations. Nor should the then-future president's efforts and accomplishments be easily dismissed. He was clearly instrumental in the subjugation of the island, and although his climb up San Juan Hill (it was actually Kettle Hill) was of greater importance to the cause of the Spanish-American War than was the charge of the Light Brigade to the Crimean War, the difference was not a monumental one. In both cases, although their heroism was decidedly real, the outcome of the war was determined elsewhere in what was, perhaps, a less spectacular style.

Resembling the 300 Spartans who defended the pass at Thermopylae in 480 B.C. against 10,000 Persians, Roosevelt and his men represented that spirit which often expresses itself in action and sacrifice. Roosevelt came to Cuba to establish and demonstrate his manhood in the only manner he thought possible—he came as a hunter (in this instance, as a stalker of man). It may be appreciated and posterity may be thankful that Roosevelt's life was not lost as he engaged in the process of spilling the blood of his fellow creatures.

One statement that would have met nearly unanimous concurrence among contemporaneous historians was that the conflict between Spain and America was a "splendid little war." Quickly coming to mind, of course, would be the exploits and derring-do of Admiral Dewey and Colonel Roosevelt. But it would not go unnoticed among the historians, as it should not go unremembered by posterity, that these two represented but a small portion of the heroism displayed during that war (on both sides).

One should not forget that which follows, but accord it as much respect as that which leads. For behind each Roosevelt foolishly leading a cavalry charge in the face of a withering barrage of gunfire, and following on the heels of every Dewey recklessly pushing into a harbor thought to be salted with enemy mines, there stands a plethora of heroes just as foolish, just as reckless, and just as determined to create a discernible footprint of their own in the sands of time.

Posterity forgets and history too seldom records these "lesser" efforts. History is, after all, created from an interesting fabric—part propaganda, part wishful interpretation, part outright distortion, part fact, part statistic, and often, though perhaps unintentional, part amnestic. Thus, mankind extols the virtues of Ulysses Grant, but utters not a word about the men under his command; we laud Horatio Nelson, but not his charges, those fellow sailors whose braveries have largely gone unrecorded; we applaud Alexander, Caesar, Napoleon, Bismarck, and on and on—but what of the common foot soldier or sailor who executed his orders efficiently, or who otherwise added meaning to his leader's deeds? Are they fellows to be dismissed by the belief that without a great commander they are mere rabble—undisciplined, unrefined, unimaginative?

During the Spanish-American War there was a hurried sort of frenzied action geared toward the creation of command. Everywhere one looked, there were generals and admirals and captains. At least in the case of the former and the latter, the number of commissions seemed to increase geometrically. Many—in fact, most—were little more than outright gifts. But there were, even in this brief "100-Day War," men of the caliber of Leonard Wood, who entered as a volunteer colonel, but rose to the rank of general and to the political/military leadership of the whole of Cuba. And if one were to look closely, he might observe a young lieutenant eager to do his duty. Even at that early date, John J. Pershing, later commander of the American Expeditionary Force in World War I, was a noteworthy if not flamboyant soldier.

And so this "splendid little war" has been entered with flourishing strokes into the pages of history. It may aptly, if too easily, be viewed as a series of battles fought between two "Christian" nations, each assured that the weight of moral turpitude and the blessings of God would alternately and ultimately crown their efforts with success and prove the righteousness of their cause. It ended with Spanish concessions and American territorial gains (plus a little international recognition, not in itself an unwelcome effect). Two verdicts are certain: Because of the Spanish-American War, Spain was never again seriously taken to be a major military power, while the United States, having tested and proven its mettle in international conflict, would henceforth be unable to effectively bury its head in isolationism.

What the U.S. Gained

- ☆ Clear title to Puerto Rico
- ☆ Clear title to the Isle of Pines
- ☆ Choice of Ladrone Islands (chose Guam)
- ☆ Right to Manila city, bay, and harbor
- ☆ Annexation of Hawaii

Postcard Connections

Postcards detailing the Spanish-American War are not as numerous as one might expect considering the exuberance and unity the war engendered, especially in the United States. Unfortunately, the largest category of cards is of the real-photo type. During this time (and also during World War I) it was quite common for soldiers and sailors to have photographs made of themselves, which they then converted into postcards and mailed home. Personal cards that are less easily connected to the war are obviously the least expensive to acquire. The identified specimens are a different matter, and many of them, being visual pieces of social, political, and military history, rightly command a premium. Also very highly prized are those real-photo cards with a connection to Dewey, Roosevelt, or battle scenes.

Chronology: Spanish-American War

Date	Event
1898	
February 15	U.S. battleship *Maine* is blown up in Havana Harbor; two officers and 266 sailors are killed.
February 16	Spain offers regrets; President McKinley accepts accident theory.
February 18	Evidence of external explosion found; Senator Mason asks for Congressional investigation.
February 19	U.S. decides to conduct separate inquiry.
February 21	Spanish officials at Havana pronounce explosion an accident.
February 22	Senate votes two new regiments of artillery; General Lee advises Americans to leave Cuba.
February 24	Ensign Povelson finds *Maine*'s keel bent upward.
February 25	Board of Inquiry is satisfied the explosion was outside the ship.
February 28	Plate bolts point to a mine as the cause of *Maine*'s explosion.
March 3	While the administration talks of indemnity, rush work is commenced in navy yards.
March 4	Spain is reported to be buying warships.
March 5–6	Pope announces for peace and urges arbitration.
March 8	$50 million voted for defenses; government plans to buy warships, an action that startles Spain; all parties unite to support the administration.
March 11	President is fully informed of Spain's guilt; plans are perfected for mobilizing the army.
March 12	Spain offers Cuba a limited independence including withdrawal of troops.
March 17	Spain refuses (semiofficially) to pay an indemnity; Flying Squadron is organized.
March 19–21	Report of Board of Inquiry is received; war speeches are made in House of Representatives.
March 23–25	Spain talks of counterdemands, orders more ships readied for service; official report blames destruction of *Maine* on a mine that could only be activated from Havana by land.
March 27	Spain and U.S. both seek to delay the crisis.
March 31	Spain refuses to give up Cuba; American ships prepare for action and more are purchased.
April 11	After heated words on both sides and Spanish intransigence, President McKinley issues ultimatum ordering Spain out of Cuba.
April 12–16	Issue debated in Congress; both Houses declare for war.
April 21	Stewart T. Woodford, American ambassador to Spain, is given his passport before he can deliver the president's message.
April 23	President McKinley calls for 125,000 volunteers.
April 25	U.S. secretary of state John Sherman resigns.
April 28	War Department calls for concentration of 10,000 troops at Tampa; the U.S. monitor *Terror* captures the Spanish steamer *Guido*.
May 1	Commodore Dewey completely routs the Spanish Fleet at Manila. Results: 8 Americans wounded and $5,000 in damage to ships, vs. Spanish losses of 1200 killed and wounded, plus property damaged or captured.
May 3–11	Spain is in a state of revolt; Admiral Sampson's fleet sails for Puerto Rico; French steamer *Lafayette* is captured while attempting to run blockade at Havana, but later released; Spanish Armada anchored at San Juan; Commodore Dewey nominated as a rear admiral.
May 12–18	Admiral Sampson bombards San Juan; battle in Cardenas Harbor (five Americans killed), city surrenders; first U.S. soldiers land in Cuba from steamer *Gussie;* Spanish cabinet resigns, new cabinet chosen by Sagosta.
May 19–30	Spanish Armada located at Santiago; Sampson's fleet at Key West; Cervera's fleet bottled up at Santiago; President issues proclamation for 75,000 more volunteers and commissions ex-Senator Butler as major general of volunteers; two more brigadier generals created.
June 1	Sampson arrives off Santiago Harbor.
June 8	Warships bombard harbor of Guantanomo.
June 11–15	Marines score victories in Cuba.
June 19–20	General Shafter arrives at Santiago and Sampson's ships prepare a landing for Shafter's troops.
June 24	First battle of Raigs Riders; Hamilton Fish killed. Shafter's army advances to Juragra.
June 28	Americans advance within three miles of Santiago; Shafter joins Wheeler at the front.
June 29	More troops—90,000—sail for Santiago.
July 1	American losses are heavy as they attack Santiago; Roosevelt leads charge up Kettle Hill.
July 3	General Shafter demands surrender of Santiago; Admiral Cervera's fleet attempts to escape from Santiago Harbor and is destroyed by American ships.
July 4	Shafter sends a surrender ultimatum to Santiago.
July 9	American losses at Santiago: 22 officers killed, 208 men killed, 81 officers wounded, 1203 men wounded; 79 men missing.
July 12	Shafter sends third ultimatum, no response.
July 13	Yellow fever appears among Shafter's men.
July 15	Major General Otis and several hundred troops sail from San Francisco for Manila; martial law proclaimed in Spain.
July 17	General Toral finally surrenders; American flag hoisted at Santiago; 600 cases of yellow fever in American army; second expedition for the Philippines arrives at Manila.
July 19	Port Caimanera surrendered to Captain McCalla.
July 21	Deciding to keep Puerto Rico as a permanent possession, the U.S. sends General Miles there with several thousand troops and a strong convoy of warships.
July 23	General Miles lands near Ponce, Puerto Rico; total American casualties to date equal 1595.
July 28	General Shafter reports 4000 cases of sickness in the army at Santiago; General Miles accepts surrender of Ponce, takes possession for United States.
August 1	Generals Brooke and Schwan arrive at Ponce; General Cappinger is also ordered to Puerto Rico.
August 4	Engagement between Spanish cavalry at Guayama, Puerto Rico, and U.S. troops; former defeated with no American losses.
August 7	Spain tentatively accepts peace.
August 8	General Miles advancing, now 20 miles from San Juan.
August 9	Coamo, Puerto Rico captured; news that Americans had defeated Spanish at Camp Dewey, Philippines, is received. Losses: 350 Spanish killed, about 950 wounded; 13 Americans killed and 48 wounded.
August 12	Spain officially signs peace treaty; President McKinley orders a cessation of hostilities.
August 13–14	Unaware of treaty, Commodore Dewey and General Merrit attack Manila; Spanish surrender Philippines.
September 2	Total number of U.S. soldiers dead: 1299.

1899 February 4	War begins between Philippine insurgents and U.S. occupation forces.	**1901** March 23	Filipino revolutionary leader Emilio Aguinaldo is captured.
1899	U.S. sends more forces and creates more officers for Philippine war.	**1902** July 4	Philippine War declared at end by President Roosevelt.

Part II: Details of War

Military Leaders

American

Name	Position/Significance
Lt. Ahern	Army; hero
Brigadier General Adelbert Ames	
General Anderson	Served in Philippines
Brigadier General John N. Andrews	Commanded 12th Infantry
Lt. Colonel John Jacob Astor	(The millionaire)
Brigadier General John B. Babcock	Assistant adjutant general
Ensign Worth Bagley	First officer killed in the war
Brigadier General William A. Bancroft	
Major General J. C. Bates	
Colonel James Bell	1st Cavalry, Philippine war commander
Lt. J. B. Bernadon	Commander of *Windlow*
Lt. Victor Blue	Navy; hero
William H. Boardman	Only naval cadet killed
Lt. F. R. Brainard	Commander of *Uncas*
Major General Joseph E. Breckenridge	Inspector general
Major General John Rutter Brooke	Commander 1st Corps
Captain W. H. Brownson	Commander of *Yankee*
Flag Lt. T. M. Brumby	Served on the *Olympia*
Major General Butler	An ex-senator, Butler was appointed by the president as major general of volunteers
Captain Allyn K. Capron	Army; hero
Captain F. E. Chadwick	Commander of *New York*
Brigadier General Adna R. Chaffee	
Captain Chester	Commander of *Cincinnati*
Colonel Gracey Childers	Tennessee Volunteers
Commander Charles F. Clark	Commander of *Oregon*
Brigadier General Jacob Cline	
Captain C. G. Coghlan	Commander of *Raleigh*
Colonel A. B. Coit	
Brigadier General Leonard W. Colby	
Brigadier General Nelson Cole	
Captain Francis A. Cook	Commander of *Brooklyn*
Captain P. H. Cooper	Commander of *Chicago*
Major General John J. Coppinger	Commander 4th Corps
General John J. Coppington	
Brigadier General Henry C. Corbin	Chief of U.S. Army personnel
Colonel L. A. Craig	6th Cavalry, Philippine war commander
Commander Craig	Hydrographer of the Navy
Commander A. S. Crowninshield	Chief of Bureau of Navigation
Commander James H. Dayton	Navy
Lt. Commander Daniel Delehantz	Commander of *Suwanee*
Commodore Dewey	Victor at Manila Bay
Captain F. W. Dickens	Navy
Captain Dorst	Commander of *Gussive*
Brigadier General Henry T. Douglas	
Colonel Duboce	First California Regiment
Brigadier General Henry M. Duffield	
General Duffield	33rd division, Michigan
Captain N. M. Dyer	Commander of *Baltimore*
Brigadier General Charles D. Eagen	Commissary general
Brigadier General Oswald H. Ernst	
Captain Robley D. Evans	Commander of *Iowa*
Brigadier General Charles Fitzsimmons	
Brigadier General D. W. Flagler	Chief of ordnance
Colonel Frost	South Dakota Regiment
Colonel Cornelius Gardener	19th Infantry; Philippine war commander
Brigadier General George A. Garretson	
Brigadier General George L. Gillespie	
Brigadier General John C. Gilmore	
Captain Gilmour	Commander of *Yorktown*
Captain Glass	Commander of *Charleston*
Brigadier General William F. Gordon	
Major General William H. Grahm	Commander 2nd Corps

Name	Position/Significance
Brigadier General Frederick D. Grant	Philippine insurgent army surrendered to him
Brigadier General A. W. Greely	Chief signal officer
Brigadier General Francis V. Greene	
Captain Charles V. Gridley	Commander of *Olympia*
Colonel Grigsby	Commander, 3rd Regiment of Cowboys
Major Grimes	Maintained an important battery for shelling purposes
Brigadier General P. C. Hains	
General Hale	Served in Philippines
Brigadier General Hall	Philippine war commander
Colonel Edward Hardin	7th Infantry, Philippine war commander
Colonel Luther R. Hare	7th Cavalry, Philippine war commander
Captain P. F. Harrington	Commander of *Puritan*
Brigadier General Peter C. Harris	
Brigadier General Henry C. Hasbrouck	
Major Heistand	Assistant adjutant general
Lt. J. M. Helm	Commander of *Hornet*; hero
Brigadier General Guy V. Henry	
Captain F. J. Higginson	Commander of *Massachusetts*
Lt. B. W. Hodges	Commander of *Nanshan*
Captain D. B. Hodgson	Commander of *McCulloch*
Lt. Jack Hood	Commander of *Hawk*
Brigadier General Lucius F. Hubbard	
Brigadier General Joseph R. Hudson	
Brigadier General Robert P. Hughes	Inspector general
Lt. Colonel R. W. Huntington	Marine commander
Captain George E. Ide	Commander of *Yosemite*
Lt. Carl W. Jungen	Commander of *Wampatuck*; hero
General Jacob F. Kent	
Lt. Commander W. W. Kimball	Commanded a torpedo-boat flotilla
Brigadier General Charles King	Well-known novelist; served in the Philippines
W. A. Kirkland	Rear admiral
Colonel William A. Kobbe	3rd Artillery, Philippine war commander
Commander B. P. Lamberton	Navy
General H. W. Lawton	
Major General Fitzhugh Lee	Commander 7th Corps
Commander E. H. C. Leutze	Commander of *Monterey*
Brigadier General G. N. Lieber	Judge advocate general
Brigadier General James Rush Lincoln	
Brigadier General M. T. Ludington	Quartermaster general
Captain Nicoll Ludlow	Commanding *Terror*
General Ludlow	Engineer Corps
Major General William Ludlow	
General MacArthur	Served in Philippines
Captain A. T. Mahan	Navy
Lt. Commander Adolf Marix	Commander of *Scorpion*
E. C. Matthews	Rear admiral
Commander Washburn Maynard	Commander of *Nashville*
Brigadier General Arthur McArthur	Father of Douglas McArthur
Commander McCalla	Navy; captured Caimanera; Commander of *Marblehead*
Brigadier General William J. McKee	
Commander M. R. S. McKenzie	Commander of *Mayflower*
Major General H. C. Merriam	
Major General Merritt	Commanded troops in the Department of the Pacific
Major General Nelson A. Miles	Commanding general of the Army
Brigadier General Marcus P. Miller	
J. N. Miller	Rear admiral
Colonel M. T. Moore	
Lt. Frank Newcomb	Commander of *Hudson*
C. S. Norton	Rear admiral
Brigadier General William C. Oates	
General Harrison Gray Otis	Served in Philippines (Anti-Union, Otis was the owner of the large daily newspaper in Los Angeles; he opposed Clarence Darrow in the latter's defense of the McNamara brothers.)
Major General Elwell S. Otis	Commander of the 2nd Detachment to Manila
Lt. Parker	Army; had a Gatling Battery
Ensign H. A. Pearson	Commander of *Zafiro*
Naval Constructor Richard Pearson	Responsible for sinking of *Merrimac* in Santiago Channel
Commander Thomas Perry	Commander of *Lancaster*
Lt. Pershing	Later a general; "Blackjack"
Colonel James Petit	1st Infantry, Philippine war commander
Captain John W. Phillips	Commander of *Texas*
Lt. Commander John E. Pillsbury	Served on the *Vesuvius*
Lt. Commander Potter	Navy
Lt. John L. Purcell	Commander of *Oceola*
Brigadier General Wallace F. Randolph	Commanded Light Infantry at Tampa
Colonel Edmund Rice	3rd Infantry, Philippine war commander
Captain William V. Richards	Also nominated assistant adjutant general with the rank of lt. colonel
Major Robe	Commander 14th Infantry
Colonel Theodore Roosevelt	
Lt. A. S. Rowan	Army; hero
F. M. Runce	Rear admiral
Lt. T. W. Ryan	Navy; commanded *Peoria*
Captain Sampson	Navy
W. T. Sampson	Rear admiral
Brigadier General Joseph P. Sanger	

Name	Position/Significance
Lt. General J. M. Schefield	Commander of the U.S. Volunteer Reserves
Commodore Schley	Commanded the Flying Squadron
Major General William R. Shafter	Commander of U.S. Army in Cuba; commander 5th Corps
Lt. Alexander Sharp	Commander of *Vixen*
Brigadier General Michael V. Sheridan	Brother of General "Phil" Sheridan
Montgomery Sicard	Rear admiral
Captain D. Sigsbee	Commander of *Maine*; later commander of *St. Paul*
Major Simpson	Chief of artillery
Colonel Smith	Tennessee Volunteers; died, replaced by Childers
Brigadier General Simon Snyder	
Lt. W. H. H. Southerland	Commander of *Eagle*
Brigadier General T. H. Stanton	Paymaster general
Brigadier General George M. Sternberg	Surgeon general
Brigadier General Roy Stone	
Lt. Commander D. D. V. Stuart	Commander of *Mangrove*
General Summer	
Brigadier General S. S. Sumner	
Captain N. C. Taylor	Commander of *Indiana*
Major Thompson	Signal Corps
Commander B. F. Tilly	Commander of *Newport*
Commander C. C. Todd	Commander of *Wilmington*
Captain C. J. Train	Commander of *Prairie*
Major General James F. Wade	Commander 3rd Corps
Lt. Commander Wainwright	Lt. commander of *Maine*
Lt. Commander Richard Wainwright	Commander of *Gloucester*
Commander Asa Walker	Commander of *Concord*
Lt. Colonel Wallace	Montana Regiment
Lt. Aaron Ward	Commander of *Wasp*
Brigadier General James R. Waties	
Commodore John Crittenden Watson	
Brigadier General Loyd Wheaton	
General Joseph Wheeler	Commander of all Cavalry forces
Lt. Henry H. Whitney	Army; carried a secret message to General Gomez, was made Captain afterward
Captain F. Wildes	Commander of *Boston*
Brigadier General John A. Wiley	
Major General James H. Wilson	Commander 6th Corps
Brigadier General John W. Wison	Chief of engineers
Colonel Leonard Wood	
Commander E. P. Wood	Commander of *Petrel*
Brigadier General S. B. M. Young	
Lt. Lucien Young	Commander of *Hist*; hero

Cuban

Name	Position/Significance
Colonel Bosa	Chief of Gómez's staff
General Maximo Gómez	Commanding general of Cuban Army
Antonio Maceo	Died in battle, December 1896
José Marte	Started 1895 revolution, then appointed Gómez to command the Army of Liberation

Others:
- General Carillo
- General Castillo
- Major Estrada
- General Calixto García
- General Emilio Nunez

Spanish

Name	Position/Significance
General Alejandrino	
Captain Alvargonzales	Commander of *Azor*
General Augusti	Governor general of the Philippine Islands
General Ramon Blancos	Replaced General Weyler
Admiral Camara	Commander of Cádiz Fleet
General Martinez Campo	
Captain Carlier	Commander of *Furor*
Admiral Cervera	His armada was destroyed
General Escario	
Captain Eulate	Commander of *Vizcaya*
General García	
General Fernain Juadenea	Replaced General Augusti upon the latter's resignation
Captain Lasaga	Commander of *Oqendo*
General Linares	Army commander at Santiago
General Manuel Macía	Captain general of Puerto Rico
General Mascardo	
Admiral Montojo	Philippine squadron commander
Captain Moreau	Commander of *Colon*
General Pando	
General Primo de Rivera	
Captain Rizo	Commander of *Rayo*
Captain La Rocha	Commander of *Terror*
Captain Somoza	Commander of *Ariete*
General Toral	Commander at Santiago
Don Vincente Trillo	Spanish vice -admiral
Captain Vasquéz	Commander of *Pluton*
Admiral Santiago Villamil	Vice commander of Cape Verde Squadron; killed at naval battle
General Weyler	Ex-governor general of Cuba

Philippine Insurgent Leaders

Name	Position/Significance
General Aguinaldo	Commander of Philippine insurgents
General Callies	
General Forres	
General García	
General Luga	
General Mascardo	
General Pilar	

American Military Outfits

First Invasion Army, Select Breakdown

Engineer Battalion	205
Regular Infantry	11,000
Signal and Hospital Corps	300
2nd U.S. Cavalry	500
1st, 3rd, 6th, 9th, and 10th U.S. Cavalries, two squadrons each	2,000
1st U.S. Volunteer Cavalry (Roosevelt's), two squadrons of four troops each	560
1st U.S. Light Infantry, Batteries E and K	160
2nd U.S. Light Infantry, Batteries E and K	150
4th U.S. Heavy Artillery G and H	200
Volunteer Infantry	2,000
Total	**17,075**

Prepared to follow was an army of 128,000 men.

American Military Outfits, Further Breakdown

2nd Cavalry	
9th Cavalry	Black outfit
10th Cavalry	Black outfit like 9th
1st Corps	Department of the Gulf, commanded by Major General Brooke
2nd Corps	Headquartered in Falls Church, Virginia; commanded by Major General William H. Grahm
3rd Corps	Chickamauga (commanded by Major General James F. Wade)
4th Corps	Mobile, Alabama (Major General John J. Coppinger)
5th Corps	Tampa, Florida (Major General William R. Shafter)
6th Corps	Chickamauga (Major General James H. Wilson, reporting to Major General Brooke)
7th Corps	Tampa (Major General Fitzhugh Lee)
23rd Division	Michigan
12th Infantry	Brigadier General John N. Andrews
14th Infantry	Regulars
18th Infantry	Regulars
20th Infantry Regiment	
24th Infantry	Black outfit like 25th
25th Infantry	Black regiment
20th Kansas	One of the most famous
22nd Kansas	
2nd Massachusetts Volunteers	
6th Massachusetts Volunteers	
10th Pennsylvania Infantry	
71st Regiment	New York
3rd Regiment of Cowboys	
Astor Light Brigade	(Millionaire John Jacob Astor offered to equip a complete battery of artillery; the offer was accepted and Astor himself was appointed a lieutenant colonel in the inspector general's department and detailed as a member of the staff of General Shafter.)
Leonard Wood's Rough Riders	
Major General Elwell S. Otis	Reported to Major General Wesley Merritt for duty with troops in the Department of the Pacific

Other American Outfits in the Philippines

- ☆ 7th Infantry
- ☆ 8th Infantry
- ☆ 12th Infantry
- ☆ 16th Infantry
- ☆ Iowa Volunteers
- ☆ Tennessee Volunteers

On July 6, 1898, an order was issued for ten new regiments for service in the Philippines. The regiments consisted of 50 officers and 1309 men each and were as follows:

26th regiment of Infantry Volunteers
27th regiment of Infantry Volunteers
28th regiment of Infantry Volunteers
29th regiment of Infantry Volunteers
30th regiment of Infantry Volunteers
31st regiment of Infantry Volunteers
32nd regiment of Infantry Volunteers
33rd regiment of Infantry Volunteers
34th regiment of Infantry Volunteers
35th regiment of Infantry Volunteers

Later Regiments:
- ☆ 4th Cavalry
- ☆ 38th Regiment

Notable American Volunteers

John Jacob Astor
Oliver H. P. Belmont
William Astor Chandler
Woodbury Kane
Colonel Edward Morrell
Colonel Thomas Potter
Lt. Colonel Theodore Roosevelt
William Tiffany
Craig W. Wadsworth
Captain Barclay H. Warburton
Colonel Leonard Wood

Contingents

American Army Contingents

Infantry Regiments

Included:
- ☆ 1st, 2nd, 3rd, 6th, 7th, 8th, 9th, 10th, 12th, 13th, 16th, 17th, 20th, 21st, 22nd, and 24th United States Regulars
- ☆ 2nd Massachusetts Volunteers
- ☆ 71st New York Volunteers

Total: 561 officers and 10,709 men

Cavalry

- ☆ Two squadrons of four troops each from the 1st, 3rd, 6th, 9th, and 10th United States Regulars
- ☆ Two troops from the 1st United States Volunteer Cavalry under the command of Colonel Leonard Wood, with Lt. Colonel Theodore Roosevelt his second-in-command (This outfit, called the *Rough Riders,* was composed primarily of Western ranchers, college athletes, and sportsmen.)
- ☆ One mounted squadron of the 2nd U.S. Cavalry, comprising nine officers and 280 men
- ☆ Also, 4th, 8th, 15th, and 25th Regiments

Total: 167 officers and 3675 men

Artillery

Composed of:

- ☆ Light Batteries E and K of the 1st U.S. Artillery
- ☆ Light Batteries A and F of the 2nd U.S. Artillery
- ☆ Also, Batteries G and H of the 4th U.S. Artillery for siege work

Total: 18 officers and 455 men

Others

- ☆ Two companies of engineers and 15 staff officers
- ☆ Representatives of the armies and navies of Europe
- ☆ 50 newspaper correspondents
- ☆ 5th Artillery, which served in Puerto Rico

American Contingents in the Philippines: Regiments

- ☆ 1st California, 1st Idaho, 1st Washington, 1st Wyoming
  (General Charles King commanding)
- ☆ 1st Colorado, 1st Nebraska, 1st South Dakota
  (General Hale commanding)
- ☆ 1st Montana, 3rd Artillery, 10th Pennsylvania, 20th Kansas
  (General Harrison Gray Otis commanding)
- ☆ 1st North Dakota, 4th Cavalry, 6th Artillery, 14th Infantry
  (General Anderson commanding)
- ☆ Batteries A and B of Utah Light Artillery
  (General MacArthur commanding in support of General Hale)

Total: 13,000 men

Manila Bay Contingents

U.S. Asiatic Squadron, commanded by Admiral Dewey, composed of the following ships:	vs.	Spanish Squadron, commanded by Admiral Montejo, which included these vessels:
Baltimore		*Castilla*
Boston		*Don Antonio de Ulloa*
Concord		*Don Juan de Austria*
McCulloch		*Isla de Cuba*
Olympia (Dewey's flagship)		*Isla de Luzón*
Petrel		*Reina Christina*
Raleigh		*Velasco*

Vessels

American Naval Vessels

Cruisers

Atlanta
Baltimore
Boston
Brooklyn
Charleston
Chicago
Cincinnati
Columbia
Detroit
Dixie
Eagle
Marblehead
Minneapolis
Newark
New Orleans
New York
Olympia
Peoria
Philadelphia
Prairie
Raleigh
San Francisco
St. Paul
Vesuvius
Yankee
Yosemite

Transports

Arkansas
Australia
Breakwater
Centennial
China
City of Peking
City of Sydney
Nanshan
Matteawan
Morgan
Stillwater
Yale
Zafiro

Battleships

Indiana
Iowa
Maine
Massachusetts
Oregon
Texas

Gunboats

Bennington
Castine
Hawk

Helena
Machias
Montgomery
Nashville
Newport
Petrel
Scorpion
Vixen
Wilmington
Yorktown

Torpedo Boats
Cushing Mayflower
Dupont
Ericsson
Farragut
Porter
Winslow

Flying Squadron
Brooklyn
Eagle
Iowa
Massachusetts
Porter
Texas

The Flying Squadron, in pursuit of the Cape Verde Fleet, finally bottled up Admiral Cervera at Santiago. United States Commander Schley was relieved shortly thereafter by Admiral Sampson, who—along with Hobson, who sank his own ship, the *Merrimac*—was credited with the destruction of the Spanish Fleet as it tried to escape the blockade.

Other Vessels
Gloucester
Gussie (steamer)
Hist
Hornet
Hudson (revenue cutter)
Lancaster (frigate)
McCulloch (revenue cutter)
Miantonomoh (monitor)
Monterey (monitor)
Puritan (monitor)
Wompatuck

Spanish Naval Vessels

Cruisers
Almirante Oquenda
Cardinal Cisneros
Carlos V
Castilla
Conde de Venadito
Cristóbol Colón
Don Antonio de Ulloa
Don Juan de Austria
Infanta María Teresa
Isla de Cuba
Isla de Luzón
Isla de Mindanao
Marquise de la Ensenada
Quiros
Reina Cristina (flagship at Manila)
Velasco
Vizcaya

Gunboats
Arayat
Callao
El Cano
Galicía
Lozo
Mariveles
Marqués de Duero
Mindora
Pampagne
Paragua
Samen
Temerario

Torpedo Gunboats
Ariete
Azor
Destructor
Rayo
Vilialobos

Torpedo Boat Destroyers
Furor
Pluton
Terror

Other Vessels
Argonauts (steamer)
Guido (steamer)
Montserrat (steamer)
Reina Mercedes
Rita (steamer)

Cape Verde Fleet
Almirante Oquenda
Cristóbol Côlon
Furor
María Teresa
Pluton
Viscaya

Part III: Postcards

Types and Categories

Type	Category
Activities of heros	R4
After-battle scenics	R3–R4
Artillery-related	R3–R4
Battle scenes	R4
Destruction of the *Maine*	R3
Hanging of prisoners	R4
Hero-related, miscellaneous	R3–R4
Hospital ships	R4
Later memorial and celebration cards	R3–R4
Military camps, miscellaneous	R3
Military funerals	R4
Military leaders	
Cevera	R4
Dewey	R3–R4
Roosevelt	R3–R4
All others	R4–R5
Military personnel relaxing	R3–R4
Military training	R3
Naval bombardments	R3–R4
Naval crews	R3–R4
POW-related	R4
Reconnoitering	R4
Red Cross cards	R4
"Remember the *Maine*" cards	R3
Rough Rider–related	R3–R4
Setting up camps	R3
Shipboard activities	R3–R4
Shipping and unloading supplies	R3
Ships, stationary	R2–R3
Ships, wrecked	R3–R4
Ships in action	R3–R4
Soldiers departing	R3
Sunday religious services aboard ship	R4
Survivors of the *Maine*	R3
Troops passing in review	R3
Various regiments	R3–R4
Victory parades	R4
War balloons	R4
Weapon-related cards	R3–R4
Wounded soldiers and sailors	R3
Wreckage of the *Maine*	R3

Sets and Series

Arthur Strauss. Published a series of cards variously numbered through the 30s and 50s and dealing with Dewey and war-ending receptions.

E. C. Kropp. Produced a series of black-and-white multiviews of Camp Harvey and Camp Thomas.

Harris Brothers. Published a #6000 series of colored views (later cards, 1912) related to the *Maine* and other incidents.

H. H. Stratton. Published a set of eight artist-drawn color cards with the subject matter "After the Spanish-American War." These depict navy life in Cuba, both on land and shipboard, and are as follows:

1. Naval Cooks
2. Naval Orphan Asylum, Guantanamo Naval Station (sailors nursing two babies with a goat)
3. Tourist Hotels, Havana
4. Sailors falling from an airplane onto a ship
5. Sailors relaxing at a table, Guantanamo Bay
6. Sailors at Fisherman's Point
7. Proddo, Guantanamo
8. Sailors at a café, Guantanamo

Rost. Produced a set showing U.S. Navy warships—at least 14 cards. Each one is black and white except for the flag. Each card has a ship on one side of its front and a representation of Miss Liberty on the other, and a souvenir mail-card reverse side. This set was reissued later with a different reverse.

Universal Postal Card Company. Produced two series of action cards: The first series is numbered 1–4; the second series is unnumbered and includes five cards. Cards are black and white.

First Series	*Second Series*
1. Destruction of the Matanzes Batteries, April 27	Sinking of the *Merrimac* in Santiago Harbor, June 3
2. Destruction of Spanish Fleet at Manila, May 1	Bombardment of Santiago, June 7
3. Capturing a Signal Station, May 11	Charge of Rough Riders, June 24
4. Bombardment of San Juan, May 12	Destruction of Cervera's Fleet, July 3
	Generals Shafter and Toral enter a captured Santiago, July 17

Other Warship Publishers. Several additional warship postcard publishers are as follows:

Albertype	Unknown number
American Souvenir Card Company	Unknown number
Arthur Livingston	13 cards; also reissued
E. C. Kropp	10 cards, black and white except for a colored flag, eagle, or shield, or a Schlitz beer trademark

Publishers

Name	Origin
Albertype	U.S.
American Souvenir Card Company	U.S.
Arthur Strauss	U.S.
E. C. Kropp	U.S.
Harris Brothers	U.S.
H. H. Stratton	U.S.
H. L. Browning	U.S.
Illustrated Postal Card Co.	U.S.

Publishers, cont.

Name	Origin
Livingston	U.S.
Metropolitan News Co.	U.S.
Rost	U.S.
Squires, Bingham & Co.	Manila
Universal Postal Card Company	U.S.

"Battleships endeavoring to force a landing." Illustrated Postal Card Company. R3

"Training ship Reina Mercedes, captured from Spain." Metropolitan News Company. R3

"Cofferdam work to dig out the Maine.*" Anonymous. R3*

Wreckage of the Maine. *Cuban governmental postal. R3*

"Towing the Maine *to Sea for Burial." Harris Brothers. R3*

"Manila Bay." Squires Bingham & Company. R2

Anchor of the Battleship Maine *at Arlington National Cemetery. Raphael Tuck. R3*

"Smoker on board battleship," Guantanamo Bay, Cuba. H. H. Stratton series. R4

Monument to Spanish-American War heroes at Arlington National Cemetery. Raphael Tuck. R2

5
The Boxer Rebellion

Part I: History and Chronology

Foreign Exploitation of China

After a disastrous military experience with the Japanese in 1894, China found herself ill-prepared to prevent a series of incursions into her territorial and—in some measure—political spheres. For their part, the major European powers viewed the Celestial Empire as so much acreage, raw material, and strategic position ripe for acquisition and exploitation. Thus began what appeared to the Chinese to be an unending string of concessions to greedy, uncultured, and ill-mannered barbarians. Travesty was heaped upon travesty as Germany, France, England, and Russia routinely and casually went about the business of cordoning off, after slicing up, this most ancient of civilizations. Like Africa before and concurrent with her, China was a nineteenth-century anachronism unable to completely forestall progress, but at the same time unwilling to embrace new ideas and new methods. Again, like Africa, she presented an inviting target for outside plunder and the insult of forced colonialism

A textbook example of military strength and sophistication proving superior to untested and unprepared armed forces, the Boxer Rebellion was a regrettable exercise in futility for the native Chinese. But the reason for Chinese chagrin was real and deeply felt. Their dignity trampled upon by those they considered culturally inferior, and the land of their ancestors being given away to these same "foreign devils," was too much for Chinese pride. A secret society known as the "Righteous Harmonious Fists," or "Boxers," began a campaign of terror against Europeans in China.

The Rebellion Begins

Openly encouraged by a sizable portion of the Chinese population and surreptiticusly supported by Empress Tz'u Hsi, the Boxers began with a series of atrocities. Determining to rid their homeland of the presence of all foreigners and committed to the eradication of all alien ideas, they focused their attention on the areas of religion and politics. Not satisfied with the murder of 200 Christian missionaries, they next vented their anger and frustration on some of their own people, slaughtering almost 20,000 Chinese Christian converts.

In 1900 the Boxers turned their attention to the foreign legations in Peking, where European diplomatic officials and the foreign citizens with sufficient foresight had barricaded themselves. Marching upon the city's legation quarter, they fully intended to execute judgment on their country's oppressors. It was at this time that the eyes of the world were focused on this most venerable of nations. In actuality, the situation was only different in degree from what had occurred during the preceding five years. As early as 1895, victims of a similar hatred, a number of British missionaries had been murdered; two years later a pair of German missionaries met with a similar fate.

For the non-Chinese world, the rebellion began in 1900, but it had been manifesting itself to the Chinese for some time. The following chronology of events details the before, during, and after of what happened, and numerous pieces of literature, histories, and celluloid productions tell the story, each with its own slant. One sort of common denominator seems to be an assumption that the Chinese were the aggressors, bent upon committing atrocities against helpless women and children—yellow-skinned monsters with a proclivity to torture and murder the other humans with whom they shared the planet.

Yet it is more than worthy of observation that, internal conflicts notwithstanding, the Chinese have engaged in fewer external wars than any European nation, Eastern or Western.

As all such rebellions must, the Boxer outbreak came to a swift conclusion beneath the armed might of stronger power. In this instance, there were a number of stronger powers, including a united expeditionary force of British, American, Japanese, German, Russian, and French troops. Unlike the American rebellion (and a few others), this one reached a foregone conclusion. For the Chinese, the results were the setting in motion of forces that eventually were to end the countless centuries of seclusion and isolation, although not all at once, nor totally. Even today the Chinese are still entering the twentieth century as they examine its ideals and technologies. It is a process that will not be completed for many years to come—maybe never.

For the "victors," the Boxer Rebellion represented the last time those nations would use their combined forces in a unified effort. It is perhaps most regrettable that the effort was devoted to economic and geographic exploitation at the expense of a nation that had sustained an advanced civilization almost a thousand years before Europeans progressed beyond animal skins, spears, the plow, and pagan sacrifices to the gods of nature.

Chronology: Boxer Rebellion

Date	Event
1895	
August	In China, massacre of several British missionaries at Ku-cheng.
1897	
November 15	Kiau Chau occupied by a German force in reparation for murder of two missionaries.
December 19	A Russian fleet enters Port Arthur to winter there.
1898	
January	China forced to cede Kiau Chau Bay and the adjacent territory to Germany for trade purposes; lease becomes active March 6 and is valid for 99 years.
March 24	Port Arthur, previously seized by Russia, is now leased to Russia for 25 years.
April 5	France, which had taken the Chinese island of Hainan, obtains the cessation of territory in Southern China for commercial purposes.
May	Wei-hai-wei is occupied by the British.
June	A concession for a railway from Peking to Hankow is granted to a Belgian syndicate acting in the interest of France and Russia.
September 21	After a coup d'état, the dowager empress assumes the regency to the virtual exclusion of the emperor Kuang Hsü.
October	Foreign legations in Peking are threatened by mob activity; troops are summoned from the coast.
1899	
April 30	An agreement is signed between Russia and Great Britain preventing either from interfering with the other regarding their respective railway policies in China.
1900	
January	An imperial edict announces the virtual abdication of the emperor Kuang Hsü and names a son of Prince Tuan as successor.
March	China promotes the so-called "Open Door" policy, a pledge given to the United States that no interference with commerce on the basis of nationality shall be permitted.
April	Antiforeign feeling culminates in outrages committed by the Boxers against Christians in Northern China.
May 31	More Boxer actions result in the assembling of foreign warships at Taku; guards are summoned to protect foreign legations at Peking.
June 10	An international force leaves Tien Tsin for the relief of the Peking legations; Chinese government appears to support Boxers.
June 17	Taku forts fire upon the European fleet and in turn are demolished and captured by the fleet.
June 20	German ambassador at Peking is murdered.
June 26	Foreigners in Peking are besieged in the legations.
July 13–14	Allied forces subdue Tien Tsin; Chinese forces in Manchuria bombard Blagovestchensk, capital of the Russian territory of the Amur.
August 4	An Allied force of 20,000 men sets out from Tien Tsin for relief of Peking legations; Russians occupy Niu-chwang in Manchuria.
August 14	Allies capture Peking and rescue prisoners in the legations; Chinese court flees to the West.
August 28	Allied troops march through the Forbidden City.
September	Massacre of Christian missionaries continues; primitive expeditions are sent out by Allied powers.
October 16	Great Britain and Germany enter into an agreement to maintain the rivers and ports of China open to trade and to take common action against any government hostile to such a purpose.
December 24	Allied powers present a joint note to Chinese government, the terms of which are embodied in a subsequent peace protocol.
1901	
February	Revelation of Russian diplomacy in China aiming at the establishment of a virtual protectorate over Manchuria.
March	China appeals to powers against Russian exactions and is supported by the U.S., Great Britain, and Japan.
April	Russia protests its disinterestedness and abandons pressure on Chinese government.
September	Peace protocol is signed with the powers agreeing to all details, including punishment of officials connected with the uprising, and payment of a war indemnity equaling 450 million taels of silver.

Part II: Details of War

Military Leaders

American

Name	Position/Significance
Adna Chaffee	Commanded troops sent from the Philippines
Lt. Jayne	Marine officer on U.S. warship *Newark*; commanded a dangerous mission up the Peiho River
Admiral Kempff	
Colonel Emerson H. Liscum	General commander of 9th U.S. Infantry; killed July 13, 1900, in the fighting at Tien Tsin
Captain McCalla	Commander of the American Marines in Admiral Seymour's expedition
Captain Reilly	5th U.S. Artillery; killed when the Allies were taking Peking
Admiral Remey	

British

General Dorward	
General Sir Alfred Gaelee	Commanded the British Indian contingent
Vice Admiral Edward Hobart Seymour	First leader of the 2000 Allied troops (British, American, French, German, Italian, Russian, and Japanese) dispatched on June 10, 1900

Chinese

General Kek	Died in the fighting at Tien Tsin

German

Field Marshal Count von Waldersee	Accepted by the Allies as chief commander of all troops in China after his arrival in 1900

Japanese

General Fukushima

Part III: Postcards

Types and Categories

Type	Category
Artist-drawn cards of military leaders	R4–R5
Artist-drawn caricatures, black-and-white or color	R4–R5
Celebration and victory cards	R4–R5
Real-photo cards of all related activities	R4–R5
Real photos of military leaders	R4–R5
Real photos of soldiers, armaments, or locations	R4–R5
All other cards	R4–R5

Sets and Series

Bürger and Ottillie. Produced a set (#6300) of at least 20 artist-drawn colored sketches titled *Der Krieg in China*. Some of these illustrations are quite energetic in their descriptive portrayals of the various peoples and arenas of the Boxer Rebellion. Clearly anti-Boxer, if not anti-Chinese, the favorite theme is one in which the Chinese are portrayed as alternately weak and wicked, a curious combination by any account. Once they are subdued by the multiple forces battling them, they are characterized as ridiculous or stubborn, or both. These are historically significant pieces of propaganda.

Unknown Publisher (French). Published a series of cards titled *La Guerre en Chine*. Like the Bürger and Ottillie cards, these are artist-drawn and colored. Also like Bürger and Ottillie cards, these are numbered in a #6300 series. Other matching identifications may exist.

Publishers

Bürger and Ottillie
Peter Goh
Unknown French Publisher

Artists

A. Michaelis

"Der Krieg in China" (The War in China). Bürger and Ottillie series; #6303. R4

6 The Russo-Japanese War

Part I: History and Chronology

Like the 1898 conflict between the United States and Spain, the Russo-Japanese War of 1904–5 is remembered more for its naval battles than for its military encounters on land. Since their defeat of the Chinese in 1894–95, Japan had become increasingly belligerent; and they had not forgotten Russia's role in forcing terms on her in that war. A growing confidence based on their navy and a desire to create an empire to accommodate both a growing population and a need for more raw materials were two of the key ingredients forcing the Japanese out of their traditional semi-isolationist stupor. That their budding arrogance was also a factor should not be forgotten. Once set on an outward course of action, Japan refused to be deterred either by an enfeebled China or that geographical monster, Russia. A tiny island nation known for its samurai, geishas, and volcanoes was poised and prepared to assert its international identity.

Russian Expansionism in the East

Having stepped in on the side of China after the Sino-Japanese War, Russia managed to wrangle for herself certain territorial concessions. Claiming to be concerned primarily with Chinese integrity, Russia deprived Japan of any acreage on the Chinese mainland while obtaining rights to parts of Manchuria for herself. The Japanese could see through the ruse, but responded initially via diplomatic channels to secure their objectives. The first cautionary action was an Anglo-Japanese alliance in 1902 which specified that in the event of war between Russia and Japan, neither Korea, China, France, nor any other power would come to Russia's aid. Actually, Japan had no reason to fear England's wrath. Already alarmed by the turn of events whereby Russia created the Russo-Chinese Bank and obtained Port Arthur in Manchuria, Britain determined to oppose Russian expansionism either eastward or southward toward the Mediterranean.

Everyone, so it seemed, was involved in the partition of China. Everyone, that is, except Japan. While Russia obtained Port Arthur and Talien-wan, Germany acquired Kiao Chau Bay, Great Britain occupied Wei-hai-wei, and France gained territory in South China. The Japanese received only the privilege of observing others slice up the Chinese pie. These "leases" and "spheres of influence" even witnessed the incursion of the United States into China. Claiming there should be an "Open Door" policy in the Far East, America also moved in as Japan watched.

According to the terms of the treaty between China and Russia, Russia had promised to evacuate Manchuria around 1903. Dragging its feet on one pretext after another, it became obvious that the Russian government had no intentions of leaving the area. Not only was it of strategic importance for protecting their Pacific Ocean interests, but many Russian settlers had immigrated there to join an already deeply entrenched Russian army. Great Britain protested, but to no avail, and the Japanese seethed.

The Korean Issue

The final bit of friction between Russia and Japan occurred over the Korean Issue. Although both countries had guaranteed Korean autonomy, Russia had been involved in various ventures of an economic nature—and to a limited extent, of a political nature—with the island nation. To Japan's consternation, her persistent questions on the matter evoked evasive answers from the Russians, who maintained that their long-range designs regarding Korea were only such as would enhance the Eastern country's benefits. All was well, Japan was advised.

To the Japanese, Russia's diplomatic maneuvering was a mask to camouflage her real intentions, which were to bring much of the Eastern world under Russian suzerainty. First would come the annexation of Manchuria, and then, that of China itself; this would be followed by control of Korea, and eventually Japan would be gathered into the fold. Whether, in fact, Russian designs were this far-reaching is debatable, but surely beyond question was the fact that since the Napoleonic wars, Russia had been desirous of securing her own borders—a task that would be made easier by the acquisition of ports in both the Mediterranean and the Atlantic. Also of primary importance was the policing of those borders, an uncertain business that often required interfering in the affairs of Japan's neighbors.

Feeling the strength of her aggressive army and navy and enjoying friendly relations with the United States and Great Britain—two nations already distrustful of what they perceived to be Russian interventionism—Japan began to make ready her military forces for an encounter. In February 1904, after waiting three weeks for Russia's answer to a diplomatic note, Japan abruptly presented the Russian ambassador with his traveling papers. A hurried speech by the Japanese ambassador to Russia, which underscored Japanese chagrin with Russia's expansionist policies in the Near East, paved the way for the series of actions that followed.

On February 7, 1904, the Japanese navy took possession of a port on the southeastern coast of Korea; two days later they fired on the Russian fortifications at Port Arthur. War had begun.

Unexpected Results

That Japan would be the victor in this conflict was hardly a foregone conclusion. Few outside Japan's borders expected a small, crowded island of 50 million people to defeat Russia, with her boundless land mass and incredibly large army (by some estimates 2–4 million). Although Japan had flexed its military muscle in subduing the four-hundred million inhabitants of China ten years earlier, this was altogether a different matter. Tactically speaking, China was essentially unschooled and unenlightened regarding advanced military techniques. Modern advances in weaponry had not penetrated the celestial empire to any appreciable degree, and military training itself existed on a rudimentary, unrefined level.

With Russia, the opposite was thought to be the case. Unfortunately for her, however, there were glaring similarities to her Eastern neighbors. Entrenched in a military system both outdated and controlled by generals of dubious tactical ability whose skills were also questionable, Russia was ill-prepared to combat the tenacity and efficiency displayed by her Japanese counterparts. And although Russia's naval vessels were nothing to be ashamed of, their captains and admirals had had precious little opportunity to sharpen either their defensive or offensive skills in combat situations for more than a decade. The brief encounter of the Boxer Rebellion in 1900 was a combined effort that required little ability and offered little opportunity for any one nation to exercise or sharpen its military prowess.

This is not to suggest that the Russian army and navy were not formidable opponents for anybody—they were—but the suddenness of the war, the breakdown in communications from the Russian capital to the actual fighting arenas, and the problems of supply transport proved in the end to be insurmountable. Coupled with the winning strategy of Admiral Togo at Tsushima and the intransigence of a Russian czar whose military intelligence seldom exceeded orders to push forward against any and all odds was the disaffection of Russia's poor toward a monarch who would lead his people thousands of miles into the jaws of death for what most of his subjects believed was just so much territorial dust in the Far East. Like the philosopher Voltaire, lamenting that the Seven Years War was fought over "a few acres of snow in Canada," the Russian lower orders considered this conflict with Japan an outrage against common sense. Their protests, accompanied by the mutinies of returning veterans, were the first rumblings that were to become the volcano of the Communist Revolution 12 years later.

Russo-Japanese War Postcards

Ever popular with collectors, postcards related to the Russo-Japanese War are represented by a pleasing number of types. In addition to the individual cards are sets and series that were printed by both combatants as well as a few by neutral countries. None, it must be noted, are easy to locate once one ventures beyond the realm of the larger postcard dealers.

Among the most exquisitely executed specimens are the minipaintings of British artist R. Caton-Woodville, which were produced by the London-based firm of Valentine and Sons.

Perhaps the most popular postcards of this war were those produced by German, French, and a couple of British companies. Most of these renderings are very well received by today's collectors of militaria, and all have prices commensurate with their scarcity and desirability. It is reasonable to expect that prices will continue to escalate as more collectors enter the field. The bulk of the postcards are artist-drawn, colored specimens that are either caricatures, special comments, or portraits of heroes, leaders, regiments, or types of military personnel engaged in the war.

Of them all, the most historically accurate and therefore historically useful are the postcards produced by the antagonists. It is through these cards that we see the armies and navies firsthand—their various commanders and vessels, the armaments, the battles in action and other sorts of assaults, the retreats, the captured supplies, the resting armies, the smiling victors, and the careworn look of defeat upon the vanquished.

These postcards are visual analyses: They show the contrasts of war—both victorious elation and celebration on one side, bitterness and recriminations on the other. While these moods are not less than genuine, as later postcards illustrate and as hindsight always tells us, they are also not of lasting substance. We recover or we forget; or failing that, we go to war again. And again.

Chronology

Date	Event
1904	
February 6	Japan severs diplomatic relations with Russia over disagreements concerning Manchuria and Korea.
February 8	Japanese fleet attacks the Russian navy at Port Arthur with a sneak attack; much damage is inflicted.
February 9	Japan sinks two Russian battleships at Chemulpo; Korea is invaded later in the month.
April 7	Japan succeeds on the Yalu River.
April 13	Russian flagship *Petropavlovsk* is blown up by a Japanese mine.
May 26–27	Japanese defeat Russians at Kinchow and Nanshan.
June 15	Russians suffer defeat at Telissu; Japanese advance against Port Arthur fortifications.
July 9–27	Japan sees victories at Kaiping, Tashihchao, and Niuchwang.
August 10–24	Russian fleet is unable to break out of Japanese squadron surrounding Port Arthur; Russian fleet is defeated at Vladivostok.
August 24–September 4	Russians are driven from their position at Liao Yang after fierce fighting.
October 5	Russian general, Kuropatkin, goes south from Mukden.
November 30	Further bombardment of Port Arthur.
December 31	General Stoessel, commanding Port Arthur, seeks armistice.
1905	
January 1	Port Arthur fleet is blown up; Port surrenders with its 24,000 men; General Stoessel, military commander of the Port, sends telegram saying, "Great Sovereign, forgive. . . . " to the Czar
January 27	General Kuropatkin announces Russian successes with capture of Sandepas and other positions.
January 29	Russians are forced to withdraw across the Hun.
February 12–28	Japanese cut railroad between Mukden and Harbin, February 12; Japanese shell Mukden, February 27–28.
March 10	Mukden and Fushen are occupied by Japanese (Russian losses: 27,000 dead, 110,000 wounded, 40,000 captured; Japanese losses: 41,000 total).
March 17	General Linevitch replaces Kuropatkin.
March 23	Japanese loan to government to raise $150,000,000 for war.
March 24–April 24	Further Russian losses on Liao River and elsewhere.
May 27–28	Russian Baltic Fleet, under Rozhestvenski, routed in Korean Straits. At the battle of Tsushima Strait, 14,000 Russians go down with their ships, 3000 are taken prisoner, and 1000 escape; Japanese losses are three torpedo boats and about 800 men.
June 16	A Russian army is defeated and driven from Liao Yang.
June 20	Japanese begin to surround Manchuria and threaten Vladivostok.
July 8–24	Japanese capture Russian penal island of Saghalien (in later spelling, *Sakhalin*); Russians are defeated outside Nanshan-chentse.
August 4	Japan presses upon Vladivostok.
August 29	Members of peace plenipotentiaries reach agreement: Japan waives indemnity, possession of interred warships, limitation of Russian naval power in Far East; Saghalien is divided.
September 5	Treaty signed by plenipotentiaries.
September 15	Armistice is signed in Manchuria.
October 14	Peace treaty is ratified; war cost to Russia is $1,200,000,000.

Part II: Details of War

Military Leaders

Russian

Name	Position/Significance
Vice Admiral Alexieff	Russian viceroy of the Far East; took temporary command of Port Arthur fleet after death of Makaroff
Grand Duke Alexis	Czar's uncle who was Commander in Chief of the Russian navy
Grand Duke Cyril	Czar's cousin; narrowly escaped death after being thrown into the water by the force of an explosion on the battleship *Pobieda* after it struck a mine (April 13, 1904) at Port Arthur
Lt. General Count Keeler	First Russian officer killed in the war (August 2, 1904, in Manchuria)
General Keller	Repulsed Japanese at Mo-tien-ling
General Kondratovitch	Commander of Russian troops at Newchang
General Kuropatkin	Former secretary of war who took command of the army in the Far East
General Linevitch	Replaced General Kuropatkin March 17, 1905
Vice Admiral Makaroff	Succeeded Vice Admiral Stark as commander of Port Arthur fleet; was killed in the sinking of the battleship *Petropavlovsk*
Admiral Nebogatoff	Commander at the Battle of the Sea of Japan
Admiral Rozhestvenski	Commander of the Baltic Fleet defeated in Korean Straits
Vice Admiral Skrydloff	Commander of the Russian navy in the Far East after the death of Makaroff (replaced Alexieff, who himself had replaced Rear Admiral Uchtomsky, the first commander to follow Makaroff)
General Stakelberg	Commanded the army at the battles of Vafangow and Telissu (55 and 25 miles north of Port Arthur, respectively)
Lt. General Stoessel	Commander of the troops at Port Arthur

Russian Military Leaders, cont.

Name	Position/Significance
Admiral Wirenius	Commander of Russian Mediterranean fleet
General Zasselitch	Relieved of command for failure to follow the orders of General Kuropatkin during his fighting in Korea; was reassigned to duty in Russia

Others: Grand Duke Boris, General Baron Kaulbars, Grand Duke Nicholas

Japanese

Name	Position/Significance
Lt. General Sadanaru Fushimi	Commander of 1st (Tokyo) Army Division
Lt. General Baron Hasegawa	Commander of the Imperial Guard Division
Commander Hirose	Died while attempting to rescue one of his men; one of the commanders trying to block the entrance to Port Arthur
Vice Admiral Ijuiu	Assistant chief of the Naval Board under Admiral Ito
Lt. General Inouye	Commander of the first army of invasion
Admiral Ito	Chief of staff of the Japanese Navy
General Kuroki	Commanded 1st Japanese Army in Manchuria; outwitted and defeated Russians at crossing of the Yalu
Admiral Marshuri	Commander aboard the flagship *Hatsuse* when it struck two mines; he was rescued
Lt. General Nodzu	Commander in 3rd Japanese Army
General Nogi	Commander of Japanese 3rd Army attacking Port Arthur
Lt. General Oku	Commander of 2nd Japanese Army
Lt. General Baron Oseko	Commander of 7th (Hokkaido) Army Division
Lt. General Baron Oshima	Commander of 3rd (Nagoya) Division
Field Marshal Oyama	Commanded the armies attacking General Kuropatkin
Commander Takayangi	Commander of the steamer *Yeddo Maru*
Lt. General Terauchi	Minister of war; in Chinese War had been vice chief of the general staff
Admiral Togo	Victor at battle of Tsushima
Vice Admiral Uriu	Commanded the Japanese fleet that caused the destruction of Russian ships in the harbor of Chemulpo
Admiral Yamamato	Minister of Marine and promoter of Japan's naval expansion

Others: General Fuji, Lt. General Fukushima

Vessels

Russian Ships

Torpedoed at Port Arthur (February 8, 1904)

Czatevitch (battleship)

Vessels, cont.

Pallada (cruiser)
Retvizan (battleship)

Ships Sunk in Battle of Sea of Japan

Alexander III
Borodino
Navarin
Oslayba
Sissoi Veliky

Vessels at Battle of Chemulpo, Korea

Korietz (cruiser)
Variag (cruiser)

Battleships for Home Defense (if necessary)

Borodino
Imperator Alexander III
Kniaz Suwaroff
Oriel
Slava

Other Vessels of Importance

Mandjur Gunboat; stationed on the Yangtse-Kiang river in China. The Japanese insisted the vessel's guns and vital machinery be removed to prevent it from being used for war purposes. Had the *Mandjur's* captain refused, his ship undoubtedly would have been either bottled up or destroyed. He complied.

Petropavlovsk Battleship; sunk in the harbor of Port Arthur on April 13, 1904. On April 12, Japanese torpedo boat *Karyu Mara* miraculously slipped close by the harbor and planted a series of mines, at least one of which the *Petropavlovsk* encountered, thus sinking and killing almost 600 men, including the commander, Admiral Makaroff.

Pobieda Battleship; also struck a mine, same time and location as the *Petropavlovsk*; Grand Duke Cyril almost lost his life (see Russian leader profile).

Rastoropony Torpedo boat destroyer; after delivering a message, the *Rastoropony* was blown up by the Russians to prevent it from falling into the hands of the Japanese.

Yeninsei A torpedo transport that accidentally struck a mine at Port Arthur.

Miscellaneous Russian Vessels

Almaz (cruiser)
Askold (cruiser)
Aurora (cruiser)
Bogatyr (protected cruiser)
Diana (cruiser)
Izumrud (battleship)
Jeimtchug (cruiser)
Nokolai I (battleship)
Novik (cruiser)
Oleg (cruiser)
Orel (battleship)
Rossia (cruiser)
Ryeshitelni (torpedo-boat destroyer)
Sevastopol (battleship)

Vessels, cont.

Smolensk (cruiser)
St. Petersburg (warship)

Japanese Ships

Hatuse Battleship; sunk off Port Arthur after hitting two mines, May 5, 1904

Karyu Mara Torpedo boat responsible for mining Port Arthur; commanded by Commander Oda

Kesaga Cruiser; collided with the *Yoshimo* off Port Arthur, May 5, 1904

Kinshiu Maru Transport

Yedo Maru Steamer destroyed at the third attempt to blockade Port Arthur, May 3, 1904

Yoshimo Cruiser; sank May 5, 1904, after colliding with the *Kesaga*, another Japanese cruiser, in the fog off Port Arthur.

Part III: Postcards

Types and Categories

Type	Category
Armies being reviewed	R3–R4
Armies on the march	R3
Artillery-related	R3–R4
Battle scenes, Japanese	R3–R4
Battle scenes, Russian	R4
Building fortifications	R4
Captured weaponry, supplies, or vehicles	R3
Christmas cards	R5
Civilian war-related activities	R3–R4
Czar with troops or commanders	R4–R5
Female military personnel	R4–R5
Fighting in China (on land)	R3–R4
Flag cards	R3
Hospital- or wounded-related	R3–R4
Mikado with troops or commanders	R4–R5
Military commanders	
Formal poses	R3–R4
In the field	R4
With their staffs	R3–R4
Military funerals	R4
Patriotic	R3–R4
Peace treaty cards	R3–R4
P.O.W.-related	R4–R5
Propaganda	R4
Red Cross cards	R3–R4
Russian defeat at Port Arthur	R3–R4
"Russian Outrage" (On October 21, 1904, while the Russians were sailing toward the Japanese fleet, they fired on a group of British merchant ships in the North Sea; the incident required an international commission to prevent the British from taking action against the Russians)	R3–R4
Ships, in action	R4
Ships, stationary	R3
Soldiers enjoying themselves	R4–R5
Spy-related	R4–R5
Unfavorable caricatures	R4
Uniformed military types	R3–R4
Victory-related	R3
Views of battle sites or strategic locations (non--action-related)	R2–R3
Weapons, armaments, or military vehicles	R2–R3

Sets and Series

Collier's Weekly. Published a set of at least six black-and-white view cards titled *La Guerre Russo-Japonaise.* Included are pictures of the Russians and of the Japanese. Views show soldiers and sailors, battles and marches, parades, and numerous other war-related activities. A desirable, historically significant group of cards that is most elusive.

Hildescheim & Company. Produced a sepia-toned #5300 series of war-theme cards that includes some of the Russian commanders.

Japanese Government. Published a set of 48 cards (printed by Tokyo Printing Company) related to many details of the war. Issued through the Department of Communications, these have scroll-like embellishments around the periphery and several have a photo inside; reportedly given to the families of servicemen killed in battle.

O. E. P. Produced an artist-drawn (R. Salles) set of cards related to both military and nonmilitary aspects of the war.

Raphael Tuck. Produced a #100 series depicting the war from the Japanese viewpoint, and produced a #700 series of humorous cards about *Jap the Giant Killer* (six cards).

The numbers and titles of other Raphael Tuck series are as follows:

☆ #5100
Russo-Japanese War

☆ #6460
Japanese Celebrations (Oilette)

☆ #6480
Russo-Japanese War (Oilette)

☆ #6500
Russo-Japanese War

Scott Russell & Co. Published a set about the Hull Trawlers, the Russian Outrage incident against Britain.

Sherer, Nabholz & Co. Published a set of 15 cards related to Russia and the war. Included are pictures of ships, the building of Port Arthur, Russian soldiers, and several Red Cross cards.

Valentine and Sons (various series). Include an unnumbered set of battle scenics and action cards and a set of six cards on the Russian Outrage (black and white, numbered).

W. and A. K. Johnson. Produced a numbered series (#300) of vignettes of the various armies.

Unknown Japanese Publisher. A numbered set of at least 70 artist-drawn colored cards dealing with the emperor, Japanese life, and the military (including the war).

Other Unknown Publishers. A set of eight blue-and-white sketches of battle scenes and life in the field, and a rare set of generals and admirals.

Other series include cards by Delittle, Fenwick & Co. and other publishers about which little is known.

Publishers

A. R. Co.
B. H. Publications
B. K. W. I.
Canney's Music Store
C. W. Faulkner
Davidson Bros.
Delittle, Fenwick & Co.
F. Berte
Franz Huld
H & M
H. C. Leighton
H. Pearson
Japanese Government
Kokusansha
Marco Marcovici
Nellie B. Van Slingerland
O. E. P.
Raphael Tuck
Rochester News Company
Rotograph
Scherer, Nabholz & Co.
Scott Russell & Co.
Somers
Valentines
W. & A. K. Johnston
W & T Gaines
W. L. Julian

Artists

S. Begg
R. Caton-Woodville
Dudley Hardy
Ch. Laborde
Lovichi
Rostro
R. Salles

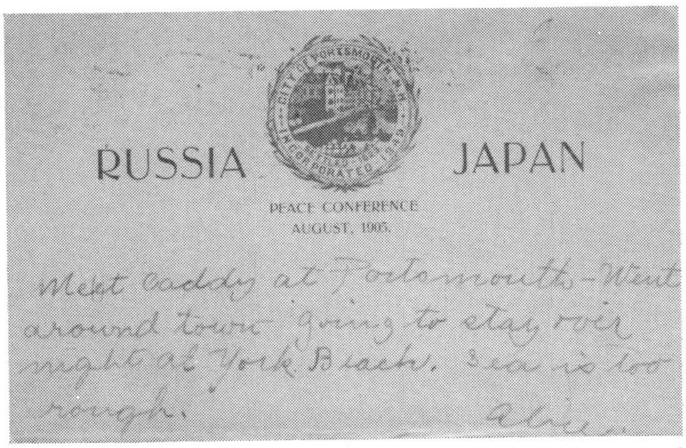

Peace conference commemorative; postmarked at Portsmouth while negotiations were in progress before signing. Anonymous. R4

Peace treaty commemorative showing the principals. Rotograph. R3

"Japanese soldiers marching to Manchuria." Kokusansha. R3

View of Port Arthur. Anonymous. R3

"Wounded Russians being conveyed to Japanese military hospitals." Anonymous. R4

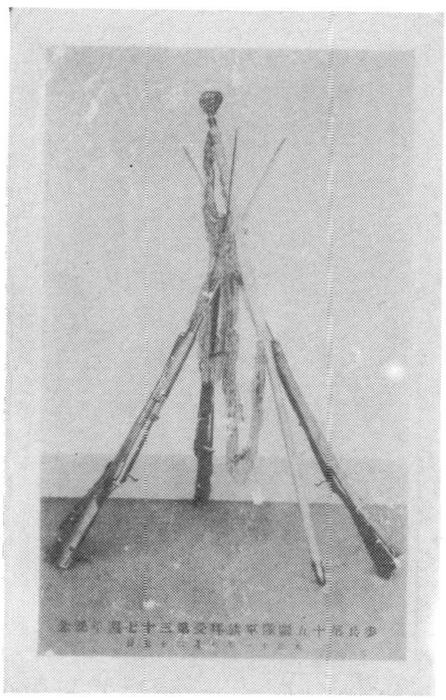

Japanese rifles. Anonymous. R3

General Stoessel, commander at Port Arthur. S. Hildesheimer & Company Ltd. R3

General Fukushima and General Oku, here seen as protectors of Japanese citizenry. Anonymous. R4

Japanese Officer Corps. Anonymous. R3

Japanese forces in the field. Anonymous. R3

Japanese General Kuroki inspecting captured Russian guns. Anonymous. R3

Battle near Tschang Tschu: Russians putting Japanese to flight. Anonymous. R4

Russo-Japanese Peace Conference. Berte. R2

Peace conference building on right. Hugh C. Leighton. R2

Decorated electric cars celebrating Japanese victory. Anonymous. R3

A captured Russian gun on display. Anonymous. R3

Russian soldiers in their barracks at inspection time. Anonymous. R4

Artillery battle at the River Yalu. Anonymous. R4

"Negligence is a great enemy; Japanese warning card." Anonymous. R4

General Oyama, Commander of Japanese armies in Manchuria. Anonymous. R4

A Russian soldier in winter foot dress. Anonymous. R4

A military conference between commanders. Anonymous. R4

Japanese warship in action. Anonymous. R4

Japanese General Nogi in full military dress. Anonymous. R4

Another of Japan's victorious generals. Anonymous. R4

7
The Mexican Revolution

Part I: History and Chronology

Many people tend to think of the Mexican Revolution as a series of events that took place from the sixteenth through the nineteenth centuries. So far as antecedents go, this thinking is correct, for it was during these earlier times that the seeds of Mexico's ultimate revolution were sown. A string of unwise leaders exercising unwise leadership, repeated attempts (always thwarted) at establishing some level of social and economic equality for the landless peons, and intervention by foreign governments—all these incidents were as carpenters, building the stage upon which was played the final series of actions in Mexico's political drama. Finally, Act IV arrived—played not in the 1600s nor the 1800s, but rather in the second and third decades of our own twentieth century.

While the heroes and the villains of those earlier times would always be alternately venerated and despised, it was to the latter generation of armed crusaders and politicos that Mexico needed to turn in order to realize some measure of political stability. They were a unique group of men, and the mention of their names even today evokes an aura of magic the non-Mexican world finds difficult to comprehend: handsome and somber Emiliano Zapata, a friend of the friendless Indians—Mexico's first inhabitants; General Pascual Orozco, Francisco Madero's primary chieftain and fighter in the northern deserts; Francisco "Pancho" Villa, half-legend, half-cutthroat—a man of action and ideas (though not ideals), the very substance of romance and intrigue.

Walking in the forefront and casting a lesser shadow than did his more notorious contemporaries was that man of vision who lacked the practical qualities necessary for effective leadership, the gentle and gentleman farmer Francisco Indalecio Madero. The forces Madero unleashed with his proclamation of November 11, 1910 ("... now the Revolution has begun ...") were to change Mexico forever—creating, almost overnight, a set of historical personages and leading, at last, to his own death through covert assassination.

The cast of characters for which the Revolution served as an omnipresent backdrop contained as varied a set of human personalities as ever may be. Of them, more will be said later. For now, it might be wise to start at the beginning.

Seeds of Discontent

To trace human conflict back in time to its inception is a hazardous enterprise at best. Although the initial spark of hostility may be easy enough to isolate, one is always left to wonder where it is that the other pieces of the mosaic may be placed. One historian indicates his version of cause and effect while another points a learned finger in the opposite direction. A third disagrees with both. All have the same answers. All add to the confusion. And if the single question *Why?* is difficult enough to answer, what is one to do with the even more perplexing query, *Why now?*

For Mexico, the answers, like the questions, have never been simple—neither at that time nor in retrospect. With the people having endured foreign domination and oppression since the 1500s, why, one might ask, was the nineteenth century a period of nascent revolt? Why didn't the necessary forces coalesce earlier? The reasons are hardly simple.

During the initial period following the conquests of Cortés, the indigenous Indian population of Mexico was treated with a "perfunctory" harshness. Thinking the Indians culturally barbarous, Spanish overlords saw no contradiction in enslaving them on the one hand while introducing them to Christian faith on the other. In their desire for wealth and personal fame, the Spanish governors brandished a heavy-handed whip on the captives. With the coming of more Spanish settlers to whom land grants had been given, the number of acres under cultivation became greater and greater, thus necessitating both an increase in the use of the native labor force and an increase in the amount of labor expected from each Indian. Although these conditions seem (as well they were) brutish and inhumane, an even sadder fact was to be found in the reality that the laborers' only comfort (nominal at best) and solace came from a growing number of the Catholic clergy sent to the New World both to Christianize it and to set up churches for the benefit of the Spanish colonists.

The progression of time only brought a worsening of conditions. Even the priests, or at least, a sizable number of them, felt more inclined to champion the cause of the New World aristocracy from Spain than to care for or about Mexico's poor. Admonitions to the native population that it was God's will for Europeans to be in superior positions while the Indians should content themselves with such stations as their intelligence and level of culture predestined them began to fall on deaf ears. When the Indians did listen, what they heard made them angry; what they saw made them angrier. They were prisoners in their own land and powerless in the bargain. What was worse, as far as any attempt to alter existing situations was concerned, was the pathetic fact that they were unorganized.

The first substantial rebellion, which occurred in 1810, was led by the most unlikely of candidates—a Catholic priest. Saddened by the plight of his poor charges and sickened by the attitude of a Spanish government that cared more about the silver in Mexico's mines than it did the rape of its native citizenry, Hidalgo y Casilla became the leader of a poorly structured insurgent army. An anomaly in both politics and religion, Hidalgo and his guerillas fought on, finally securing independence for Mexico in 1823.

Politically speaking, this giant step was in the direction of more problems. Liberals and conservatives openly and aggressively opposed each other for 40 years amid the rising and falling fortunes of such individuals as the legendary General Santa Anna and the would-be emperor Maximilian of the Austrian House of Hapsburg. The young republican was ill-prepared to understand or appreciate the fact that revolutions lead, most frequently, not to stability, but rather to its opposite. Foreign internationalism coupled with the emergence of the soldier-politician merely served to exasperate what were already tumultuous conditions.

Under these auspices, it is not surprising that General Porfirio Díaz was able to seize power in 1876. Presented with an excellent opportunity to earn the respect of the indigenous population, Díaz spurned the chance. Instead, he purposely rejected all legislative attempts at land redistribution and became part of the process whereby more and more Indian land was taken over by the large estates. The excesses of Díaz paved the way for the entrance onto the political scene of Francisco Madero, and with him, the page is turned to the final chapter.

The Principal Players

Francisco Madero

Any conversation about the twentieth-century Mexican Revolution that omits the name of Francisco Madero is largely meaningless. Without him and without the universal perceptions of his nobility and gentleness, the Revolution would have swiftly degenerated into a series of squabbling feuds among rival chieftains. Without Madero as a focal point—his lack of mean-spiritedness as an emotionally leveling influence, and his humanitarian philosophy to rally around—the efforts of others would have been disjointed and thus have had a negligible impact. The bandit Villa, the justice-seeking Zapata, and even the eventual rule of Obregón owe a debt to Madero's memory. The foolishness of which he was later a part merely indicates that men of his moral stripe and kindly, if high-strung, disposition fare ill when placed in influential positions.

Born into landed aristocracy, Madero could have chosen any life or lifestyle that suited him. At an early date, "little Paco" decided in favor of some form of social work. Rather than spend his time with the sort of trivial activities his economic and social status afforded him, Madero chose to educate the children of the peons who flocked around him to hear his diatribes on vegetarianism, upright conduct, and universal brotherhood. Not a pseudo-saint, Madero selected the path of priestly celibacy rather than the career of law his parents wanted for him. It was this other-worldly mentality that placed him at variance with family and friends and ultimately led to his undoing.

In the beginning, Madero's political motivations were in the abstract: While he spoke in favor of universal suffrage, better living and working conditions for the lower social orders, and a state-supported education system, he himself had no aspirations of actually seeking public office in order to effect them. He was content to vocalize his displeasure and to formulate theories, hoping that in some yet-unknown manner the concept of equality would eventually become social reality. Like other men of vision and hope, he finally arrived at the conclusion that his private conversations would need to become public utterances if they were to receive serious attention.

What Madero could not have known, given his proclivity for seeing the best in everyone, was that Mexico's strongman ruler was quick to employ ruthless methods at the first sign of political dissension, especially that of a serious nature. Díaz may have been nearly 80 years old and fast approaching senility, but he was still supremely capable of dealing with all opposition thrown in his path. For a brief period, Madero's speeches in village squares and haciendas were ignored. Díaz even went so far as to invite the little man to the palace, where they discussed social justice. Madero emerged from the meeting with mixed emotions. He was overjoyed with the opportunity of speaking to Mexico's ruler; he was less than thrilled by the cold eyes and recalcitrant antagonist he faced. Díaz promised limited reform, but Madero knew better.

So it was back to the stump for Madero until he eventually learned something of which he had previously had no knowledge—the nature of prison life. First placed in a cell, he was later given the area around San Luis Potosí as his territory and his prison. Madero managed to escape on October 4, 1910, by shaving off his beard and riding out disguised as a railroad worker. He sought refuge across the border in San Antonio, Texas, where he detailed the *Plan of San Luis,* which he had written while a prisoner. His initial step was to issue a proclamation calling for a general uprising on November 20, 1910. With this, the die was cast, and although the Revolution had an uncertain, inauspicious beginning, it was obvious from the start that Madero's stirring speeches had the desired effect. Large blocks of dispossessed Indians and even greater numbers of disenfranchised Mexican day laborers grouped themselves under the broad banner of his rhetoric. While few were sufficiently literate to read his book *The Presidential Succession of 1910,* they knew the message it contained, and they joined the growing hordes clammering for free elections and the hope of a piece of land for each to till for himself.

Many entered the various emerging armies and served under one chieftain or another. In the North, around Sonora and Chihuahua, "Pancho" Villa held sway. The South was controlled by the splendid figure of part-Indian Emiliano Zapata. Madero aligned himself with the lean Spartan, Pascual Orozco, who was himself first commander of, and later teamed with, Villa. They were all men who could be brutal; none were less than forceful. One story credits Orozco with sending some bloodstained federal uniforms to Díaz with the message *Here are the leaves in which the tamales I ate were wrapped. Please send me some more.*

By contrast, Madero cut an unimposing figure. Measuring little more than five feet in height and having a voice that frequently assumed a shrill falsetto quality, Madero was also given to nervous gestures and, according to some accounts, uncertain footing. But what he lacked in forcefulness was more than compensated for by the earnestness of his pleas and his burning determination to see Mexico take the path toward democracy.

The rest of his story may be told with brevity and sadness. After a series of victories by Orozco, Madero was poised for political office. First came the vote, then the presidency. But this step was one too many for Madero, and here the trouble began. Intellectually prepared to deal with some, if not most, situations, he was inadequately schooled in the rough-and-tumble, sometimes contradictory, and always changing business called *political reality.* Moreover, the insulation of public office removed Madero from the personal contact with his constituents and fellow Mexicans which had always been the abiding sense of his strength. Add to this state of affairs a group of advisors zealous of promoting their own agendas, a veritable mountain of paperwork, and the infighting of military chieftains who refused conciliation with one another, and the problems of the "Little Giant" come into sharp focus.

A man accustomed to operating in such a highly charged atmosphere might look for opportunities and ways of exploiting weaknesses—of playing one side against another. In other words, a true politician would have jumped readily into the fray and sought the sorts of compromises that might eventually lead to the actualization of some part of his goals. Francisco Madero was not such a man. Because of this, his fate was sealed and determined by those who were more opportunistic and more determined.

Conservatives disliked his reforms of press, labor, and agriculture, while the more hard-core revolutionists thought he was dragging his heels and not introducing truly progressive legislation. Harrassed by his own congress, by the Mexican press, and by America's ambassador, Madero seemed incapable of maintaining his personal rule. It came unraveled after a series of rebellions in Mexico City on February 9, 1913, which culminated in his betrayal by the commander of the federal troops, Victoriano Huerta. The end was swift and inevitable. Shortly after his arrest, Madero was assassinated while being transferred from jail to prison. His captors knew he could not be allowed to remain alive as a rallying point for contentious rebels, so he was murdered. And with his death, the poetry appeared to desert the Revolution, but not, as shall be seen, the fire or the antagonism.

Emiliano Zapata

If asked to identify the first name that comes to mind in connection with the Mexican Revolution, it would be a safe assumption that the bulk of Mexico's people would focus on Emiliano Zapata. Nor would this reaction be an unreasonable one. Unlike the other figureheads—even including, to his shameful discredit, Francisco Madero—Zapata lost neither the dream nor the righteous indignation that fires the spirit of the true revolutionary. His personal goals and his political ideals were the same, and they never changed. To him, and to the mass of his followers, the Revolution could be justified on the basis of one tenet: land reform.

Born poor, although not destitute, Zapata clawed and worked his way to a position of economic well-being. Orphaned at the age of 15, he explored more of the world outside his village in the Southern states of Morelos than had his neighbors or his later compatriots. Zapata was a small-scale farmer and rancher who also trained horses and hired out to steer herds of pack mules. A man who liked good clothes and who was ever conscious of his appearance, he presented a daring figure on his infrequent forays into Mexico City. Although not a city dandy, Zapata was pleased to display the fact that his own honest labor and a bit of ingenuity were all he needed to rise above the abject poverty that had characterized his youth. Thin and muscular, Zapata possessed a stance and penetrating stare that were often sufficient to make men of lesser fiber feel ill at ease in his presence.

Just entering the third decade of life when the Revolution began, the Southern rebel preferred to remain anonymous. His own life was progressing suitably, and the prospects for his children were promising. Tied to the landless Indians by bloodlines and sympathy, Zapata was nonetheless willing to permit Madero, Orozco, and the rest to overthrow the corrupt government in Mexico's capital. History had other ideas—and those were the ones that prevailed.

For Zapata, the entry point came as early as 1911, which was as soon as he could determine that the rebels in the North harbored little sympathy for agrarian reform. To him, these "other guerrillas" were nothing more than opportunists cashing in on a chance for wealth, position, and social approbation. Zapata thought them no different in attitude and in possession of no more social conscience than those they were attempting to displace. This perception applied initially to the military chieftains, but in time, Zapata came to paint Madero with the same brush.

Zapata's enemies could, he soon discovered, give as much grief as they received. Although superficially and to all outward appearances they were aligned with him, the Northern insurrectionists viewed their Southern compatriot as a country bumpkin—unsophisticated in the ways of politics and social behaviors. Their ungenerous perspective was that Zapata had his nose too close to the dirt—a poor position, they reasoned, from which to appreciate the complexities of government.

They may have been correct with this indelicate and uncharitable analysis. In the end, Zapata's political philosophy was somewhat modified, but not by a great deal, and not soon enough: He was murdered in 1919 by one of his own men. For Zapata, the difference was not an alteration, but rather an addition; his final solution was to seek a combination of agrarian reform and an appreciation of the plight of the urban unemployed and the need for strong labor unions.

Yet, to his death, the Southern chieftain pursued a dream of land redistribution as spelled out in his *Plan de Ayala*. Not altogether unrealistic, his idea was that one-third of the haciendas' lands should be relinquished to the peons who would work it and, in turn, repay their land barons as the money became available to do so. Only in those cases where the land owners refused to negotiate did Zapata sanction the confiscation of property.

What Zapata could not understand was that his vision of an agriculturally egalitarian Mexico had no chance to reach fruition in an atmosphere where rival political ambitions and military commanders lived amid a daily round of intrigue and assassination. His dream was more suitable to a smoothly operating system than to one in which greed and envy had yet to complete their course. Although the murder of Madero and the ousting of first one and then another politico should have been sufficient to induce Zapata to walk slowly and softly, these merely confirmed his belief that his position would eventually be the dominant one—and the final one.

Rallying the native Indians of the South and the other dispossessed around his banner, Zapata held off attempt after attempt on his life. It made little difference who was sent against him; the result was the same—failure. A final peace offering came to naught as Carranza became the last in a long line to discover that the revolutionary would neither bargain nor sell his principles. That his platform might be unrealistic never occurred to Zapata, and this fact caused his enemies no end of dismay and chagrin. The only solution was to murder him through trickery. Fortunately for the future of Mexico, Zapata's dream could not be so easily dispatched.

In fact, as is so often the situation, his death as a martyr made his ideals all the more palatable to even larger numbers of Mexico's population than was the case during his lifetime. A final tragic note is that Zapata's single-minded efforts for everyone else's welfare caused his family to suffer. After his death, they were forced to accept charity to prevent their deaths through starvation or disease.

Francisco "Pancho" Villa

In contrast to the Mexican response, most Americans would think first of "Pancho" Villa if the subject of the Mexican Revolution presented itself. Alternately seen as a Robin Hood and a rogue, Villa had more in common with the latter designation than with the former, and the evidence furnishes example after example to validate the claim. Murderer, thief, opportunist—Villa was all three and more, including a bigamist, which may have been the least serious of his many offenses. One thing is certain: He was no committed social reformer.

Having entered the world on July 7, 1878, as Doroteo Arango, the young man changed his name to that of a bandit chief he rode with. By his thirtieth birthday, Villa was leading his own group of lawbreakers—criminals whose chief occupation was cattle rustling. Already sought by the authorities on a charge of murder, the social pariah joined the ranks following Madero and General Pascual Orozco at the Revolution's outset in 1910. Why Villa offered the reformer his services is still a matter of debate, but perhaps it will be sufficient to let the record speak for itself.

After seeming to align himself with the dispossessed, Villa had little reason to fear legal exaction for his many crimes. Indeed, in a sort of strange twist of justice, the "erstwhile" bandit placed himself in the enviable position of persecuting some of the very authorities who were about the business of apprehending him. The irony should not be missed that he was doing this in the name of social and political reform. The Revolution gave Villa the occasion to wear the laurel wreath of goodness. Moreover, like all such civil wars, it also furnished the oportunity for the unscrupulous to enrich themselves at the expense of former owners of property and business whom the Revolution mandatorily impoverished. The opportunities were presented over and over, and Villa took full advangage over and over.

Among his acquisitions as a result of the Revolution were a butcher shop, gambling casinos, several haciendas, a meat-packing plant, and various other businesses and land holdings. So great was the number of properties he owned by 1920 that Villa was able to gift many of his subordinates with property and businesses.

Unwilling to change his methods of operation, the Northern bandit continued to murder, steal, and lie. Unable to maintain fruitful relations with any military leader as his boss, Villa eventually controlled his own army. Not all of his men were cutthroats: Most were the landless and the destitute; disenchanted with their country's political leadership, they tended to idolize Villa and what they presumed he represented. However, a few of his chief officers were characters whose cruelty matched that of their commander, and in come cases, exceeded it.

Another obvious fact was that Villa was no fool. Although he could not abide the selflessness of Zapata nor share his ideals, the bandit was quick to capitalize on the former's popularity, and readily agreed to his plans for agrarian reform. There can be little doubt that his championing of Madero's philosophy (which differed in some fundamental ways from that of Zapata) was but the first in a long line of examples illustrating Villa's ability to manipulate public sympathy on his behalf. Conversely, the murder of 16 American miners as retaliation for the U.S. government's snubbing of him in favor of Carranza gives a brief glimpse into the substantive character of the man. It is interesting that even in this situation Villa was wearing his thinking apparatus. He anticipated that his act would lead to war between the United States and Mexico, a situation he proposed to use to his advantage.

The lone example of Villa seeming to implement land reform (in Chihuahua) was an obvious (although perhaps not obvious at the time) sham. The visible signs indicated that agrarian equity was the proposed goal, but the fact was that no state funds were allocated to the local agrarian commission. Villa's *Aguascalientes* proposal was equally hypocritical. Thinking to present himself as the champion of the landless, Villa proposed, among other things, to force prior payment for the land from this penniless group he knew was incapable of paying.

Finally persuaded to lay down his arms, the Northern insurrecto was given a large hacienda that would permit him to live a life of wealth and comfort. Even in retirement, however, Villa's tactics were typical of him and included the subverting or outright stealing of government subsidies and making money from both his neighbors and from the already poorly rewarded laborers in his employ. It is perhaps fitting that Villa's assassination in 1923 came at a time when he was engaged in another attempt to overthrow the reigning Mexican government.

Epilogue

America's entry into World War I in 1917 spelled the end of the fascination for Mexican politics among the citizenry of the United States. The kaiser's unrestricted submarine-warfare attacks and the unpleasant reality of trench warfare quickly reduced Pershing's Southern foray to romantic memories. For the soldiers trekking across Mexico's arid landscape, or those stationed along the Mexican border, however, their neighbor's civil war was a disagreeable, albeit brief, experience.

This poem written by an American soldier temporarily stationed in Texas reflects the infantryman's sense of frustration and discomfort—and humor—during the Mexican Revolution.

Soldier Life in Texas

Soldier life in southern Texas
Is not heaven by a mile
Tho' there's many things to vex us,
We just smile and smile and smile.

We were sent here for some reasons
That we do not understand,
And must spend this sweltering season
On a bed of blistering sand.

Oh, the mesquite and the cactus
Can be seen for miles around
And mosquitos fierce attack us
Which by millions here abound.

And at night the coyote's howling
Does our peaceful slumbers break
And the greasers round us prowling
Scalps like ours would like to take.

And the eats we have, don't mention
Not like mother use to make
But to them there's no attention
For we sure have them to take.

Yet all things are kept in order
For a fearful bloody fray,
And there'll be hell on the border
If old Villa comes this way.

But we long for home and pleasure
And God's country long to see,
For each soldier boy's a treasure
That from warfare should be free.

Pvt. Lowell Seaton Martin
July 4, 1916

Chronology: Mexican Revolution

Date	Event
1910	
November 11	Madero proclaims the beginning of the Revolution.
November 22	Madero proclaims himself president of Mexico; Francisco Villa and Pascual Orozco join the revolt.
1911	
March 7	20,000 American soldiers are ordered to the border because of the seriousness of the Revolution.
March–May	Zapata begins full-scale revolutionary activity in Morelos.
May 25	Juarez is captured by insurgents; Porfirio Díaz resigns.
June	The International Boundary Commission gives Mexico part of the Chamiza tract near El Paso. (El Paso was headquarters for a large number of U.S. troops sent to the Mexican border. It was also here that many Mexican refugees fled across their own border for protection against both the insurrectos and the federal soldiers.)
October 1	Madero is elected president.
October 16	Fighting breaks out between the followers of Madero and those of Zapata.
1912	
January	Revolts against Madero's government occur in various places.
April 17	Mexico refuses to permit the U.S. to interfere in her affairs.
October 16	Revolution in Vera Cruz, American action imminent; revolt is suppressed.
1913	
February 18	Madero is taken prisoner after serious outbreaks in Mexico City; Huerta becomes provisional president.
February 23	Madero is assassinated while being taken to the penitentiary in Mexico City.
May	Rebellion in the North against Huerta government.
November 14	England and Germany advise Huerta to accept U.S. demands.
November 27	Rebels capture Mazatlán.
December 28	The insurrectos attack Ojinaga, last federal stronghold in the North.
1914	
January 10	Rebels conquer federal troops at Ojinaga; rebel commander is Francisco "Pancho" Villa.
March 21	Villa attacks Torreón and subdues it after 11 days of fighting (April 2).
April 10	U.S. Marines landing for supplies at Tampico are arrested; Huerta first apologizes, then refuses to salute a U.S. flag; finally agrees to mediation by ABC (Argentina, Brazil, and Chile) Powers.
May 13	Tampico is captured by rebels.
June 2	Mexican delegates at Nicaragua announce Huerta is willing to resign.
June 24	Rebels capture Zacatecas.
July 9	Guadalajara is seized by the rebels.
July 15	Huerta resigns.
August 15	General Carranza is appointed secretary of foreign affairs; provisional president Carbajal resigns after appointing Carranza.
August 21	Carranza enters Mexico City—his inaugural address includes promises of justice and reform.
1915	
January 15	Ex-president Gutiérrez surrenders to Carranza.
June 27	General Huerta and Orozco are arrested by U.S. officials near the border and are charged with planning further revolutionary activities against Mexican government.
August 19	General Villa is warmly applauded by the United States.
October 19	The U.S. and other American republics officially recognize General Carranza as leader of prevailing power in Mexico.
October 20	U.S. declares embargo on arms for Mexico except those going to Carranza or his forces.
1916	
January	19 American employees of a mining company are taken from a train near Chihuahua, Mexico, and shot by Villa's men.
January 13	General Victoriano Huerta dies in Texas.
March 9	Villa raids Columbus, New Mexico.
March 15	General Pershing marches into Mexico (accompanying him is a young lieutenant named George Patton).
March 29	U.S. Cavalry under command of Colonel Dodd fights Villa's troops at San Geronimo, Guerrero, Mexico.
May 6	Glen Springs, Texas, is raided by Villa.
May 31	General Carranza demands withdrawal of U.S. troops from Mexico.
June 17	American troops again enter Mexico; Carranza's consul in Brownsville, Texas, protests to General James Parker and promises Carranza will fight.
June 18	President Wilson calls out organized militia of 45 states and District of Columbia for duty along the Mexican border (National Guards of Texas, Arizona, and New Mexico are already on active service along their respective borders); eventually, 100,000 are called into active service.
September 7	Partial demobilization of National Guard begins.
1917	
January 28	Assassination of Zapata.
June 15	American troops cross the border to protect El Paso from Mexican bandits.
1920	
May 22	President Carranza is slain by his own escort near Tlaxcalatongo, following his flight from the capital.
September 5	Obregón is elected president of Mexico.

Part II: Postcards

Types and Categories

Type	Category
After the battle	R3
Americans observing battles	R3–R4
American troops in "welcome home" parades	R4
Armies in the field	R3–R4
Artillery-related	R4
Battle scenics	R3–R5
Columbus, New Mexico–related	R4
Deceased-related	R3–R4
El Paso, Texas (U.S. Army headquarters)–related	R3–R4
Execution of spies	R4
Field kitchens and mess halls	R4
Funeral procession for 17 Americans killed during siege of Vera Cruz	R4
George Patton–related	R5
Hangings	R3–R4
Indian troops	R3–R4
John J. Pershing–related	R3–R4
Later cards with a tie-in	R2–R4
Mexican federal troops	R3
Mexican leaders:	
Carranza	R4
Huerta	R4
Madero	R3–R4
Obregón	R4
Villa	R3–R4
Zapata	R3–R4
Others	R3–R5
Mexican refugees	R3–R4
Mexican sharpshooters	R3
Miscellaneous American or insurrecto involvement	R4
Miscellaneous execution-related	R4
Miscellaneous significant military characters	R4
Officers' headquarters	R4
Pitching tents	R3
P.O.W.–related	R4–R5
Preparing fortifications, repairing telegraph wires, and other necessary activities	R4
Pursuing Villa	R3–R4
Soldiers relaxing	R4
Soldiers with girls	R4
Types of bullets	R5
U.S. troops marching or parading through towns in Texas, New Mexico, Arizona, or California	R3–R4
Various routine activities at camp	R3–R4
Vera Cruz–related	R3–R5
Women with weapons	R4
Wounded soldiers	R4

Sets and Series

Army Y.M.C.A. Produced a series of sepia cards showing the Mexican soldier, Mexican army, "Pancho" Villa, and a number of interesting Mexican and American scenics.

Cal Osborn. Produced a series of cards depicting various aspects of the war. Included are pictures of posing American and Mexican army personnel, "Pancho" Villa, and gruesome pictures of dead or half-buried bodies.

H. H. Stratton. Published a series of real-photo cards that portray Mexican generals, American troops, Mexican troops, and so on.

International Film Service. Published a numbered (#900) series of sepia postcards, which includes such diverse topics as field artillery, infantrymen in action, setting up camp, various weaponry, battle destruction scenes, and more. Represented are both Mexican and American soldiers.

International News Service. Various scenics as just described.

Kavanaugh War Postals. Produced a series of black-and-white cards showing scenes in Columbus, New Mexico, and pictures of the U.S. Army.

Valentine Souvenir Company. Published a numbered series (200,000) dealing with Zapata as a colonel as a general, and with the U.S. Army, Navy, and Marines.

W. H. Horne. Photo cards of various locations and army personnel, as well as cards of Mexican refugees in American camps, and military atrocities.

Publishers

Army Y.M.C.A.
A. W. Long
Cal Osborn
Curt Teich
C. V. Williams
Doubleday-Heuther
D. W. Hoffman
Hecox
International Film Service
International News Service
J. G. Hatton
J. K.
Jones & Gullen
Judd
Kavanaugh War Postals
Max Stein
Scott Photo Company
Shannon
Stratton
Valentine Souvenir Company
W. H. Horne Company

"Federal Camp, Ojinaga." C. U. Williams. R3

Irregular Army of the North, 1912. Anonymous. R3

U.S. Infantry entrenching in Mexico. International Film Service. R3

"U.S. Army camp at Corallitos, Mexico." International Film Service. R3

U.S. Field Artillery on Mexican border. International Film Service. R3

Adobe house destroyed by artillery. International Film Service. R4

"Villa's troops." Anonymous. R3

Virginia troops marching through Brownsville, Texas. Anonymous. R4

General Francisco "Pancho" Villa in resplendent dress. Anonymous. R4

U.S. motor truck carrying machine gun. International Film Service. R4

"Maximo Castillo, El Bandido." Anonymous. R3

Installing telegraph lines. Anonymous. R4

"Mexican sharpshooters." Anonymous. R3

Federal troops on the march. Anonymous. R3

"Americans with insurrectos." Anonymous. R4

"General Blanco's army." Anonymous. R3

"Red Lopez." Anonymous. R4

"Red Lopez at Agua Preita, Mexico." Doubleday-Heuther. R4

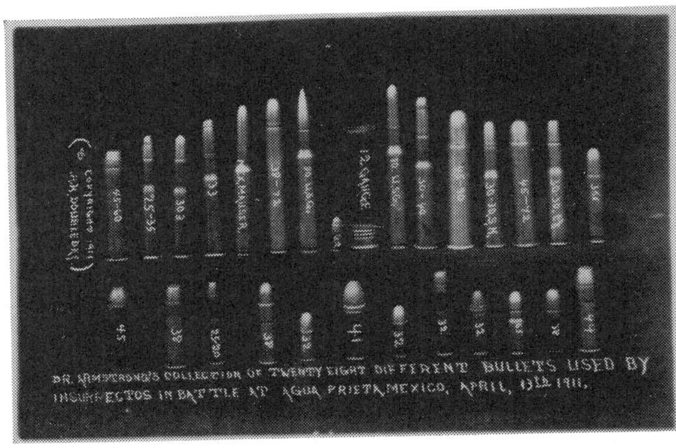

Bullets used by insurrectos at Agua Preita. Doubleday. R5

General Mosby and Adjutant Laflin, insurrectos. Anonymous. R4

Federal cavalry, Juarez. Anonymous. R3

An "after battle" card. Anonymous. R3

"General Orozco and his staff." Anonymous. R4

Indian troops. Anonymous. R4

"General Villa on road into Torreón." Max Stein. R3

Federal troops. A. W. Lohn. R3

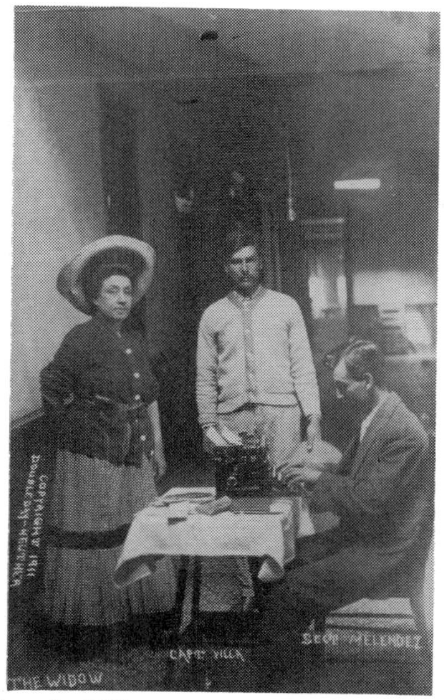

Captain Villa, secretary Melendez, and the widow; note the lady's pistola. Doubleday-Heuther. R4

General Villa, General Ortega, and General Fierro. A. W. Lohn. R4

More freedom fighters, including women with rifles. Anonymous. R4

"U.S. officers watching Battle of Ojinaga." Anonymous. R4

Soldiers gambling at a refugee camp in Ft. Bliss, Texas. C. U. Williams. R4

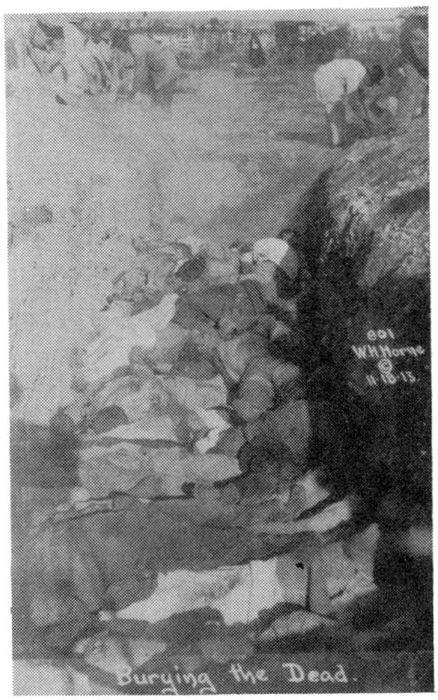

"Burying the Dead, the ultimate cost of war." W. H. Horne. R3

Porfirio Díaz. J. K. R3

"Mexican refugees preparing first meal at Fort Bliss, Tex." Anonymous. R3

"Wash day—refugee camp, Ft. Bliss." C. U. Williams. R3

"Prisoners at Fort Bliss." Anonymous. R4

"The grave of a Federal officer executed in Juarez." Anonymous. R4

8
The Balkan Wars

Prologue to World War I.

The Eastern Question

Daniel Spitzer, a nineteenth-century Viennese journalist, once observed that "We have the East to thank for opium smoking, hashish use, and the Eastern Question. All these have the common property of rendering extraordinarily stupid those individuals who are involved with them for a long time."

One can argue that the Eastern Question has been the most serious diplomatic problem confronting European states during the past 300 years. In its simplest form, the Eastern Question can be defined as *Who is to succeed the Ottoman Turks as the ruler of the Balkan Peninsula?* From the repulse of the Turks before Vienna in 1683 to the final loss of Ottoman territory in the aftermath of World War I, Turkish rule in the Balkans was in constant, irreversible decline. European Great Powers—most notably the Hapsburg Empire, Russia, and Great Britain—usually tried to control the rate of Turkish decline and to superintend the outcome. More recently, the subject peoples and the small nations of the Balkans have played an ever-increasing role in determining their own fate.

At all times, Balkan history has been complex, stemming primarily from the large number of forces at work on a very limited physical stage. For example, the area is precisely the meeting point of East and West. Within very narrow confines we find Orthodox, Roman Catholic, and Moslem societies. The ethnic mixture is even more confusing. Greeks, Slavs, Rumanians, Albanians, and Turks are the principal groups, but there are a host of lesser-known peoples such as Vlachs, Macedonians, and Szeklers who also inhabit the area. Generally speaking, most of these groups have a long history of xenophobia and mutual mistrust.

Differences in race and religion have been heightened by the physical characteristics of the Balkans. For the most part, the area consists of rugged mountains and highlands; poor, barren soil; and limited, difficult trade and transportation routes. These barriers have contributed to the isolation of the various peoples and nations and have accentuated the struggles for the fertile land and accessible trade routes.

As time has passed, modern forces such as nationalism, imperialism, and militarism have mixed with historic conditions to create a perpetually volatile situation in the Balkans. Nationalism, epitomized in the rise of the omnipotent nation-state, fostered a sense of self-awareness and ethnic pride on the part of the small states of the peninsula. That spirit coupled with militarism made for conflict in the latter nineteenth and early twentieth centuries. The same factors plus imperialism led the Great Powers of Europe to intervene in Balkan affairs for their own aggrandizement. Ultimately, all these forces came together to help bring about World War I, which, at least for the time being, settled the Eastern Question.

Shifting Sands in Europe

Although it predates the use of postcards by a few years, an appropriate starting point for modern Balkan history is the year 1871. While little of significance happened in the peninsula itself that year, several events occurred in the wider European context that were of great importance for affairs in Southeastern Europe. Specifically, diplomatic and power relationships among the great states of Europe changed drastically. Let us briefly review the positions and aspirations of the Great Powers before we proceed to Balkan affairs.

A Unified Germany

The year 1871 was most significant. In January, Otto von Bismarck, the Hohenzollern dynasty, and Prussian military might created a unified German state. The crushing defeat of France in the Franco-Prussian War ensured the primacy of the New Germany in Central and Western Europe. Germany's acquisition of the provinces of Alsace and Lorraine from France ensured implacable French opposition toward virtually any German foreign-policy initiative. The Franco-Prussian war also demonstrated that Austria-Hungary would have to relinquish any hope of hegemony in Central Europe, and would have to look torward the Balkans as an area for economic and territorial expansion.

Once he achieved the unification of Germany, Bismarck's foreign policy goals may be summed up in one word—*peace*. The chancellor had no further territorial aspirations, and the empire, particularly Prussia and the South German states, needed time to coalesce.

In order to gain the time and tranquility necessary for his country to come together, Bismarck had to ensure that France did not try to gain revenge for the Franco-Prussian War. Bismarck's work was aimed at keeping France diplomatically isolated and without military allies. Part of this effort involved an attempt either to maintain the existing European territorial arrangement or to ensure that any changes were made peacefully and cooperatively.

France in Isolation

The primary objective of France, subsequent to 1871, was to secure reliable allies against Germany. Unfortunately, France had little to offer a potential ally. The French army had just been decisively defeated by the Prussians, and internally, France seemed unable to choose between monarchical and democratic forms of government. Thus, in the 1870s, the only course of action open to the French government was to work slowly and carefully to revitalize the nation and its military forces in order to take advantage of any opportunity to end the country's diplomatic isolation and strike a blow at Germany.

The Problem with Italy

Italy faced problems similar to those of France, but in the Italian case, the difficulties arose primarily form Italy's recent and precarious attainment of Great Power status. None of the Italian states had been able to emulate Prussia and unify the Apennine peninsula; rather, unification came only with the assistance of France and Prussia and in spite of Austrian victories over Italian forces. Nor could Italians really consider unification complete since there were tremendous economic and cultural differences between Northern and Soutern Italy, and since substantial numbers of ethnic Italians still lived under Austrian rule in Istria and Southern Tirol.

The primary goals of the Italian government during the 1870s were to create a cohesive state and to guard zealously Italy's position as a Great Power. Territorially, Italy desired to expand its influence into Northern Africa and the Western Balkans. However, in view of its weakness, Italy required either an ally or a crisis in European diplomacy to think seriously about attaining its territorial goals. Ostensibly, an alliance with France was possible; however, there was an increasing likelihood of Franco-Italian rivalry in North Africa. In addition, an alliance between Rome and Paris would arouse the enmity of Bismarck and Germany. Any understanding with Austria-Hungary was out of the question because of Italian remembrance of long years of Hapsburg rule in the Apennine peninsula, and because Italian and Austro-Hungarian interest clashed in the Balkans. Germany was a possible ally, but Berlin favored closer ties with Vienna instead of with Rome. Russia was a potential ally, particularly in regard to the Balkans, but Russia and Great Britain were not on good terms, and as an ally of Russia, Italy would be subject to pressure from British naval strength. With all these considerations in view, Italy, like France, was forced to adopt a cautious yet opportunistic foreign policy during the 1870s.

Austria-Hungary's Predicament

In a general sense, the problems and aspirations of Austria-Hungary were similar to those of France and Italy. In the dozen years preceding 1871, Austria-Hungary had been defeated in two wars, had lost its territorial possessions in Italy, was expelled from a position of leadership in Germany, and faced a major threat to its unity from its Magyar—or Hungarian—populace.

In view of the Dual Monarchy's tarnished reputation, one of the primary goals of Austria-Hungary's leaders in the 1870s was to demonstrate that, despite its recent setbacks, the Dual Monarchy was a viable and resilient state. However, in order to revitalize itself internally and militarily, the country needed a period of external peace. The best guarantee of that peace was alliance with a strong power. The only realistic candidates were Germany and Russia. For his part, Bismarck decided on peace and friendship between Germany and Austria-Hungary; however, an influentual faction within the Hapsburg Empire could not forget or forgive Prussia's defeat of Austria in the Seven Weeks War of 1866.

The situation vis-à-vis Russia was much more complex. Relations between Vienna and St. Petersburg had been quite cool since Austria's "treachery" during the Crimean War in the 1850s. During that conflict, Austria refused to allow Russian troops to pass through the Balkan Peninsula (so Russia could attack the Ottoman Empire), with the result that Russia was severely hampered in its efforts to wage war against the Turks. In addition, there was a strong probability of a conflict of interests between the Hapsburg and Romanov empires in the Balkans.

Russia's Continued Goal of Expansionism

In contrast to France, Italy, and Austria-Hungary, Russia was not searching desperately for allies during the 1870s. The country was on good terms with Germany and there were no significant potential points of conflict between them.

In terms of foreign policy, Russia wanted to resume her age-old drive toward Constantinople and access to the Mediterranean Sea. That drive had been blunted, even temporarily reversed, some 20 years earlier by the defeat Russia suffered in the Crimean War. Any Russian penetration of the Balkans would have to be cautious and skillful in order to avoid driving Austria-Hungary and Great Britain into an alliance. An alternative to the unilateral course of action would be to attempt to partition the Balkans in cooperation with Austria-Hungary at the expense of the Turks. A second possibility would be to ally with Germany in order to overawe Austria-Hungary into acquiescing to Russian penetration into the Balkans.

Complacent Great Britain

Little has been said about Great Britain thus far, because while it was certainly a Great Power, Great Britain was not interested in being a European Great Power in 1871. There was a mild concern on the part of Her Majesty's government regarding Bismarck's intentions after the Franco-Prussian War, and there was also friction with Russia over central Asia, but on the whole, Great Britain was one of the strongest powers, existing in isolation and with little need to concern itself over continental events.

In summary, in the era immediately after the the Franco-Prussian War, Bismarckian Germany was content with the existing situation, but also had to be constantly vigilant in regard to France; Great Britain held itself smugly aloof from Continental affairs; and Russia desired to reassert its power and prestige—which might well be an aggressive policy in the Balkans. The other three powers—France, Italy, and Austria-Hungary—because of reasons such as recent miitary defeats or lack of internal unity, were more likely to play a secondary role in European diplomacy since they all required a period of tranquility to refurbish their Great Power status.

Minor Players in the Balkans

Having examined the positions and aspirations of the Great Powers, let us now look at some of the minor players in the Balkans during the early 1870s. In 1875, when the most serious of the nineteenth-century Balkan disturbances began, much of the peninsula was ruled by the Ottoman Empire. Turkish rule had not been effective for several centuries. The rule of Constantinople over its Balkan provinces was inefficient, endemically corrupt, and chaotic. Indeed, the farther removed an area was from Constantinople, the more tenuous the sway of the central government, with the result that local rulers were often virtually autonomous. The peasantry, both Christian and Moslem, was heavily taxed and oppressively exploited. The result was frequent, violent peasant revolts. In the views of several of the Great Powers, Turkish control over its Balkan possessions was so fragile that the issue was one of how and when to divide the Turkish territory rather than one of how to reform and preserve the Ottoman Empire.

In 1875 the Balkan states of Serbia, Montenegro, Rumania, and Greece all enjoyed some degree of independence—either legally recognized or actually attained. All of them were militarily and economically weak. As a general rule, they all had internal consolidation of the strength and authority of the central government and external expansion to bring all of their race within the borders of a single state—except for Rumania. Rumania's expansion was aimed primarily at the Ottoman Empire because that state was the weakest one having sovereignty over its ethnic brethren. However, Austria-Hungary in particular also contained a large South Slav population and was therefore a potential target of Serbian and Montenegrin aggrandizement.

Before delving into the details of the crisis of 1875–78, we must briefly examine one specific ideology that played an important role in the events of those years. Pan-Slavism was a Russian movement that had originally exalted linguistic, cultural, and ethnic ties among Slavs. By the 1870s, however, it was in a transition to what amounted to Pan-Russianism. This is to say, proponents of the movement advocated the union of all Slavs under the auspices of Mother Russia. One of the foremost Pan-Slavs was the Russian ambassador at Constantinople during the 1870s. His influence extended into the Balkans as well, with the result that in many quarters it was assumed that Russia would help her little brother Slavs of the Balkans in their efforts to strengthen and unify their peoples.

The Crisis of 1875–78

Now let us look directly at the crisis of 1875–78. Regardless of Great Power intrigues and aspirations, the original problem was purely indigenous to the Ottoman provinces of Bosnia-Herzegovina. Poor harvests combined with onerous taxation sparked a revolt in Herzegovina that quickly spread over an extensive area.

The initial response of the Great Powers was an effort to contain the revolt so that the Turks could suppress it. This effort was led by Austro-Hungarian foreign minister Count Gyula Andrássy as spokesman for the Three Emperors' League. This League was a conservative alliance of Germany, Austria-Hungary, and Russia that had resulted from a series of personal meetings between the rulers of those countries during the early 1870s. The League had great significance for the Balkans because Russia and Austria-Hungary agreed, albeit verbally and informally, to maintain the existing situation in the Balkans. This was precisely what Austria-Hungary wanted at the time and for the foreseeable future. St. Petersburg, however, probably intended to use the Three Emperors' League as a means to improve relations with Austria-Hungary so that eventually Vienna could be persuaded either to participate in a joint partition of Ottoman territory or to acquiesce to Russian acquisition of Turkish territory.

The Berlin Memorandum

Austria-Hungary's initial effort to suppress the revolt in Bosnia-Herzegovina consisted of several related initiatives. At Andrássy's insistence, the consular representatives of the Great Powers met with the insurgent leaders and attempted to mediate a peaceful resolution of the dispute. The rebels refused to lay down their arms because the Great Powers would not guarantee the necessary reforms of Ottoman governmental administration. Andrássy then, in December 1875, formulated a reform program that included full religious liberty, an end to tax farming, and the amelioration of the lot of peasant farmers. These proposals were accepted by all the Great Powers and by the Turks, but were rejected by the rebels—again because the European powers would not guarantee their implementation.

In view of Andrássy's two failures to end the fighting, Prince Alexander Gorchakov, the Russian foreign minister, stepped forth with another plan in the summer of 1876. Among other conditions, Gorchakov proposed that Austria-Hungary occupy Turkish territory in order to guarantee reform, and that Montenegro receive territory from the Turks.

Such a plan was absolutely unacceptable to Andrássy, who quickly wrestled the diplomatic initiative from his Russian counterpart. Andrássy refashioned Gorchakov's plan into the Berlin Memorandum of May 1876. That document was essentially a restatement of Andrássy's earlier proposals. France and Italy quickly agreed to the memorandum; Great Britain just as swiftly and very decisively rejected it. British prime minister Benjamin Disraeli was extremely suspicious of the Three Emperors' League and regarded the terms of the Berlin Memorandum as a distinct threat to the territorial integrity of the Ottoman state. In the face of British opposition and chaotic conditions in the Turkish government, the Berlin Memorandum was quietly laid to rest.

Serbia and Montenegro Declare War

A direct result of the failure of the Great Powers to negotiate an end to the revolt, which had spread from Bosnia-Herzegovina to Bulgaria as well, was a declaration of war by Serbia and Montenegro against the Ottoman Empire in the summer of 1876. The two principalities had been held in check for a year by strong Austro-Hungarian and Russian pressure, and diplomatic pressure. By mid-1876, however, the two little countries were overflowing with both embittered refugees from Bosnia-Herzegovina and with an excess of enthusiasm for the Slavic cause. When reform efforts appeared hopeless, war became inevitable.

The attack of Serbia and Montenegro on the Turks signaled a new phase of the Balkan crisis. It was now almost a certainty that the pre-1875 situation could not be restored. It was quite possible that the conflict might become a kind of Slavic Christian crusade against the Turks that would be sure to bring in its wake increased Russian activity in the Balkans. Russia would have to protect its Slavic kinsmen if the war went against them, and conversely, if the Turks were defeated, Russia was unlikely to refrain from adding to the Czar's territory. Austria-Hungary, too, had to reevaluate its position. If the pre-1875 situation could not be maintained, Vienna had to make sure that Hapsburg power and prestige were preserved and that the possibility of territorial expansion into the Balkans was safeguarded. Vienna had several considerations in mind regarding expansion to the Southeast. First, Dalmatia, a long coastal province immediately west of Bosnia-Herzegovina, had to be protected because that area contained the primary Austro-Hungarian naval bases and ports. Second, and more important, Austria-Hungary had to be certain Serbia and Montenegro did not gain so much territory and prestige as a result of a successful war against Turkey that the South Slavic peoples of Austria-Hungary would be enticed to try to break away from the Dual Monarchy and join their Slavic brothers.

In addition to increased Russian and Austro-Hungarian activity, the outbreak of war also brought with it the prospect of greater British involvement in Balkan affairs. If Russia were to be more active and pose a threat to Constantinople, Great Britain would have to defend its interests in the Eastern Mediterranean.

Possible Solutions

Each of the three Great Powers most closely involved had several options available. The two land powers could arrange a partition of the Turks' Balkan provinces, which Great Britain would be unable to oppose; however, any such partition would be regarded as an unpalatable last resort by Austria-Hungary. Great Britain and Austria-Hungary could ally for the purpose of denying Russia any increase in territory or influence, but if hostilities among the three Powers resulted, the brunt of the land fighting would fall upon Austria-Hungary, and Vienna did not feel strong enough to risk war with Russia. Austria-Hungary could also attempt a variation of its original course of action and try to forestall active Russian intervention in the Balkans for as long as possible. That might give the Turks enough time to defeat Serbia and Montenegro and restore an approximation of the prewar situation.

With the variety of diplomatic possibilities that lay open to the Great Powers, it is hardly surprising that the second half of 1876 witnessed an intent exchange of notes and ideas among the capitals of Europe. The one concrete result was the Reichstadt agreement between Austria-Hungary and Russia. In July 1876, Emperor Franz Joseph I of Austria-Hungary and Andrássy met with Emperor Alexander II and Gorchakov for the purpose of resolving potential conflicts that might result from the Serbo-Montenegrin-Turkish War. Andrássy and Gorchakov quickly settled the points at issue; however, an authoritative text of their agreement was not prepared, so each side came away with a different version of the settlement. The two sides both believed that if the Turks won the war, peace would be reestablished on the basis of the prewar status quo in Serbia and Montenegro, and that the reforms Andrássy proposed several times before would be implemented in Bosnia-Herzegovina. If the principalities triumphed, Austria-Hungary, Serbia, and Montenegro would divide Bosnia-Herzegovina. In the Russian version, Austria-Hungary would receive only a relatively small part of Bosnia. The two Powers also agreed that a large Slavic state would not be established in the Balkans. As its share of spoils, Russia would receive the part of Bessarabia that the czardom had lost to Rumania in 1856, as well as Turkish territory in Central Asia.

Conference at Constantinople

Once Austria-Hungary and Russia settled their differences, they could afford to sit back and watch the progress of the war. The course of the conflict was surprising—the Turks won quickly and decisively. Their success was so far-ranging that in September they implemented a unilateral armistice in order not to provoke Russia into intervention to save Serbia and Montenegro. When the principalities refused to yield, the Turks resumed hostilities until the end of October, when Russia coerced Constantinople into another armistice.

This armistice was followed in short order by a conference of the Great Powers' representatives at Constantinople in December. The Powers proposed the division of Bulgaria into Eastern and Western provinces. These provinces, along with Bosnia-Herzegovina, would have substantial control over local affairs. In addition, Serbia would retain its prewar boundaries, while Montenegro would retain the territory her troops conquered in Herzegovina and Northern Albania. Despite the unanimity of the Great Powers, Constantinople rejected the conference proposals. The Turks insisted that a newly promulgated constitution would guarantee reform of the Ottoman Empire, and that, therefore, the proposals had become moot.

The rejection of the reform proposals was viewed by Czar Alexander II and the Pan-Slavs as an affront to Russian honor. The proper response to each insult was war; however, prior to opening hostilities, Russia had to ensure that her diplomatic fences were mended. The most important item of business was to reach an understanding with Austria-Hungary about Vienna's role in a Russo-Turkish war. The benevolent neutrality of the Dual Monarchy was absolutely essential to Russian war plans since Russian armies could not attack the Turks through the Balkans with a hostile power on their right.

From Vienna's perspective, an agreement with St. Petersburg was the only practical course of action available. In late 1876, Austria-Hungary and Great Britain exchanged notes and information, but had not been able to agree on a common policy in the event of a Russo-Turkish war. For their part, the Austrians were afraid the British would leave them in the lurch if hostilities broke out among the three Powers, and in any event, Hapsburg troops would have to bear the brunt of land campaigns. The British, on the other hand, doubted Austria-Hungary's ability to sustain a war against Russia and could not rule out the possibility of a diplomatic trap set for Her Majesty's government by the Three Emperors' League.

Austria-Hungary Agrees to Neutrality

Having no other ally to turn to, Austria-Hungary and Russia reached a compromise agreement in Budapest on January 15, 1877. Austria-Hungary agreed to remain benevolently neutral in the event of a Russo-Turkish war and to decline to participate in European mediation of any such conflict. In an additional agreement signed on March 15, 1877, Austria-Hungary obtained the right to annex Bosnia-Herzegovina, while Russia was to get Bessarabia. Other conditions stipulated that the fate of the Turkish province of Novi Pazar, which separated Serbia and Montenegro, would be decided later, and that no large Slavic state was to be created in the Balkans.

The Budapest Conventions were an Austro-Hungarian diplomatic victory. The Dual Monarchy obtained a guarantee of Bosnia-Herzegovina and limited Russian expansion in the Balkans. For the Russians, the Conventions were harsh necessities if Russia was to attack the Ottoman Empire. There did remain the possibility that St. Petersburg might be tempted to try to implement a postwar revision of the terms.

Russian Victory over Turks

As soon as diplomatic preparations with Austria-Hungary had been completed, Russia declared war on the Ottoman Empire (April 1877). Initially, the Russians enjoyed rapid and spectacular success—so much so that Austria-Hungary and Great Britain became alarmed that the Ottoman Empire might be completely fragmented. The gallant Turkish defense of Plevna temporarily blunted the Russian drive, but the Turks also faced the Rumanians and Montenegrins, and Serbia appeared ready to enter the fray again. In fact, Montenegro made substantial gains along the Adriatic coast in Northern Albania, a situation Austria-Hungary found totally unacceptable.

On December 10, 1877, Plevna fell, and the Russian army resumed its surge southward. War fever mounted in Great Britain, and Austria-Hungary reconsidered an alliance with Her Majesty's government. Meanwhile, Russian troops advanced to the outskirts of Constantinople.

On March 3, 1878, Russia and the Ottoman Empire signed the Treaty of San Stefano, ending the Russo-Turkish War. By the terms of that treaty, Bosnia-Herzegovina was to receive local autonomy and the implementation of reform measures proposed in the past. Serbia and Montenegro were to gain complete independence and some territory as well. Likewise, Rumania was to become completely independent, although the country would also have to give up Bessarabia to Russia. A very large autonomous Bulgarian state was to be created and occupied by Russian troops for two years. In addition to Bessarabia, Russia was to receive territory in Central Asia.

The Treaty of San Stefano was completely unsatisfactory to everyone except Russia. Both Austria-Hungary and Great Britain objected to the provisions regarding

Bulgaria, and the Dual Monarchy was also concerned about the status of Bosnia-Herzegovina. Greece, Serbia, and Montenegro all fumed about the extent of Bulgaria, while Rumania mourned the loss of Bessarabia.

It seems quite likely that St. Petersburg demanded more than it could hope to gain in the expectation of obtaining what it regarded as absolutely necessary. For their parts, the other Powers demanded a conference to revise the treaty settlement.

Treaty of Berlin

The Congress of Berlin that met in June 1878 and finally ended the protracted Balkan Crisis of the 1870s was really rather anticlimactic. For the most part, the congress formalized several agreements that had been negotiated prior to its convocation. In late May 1878, Great Britain and Russia resolved their main point of conflict when they reached a bilateral agreement on the extent of the Bulgarian state. A week later, Austria-Hungary agreed to support Great Britain on the Bulgarian issue in return for British support of Austria-Hungary's claim to Bosnia-Herzegovina.

By the terms of the Treaty of Berlin, "Bulgaria" was divided tranversely along the Balkan mountain range. The northern area, known as Bulgaria, was granted autonomy under an elected prince. The area south of the Balkan Mountains was designated Eastern Rumelia. Constantinople continued to govern the area, although it did obtain a substantial degree of autonomy. The province of Macedonia, granted to Bulgaria by the terms of San Stefano, reverted to the Ottoman Empire. Serbia, Montenego, and Rumania all gained complete independence, as well as some territory. However, Rumania lost Bessarabia to Russia, and Serbia did not get the fervently desired Bosnia-Herzegovina access to the Adriatic Sea. Austria-Hungary received Bosnia-Herzegovina to occupy and administer and also received the right to occupy the province of Novi Pazar, although, titularly, the province remained Turkish territory. Russia, as already mentioned, regained Bessarabia as well as territory in Central Asia. Great Britain obtained the island of Cypress from the Turks.

Unsolved Treaty Problems

While the Congress of Berlin brought open hostilities to a close, it did not satisfy many of the participants, and its provision contained the seeds of further discord. The foremost problem the Congress created involved the fate of Macedonia. That area became the focus of the territorial ambitions of the small Balkan states. Specifically, Bulgarians felt the area belonged in a "greater Bulgaria"; Greeks coveted the province because Greece had received nothing from the Congress of Berlin and regarded the creation of Bulgaria as an insult, while Serbia and Montenegro—blocked by Austria-Hungary in Bosnia-Herzegovina and Novi Pazar—had no other area in which to expand. The stage then was set for fratricidal conflict, which came early in the twentieth century.

The fate of Bosnia-Herzegovina constituted a second major problem which the Congress of Berlin had failed to resolve. Austria-Hungary had the task of occupying and administering the area, but the province remained legally a part of the Ottoman Empire. It was assumed by the Powers that the area would not revert to actual Turkish control; however, until Austria-Hungary formally incorporated Bosnia-Herzegovina into the Hapsburg Empire, Serbians, Montenegrins, and Turks continued to covet jealously the two provinces.

The Years Preceding the Balkan Wars

In the years between the Congress of Berlin and the outbreak of World War I, Austria-Hungary and Russia remained the protagonists on the Balkan stage. Infrequently they cooperated; usually they regarded each other with wary eyes and thinly veiled hostility. Throughout the late nineteenth and early twentieth centuries, Russia continued to support Balkan client states in an effort to expand her own power and prestige. Austria-Hungary worked steadily to counteract any possible Russian gains. Vienna was primarily concerned with nullifying the effect of Pan-Slavic propaganda on the Slavs of the Dual Monarchy, since such agitation could stimulate a separatist movement within Austria-Hungary. The Hapsburg Empire also tried to manipulate relations with Serbia to ensure that the principality's territorial aspirations were directed away from Bosnia-Herzegovina, and southward toward Macedonia.

One of the instances of Austro-Hungarian-Russian cooperation occurred immediately after the Congress of Berlin and was primarily due to Bismarck's influence. The German chancellor was most eager to repair the damage done to the Three Emperors' League by the Balkan Crisis. In 1881, he fostered a renewal of the League. As a part of the alliance agreement, Russia and Germany vowed not to oppose Austro-Hungarian annexation of Bosnia-Herzegovina should the Dual Monarchy decide to do that. In return, Austria-Hungary agreed not to object to the eventual union of Bulgaria and Eastern Rumelia. The alliance also provided that if the territorial status of Turkey was altered, the three empires would agree on a unified course of action.

Austria-Hungary Improves Its Position

Around the same time, Austria-Hungary also took several other steps to strengthen its Balkan position. Rumania resented deeply the loss of Bessarabia to Russia and was quite willing to enter into an agreement with Austria-Hungary. The two countries concluded an alliance in 1883 requiring each to aid the other in the event of an attack by Russia.

The Dual Monarchy improved its relationship with Serbia as well as with Rumania. Protestations of Slavic leadership and unity notwithstanding, Russia had not supported the Serbs at the Congress of Berlin. As a result, Serbian territorial gains were quite modest, particularly when compared to its sacrifices during the 1875–78 period, and were made primarily due to Austro-Hungarian assistance. In 1881, Vienna and Belgrade concluded both a commercial treaty and a diplomatic accord: Austria-Hungary agreed to support Serbian expansion southward, while Serbia agreed to make no treaties with other Powers without Austria-Hungary's approval. The diplomatic agreement was kept highly secret and depended on the personal power and prestige of the Serbian ruler, Prince Milan Obrenovich. It probably could not have been sustained among the populace had its terms become known, but at least Austria-Hungary had the temporary assurance that the Serbian government was not fostering intrigues against Vienna.

Serbo-Bulgarian War

In the years just after the Congress of Berlin, Russia continued to try to enhance its power and prestige by working through the Bulgarians. However, the Bulgarians proved themselves increasingly unruly vassals and ultimately became entirely unmanageable. In 1879, the Bulgarians adopted a liberal constitution and chose Alexander of Battenberg, a minor German prince, as their ruler. For the next few years, Alexander, his Bulgarian subjects, and the Russians waged a three-way struggle for control of the country. Eventually the prince and his people united against the Russians; however, without Great Power support, Alexander could not implement a complete break with St. Petersburg. At this point, in 1885, the people of Eastern Rumelia revolted against their Turkish governor and announced union with Bulgaria. Paradoxically, St. Petersburg opposed this union because it occurred under Prince Alexander; however, popular sentiment could not be undone.

At this point, the Serbians entered the fray. Prince Milan, in his secret treaty with Austria-Hungary, had committed Serbia to expand to the south. Now, with the union of Eastern Rumelia and Bulgaria, it looked as though that direction might soon be blocked. In order to preserve his throne, Milan felt obliged either to attack Bulgaria or to fight the Turks for Macedonia. Austria-Hungary counseled an attack on Bulgaria as the lesser of evils, and in late 1885, Serbia declared war. The result was decisive and surprising; the Bulgarians won such a resounding victory that Austria-Hungary had to threaten intervention to save Serbia.

The Macedonian Issue

The crisis surrounding Bulgarian unification is important because it disrupted the Three Emperors' League once again and for good, since Austria-Hungary and Russia had supported their respective warring vassals in the Serbo-Bulgarian War. It is equally important because it brought to the forefront the Macedonian issue.

Macedonia may be generally defined as the area around the city of Salonika. Historically, the territory was coveted because it controlled the North-South trade route through the Balkans, along the Vardar-Morava River Valley. In addition, the area nearest Salonika was a fertile lowland that produced an abundance of food crops. Finally, the focal point of Macedonia was the prosperous port of Salonika. In addition to these obvious economic benefits that would accrue to the owner of Macedonia—Bulgaria, Greece, and Serbia also quarreled over the province because there was no other area into which they could expand. The result of this rivalry was a bitter, protracted struggle for domination.

The torturous twists and turns of intrigue involving Bulgars, Greeks, Serbs, and even Rumanians are too intricate to detail here; however, several results of the struggle had a great impact on later events in the Balkans. The primary effect of outside attempts to control Macedonia was the creation of the Internal Macedonian Revolutionary Organization, or IMRO. IMRO began in 1893 as an indigenous effort to unite Macedonians for Macedonia and drive out the Turks who still maintained at least titular control over the area. After a decade of plotting and conducting terrorist activities, the IMRO led a revolt against the Turks in 1903. The result was typical of much of Balkan history: Ottoman troops quickly laid waste to Macedonia and suppressed the revolt. The Great Powers, led by Austria-Hungary and Russia, forced the implementation of reforms that Constantinople honored more in spirit than in fact. Thus the Turks maintained a precarious hold on the one remaining Balkan territorial prize, but all the players were determined to continue gambling for it.

Bosnia-Herzegovina was the second major Balkan problem left over from the Congress of Berlin. The situation there was not as explosive as in Macedonia, but it was no less troublesome. The problem was what to do with the territory. Theoretically, the Ottoman Empire owned the area, but Austria-Hungary occupied and administered it. The obvious thing to do was to turn the actual Austrian ownership into a legal one; however, such a course of action would encounter serious difficulties. From a foreign policy standpoint, Austria-Hungary could expect to face adamant opposition from Serbia and Montenegro. Those two states still dreamed of incorporating Bosnia-Herzegovina in a large, independent South Slavic state. Their opposition to the Dual Monarchy's annexation of Bosnia-Herzegovina would undoubtedly be supported by Russia. At the very least, Russia would require something in return for acquiescing to an Austrian annexation of the provinces. Internally, the acquisition of Bosnia-Herzegovina would be strongly opposed by the Hungarians, and there would be the practical problem of which half of the Dual Monarchy would govern the area.

Young Turks

In 1908, an event took place that began to mix the volatile elements of Balkan politics, setting the stage for the explosion in 1914. For centuries, reformers had tried to modernize the Ottoman government and administration in order to create a viable state. By the first decade of the twentieth century, the danger to the antiquated and impotent Turkish government was acute. Continuing problems in Macedonia resulted in various Great Power proposals to reform the Turkish state. In the minds of loyal Ottomans, reform was often regarded as synonymous with "partition" or "destruction" of the Turkish empire. Unending European meddling in Ottoman affairs finally led a group of army officers known as *Young Turks* to rebel against Sultan Abdul Hamid II. In 1908, the Young Turks forced a restoration of the 1876 constitution, and in 1909, they deposed the sultan and replaced him with a figurehead of their choosing.

The vigor of Young Turk actions and the potential power of their ideology had momentous consequences for the Balkans. The Young Turks believed in basic freedoms for all citizens of the Empire if, in return, those citizens would support the idea of the Empire and its existing territorial status. The Young Turks did believe in the predominance of Turks over other ethnic groups and expected those other groups to become more like Turks as a part of their support of the Ottoman Empire. Their dynamism indicated that the government of the Young Turks might actually be able to sustain and possibly even reinvigorate the empire. Any such renewal would obviously threaten the Austro-Hungarian position in Bosnia-Herzegovina and might also deprive the minor Balkan states of the opportunity to expand into Macedonia.

The ambiguous status of Bosnia-Herzegovina was resolved before that of Macedonia. A combination of circumstances worked to bring this about. Austria-Hungary felt a growing pressure to annex Bosnia-Herzegovina in order to put that prize beyond the grasp of both the Young Turks and the Serbians. In 1903, the Obrenovich dynasty was replaced by the Karageorgevich dynasty in Belgrade. The new ruler was anti-Austrian, and there was a growing clamor for the expansion of the country to include all Serbs in a "greater Serbia." Austria-Hungary also had to deal with a more aggressive Russian foreign policy in the Balkans. This came about because the czardom's defeat in the Russo-Japanese War had temporarily ended Russia's Far East ambitions. Russia then turned to the Balkans to salve its pride and refurbish its prestige.

Austria Annexes Bosnia-Herzegovina

The actual annexation of Bosnia-Herzegovina by Austria-Hungary owed a great deal to the personalities of the foreign ministers of the Dual Monarchy and Russia at that time. Count Alois Aehrenthal, the Austro-Hungarian foreign minister, was a vain and aggressive man bent on personal aggrandizement and a throttling of Serbian ambition. Russia's Alexander Izvolsky was also extremely ambitious about enhancing his country's authority.

In order to pave the way for a more aggressive Russian policy in the Balkans, Izvolsky first had to secure an understanding with Austria-Hungary. In the summer of 1908, he proposed to Aehrenthal that Russia would support an Austrian annexation of Bosnia-Herzegovina if Austria-Hungary would agree to a Russian attempt to have the passage from the Black Sea into the Mediterranean Sea opened to Russian warships. In September 1906, this understanding was refined during a personal meeting between the two foreign ministers, but they failed to prepare a definitive written statement of their agreement.

Aehrenthal wasted no time implementing his view of the bargain. On October 6, Austria-Hungary announced the annexation of Bosnia-Herzegovina. Although this action merely legitimized a situation that had existed for 30 years, it incensed Serbia, Montenegro, and the Ottoman Empire, and offended Russia as well.

In part, the Russian government was upset because Izvolsky had acted independently in making his agreement with Aehrenthal. As a result of that understanding, Austria-Hungary got Bosnia-Herzegovina, but Izvolsky was not able to get the other Great Powers to agree to a modification of international treaties relating to the Straits, so Russian warships remained bottled up in the Black Sea. In effect, Russia's brother Slavs in Bosnia-Herzegovina had been sacrificed to Austria-Hungary, while Russia got nothing in return.

The Serbs likewise were furious over the fate of their fellow Slavs. They refused to recognize the annexation and threatened war against the Dual Monarchy. Their agitation received strong popular support in Russia.

Eventually, the festering crisis was brought to a conclusion by Germany. In the face of a serious possibility of war between Austria-Hungary and Serbia with the likelihood of Russian intervention, the German government issued an ultimatum to Russia to recognize the annexation and to cease supporting Serbia in opposition to Austria-Hungary's action. As a result, both Slavic nations ceased their clamor and the crisis faded away.

The Balkan Wars

The annexation of Bosnia-Herzegovina had several significant effects on subsequent Balkan history. The Austrian action clearly demonstrated the opposing sides in the Balkans. There was no further hope of cooperation between Vienna and St. Petersburg because of Russia's loss of face. The Serbs were incensed and inflamed with ideas of revenge against Austria-Hungary, a feeling which came to fruition in 1914.

The annexation of Bosnia-Herzegovina also contributed directly to the formation of the alliance which was known as the Balkan League, that instigated the First Balkan War (1912). This struggle and its subsequent round, the Second Balkan War (1913), were the last major developments in the Balkans prior to World War I.

In view of the deep-seated rivalries among the Balkan states, the motivating force for any alliance had to be quite strong and conditions had to be just right for the union to come into being. Such was the case in the years just after the annexation of Bosnia-Herzegovina. Indeed, as indicated above, the annexation itself was one of the foremost stimuli for an alliance. The Austrian action had seemed high-handed and arbitrary to the Balkan states, but it had also been successful. There was certainly no guarantee that Vienna might not try to annex the province of Novi Pazar as well, and even if the Dual Monarchy refrained from taking additional territory itself, it might well try to sit in judgment on acquisitions by the Balkan states. In short, the annexation crisis proved that the Balkan states had to band together if they were to have any chance of defying the Hapsburg Empire.

A second force pushing for Balkan unity was Russia. St. Petersburg was humiliated by its diplomatic defeat in the Bosnian-Herzegovina annexation crisis. Russia could ill afford another such loss of face; however, the events of 1908–9 had shown that there was scant prospect of success in supporting only one of the Balkan states against Austria-Hungary. Perhaps the answer lay in an alliance of all the Balkan states. While Russian diplomacy—as embodied in the czardom's representatives—was somewhat confused as to what the proper goal of any alliance should be, there was no mistaking the anti-Hapsburg emphasis and the encouragement St. Petersburg provided to Athens, Belgrade, Cetinje, and Sofia.

The situation in the Ottoman Empire also favored an alliance of Balkan states. There were several factors at work. The Young Turks' ideology mentioned earlier provoked violent and unrelenting opposition among the non-Turkish subjects of the empire. Indeed, the Albanians seemed perpetually in revolt against the Ottoman government. In addition, the Turks were attacked by Italy in late 1911 as a result of a dispute over North African territories. The war went against the Ottoman Empire, with the result that the Balkan states were encouraged to band together to further their own territorial ambitions.

The Balkan League

The Balkan League, while a direct result of the annexation of Bosnia-Herzegovina, did not come into being immediately after that crisis. The delay was due primarily to the parties' conflicting interests. Negotiations were slow and sometimes the agreements reached were ambiguous. The League itself was not a common treaty entered into by all parties, but rather a network of interconnecting treaties, usually between two of the various countries. The League began with an agreement between Bulgaria and Serbia, which was concluded in the spring of 1912. At its simplest level, this provided that the two countries would assist each other if one were attacked, and that they would act together to resist any attempt by a Great Power to annex Ottoman territory. The two nations also specified a partial division of Macedonian territory in the event that it should become necessary. They could not, however, reach a definitive understanding on the division of Macedonia because their respective territorial claims overlapped.

The second part of the Balkan League to fall into place was an agreement between Bulgaria and Greece. While the Bulgaro-Serbian treaty had been directed at least in part against Austria-Hungary, the accord between Athens and Sofia was aimed at the Ottoman Empire. As had been the case with Serbia and Bulgaria, Greece and Bulgaria could not reach a definitive understanding on a future partition of Macedonia. The crux of the dispute was the fate of the port of Salonika, which both countries ardently desired to have.

The final part of the Balkan League was the alliances Montenegro arranged with Bulgaria and Serbia. Both of these agreements were offensive in nature and directed against the Ottoman Empire. In fact, the accords called for an attack on the Turks in the early fall of 1912.

The First Balkan War, 1912

In accordance with its treaty obligations, Montenegro declared war on the Ottoman Empire in October 1912. Montenegro was followed in short order by its allies, so for the first time, the Turks were confronted with a united Balkan front.

The allies were victorious on all fronts. The Bulgarians bore the brunt of the fighting as they advanced toward Constantinople. The Greeks and the Serbians first cleared the Turkish forces out of Macedonia, and then the Serbians and Montenegrins occupied Novi Pazar while the Greeks moved into Southern Albania. Later, the Serbians also attacked Albania and captured the Adriatic port of Durazzo. By late April 1913, an armistice had been instituted, and in May, the Ottoman Empire signed the Treaty of London, which virtually eliminated Turkish possessions in Europe.

Obviously, the problem that arose in the aftermath of the First Balkan War was how to divide the spoils. The problem was multifaceted. For one thing, the Great Powers intervened to see that an Albanian state was created. In part, this was recognition of the Albanians' vigorous struggle for independence. It was also, however, a thinly veiled Austro-Hungarian effort to limit the territorial gains of Serbia and Montenegro and to prevent either of them from gaining an outlet to the Adriatic Sea. Indeed, it was an Austrian ultimatum that finally compelled Serbia to abandon Durazzo to an international peace-keeping force.

A second and more serious part of the problem was the interrelated issue of Bulgaria and Macedonia. Necessity had channeled the primary Bulgarian military effort toward Constantinople and away from Salonika and Macedonia. The Greeks had captured Salonika and refused to relinquish it. The Serbians, having lost territory to the unforeseen Albanian state, wanted compensation from Bulgaria in Macedonia.

The Second Balkan War, 1913

As the stalemate dragged on without resolution, skirmishing occurred in Macedonia, with Greek and Serbian troops on the one side and Bulgarian troops on the other. Eventually, in June 1913, Greece and Serbia concluded an alliance directed against Bulgaria, and in late June, fighting broke out between the two sides in Macedonia. Montenegro, Rumania, and the Ottoman Empire also promptly attacked Bulgaria. By the end of July, the fighting was over—Bulgaria had had no chance. Succinctly stated, Bulgaria's neighbors benefited at its expense. Sofia was allowed to keep only a very modest portion of Macedonia, despite the fact that Bulgarian troops did most of the serious fighting in the First Balkan War.

As a result of the two Balkan Wars, the Balkan League was shattered, with each of the small states looking greedily to protect its own interests. Bulgaria—isolated and frustrated—was intent on revising the territorial division and finding any ally against its neighbors. The issue of Albania continued to be a sore spot with Serbia and Montenegro. Albania's northern frontier had not been settled at the outbreak of World War I, and both Serbia and Montenegro hoped to make future gains there.

The fact that the Balkan states had acted independently concerned the Great Powers, particularly Austria-Hungary and Russia. Those nations attempted to reestablish some sort of control over their erstwhile vassals; obviously, the easiest way to do this was to hold out the prospect of support for future territorial gains. In short, by 1914 the Balkan peninsula was in more turmoil than had been the case for some time.

With the close of the Balkan Wars, we come to World War I, a conflict that some observers maintain should be called the Third Balkan War. In many respects, the events recounted in this chapter are merely prologue to World War I. We have seen how age-old factors such as religious and ethnic differences contributed to suspicion and disunity, with the result that the peoples of the Balkans were never able to unite for any length of time. Because they could not unite, they also could not fend off the selfish machinations of Great Powers such as Austria-Hungary and Russia. As we draw closer to our own time, we see that the small states of the Balkans were increasingly better able to protect their own interests. We also see, however, that they tended to operate out of a typically late-nineteenth and early-twentieth century world view that emphasized nationalism, imperialism, and militarism. Given the mixture of mutual antagonism, a competitive outlook, and fragile control over their own destinies, it is hardly surprising that eventually the small states of the Balkans involved the entire world in their conflicts.

Balkan Military Postcards, 1870–1914

Military postcards of the Balkans prior to World War I were not issued in large numbers and are decidedly scarce today. As mentioned in the preceding narrative, the Russo-Turkish War and the First and Second Balkan Wars were the major Balkan military conflicts between 1870 and 1914.

There are a few postcards available relating to the Russo-Turkish War. These are primarily portrait cards of the military and/or political leaders of the two sides. The Turks' defense of Plevna also generated a few cards, but on the whole, cards are not abundant. The war simply predated the massive, popular use of postcards and involved two relatively backward nations who were a step behind general European usage of postcards.

The Balkan Wars, coming early in the twentieth century, did generate a number of postcards despite the overall low level of culture—at least as measured by postcard usage—of the countries involved. Most of the examples currently in existence seem to have come from the Balkan League nations and depict their victories over the Turks in the First Balkan War. There are a few examples from the Second Balkan War, but that was an extremely short-lived conflict.

The Austro-Hungarian occupation of Bosnia-Herzegovina, while not a declared war, was resisted militarily by the Turks and resulted in a number of cards depicting the exploits of the Hapsburg army. Likewise, in the years immediately after the occupation, the Austrians had to combat sporadic armed resistance, and this, too, generated several cards extolling the bravery of Austro-Hungarian troops.

In view of the scarcity of military cards relating to the Balkans, collectors sometimes turn to propaganda cards. These cards often illustrate a nationalistic theme using a military motif. They are not abundant, but probably are a bit more plentiful than the strictly military cards. The pictorial and verbal messages of these cards are generally quite keen. One may, however, encounter difficulty in determining the precise date of the card, and it is sometimes hard to fathom the exact subject of the card without some knowledge of Balkan history.

As a general rule, Balkan cards are not as "exciting" as many other categories of military cards—artwork and quality of printing are usually a little below contemporary Western European standards, and the languages used can be a hindrance to determining the subject of the cards. However, if one is willing to put forth some investigative skill, one will frequently be rewarded with a rare and unique addition to his or her collection of military cards.

1878

K.u.k Infantry Regiment Alfonso XIII. Anonymous. ***R4***

Russian officers. Anonymous. ***R5***

1912–13

Balkan leaders with battle scenic. N.P.G. ***R4***

Prince Danilo of Montenegro sharing Christmas with his troops. Anonymous. ***R4***

Encampment of Montenegrin troops at Uraka. Anonymous. ***R4***

The Balkans' leaders attack Turkey from all directions. B. K. W. I. ***R5***

9
World War I

Part I: History and Chronology

A War to End All Wars

Called by contemporaries "The War to End All Wars," World War I was vastly unlike any conflict preceding it. Not only did World War I utilize armies of nations geographically distant from one another, it also expended, pellmell fashion, resources of raw material and labor, pushing the combatants to near economic and social ruin.

Fifteen years of British suspicions concerning the German naval buildup, almost 30 years of German armaments production, and more than 40 years of French animosity were not to be denied their disastrous consequences. War would come.

Once the fighting began, the most terrible instruments of destruction ever devised by man were placed in the field and in the oceans and in the air. Among the new or improved weapons were the tank, flame throwers that propelled liquid fire, mustard gas, the airplane, a redesigned and more deadly efficient machine gun, the inconceivably huge and unwieldingly unreliable dirigible, the hand grenade, massive missiles launched from gigantic cannons, and that omnipresent sea-going vessel, the submarine. A new type of super battleship called the *dreadnought* (after the prototype British vessel of that name) was produced by the larger countries and—along with the items just listed—saw immediate and unlimited use.

Allied Commitment to the War

England and France may have committed themselves to the war because of treaty violations, but their spirits found freer and firmer expression for other reasons. For France, hatred of Germany, which traced its strongest point of reference to the humiliation of the Franco-Prussian War, was the sauce that garnished the meaty substance of a willingly accepted military conscription. In England, the violation of Belgian neutrality was a less convincing inducement to potential soldiers than the murder of one of their own, Edith Cavell, and the dirigible bombings of London. As the numbers indicate, it was events like these that really caused the enrollment numbers to swell. Even the "colonials" sublimated their energies to fight beneath the banner of the British Empire or for the benefit of Greater France, thereby forging a protracted identity for themselves.

As for America's entry into the war, one may note that it came not as a result of the ill-fated sinking of the British passenger ship *Lusitania,* but actually ensued only after the sinking of six American vessels and the dispatch of the insulting Zimmerman telegram. Then and only then had national honor been maligned; then and only then was war dignified as the proper course of action. In this connection, it is also worth observing that American troops insisted on being commanded by their own officers.

Indecisive Russia was something of an anomaly and should be viewed from a separate perspective. She pursued her own agenda, a policy consistent with her continuing desire to guard her borders against agitation or encroachment. Less interested in territorial gain than in preserving her geographical integrity, Russia viewed the war as an opportunity to cement the alliances with her Southern Slavic neighbors by defying the empire of an Austria-Hungary she both feared and despised.

The War Recorded on Postcards

Presented with an unequaled opportunity to pursue a myriad of war-related topics and subjects, producers of picture postcards quickly came to the fore, painting, drawing, and photographing any and everything connected to the conflict. Heroes, military commanders, national leaders, weapons, men in action, men at rest, wrought destruction—all and more were the object of observation, and all were duly portrayed by camera, drawing pencil, and brush. Nor were the folks at home who represented the audience for the postcard publishers forgotten. War bond drives, admonitions to persevere, sentimental montages, view cards of the men at the front, and pictures of every imaginable weapon or activity were only a few of the types of postcards that kept them ever mindful of the war surrounding them.

Displayed in abundant numbers were tearful and pride-filled departure scenes. Leaving with a look of determination, many must have hoped, in the best tradition of all the heroes who had preceded them, to etch their names and their deeds on the pages of history. Had they known the reality of trench warfare, had they been apprized of the miles of booby traps and barbed wire, the stench and death caused by mustard gas, the endless trudges through mud-packed fields, the various diseases waiting to ravage young and old alike—had they been aware of the very real and abiding face of war, and death in the most unglorious of fashions as its ever-attendant companion, their feelings and inclinations may have developed along different lines. Thankfully for these men, and for the safety of their civilian counterparts, they did not know.

Patriotism and nationalism were also fathomless reservoirs to be tapped, and they were not used sparingly. Card after card was produced, each and all feeding the public appetite for approbation and national identity. As the postcards proved, altruism may be the most noble appeal to man's higher self and side, but it was a tame liquid when offered alongside the headier brew of ethnocentricity.

Looking at World War I–era postcards, one is reminded that each country relished its individual contributions to the war effort and each manifested the inclination to produce pictures of the country's leaders, weapons, men in action, and the like. To be sure, there was much cooperation, and the sense of comradeship was both genuine and keenly felt. But as the postcards illustrate again and again, the war furnished an unparalleled occasion for each country to demonstrate its own talents and abilities, and each did so—immodestly and unflinchingly. President Woodrow Wilson's statement at the time the United States was deciding in favor of entering the conflict is most revealing:

> There is one choice we cannot make—we are incapable of making. We will not choose the path of submission.

Unsurprisingly, the Central Powers had a set of rationales all their own. Germany, with its larger army and more sophisticated weaponry, exercised a martial suzerainty over its compatriots that they were eager to accept. This is also reflected in the postcard record. Although regiments, commanders, and battle scenes relating to Austria-Hungary, Bulgaria, and Turkey do exist, many of these have a strong Teutonic flavor.

It was as if Germany's allies were only expected to supply the bodies, while the Germans would be responsible for strategy, know-how, and more sophisticated weaponry. The Austro-Hungarians did have a fair share of postcards devoted to them and, at least in the beginning, also had some limited military autonomy in campaign planning, but there can be little doubt that the German High Command had the swagger stick and the hoop; their subordinates learned, like Pavlov's dog, how to salivate and jump on command.

Implements of Destruction

If ever the world could have been said to be mechanically prepared for war, the period 1914–18 certainly would represent such a time. Indeed, World War I witnessed the introduction of a plethora of weaponry guaranteed to wreak havoc, decimate property, and not least of all, cost the lives of millions of antagonists.

The old saw proclaiming invention as the mother of necessity certainly applied here, and even those weapons and military objects devised and copyrighted prior to World War I may have been invented with the future cataclysm in mind. For decades, France and Germany had been preparing for war with one another. Plans were made, proposed actions reviewed, and general staffs considered options. Germany had its Schlieffen Plan and France, bravado being the continuing order of the day, was outlining its potential offensive operations.

While they maneuvered and plotted, each was laying groundwork not only for themselves, but most decidedly for their allies as well. The watchword was *preparation*—preparation of the sort that demanded the deployment of newer, deadlier weapons. Nations vied with one another to be first. Germany introduced mustard gas, England produced the tank, and France dropped flechettes on the terrified soldiers fleeing for cover. To a world that had previously viewed war in terms of cavalry charges and bayonet thrusts, the new weaponry must have seemed awesome. Automatic guns that fired 1¼-pound shells at the rate of 120 a minute; 4000-pound bombs dropped from airplanes and missiles weighing more than a ton; targeting distances exceeding 25 miles: War had indeed become hell.

Postcard Propaganda

It has been suggested that the first use of the printing press for purposes of propaganda was during the American and French Revolutions. Evidence supporting this claim is fairly solid: In both conflicts, leaflets, pamphlets, newspapers, and other forms of printed material lauded the position of those opposed to royal prerogative, while unflattering caricature and invective in the print media were the brushes used to color their enemies.

By the time the First World War made its unsightly appearance, the press had become a complex and refined tool both for extolling virtue and condemning vice. News writers, rarely the impartial creatures they frequently claim to be, crusaded for one position or postured for another, positive they were discerning good from evil for those less adept at making that distinction. And if one were still confused, there were the words from the mouth of one of the philosopher Voltaire's literary creations—a simple enough fellow who assured all who would listen that God was on the side with the largest army. Even in Voltaire's day it seemed that propaganda could espouse an occasional ridiculous position or two.

World War I opened one Pandora's Box after another, examining in an all-too-superficial manner the various ethical and social dilemmas presented by this particular war. It would be incorrect to assume, as some revisionist historians have, that all the participants of this struggle acted inhumanely; it would be equally incorrect to assume that the reports of German atrocities were much ado about nothing. As in most such matters, the truth lies somewhere between the two extremes.

German Atrocities

What there is no way of avoiding, however, is the fact that German behavior reflected new lows in modern barbarity. The execution of nurse Edith Cavell is an illustration of this, although clearly not the only one. At least part of the "Belgian atrocity" reports may be dismissed as mere attempts to engender hatred of the Hun, but there were real incidences that cannot be so cavalierly disregarded. Nor were all the stories told of Germany's treatment of her P.O.W.'s just so much propaganda. Additionally detestable was Germany's indiscriminate bombing of London and Paris sites that included hospitals and orphanages. And although the French developed the much-feared flechette (a six-inch steel arrow which, when dropped from an airplane, would pass completely through the human body with deadly rapidity), and the British must be credited with the ominous tank, these items pale in comparison with certain developments of German manufacture. Among them were mustard gas, the flame thrower, and cannons capable of discharging 200-pound shells to distances exceeding 75 miles. The random targets of these projectiles could not even be approximated, making them the more to be feared. Unrestricted submarine warfare was yet another regrettable German military paradigm, giving the Germans carte blanche to make war on merchant and passenger ships. In this climate, ammunition for the propaganda mills was provided daily, and picture postcards were not slow about jumping on board. Contemporary analysts knew the historical verdict had already been rendered. Individual soldiers may have been merciful or compassionate in given situations, but the German High Command was relentless in its prosecution of the war, and it set a policy that was at once bottomless and indefensible. Even in war there are rules of behavior—codes of conduct to which most civilized nations subscribe. That Germany did not acquiesce to them in 1870, in 1914–18, or in 1939–45 is lamentable, but true.

British Pride

Barbarity and cruelty aside, postcard propaganda of World War I was incredibly multifaceted. British jingoism, at least in the war's early stages, is one of many examples. Although it seems a quaint notion to their more dignified descendants, most of the English were pleased to step to the popular tune "It's a Long Way to Tipperary." Patriotism might have been a slogan, but it was also a word spoken with pride, embellished with all sorts of honorable images. Artist-drawn cards of proud "Tommy" strutting with expanded chest in his new suit of khaki were not sources of humor, but symbols embracing pride and national honor.

Perhaps it is true that all propaganda postcards relate either directly or indirectly to patriotism. Racial and ethnic bigotry, an excessive sense of nationalism, and a belief that all the forces of righteousness are mustered on one's side are images that have been used repeatedly, and all have some casual relationship to patriotism. When a nation's leaders are able to use propaganda to include such sentiments, these leaders quickly discover at their disposal an effective way of marshaling the energies, emotions, and intellect of their people.

Britain was able to do this through humor, and it is worth observing that innumerable "Tommy" cards used jocularity to good effect. Of course, many of the cards were more direct with their messages of determination and sacrifice, but the English often responded to their own brand of humor when psychological efforts to coerce their thinking or manipulate their feelings failed.

German Strength and Austrian Patriotism

For the Germans of this period, sophistication was an unnecessary commodity. The government relied on attempts to strengthen their inbred sense of national identity and legendary obeisance to leadership figures. Proud of their traditions, militaristic tendencies, desire to excel, and inclination toward self-sacrifice, German citizens needed little prodding in order to sustain their commitment. Their sense of duty was complete, a fact well attested by the postcard record. The "enemy" was depicted as cowardly or stupid, or both. The German's own postcard record was not complete without countless pictures of the kaiser and the general staff, and unlimited reminders of military prowess and a history of success. How it was that an aggressive Germany could justify depicting the allies as unfeeling, intolerant, greedy, and cruel warmongers while showing them as docile, weak, and effeminate is one of those paradoxes of war. What this demonstrated for Germany and other countries as well was that as far as propaganda was concerned, the postcard performed the dual task of exalting one side's virtues while denigrating everything related to the other side.

Turning to Austria, we quickly see that propaganda postcards made use of two elements: tradition and religion. With a military link to the Middle Ages through decades of conquest, and religious ties through the Holy Roman Empire, Austria's people were well connected to propagandist tools. In short, it should have been a simple matter to elicit patriotic fervor from such a people, and as long as their militarily superior ally Germany was on the offense—and winning—the Austrian soldiers were dedicated fighting machines. However, as they began to suffer reverses in the field and the Allies became successful aggressors, the number of patriotic and propaganda postcards increased, but were fast losing appeal and utility.

French Sentimentalism

Given the sentimental and basically romantic nature of the French (as seen by the rest if the world), it is hardly surprising that French postcards should reflect such a mind set. Wistful goodbye scenics, religious montages, and allegorical images immersed in emotionalism characterize many of their offerings. Usually quite colorful, they are eagerly sought.

Propaganda Around the World

Other countries also produced propaganda cards for all the same reasons. Occasionally the theme was one of unity, and countries expressed their togetherness through clasped hands and crossed flags. For the military enthusiast, these particular cards are thought to illustrate the reason and justification for the fight. Perhaps the reality is somewhat different—perhaps they are merely what they seem to be: tools of propaganda.

Always preparing to show the world's places and activities, postcard producers furnished an inquisitive public with pictures of the implements and engines of war both in use and at rest—tanks on the move, airplanes engaged in dogfights or dropping their death-giving payloads, cannons unleashing limitless destruction, flame throwers spewing their fiery offerings. Camera and brush were omnipresent, clicking and painting and drawing, capturing life and and death in the field. Images of smiling men enjoying a "smoke," their rifles ever at the ready; grimacing men enduring aerial bombardments and gas attacks; frightened men fleeing approaching tanks; angry, determined men rushing pill-box machine-gun locations—in these scenics, the men are seen as both heroic and fearful, two sides of the same coin.

Impact of World War I

Quite apart from human life and injury, it is inconceivable that any war has escaped the multiple ravages for which wars are so well known. World War I was more disastrous than those preceding it, and that by large measure.

Although statistics are merely numbers reflecting the bare bones, they do provide something of a necessary outline around which historians may write. While the carnage, casualties, and ultimate costs may not fully engage our imaginations as mere numbers, for the participants of war, they represent what was real.

☆ Because of World War I, the Russians were swept into their last revolution.
☆ Fall of the Old Royal Order in Europe (Hohenzollern, Hapsburg, Romanov, German States, Montenegro, and so on) occurred as a result of the war.
☆ World War I led to the "redrawing" of the European map.
☆ It was the war with the most heightened sense of patriotic fervor and ardor (jingoism, idealism, romanticism, and so on); in this capacity, even World War II paled in comparison.
☆ More people were killed than in any preceding conflict.
☆ World War I was the first fully mechanized war, the first "world" war, and the last war in which horses, dogs, and pigeons were used.
☆ The results of World War I (especially the harshness of the treaty of Versailles) were partially responsible for World War II.

Monetary Costs

Money owed to U.S. by Allied Governments	
Great Britain	$ 4,000,000,000
France	4,000,000,000
Italy	2,000,000,000
Others	Remainder
Total	**$11,786,420,944**
Direct Cost of War	$186,000,000,000
Indirect cost of War	$152,000,000,000
Total	**$338,000,000,000**
Property Damage	$36,000,000,000
Allied Debt Increase (Domestic and Foreign)	From $20,000,000,000 to $100,000,000,000
U.S. National Budget Increase	From $1,000,000,000 to $3,000,000,000
Amount of Budget Allocated to the War	85%

Postcard Addendum

The various engagements were more than worthy of postcard reproduction, but few of them were thus employed. Rather than relay such information as troop deployments and the size of various armies through the mail, where it might fall into the wrong hands, most postcards that were battle-related either illustrated specific acts of bravery or were propaganda types ("They Shall Not Pass," referring to Verdun, and the like).

The campaign at Verdun, which lasted from February 21, 1916, to July 1, 1916, was a classic series of battles with which many of the noncombatants identified the war itself. It contained all the key elements: a massive struggle for a key position where bravery and foolishness wrestled in near equal proportions in a bloodied, mud-splattered terrain. One of the most heavily fortified areas in France, Verdun was of vast strategic importance to both Germany and France. Hoping to capture it, the Germans committed 500,000 men and a vast array of armaments to the area.

During the first few weeks of the struggle, Germany made impressive gains, securing one fortification after another. The French fought with a vengeance, but the Germans continued to edge forward. Teutonic tenacity met the stoutness of French resistance. Finally, by June 24, the Germans had penetrated Verdun's inner defenses, and the city seemed doomed. Ultimately, the German Crown Prince had to withdraw his armies when on July 1, 1916, a contingent of British and French forces smashed against the German lines, ten miles from the Somme river. This counteroffensive, which lasted until March of 1917, was begun too late in the year to reach a fruitful conclusion. The rainy season that had just set in made troop and weapon movements impossible. Still, it was an Allied success as 700,000 Germans (including 95,000 prisoners) were lost to the war effort. Additionally, a large amount of weaponry was captured. Similar to that at Verdun, the Somme River engagement had few "action" cards devoted to it. Save for the occasional individual acts of heroism, before/after scenics, a few artillery barrage cards, and the omnipresent propaganda postcards, the encounters went largely unrepresented.

Overall it must be noted that the photographic and artistic record of World War I is very inclusive, as almost everything one may imagine was printed or otherwise reproduced on postcards in greater or lesser numbers. Humor and pathos, wit and sorrow, tragedy and victory, pride and shame, bravery and cowardice—all this and more were illustrated on pasteboard. The following chronology is the skeleton; breathing life into it and putting substance and definition on its form is that revealer of all things human, the picture postcard.

Chronology

Date	Event
1914	
June 28	Archduke Franz Ferdinand, heir to the throne of Austria-Hungary, and his morganatic wife, Sophie Chotek, are assassinated by Serbian anarchist Gavrillo Princips in Sarajevo, Bosnia.
July 5	German kaiser holds war council at Potsdam.
July 27	Britain's Sir Edward Grey is unsuccessful in his attempt to convene an international conference to avoid a European war.
August 1	Germany declares war on Russia.
August 2	German forces enter Luxembourg.
August 4	President Wilson proclaims American neutrality; England's ultimatum is ignored as Germany attacks Liège and declares war on France (von Kluck's army crosses the Belgian border).
August 5	England declares war on Germany; Kitchener is appointed secretary of state for war; German mine-layer *Koenigin* is sunk by British ship *Amphion.*
August 6	Austria declares war on Russia; British ship *Amphion* is sunk by mine in North Sea.
August 7	French invade Alsace; Germans enter Liège; Montenegro declares war on Austria (possibly August 8); British Expeditionary Forces land at Calais, Ostend, and Dunkirk.
August 8	Portugal declares to be an ally of Great Britain; Italy proclaims neutrality; Serbia declares war with Germany; Britain seizes German Togoland.
August 10	France declares war with Austria.
August 12	Montenegro declares war on Germany; Great Britain declares war with Austria-Hungary.
August 13	German cruisers *Goeben* and *Breslau* seek refuge in Constantinople.
August 15	Japan sends an ultimatum to Germany to evacuate Kiaochau in China.
August 20	Germans occupy Brussels; Serbians defeat Austrians at Lonitza.
August 21	Germans attack Namur.
August 23	Japan declares war on Germany and attacks Tsingtau; Austria stops hostilities against Serbia (temporarily).
August 24	Germans approach Lille and German dirigibles bomb Antwerp; British driven from Mons.
August 25	Austria declares war on Japan.
August 26	Germans sack and burn Louvain in retaliation for supposed hostilities by the citizens; British seize German Togoland in West Africa; German ship *Kaiser Wilhelm der Grosse* is sunk by British cruiser *Highflyer.*
August 27	Russians capture Tilsit.
August 28	British win naval engagement at Helgioland; French withdraw from Alsace.
August 29	Germans seize La Fere; British forces from New Zealand capture German Samoan Islands; Russians attack Konigsberg (Prussia).
August 30	Germans occupy Amiens; Russians under Rennenkampf defeated by Von Hindenburg at Tannenburg, East Prussia.
August 31	St. Petersburg changed to Petrograd by Imperial decree.
September 1	Russia defeats Austrians at Lemberg, capturing 82,000 prisoners.
September 3	Germany takes Rheims; Russians enter Lemberg.
September 5	German submarine sinks British cruiser *Pathfinder.*
September 6–10	Battle of the Marne; von Kluck is beaten back, along with von Bulow on his left; Germans retreat to Soissons under fierce fighting by Joffre's army.
September 7	Austrian left wing defeated at Ravarusska.
September 10	German crown prince attacks Revigny; Serbia subdues Semlin.
September 11	Australian expedition captures Bismarck Archipelago and Solomon Islands.
September 12	Crown prince of Bavaria (Rupprecht) retires to Lorraine after inability to capture Nancy.
September 13	German cruiser *Hela* is sunk by the British submarine E-9.
September 14	France reoccupies Rheims.
September 20	German cruiser *Koneigsberg* defeats British cruiser *Pegasus* at Zanzibar harbor.
September 22	Russians capture Jaroslav; British cruisers *Aboukir, Cressy,* and *Hogue* are sunk by German submarine U-9.
September 24	Ostend bombed; cholera breaks out among Austrian troops admitted in Vienna; Allies occupy Peronne.
September 25	Australians seize German New Guinea.
October 2	British admiralty announces intention to mine North Sea.
October 4	Berlin admits outbreak of cholera among German army.
October 6	Japan captures Marshall Islands.
October 9	Germans occupy Antwerp.

October 13	British occupy Ypres.
October 14	Canadian Expeditionary Force of 32,000 lands at Plymouth.
October 15	Germans occupy Ostend.
October 16	A German submarine sinks the British cruiser *Hawke*.
October 17	British cruiser *Undaunted* sinks four German destroyers off the Dutch coast.
October 18	German warship destroys British submarine E-3.
October 29	Turkish warships shell Russian Black Sea ports; German cruiser *Emden* enters Straits Settlements under a Japanese flag, then proceeds to sink the Russian cruiser *Zhemtchug* and the French destroyer *Mousquet*.
October 30	Russia declares war against Turkey.
October 31	British cruiser *Hermes* is sunk by German submarine in the Straits of Dover.
November 1–3	British cruisers *Monmouth* and *Good Hope* are sunk by German squadron under command of Admiral von Spee off Chile. British rear admiral Craddock and 1500 sailors are lost.
November 5	Both Great Britain and France declare war on Turkey; Britain annexes Cyprus.
November 6	Japanese capture German fortresses at Tsingtao and Kiaochow in China; German cruiser *Yorck* is sunk by a German mine.
November 9	German cruiser *Emden* is sunk by Australian cruiser *Sydney* off the Cocos Islands, near Java.
November 11	British torpedo gunboat *Niger* is sunk at mouth of Thames by German submarine.
November 14	British super dreadnought *Audacious* is reported to have been sunk by a mine October 27; Lord Roberts dies suddenly on a visit to the Front in France.
November 20	Khedive of Egypt joins the Young Turks and Germans.
November 23	German submarine U-18 is sunk by a British patrol boat off Scotland.
November 26	British warship *Bulwark* destroyed by an explosion in dock yards on the Thames; 738 lives lost.
November 27	Czernowitz captured by Russians; German submarines sink two British steamers while raiding the English Channel.
December 1	The emperor of Russia and the kaiser of Germany join their troops at the front.
December 2	Russia captures Plock; Austria captures Belgrade after 126 days of seige.
December 3	Russians bombard Cracow.
December 8	British rear admiral Sturdee avenges the *Good Hope* and *Monmouth* sinkings by defeating the same attackers off the Falkland Islands. The *Scharnhorst, Leipzig,* and *Gneisenais* are sunk.
December 9	Turks surrender at Kurnak, giving Britain control of the Tigris-Euphrates delta.
December 10	German ship *Nurnberg* is sunk.
December 13	Turkish warship *Messirdieh* is sunk in the Dardanelles by a British submarine B-11, which dove beneath five rows of mines.
December 14	Serbians recapture Belgrade.
December 16	English coastline towns of Scarborough, Hartelpool, and Whitby are shelled by German squadron, killing 122.
December 19	Heavy fighting near Ypres and elsewhere.
December 23	Russia raises siege of Cracow in order to engage Austrians at Przemysl.
December 30	Russians defeat Austrians at Przemysl; German airships bomb Dunkirk.
December 31	Desperate hand-to-hand struggle for their possession occurs at Sennheim and Steinbach in Alsace.

1915

January 1	British battleship *Formidable* is sunk by a submarine in the English Channel; nearly 600 deaths.
January 5	Cardinal Mercier detained in Malines by Germans who think he incited civilian rebellion.
January 9	Russians reach Transylvania on way to Budapest.
January 10	Germans attack Dunkirk again, killing six.
January 13	Germans defeat French at Soissons after three days of heavy fighting; 300,000 French killed.
January 16	Russian Black Sea fleet reported to have sunk eight Turkish transports.
January 17	Russians defeat Turks in the Caucasus Mountains at Kara Urgan.
January 19	A German air raid on the English coast; six towns bombed; five are killed.
January 22	Germans capture St. Michel.
January 23	Six killed and 14 injured when German aviators raid Dunkirk; British occupy La Bassee.
January 24	German cruisers *Blucher* and *Kolberg* are sunk while attempting raid on British coast.
January 28	Turkish troops invade Egypt, engage British in heavy fighting; American bark *William P. Frye* is sunk in South Atlantic by German cruiser.
January 30	German submarine U-21 sinks three British merchantmen: *Ben Cruachan, Kilcoan,* and *Linda Blanche*.
February 5	Germany announces that after February 18 the waters around Britain will be a war zone and that all vessels must avoid those waters.
February 10	American steamship *Wilhelmina,* carrying foodstuffs bound for Germany, is held for prize court unless the food is sold for Belgian relief; Russians defeated and driven back from Masuum Lakes region by Germany.
February 13 and 16	British (and later French) seaplanes attack Belgian coast, trying to destroy German positions and the naval base at Zeebrugge.
February 18	British steam collier *Dulwich* and the French steamer *Ville de Ville* are first casualties of German blockade.
February 20	British steamship *Cambank* is sunk off north coast of Wales.
February 21	U.S. steamship *Evelyn,* carrying cotton for Bremen, is sunk by a mine off mouth of Ems river; a combined force of 32 French and British warships attack Dardanelles forts.
February 23	Second American ship carrying cotton bound for Bremen is sunk by mine outside safety zone; Norwegian ship *Regin* is sunk off Dover by submarine; British transport *Branksome Chine* is sunk by mine off Sussex coast.
February 25	Two British steamers (*Deptford* and *Western Coast*) are sunk; combined British and French fleets have destroyed Dardanelles' outer forts.
February 27	American freighter *Dacia* seized by the French. It sailed under American registry, but was German before being sold.
March 6	Russia dislodges the Austrians from Czernowitz in Bukowina.
March 10	British capture Neuve Chapelle.
March 11	Destruction of German submarine U-12 by the British destroyer *Ariel*.
March 14	German raiding cruiser *Dresden* is sunk by British squadron off Chile.
March 20	French battleship *Bouvet* and British battleship *Irresistible* are sunk by mines in Dardanelles.
March 21	Memel captured by the Russians.
March 22	Russians capture Przemysl after a 200-day siege; over 119,000 Austrian prisoners taken.

March 28	British passenger ship *Falaba* is sunk by German submarine off Welsh coast.
April 2	British aircraft attack German submarine base at Zeebrugge.
April 6	Turkish government claims destruction of British battleship *Lord Nelson.*
April 11	German auxiliary cruiser *Kronprinz Wilhelm* interns at Newport News, Virginia (has already sunk 14 Allied ships).
April 19	Von Hindenburg reportedly has assumed command of Austro-German forces in the Carpathians.
April 22	Germans use poison gas for first time in attack on Canadians at Ypres.
April 24	British capture much territory in Second Battle of Ypres.
April 29	The French armored cruiser *Leon Gambetta* is sunk by Austrian submarine U-5.
April 30	German aviators bomb Ipswich.
May 1	German submarine disables American steamer *Gulflight* off Sicily; British army headquarters at Dunkirk are bombarded from 22 miles away by Germans, near Nieuport; 65 killed and/or wounded.
May 2	British South African troops under General Botha capture German positions in Southwest Africa.
May 4	Russians, defeated in Galacia by Austria-Hungary, retreat from Hungary.
May 7	The Cunard steamship *Lusitania* is torpedoed and sunk by German submarine (1152 lives lost, 14 of which are American); Germans capture Libau on the Russian Baltic.
May 13	British battleship *Goliath* torpedoed in the Dardanelles; 500 men lost.
May 23	Italy declares war on Austria-Hungary; two Turkish gunboats and two transports are sunk by British submarines in the Sea of Marmora.
May 24	German submarine torpedoes American steamer *Nebraskan* off the coast of Ireland.
May 26	British battleship *Triumph* damaged by German submarine in the Dardanelles.
May 27	*Princess Irene,* a British auxiliary, is blown up in Thames river, losing 424 men; British battleship *Majestic* is sunk in the Dardanelles; British submarine E-11 reportedly torpedoes two supply ships in Sea of Marmora.
May 31	German zeppelins bombard London suburbs; four reported killed.
June 3	Austrians capture Przymsl; Britain captures Kut-el-Amara.
June 4–6	German aircraft bomb English towns.
June 7	Italian troops claim to have crossed the Isonzo; Canadian aviator Lt. R. A. J. Waneford explodes a bomb on a zeppelin over Ghent, Belgium (the first time an airplane has done this); all 28 aboard die.
June 15	Allied aircraft bomb Baden and Karlsruhe; 40 reported killed in German air raids over northeast coast of England.
June 19	German submarine U-29 is reported sunk by British tank steamer.
June 22	Austrians recapture Lemberg; German long-range guns bombard Dunkirk.
June 23	Torpedo damages British cruiser *Roxburgh.*
June 26	Montenegrin army enters Scutari (Albania).
June 27	French aircraft shell zeppelin station at Friedrichsahven.
June 28	German submarine U-38 sinks British freighter *Armenien,* which is carrying a cargo of horses and mules; 21 American muleteers lost.
June 29	Austro-Germans capture Tomaszow in Russian Poland.
July 2	German mine-layer *Albatross* reported lost after naval battle between Russian and German fleets.
July 6	Russians stop German advance toward Warsaw, east of Krasnik.
July 7	Austrian submarine sinks Italian armored cruiser *Amalfi.*
July 9	German forces in South Africa surrender to General Botha.
July 12	Destruction of German cruiser *Konigsberg* by British river monitors in German East Africa.
July 14	Austria retakes Przasnysz.
July 16	Russian warships reportedly sink German submarine U-51 in Black Sea.
July 18	Austrian submarine destroys Italian cruiser *Guiseppe Garibaldi* off Ragusa.
July 22	Announcement that this is first week since war began that a German submarine has not sunk a British ship; Austrians capture Ivangorod.
July 24	Austro-German army seizes Pultusk.
July 25	U.S. steamer *Leelanaw* is sunk by German submarine off Orkey Islands.
July 30	Germans repulsed near Arras.
July 31	French aircraft bomb Baden; British liner *Iberian* is sunk by German submarine.
August 5	Warsaw entered by Austro-German army under Prince Leopold of Bavaria.
August 6	New British force arrives in Suvia Bay on the Gallipoli peninsula.
August 9	Turkish battleship *Kheyr-ed-Din Barbarossa* is sunk by unidentified submarine.
August 10	Zeppelins kill 18 civilians during raid to the east coast of England; Austro-German army occupies fortress at Lomza.
August 11	Italian submarine reportedly sinks Austrian submarine U-12.
August 14	*Royal Edward,* a British transport, reportedly is sunk by a German submarine on the way to Dardanelles; nearly 1000 soldiers being transported are killed.
August 17	Germans subdue Russian fortress at Kovno.
August 18	Zeppelin attack on outskirts of London results in ten deaths.
August 19	White Star Line steamer *Arabic* is sunk off coast of Ireland; 50 passengers, including two Americans, drown.
August 20	Germans capture Russian fortress at Novo-Georgievsk and obtain a large cache of supplies, along with 85,000 prisoners.
August 21	Italy declares war on Turkey.
August 23	British fleet bombards Zeebrugge.
August 25	General von Mackensen captures fortress of Brest-Litovsk; 62 French airplanes bomb ammunition factories in Prussia.
August 28	Germans capture Lipsk.
September 4	Steamer *Hesperian* is sunk off coast of Ireland; 24 killed.
September 6	Czar assumes command of Russian army.
September 7	Zeppelin raid on east coast of England; 13 killed, 43 wounded.
September 8	Zeppelin bombing of London; 38 killed, 124 wounded.
September 13	Official total of British casualties in Dardanelles reported at 87,630, with 17,608 of those dead.
September 15	General von Mackensen captures Pinsk; since August 25, von Mackensen has advanced almost 100 miles.
September 17	A German submarine sinks the British tank steamer *Zeferino.*

September 20	Bulgaria begins mobilization of all 700,000 forces, claiming the need for armed neutrality.
September 26–27	Allies claim to have gained ground in Belgium, Champagne, and elsewhere.
September 28	General von Linsingen captures Lutsk for the Central Powers; Rear Admiral Rubin de Cerrin, the steamship commander, and 334 members of his crew are killed when an explosion in the Brindisi harbor sinks warship *Benedetto.*
October 5	King Constantine declares position of armed neutrality for Greece.
October 9	Belgrade is occupied by Austro-German army.
October 11	Bulgaria breaks diplomatic relations with the Allies.
October 12	English nurse Edith Cavell is executed as a spy by the Germans; Bulgarian forces are reported to have crossed Serbian border.
October 14	Zeppelin raid over London results in 55 deaths, 114 injuries.
October 15	Great Britain declares war on Bulgaria.
October 16	Bulgarian troops capture forts of Zaitcar.
October 18	Major General Sir Charles Monro is appointed to succeed Sir Ian Hamilton, who is recalled from command of British land forces in the Dardanelles.
October 19	Russia and Italy declare war on Bulgaria.
October 20	Bulgaria captures Vranya and Vlasotine; Russian, British, and French ships bombard Bulgarian coastline.
October 23–24	Bulgaria captures Kuprili and Uskub; German cruiser *Prince Adalbert* and Turkish transport *Carmen* are sunk by British submarines.
October 28	King George is thrown from a horse while visiting British troops at the French front; his wound is serious, but not fatal.
November 1	Austro-Germans capture the principal Serbian arsenal at Kragujevac.
November 5	French and Serbian forces gain a minor victory over Bulgarians on Serbian soil at the Babuna Pass.
November 6	Bulgaria occupies Nish (Serbia).
November 9	Italian passenger steamer *Ancona* is sunk by an Austrian submarine; 208 are killed, including several Americans.
November 12	Serbian army and Austro-German forces clash in the mountain regions west of Nish; Winston Churchill resigns from British Parliament and goes to the front after enlisting in the army.
November 14	Austrian airplane bombing of Verona (again) is followed by bombing of Vicenza and Grado.
November 20	Italians attack Goritz; French troop ship *Colvado* is sunk by a submarine with 800 soldiers lost; Kitchener confers with King Constantine.
November 23	British seize American TransAtlantic Company ship *Kankakee,* which is reportedly carrying noncontraband items bound for a neutral port; the key to Goritz (Podgora Peak) is captured by Italian army after five-month seige.
November 24	Russian troops reported to be marching on Teheran, Persia's capital.
November 27	Constantinople claims to have captured a materials section of the Allied trench at Gallipoli.
November 28	Berlin announces capture of all of Serbia, with 100,000 prisoners.
December 2	Monastir surrenders to Bulgarians; General Joffre becomes commander in chief of all French forces.
December 4	Henry Ford leads peace delegation sailing for Europe on the steamship *Oscar II.*
December 9	Germany claims military successes in Montenegro and Albania.
December 11	General de Castelnau appointed chief of staff of the French army.
December 14	General Smith-Dorrien appointed commander in chief of British forces in East Africa.
December 15	Field Marshal Sir John French is succeeded by General Sir Douglas Haig as commander of the British Army in France and Belgium.
December 20	Britain begins to withdraw troops from Gallipoli.
December 21	Lt. General William Robertson, chief of the British general staff in France, becomes chief of the Imperial Staff in London; France subdues section of German trenches in Alsace; Japanese liner *Yasaka Maru* is sunk in Mediterranean without loss of life; port of Varna in Bulgaria is seized by Russian fleet.
December 22	Sir Charles Monro succeeds Sir Douglas Haig in command of 1st British Army in France; Lt. General Sir Archibald Murray succeeds Monro in Dardanelles.
December 23	British losses in Dardanelles announced as 112,921.
December 24	French steamer *Ville de la Ciotat* is sunk in Mediterranean by submarine.
December 26	Persia renounces German agreements, announces for Allies.
December 30	Italians seize capital of Albania (Durazzo); British cruiser *Natal* is sunk by internal explosion while lying in port, with more than 300 deaths; British liner *Persia* is sunk off the island of Crete (believed sunk by a submarine).

1916

January 3	Janude, the last stand of the Germans in Equatorial Africa, is taken by British forces.
January 6	Germans bombard Nancy.
January 7	An Italian steamer from the United States carrying 425 Montenegrin recruits is sunk by a mine off Albania; 200 killed.
January 9	British battleship *King Edward VII* is sunk by a mine in the North Sea without loss of life.
January 14	Germans protest and promise reprisals for the alleged murder of German sailors following the August 12, 1915, sinking of a German submarine by the British patrol boat *Baralong*; Austrians report capture of Montenegrin capital of Cettinje.
January 16	Turks reported to have suffered reverses by Russians in the Caucasus Mountains and by British in Mesopotamia.
January 17	Montenegro reported to have surrendered unconditionally to Austria.
January 27	French aviators bombard Freiburg, Germany.
January 29	Zeppelin raid on Paris witnesses 23 deaths and 29 injuries.
January 31	Zeppelins bomb Northeastern England, killing 59.
February 1	Zeppelin attacks Salonika; 11 killed, 50 injured.
February 3	Yussuf Izzedin, Turkish crown prince, is reported to have been assassinated or forced to commit suicide by minister of war, Enver Pasha.
February 6	Field Marshal von Mackensen assumes command of Austro-German troops in Salonika campaign.
February 9	German seaplanes and zeppelins attack Ramsgate and Broadstairs, England, injuring three; General Sir Horace Smith-Dorrien retires and is replaced as commander of British South African forces by General John C. Smuts.
February 11	Germany reports sinking of British cruiser *Arabis* in the North Sea.

February 12 Austrian airplanes bomb Codigoro, Ravenna, and Bottrighe in Italy, killing 15.

February 14 Berlin reports successes against both French and British positions; Austrian airplanes bomb Monza and Milan.

February 16 Grand Duke Nicholas reports Russian capture of fortress of Erzerum; four Turkish army corps under command of Germany's General von Sanders escape before Russians storm the fort.

February 20 German airplanes bomb Lowestoft, Suffolk, and Walmer, England; heavy fighting at Ypres, in the Argonne, and between the Meuse and the Moselle.

February 21 French aircraft bombard Habsheim and Muelhausen in Alsace; assaults—by forces of the German crown prince—on forts at Verdun begin.

February 24 Fifty Austrian and German ships interned at Lisbon have been seized permanently by Portugal.

February 25 Austria reports defeat of Italian and Albanian forces near Durazzo.

March 1 First day of Austro-German submarine campaign witnesses sinking of British vessels *Thornaby* and *Malvina*.

March 2 Britisher destroyer *Viking* reportedly is lost after striking a mine on January 29.

March 5 Zeppelins raid east coast of England, killing 13.

March 9 British relief force on the Tigris fights to within seven miles of Kut-el-Amara; all previously exempted Germans between ages of 18 and 40 are called into service.

March 10 Russian fleet bombs Varna, Bulgaria, after sinking eight Turkish steamers in the Black Sea.

March 11 American steamship *Edna* seized by a British cruiser and taken to Port Stanley, Falkland Islands.

March 12 Russian forces within 150 miles of Baghdad.

March 15 Announcement is made of resignation of Grand Admiral von Tirpitz because of ill health (real reason is thought to be that the Imperial Chancellor and others disagree with von Tirpitz's submarine policy); Krupp gunworks at Essen raided by Allied aircraft.

March 16 General Charles Roques succeeds General Gallieni as French Minister of War after the latter resigns; Dutch liner *Tubantia* is sunk in North Sea by torpedo or mine (Germans blamed).

March 18 German submarine sinks the Dutch liner *Palenbang* off coast of Essex; Upper Alsace region becomes site of a great aerial battle; out of nearly 40 aircraft, four French and three German airplanes are shot down.

March 19 Fighting is hand to hand around Fort Douamount and Vaux; German seaplanes raid English coast between Dover and Margate; 9 killed, 31 injured.

March 20 Sixty-five airplanes bomb German seaplane and submarine station at Zeebrugge.

March 23 Russians advance on Galacia.

March 24 French bombard Germans in Argonne; channel steamer *Sussex* torpedoed or strikes a mine, but reaches port; 50–80 lives lost, including those of several Americans.

March 25 British Dominion liner *Englishman* is reported sunk.

March 26 British destroyer *Medusa* is lost in a collision with destroyer *Laverock*.

March 28 British cruiser *Cleopatra* reported rammed and sunk by German torpedo in North Sea, March 25.

March 29 General Chouvaieff succeeds General Palivanoff as Russian minister of war.

March 31 Announcement made of sinking of Franco-Russian hospital-ship *Portugal* in the Black Sea, with 115 lives lost, including those of a number of physicians and nurses; five zeppelins raid east coast of England, killing 28 and injuring 44; L-15 is destroyed during the raid (Turks later admit sinking of *Portugal*, but claim the vessel did not fly a Red Cross flag and was additionally being used for transport).

April 5 General Paolo Morone succeeds General Zupelli as Italian Minister of War; General Lake reports capture of Umm-el-Hanna, 23 miles from Kut-el-Amara; reported sinkings include Norwegian *Orena,* the British *Bendero,* and the Dutch schooner *Elsina Helfa.*

April 6 British steamer *Zent* torpedoed west of Fastnet; 48 drown.

April 14 British aircraft drop bombs on the Zeitunlik powder factory and airplane hangars at Constantinople (said to be longest flight made during the war).

April 18 Russians capture Black Sea port of Trebizond with both land and naval forces; Treviso, Italy, bombarded by Austrian hydroplanes.

April 19 Field Marshal Baron von der Goltz, commander in chief of 1st Turkish Army, dies of spotted fever at Baghdad.

April 20 Italian aircraft raid Trieste, killing nine civilians; Russian troops land at Marseilles.

April 21 Auxiliary German cruiser (under guise of a neutral merchant ship) and a submarine attempting to bring arms and ammunition to Ireland are prevented from doing so and cruiser is sunk; among the prisoners is Sir Roger Casement, a prominent Irish Nationalist.

April 27 British battleship *Russell* is sunk by mine in the Mediterranean, killing 24.

April 29 After the exhaustion of food supplies, 9000 British and Indian troops surrender at Kut-el-Amara (have been under siege for five months).

May 2 East coast of England raided by five German zeppelins; 36 casualties; zeppelin L-20 is destroyed.

May 7 General Pétain assumes command of all French armies from Soissons to Verdun; succeeded at Verdun by General Nivelle.

May 8 White Star liner *Cymric* is reported sunk on May 7 by German submarine off Ireland while carrying munitions from the United States; five crew members killed.

May 17 Increased aerial activity on Western front; 33 air combats reported in Verdun area, 27 on British front.

May 21 British army and Russian cavalry reported unified on the Tigris.

May 26 Bulgarian troops cross Greek border for first time; Rockefeller Foundation of New York appropriates $1 million for Polish and Balkan relief.

May 27 General Gallieni dies.

May 28 The 100,000-man Serbian army arrives at Salonika.

May 29 Britain states that 44 air raids have been made on England since the war began; 409 persons killed, 1005 wounded; three naval attacks by German warships on England cause 141 deaths and 611 injuries.

June 4 — Austria captures Italian town of Cesuna; General Brusilov's Russian army begins offensive that leads to the taking of 13,000 Austrian prisoners.

June 5 — British cruiser *Hampshire*, with British Secretary of War Kitchener and his entire staff aboard, strikes a mine west of the Orkney Islands and sinks; only 12 of the crew are saved (Kitchener was headed for a conference in Russia).

June 6 — Russians advance on Eastern front; 25,000 Austrian prisoners taken to date.

June 13 — After fierce fighting, Canadians regain ground lost at Ypres; Italians defeat Austrians in the Lagarina Valley.

June 14 — In a naval engagement between the Russians and Germans, the czar's ships are said to have sunk a German cruiser and two smaller vessels.

June 18 — Russians capture Czerowitz; Field Marshal von Moltke dies in the Reichstag at a memorial service for Field Marshal von der Goltz.

June 20 — Italian troops report capture of Posina, Arsiero, and other areas in the push toward Trentino.

July 9 — General Letchitzky's Russian army captures Dalatyn, while General Brusilov advances to within 22 miles of Kovel.

July 11 — After ten days of furious fighting, British army defeats Germans on the Somme.

July 19 — Russians advance on Hungary.

July 23 — Holland issues an Orange Book, denouncing Germany in her relations with the Dutch.

July 25 — Russians occupy Turkish fortress of Erzingan in Armenia.

July 28 — News that Captain Charles Fryatt of the British Merchant Service has been executed by the Germans for trying to ram a German submarine.

July 31 — Dutch mail steamer *Konigen Wilhelmina* is sunk by a mine on her way to Sheerness from Flushing.

August 2 — Field Marshal von Hindenburg is placed in supreme command of all German and Austrian armies on the Eastern front.

August 9 — Italian troops capture Goritz after three days of fighting; 10,000 Austrian prisoners taken.

August 10 — Russian army occupies Stanislau.

August 11 — Turkish army drives Russians out of Hamadan in Persia.

August 12 — Turkish troops reported to have occupied Bitlis (August 7) and Mush (August 8) in Persia.

August 13 — German submarine torpedoes British destroyer *Lassoo* in English Channel.

August 15 — Russians capture Jablonitza on the way to Hungary; Italian dreadnought *Leonardo da Vinci* sinks in Taranto Harbor after internal explosion.

August 16 — Petrograd announces General Brusilov's success from June 4 to August 12; totals are 358,000 captured, along with 405 cannons and 1326 machine guns.

August 17 — Bulgarian army occupies Florina five miles from Greek-Serbian border; General Nicholas V. Ruzsky has been appointed commander in chief of the Northern armies of Russia.

August 18 — British and French make a combined attack from Pozieres to the Somme.

August 19 — Allies launch an offensive against the Central Powers on the Salonika front; German submarines sink British light cruisers *Nottingham* and *Falmouth* in North Sea; British submarine E-23 damages German battleship *Westfalen.*

August 25 — Russians resume Asiatic attack; British airplanes bomb airship sheds at Namur.

August 27 — Italy declares war on Germany; Rumania declares war against Austria-Hungary; Germany declares war against Rumania. Total number of belligerents now equals 15; Bulgarian forces capture locations in Greece, which are then bombarded by British warships.

August 29 — Rumania quickly makes her presence felt by forcing the Austrians from Transylvania and joining the Russian troops in Bukowina; announcement that Field Marshal von Hindenburg has succeeded General von Falkenhayn as chief of the general staff of the German Army.

August 30 — Rumanian troops occupy two chief cities in Transylvania (Kronstadt and Hermannstadt).

September 2 — Thirteen German zeppelins raid England; one is brought down.

September 7 — German-Bulgar army seizes Rumanian fortress of Tutrakan with 20,000 men and 100 cannons.

September 11 — Belgian army in German East Africa captures Tabora, the territory's principal fortress; German leaders of Teutonic armies in France include Duke Albrecht of Wurttemberg, commanding northern sector; Crown Prince Rupprecht of Bavaria, commanding central sector, including the Somme; and German crown prince controlling the Verdun sector.

September 15 — British troops penetrate lines of Prince Rupprecht's army for a length of six miles.

September 18 — German's repulse Russians at Halicz.

September 20 — American war contributions to date are $28,896,277.

September 22 — By an encircling movement, Field Marshal von Mackensen in Dobrudja forces the enemy back.

September 23 — Austrians blow up summit of Monte Simone and take nearly 400 Austrian prisoners; Germans capture Dutch mail steamer *Prins Hendrik* and British steamship *Colchester;* 12 zeppelins raid Great Britain, killing 30—2 zeppelins grounded.

September 24 — British occupy Jenmita on the Salonika front.

September 26 — General Maschopoulos, chief of staff of the Greek army, and 500 officers address a memorial to the king demanding an end to Greek neutrality.

September 27 — Sophia reports Serbian army in retreat along the front in western Macedonia.

September 30 — Russians renew their drive to Lemberg.

October 1 — Another zeppelin brought down in a raid on London; British seize two Bulgarian positions on the Struma.

October 4 — Cunard Line steamship *Franconia* is sunk by a U-boat in the Mediterranean.

October 5 — Allies advance along Macedonian front; Russians renew Armenian drive.

October 7 — British troops on the Somme capture village of Le Sars.

October 9 — French auxiliary cruiser *Gallia* is reported sunk by submarine on October 4 while transporting 2000 Serbian and French soldiers; General Falkenhayn seizes Toerzvar in Transylvania.

October 12 — Rumanian line in eastern Transylvania is in retreat; greatest aerial battle to date fought between Franco-British and German airplanes; more than 50 aircraft participate, 15 destroyed.

October 14 — French take control of Greek railroads, telegraph, and mails.

October 15 — King Ferdinand takes command of Rumanian army.

October 18 — Serbian troops capture Brod on the Cerna river.

October 19	General von Kluck has himself placed on retirement list; Cunard liner *Alaunia,* carrying 10,000 tons of war supplies, is sunk by a mine in the English Channel.
October 20	Russian battleship *Imperatriza Maria* is sunk by internal explosion at the mouth of the Danube; 150 lives lost.
October 21	Field Marshal von Mackensen breaks through Russo-Rumanian left wing and advances on Black Sea port of Constanza (Rumania).
October 23	Field Marshal von Mackensen captures Constanza; von Falkenhayn captures Predeal.
October 28	British steamships *Marina* and *Rowanmore* torpedoed by German submarine off Irish coast; six Americans are among those killed.
October 30	Lt. General von Stein appointed German war minister to succeed General von Hohenborn, who is sent to Western front.
October 31	Lt. General Vladimir Sakharoff, former Russian commander in Galacia, takes command of the army in the Dobridja.
November 1	Italian forces open a new offensive at Goritz and on the Carso; 4731 prisoners taken, more the next day.
November 4	Berlin reports that German submarine U-41 was sunk September 19 by a British ship flying the American flag.
November 5	Italy claims to have taken 40,365 prisoners since its offensive began on August 6.
November 7	Cardinal Mercier issues protest against deportation of Belgians to forced labor in Germany; 30,000 are said to have been deported to date.
November 8	American-Hawaiian steamship *Columbian* is sunk by a submarine; crew is saved.
November 9	Seventy British and German aircraft battle over German lines northeast of Bapaume; 42 aircraft downed in one day.
November 10	German casualties reported at 3,755,692.
November 11	Russian Black Sea fleet bombards Constanza; Austrian seaplanes bomb Padua, killing 32.
November 13	General Sir Sam Hughes resigns as Canadian minister of militia and defense because of war policy differences with Premier Borden.
November 15	Major General Groener, former chief of military railways, is given wide powers to reorganize economic and social resources of German empire.
November 17	French aviator Captain de Beauchamp flies more than 400 miles to drop bombs on Munich station.
November 19	Germany admits torpedoing the *Arabia*, but claims it was an armed transport.
November 21	Emperor Franz Joseph I dies at Schonbrunn castle after reign of 68 years; German troops capture Craiova in Wallachia; Alfred Zimmerman replaces Gottlieb von Jargow as German minister of foreign affairs after Jargow resigns for health reasons; White Star liner *Britannic,* while serving as a hospital ship, is sunk by a mine off Keos in the Aegean, killing 50.
November 26	Armies of van Falkenhayn and von Mackensen meet north of the Danube, 50 miles from Bucharest.
November 28	American steamship *Chemung* torpedoed and sunk off Spanish coast without loss of life.
November 29	Army of von Falkenhayn captures Pitechti; Admiral Sir John Jellicoe appointed first sea lord of the admiralty, succeeded as commander of British fleet by Vice Admiral Sir David Beatty.
November 30	King Constantine refuses to surrender Greek artillery and munitions to the Allies; Austro-German troops capture Rumanian city of Campulung, 16 miles from Bucharest.
December 6	German forces occupy Bucharest.
December 14	Field Marshal von Mackensen has subdued most of Southern Wallachia; British horse transport *Russian* is sunk by a submarine in the Mediterranean; 11 crew members and 17 American muleteers killed.
December 15	French forces at Verdun break through German lines for seven miles.
December 20	President Wilson's peace note to the nations is made public.
December 21	British troops subdue El Arish, a Turkish position 90 miles from the Suez Canal.
December 27	French armoured cruiser *Gaulois* is torpedoed in Mediterranean; General Joffre is made a marshal of France.
December 28	Berlin proclaims total defeat of Russo-Rumanian forces in Rumania.
December 30	Coronation of Emperor Charles and Empress Zita as King and Queen of Hungary in Budapest; "Mad Monk" Gregory Rasputin is murdered in Petrograd by members of the Russian nobility.
1917	
January 2	Allies claim to have captured 583,000 men in 1916.
January 4	German-Bulgar army captures Braila, chief commercial city of Rumania.
January 8	Foscani (in Rumania) captured by Entente; Allies reissue ultimatum to Greece.
January 11	British warship *Cornwallis* reported sunk by submarine on January 9.
January 12	Official announcement of sinking of Italian battleship *Regina Margherita* on December 11 by a mine; 675 men lost.
January 16	Greece accedes to allied demands.
January 17	Russians announce recapture of Rumanian village of Vadeni.
January 19	English munitions plant near London explodes, causing 69 deaths and 400 injuries.
January 23	Naval engagements between English and Germans in North Sea results in loss of a destroyer for each participant.
January 24	Germans push back Russians in Riga region.
January 25	British auxiliary cruiser *Laurentic,* carrying a reserve naval crew, is sunk off Irish coast; 350 killed.
January 27	Atlantic transport line steamer *Minnewaska* is sunk by a mine off a Greek island.
February 1	On first day of new U-boat campaign, Germans sink ten ships.
February 3	U.S. severs diplomatic relations with Germany.
February 5	Three British steamers, a Russian bark, and the Belgian relief ship *Lars Kruse* are sunk by German submarines; to this point Germany has destroyed 31 vessels since beginning the new submarine campaign.
February 6	Germans sink 14 more vessels, including the British passenger steamer *Port Adelaide*; German steamer *Kronprinzessen Cecilie* has her engines wrecked at Boston harbor while in U.S. custody to prevent the ship from being used for war purposes.
February 7	British liner *California* is sunk off Irish coast; 13 other vessels are destroyed same day.

February 12	American schooner *Lyman W. Law*, en route to Italy with a cargo of lumber, is sunk by a submarine off the Sardinian coast.
February 13	White Star line steamship *Afric* is sunk by submarine.
February 16	Seven British ships are sunk in war zone.
February 21	Vice Admiral Capelle, German Minister of the navy, expresses satisfaction with his navy campaign program to date.
February 23	French steamer *Athos* carrying Senegalese troops and colonial laborers is torpedoed in Mediterranean.
February 24	A Dutch flotilla is attacked by German submarines after German government is believed to have promised safe passage; three vessels are sunk, four are badly damaged.
February 25	Cunard liner *Laconia*, carrying 73 passengers, is sunk without warning off the Irish coast; 13 are killed, including two American women.
February 26	British capture Kut-el-Amara.
February 28	Reported that Germany has sunk 183 vessels during the month of February; "Zimmerman" note is revealed.
March 3	Russian troops recapture city of Hamadan in Western Persia.
March 4	Germans make strong attack at Verdun, making gains at several points.
March 8	Count Ferdinand von Zeppelin dies of pneumonia.
March 11	General Maude's British forces capture Baghdad.
March 14	China severs relations with Germany.
March 15	Czar Nicholas abdicates.
March 17	British capture Bapaume; French seize Roye and Lassigny.
March 18	Germans retreat from Peronne, Noyon, and other areas along an 85-mile front; American ships *Illinois, City of Memphis,* and *Vigilancia* are torpedoed.
March 21	American ship *Healdton,* bound for Rotterdam, is sunk without warning; 21 men are lost.
April 1	American armed ship *Aztec* is sunk in submarine zone.
April 5	American steamer *Missourian* is sunk in Mediterranean.
April 6	U.S. declares war on Germany.
April 7	Cuba and Panama declare war on Germany.
April 8	Austria-Hungary severs relations with U.S.
April 9	Bolivia severs relations with Germany.
April 13	Canadians capture territory at Vimy, Givenchy, and elsewhere.
April 20	Turkey breaks with U.S.
May 9	Liberia breaks with Germany.
May 15	General Foch is appointed chief of staff; General Pétain succeeds General Nivelle as commander in chief of French armies; beginning of great Italian offensive on Isonzo front.
May 16	British capture Bullecourt; Honduras breaks with Germany.
May 22	Italians advance on Carso.
May 26	Hospital ship *Dover Castle* is sunk in Mediterranean.
June 2	Independence of Albania proclaimed.
June 7	British bombard Messines Ridge south of Ypres and take 7500 German prisoners.
June 8	General Pershing arrives in England en route to France.
June 12	King Constantine of Greece is forced to abdicate.
June 13	Airplane raids on London; 157 killed, 432 injured.
June 15	Airplane raids on London kill 104.
June 18	Haiti breaks with Germany.
June 23	P & O liner *Mongolia* is sunk off Bombay.
June 24	British approach Lens.
June 26	First American troops arrive in France.
July 1	Russian offensive begins in Galacia.
July 8	Austrian front is broken west of Stanislau.
July 9	Russians evacuate Mesopotamia; H.M.S. *Vanguard* is blown up, killing 700.
July 10	Russians capture Halicz; Turks are defeated on Euphrates.
July 16	French win back Hill 304.
July 22	Siam (Thailand) declares war against Germany and Austria.
July 22–24	Austro-Germans retake Stanislau and Halicz.
July 30	German naval mutiny at Wilhelmshaven and Kiel (a second mutiny occurs on September 2); H.M.S. *Ariadne* is torpedoed.
August 3	Austro-Germans capture Czernowitz.
August 7	Liberia declares war against Germany.
August 11	The ship *City of Athens* is sunk by mine.
August 14	China declares war on Germany and Austria.
August 15	Canadians dominate area around Lens after taking Hill 70.
August 19	Italians cross Isonzo and capture Monte Santo (August 24).
August 21	Canadians enter Lens.
September 1	Jutland naval battle witnesses destruction of four German mine sweepers.
September 3	Germans seize Riga.
September 7	Atlantic Transport liner *Minnehaha* is sunk off Irish coast.
September 16	Kerensky proclaims Russia to be a republic.
September 20	Costa Rica breaks with Germany; British begin attack on six-mile front east of Ypres.
September 21	General Tasker H. Bliss is appointed U.S. Army chief of staff.
September 25	Guynemer, the famous French aviator, is killed.
September 29	British capture Turkish Mesopotamian army under Ahmed Bey.
October 1	H.M.S. *Drake* torpedoed.
October 6	Peru and Uruguay sever relations with Germany.
October 12–16	Russians defeated in Gulf of Riga.
October 17	American transport *Antilles,* westbound from France, is sunk by submarine, with a loss of 67 lives.
October 23	First American shots fired.
October 23–26	French begin successful push north of the Aisne.
October 24	Austro-German forces start offensive against Italian positions. Italians driven back to Piave river, Asiago plateau, and Brenta river.
October 26	Brazil declares war on Germany.
October 31	Austrians retreat to the Tagliamento; British occupy Beersheba in Palestine.
November 2	Germans retreat from Chemin des Dames north of the Aisne.
November 3	First encounter between Germans and Americans; Americans suffer 20 casualties.
November 4	British troops reach Italy.
November 7	Italians continue to retreat; Russian Bolsheviks led by Lenin and Trotsky seize Petrograd and depose Kerensky; British take Gaza.
November 8	General Diaz succeeds General Dacorna as commander in chief of Italian armies.
November 10	Lenin succeeds Kerensky as Russian premier.
November 15	George Clemenceau succeeds Painleve as Premier of France.
November 17	North Sea battle involving eight cruisers.
November 18	British troops seize Jaffa (Palestine); Major General Maude (captor of Baghdad) dies in Mesopotamia.

November 20	Hindenburg line smashed on ten-mile front facing Cambrai.
November 22–December 13	Battle of Cambrai, British surprise attack under General Byng; tanks are used for first time to break down wire entanglements; German counterattacks on November 26 and December 13 are only partially successful.
November 23	Italians counterattack Germans from Asiago plateau to the Brenton river.
December 1	German East Africa is reported to be completely subdued by Allies.
December 3	Russian Bolsheviks agree to armistice with Germany (signed on December 15).
December 4	Germans attack British trenches at Ypres.
December 5	British retire from positions west of Cambrai.
December 6	U.S. destroyer *Jacob Jones* is sunk by submarine, killing 60; steamer *Mont Blanc*, loaded with munitions, explodes in collision with the *Imo* in Halifax harbor, killing 1500.
December 7	Finland declares its independence; U.S. declares war on Austria.
December 8	Jerusalem, which was reportedly held by Turks for 673 years, surrenders to British General Allenby.
December 9	Italians torpedo two Austrian battleships at Trieste.
December 10	Panama declares war against Austria.
December 12	German destroyers attack a convoy of neutral vessels.
December 14	Cuba declares war against Austria; Austro-Germans win a sector against Italians.
December 18	Airplane raid on London.
December 25	France and Germany agree to exchange prisoners 48 years of age and older.
December 27	Turkish army is defeated by British while attempting to take Jerusalem.
December 24–30	Fierce fighting between Italians and Germans.
December 30	British occupy Bireh near Jerusalem; renewed fighting at Cambrai.

1918

January 2	Germans repulsed between Lens and St. Quentin and in thrust for Venice.
January 7	Mutiny at German naval base at Kiel.
January 9	British hospital ship *Rewa* torpedoed in British Channel.
January 19	American troops capture sector northwest of Toul.
January 20	British announce sinking of Turkish cruiser *Medulla* and beaching of former *Goeben*; Allied naval forces bombard Ostend.
January 21	*Louvain* is sunk in Mediterranean; 100,000 Turkish troops are reported to have deserted.
January 27	*Andania* torpedoed off coast of Ireland.
January 28	Rumanians capture capital of Bessarabia (Kishineff).
January 29	Allied aircraft attack Zeebrugge at same time that German aircraft bomb London; Italians seize Monte di val Belle.
January 30	British forces in Palestine approach Antioch.
February 5	American steamship *Alamanse* is torpedoed and sunk.
February 6	American transport *Tuscania* is torpedoed off Irish coast, killing 101.
February 11	Italians repulse Austrians after the latter attack in fury, west of Brenta.
February 15	Germany renews war on Russia.
February 16	Bolsheviks defeat Ukrainians in battle for Kiev.
February 19	British advance on Jericho.
February 21	*Philadelphian* is sunk; Germans enter Russia and seize Minsk and Rovno; British capture Jericho.
February 24	British report that Bolshevik leaders have accepted German peace terms; Trebizond is captured by Turks.
February 25	Germans capture Reval and Pskoff.
February 26	British hospital ship *Glenart Castle* is torpedoed in English Channel, killing 166 doctors, nurses, and orderlies; Rumania contemplates peace with the Central Powers.
February 27	Japan seeks joint efforts with Allies in Siberia.
March 1	H.M.S. *Culgarian* is sunk off coast of Ireland; Germans reach Dnieper river; Bolsheviks victorious near Rostof-on-Don; Americans gain victory north of Toul.
March 1	German and Ukrainian troops occupy Kiev.
March 3	Russians sign Brest-Litovsk treaty (between Germany and Bolshevik government).
March 4	Treaty signed between Germany and Finland.
March 5	Roumania signs preliminary agreement with Central Powers; American Rainbow Division repulses German attack in Lorraine sector.
March 7	German airplanes attack London in night raid.
March 8	Germans and British engage in fierce fighting around Ypres.
March 9	Russian capital moved from Petrograd to Moscow.
March 10	British advance in Mesopotamia; British hospital ship *Guilford Castle* is torpedoed in English Channel.
March 11	Americans subdue Toul; German airplanes raid Paris; Turks recapture Erzerum from Armenians.
March 14	Germans occupy Abo (Finland); Americans advance northeast of Badonvillers.
March 17	Belgians occupy Flanders coast.
March 18	Great Britain and America take over Dutch shipping in their respective ports.
March 19	French break German line near Rheims; ignoring armistice, German troops continue advance into Russia.
March 21	Germans begin offensive on a 50-mile front from Arras to La Fere, and bombard Paris with large cannons from as far as 75 miles away.
March 22–25	Germans penetrate Croisilles, Bapaume, Peronne, Bril, and northwest of Noyon, capturing 75,000 men and 600 guns; French report enemy's loss at 600,000, which was the German maximum at Verdun in 1916–17; General Zuppeli succeeds General Aldieri as Italian war minister.
March 23–25	Demoralization occurs among Allies as they retreat before German onslaught (especially General Gough's British 5th Army); General Carey's "scratch" division keeps in touch with General Byng's 3rd Army in the North; French general Fayolle saves 3rd Army in the South, with over a 30-mile gap between it and 6th French Army.
March 28	Entire Turkish force in area of Hit in Mesopotamia is either captured or destroyed.
March 29	General Foch is chosen commander in chief of all Allied forces.
March 31	French begin counterattack; Germany envelopes Albert; Germans advance in Ukraine, capture and burn Poltava.
April 1	German naval forces capture Hango in Finland; British continue advance, threatening Aleppo.
April 4–7	Germans capture Hamel on Somme, but are defeated at Casel by the French and at Villers-Bretonneux by the British.
April 5	U.S. Army at end of first year totals 1,500,000 men; Japanese troops land at Vladivostok.
April 9	Second German offensive is begun in Flanders.

April 10	First German drive is stopped before Amiens (it was to be a 35-mile advance); German troops mutiny at Limburg.
April 12	Field Marshal Haig issues special orders of the day: "All positions must be held to the last man."
April 13	German forces occupy Helsingfors, Finland.
April 15	Second German drive is halted before Ypres (it was to be a 10-mile advance).
April 16	Bolo Pacha, Levantine resident in Paris, is executed for treason; France calls men of age 19.
April 21	Guatemala declares war on Germany.
April 22	British blockade Zeebrugge (German submarine and destroyer base); von Richtofen, ace German flier, is killed.
April 27	British troops in Mesopotamia capture Kirfa.
April 24–27	Germans dislodge French and British from Mont Kemmel.
May 1	Many Czechs and Slavs join Italians in fight against Austrians; British advance in Palestine; Allied conference held at Versailles; Germans occupy Sebastopol.
May 6	Rumania signs peace treaty with Central Powers.
May 7	Nicaragua declares war against Germany and her allies.
May 10	Italians seize Monte Corno.
May 12	French recapture Hill 44 on north flank of Mont Kemmel.
May 17	Russian transport carrying 3000 people is sunk by German submarine, killing most aboard.
May 19	Bolshevik and Musselman troops battle at Baku on Caspian Sea; Major Raoul Lufberry, famous aviator, is killed.
May 23	British transport *Moldavia* is sunk off English coast; first meeting of Russo-Ukrainian peace conference.
May 24	Costa Rica declares war against Germany and Austria-Hungary.
May 25–June 14	German submarines sink 19 vessels off U.S. coast.
May 26	British transport *Leasowe Castle* sunk by submarine in Mediterranean; Italian army breaks through German defensive at Capo Sile on lower Piave front.
May 27	Italians continue advance; third German offensive begins on Aisne-Marne front, 30 miles between Soissons and Rheims.
May 28	American troops capture Cantigny; Germans cross the Visle at Fismes.
May 29	Germans suddenly advance from west, enveloping Soissons.
May 30	Germans reach the Marne and begin to consolidate their position.
May 31	U.S. transport *President Lincoln* is torpedoed and sunk.
June 2	Schooner *Edward H. Cole* is torpedoed off U.S. coast.
June 3–6	American troops (including Marines) stop Germans at Chateau-Thierry and Neuilly after Germans have advanced 32 miles.
June 8	Czechoslovak troops reach Vladivostok.
June 9–14	Germans advance nine miles on Noyon-Montdidier front.
June 13–14	French force the Germans to retreat beyond Courcelles and Croix Richard after heavy fighting; Turks capture Tabriz in Persia.
June 15–24	Austrian push fails on Italian front.
June 23	Norwegian freighter *Augvold* sunk off Cape Race.
June 29–30	Italians capture Asiago, Col di Chelo, and Col del Rosso.
July 1	American troops capture Vaux; U.S. transport *Covington* is sunk.
July 1–4	Italians raid Monte Grappa.
July 3	Sultan of turkey, Mohammed V, dies.
July 4	Americans and Austrians capture Hamel.
July 6	Italians and French advance between the coast and Tomorico Valley; last Austrians are driven across the Piave, having suffered between 250,000 and 270,000 casualties since November; French/Italian forces capture Fieri.
July 7	Czechoslovak troops march into Siberia and defeat Bolsheviks at Chita on the Trans-Siberian railroad.
July 8	Czechoslovaks capture Nikolsk.
July 9	German foreign minister resigns.
July 11	U.S. supply ship *Westover* is sunk.
July 12	Italian forces capture Berat, Austrian base in Albania.
July 14	French seize Gramshi and Natta.
July 15	Haiti declares war against Germany; new German drive on Paris is blocked by Americans at Chateau-Thierry.
July 16	Nicholas Romanov, former czar of Russia, is assassinated at Ekaterinberg.
July 17	*Carpathia* sunk; Lt. Quentin Roosevelt, youngest son of former president Theodore Roosevelt, killed in aerial attack near Chateau Thierry.
July 18	French and American forces led by General Mangin attack right wing of German crown prince's army between Soissons and Chateau Thierry.
July 19	U.S. cruiser *San Diego* is sunk off Fire Island; Honduras declares war on Germany; Italian troops take Bouilly.
July 20	Italians recover Corno di Cabento and Marte Stabiel; the liner *Justicia,* used as a troopship, is sunk off Irish coast.
July 21	French-Italian forces gain further territory in Albania; German submarine sinks three barges off Cape Cod.
July 22	Austrians bombard Tonale region in the Brento Valley and on the lower Piave.
July 23	*Marmora* is sunk; French take Oulchy-le-Chateau and drive Germans back between the Aisne and the Marne.
July 24	British munition workers go on strike; Austrians forced from Davoli Bandle and Kuci Arch.
July 23–25	Germans counterattack fiercely, but are driven back.
July 30	Germans begin retreat to the Vesle.
August 2	French occupy Soissons after recapturing it and surrounding territory.
August 3	Allies capture entire Aisne-Vesle front; British ambulance transport *Warilda,* with 600 wounded aboard, is sunk by submarine, killing 123.
August 4	The ship *O.B. Jennings* is sunk.
August 5	*Stanley I. Seaman* is sunk; U.S. troops land at Archangel.
August 8	Allies move south and attack Bolshevik troops; new Allied push on Western Front is begun by Field Marshal Haig in Picardy, penetrates 14 miles; British General Rawlinson, with French Generals Debeney and Humbert, advance against army of von der Marwitz, south of the Somme.
August 9	Japanese General Otani is appointed commander of U.S. and Allied troops in Siberia; more vessels are sunk off U.S. coast by submarines.
August 10	Allies recapture Montdidier.

August 11	Submarines sink nine U.S. fishing boats; counterrevolution in Russia; Bolshevik leaders prepare for flight.
August 12	German ambassador flees from Russia.
August 13	Italians advance to Swiss border.
August 15	First U.S. troops land in Siberia; Canadians capture Damery and Parvillers.
August 16	American ship *Montanan* is sunk.
August 17	French cruiser *Dopetit Thouras* is sunk.
August 19	French overrun the Lassigny Massif, later take Le Hamel; British retake Mont Kemmel.
August 21	General Byng advances with 3rd British Army on Rawlinson's left; American 30th Division begins an offensive north of the Ancre; General Mangin advances to Cuts and Pontoise, outflanking Noyon (August 22).
August 22	Belgian relief ship Gasconier is sunk.
August 24	British push opens entire road from Albert to Bapaume.
August 25	Canadian steamer *Eric* is destroyed by shellfire off Miquelon Island.
August 25–26	British capture Suzanne and Capy; Byng crosses Hindenburg line between Arras and Bapaume.
August 25–29	Three American schooners are sunk.
August 27	General Debeney takes Roye.
August 28	Americans with Mangin attack Fismes and near the Vesle-Aisne junction.
August 30	Germans retreat on a 20-mile front.
August 31	Lenin is wounded twice by would-be assassin.
September 1	Australians capture Peronne; British advance in Macedonia west of Vardar river; Americans fight in Belgium, take Voormezelle.
September 5	*Mt. Vernon* is torpedoed, but not sunk.
September 5–6	Americans led by Mangin beat back Germans between Vieil Arcy and Villiers-en-Praveres.
September 5–11	Germans in retreat from the Vesle to the Aisne.
September 11	Bolsheviks defeated by Czechoslovaks near Ekaterinberg.
September 12	British capture Havrincourt, Moeuveres, and Trescault on push to Cambrai; Major General Hunter Ligget's 1st American Army attacks St. Michiel salient between Verdun and Metz, capturing 200 square miles, 20,000 prisoners, and more than 100 guns.
September 13	French capture Lassigny Massif.
September 14	An offensive on the Macedonian front begun by Allied contingents from France, Italy, Britain, Serbia, Greece, and Montenegro.
September 15	Canadians seize Damery and Parvillers; Germany makes peace offer to Belgium; *Galway Castle* is sunk, killing 120.
September 16	Czechoslovaks seek Allied assistance.
September 17	Americans take Ronvaux, Haumont, and Manhuelles.
September 18	*Buena Ventura* is torpedoed; U.S. rejects Austrian peace offer; Debeney's 1st French Army penetrates Hindenburg line northwest of St. Quentin.
September 19	General Allenby, commanding the Anglo-Egyptian Army and a group of French contingents, routs the 8th Turkish Army (led by the German general Liman von Sanders), capturing 80,000 prisoners and 500 guns; on his right, the Arab army commanded by Hussein I, King of the Hedjaz, defeats the 4th Turkish Army.
September 20	Report of the loss of the French ship Amiral Charner.
September 25	American 30th, 38th, and 27th Divisions advance on 14-mile front toward Cambrai. They take 16,000 prisoners in two days; Bulgarians retreat in Macedonia on 130-mile front.
September 26	*Tampa* is sunk; British approach Sea of Galilee; Bulgaria asks for suspensions of hostilities, request denied; Serbs and British occupy Veles, Kochana, and Strumitza.
September 27	Bulgaria requests armistice of British government.
September 28	Von Hertling resigns as German chancellor.
September 29	Noyon and Bapaume are captured by Allies; 10,000 Turkish troops surrender to British at Gaza; Americans take Bellecourt and Nauroy.
September 29–30	Belgians seize Dixmude and Roulers; British capture Passchendaele Ridge.
September 30	Americans take Apremont; Bulgaria signs armistice with Allies on Allied terms; Petrograd announces fall of Kazan to Czechoslovakia.
September 31	Eight Norwegian vessels are sunk.
October 1	British cavalry occupies Damascus; Austrian naval base at Durazzo, Albania, destroyed by Italian-American naval expedition; the cornerstone of Hindenburg line at St. Quentin is captured.
October 2	Bulgarians evacuate Serbia; Germans evacuate Lens; Debeney's troops occupy St. Quentin.
October 3	Italians drive Austrians from Albania; General Marshall, with Anglo-Indian Army in Mesopotamia, advances up the Tigris against Mosul.
October 4	Boris succeeds Ferdinand as King of Bulgaria; Spanish ship *Francoli* is attacked by submarine; Greeks occupy Demir Hassan Pass.
October 5	American and French forces advance on Western front; *Hirano Maru* is sunk, killing 300; Bulgaria demobilizes; Austrian prime minister resigns; Prince Maximilian, new German chancellor, pleads with President Wilson to ask Allies for armistice, says Germany will accept Wilson's 14 points.
October 6	General Allenby captures Zahlek and Rayak; *Oranto* is sunk after collision; 364 U.S. soldiers are lost.
October 7	French take Berry-au-Bac (the great German supply station); Allenby occupies Sidon and French Beirut.
October 8	President Wilson asks whether Prince Maximilian is speaking for the German people or for the War Lords; the *Leinster* is torpedoed in Irish Channel, last German naval atrocity; 480 killed.
October 9	Allies occupy Cambrai.
October 10	Le Chateau is captured by British.
October 12	German foreign secretary (Solf) agrees to evacuate all foreign soil as Germany accepts Wilson's terms; Serbians capture Nish; Major General Robert L. Bullard's 2nd American Army attacks northwest of Verdun; Mangin captures almost all of the Chemin des Dames.
October 13	General Allenby occupies Tripoli on the Syrian coast; Germans abandon Laon and La Fere.
October 14	Italians occupy various locations in Albania; President Wilson's specific details in reply to Germany's peace offer include referring the Germans to General Foch, who will accept armistice terms.
October 15	Allenby's cavalry invades Homs; Turkey informs Austria that she will make separate peace with Entente; U.S. transport *America* is sunk at pier; Bohemia revolts against Austria.
October 16	British 2nd Army subdues Wervicq, Comines, Halluin, and Wevel-ghem; French and Belgians capture Ingelmunster and Lechtervelde; American 1st Army takes Grand Pre in Argonne Forest.

October 17	Serbs seize Krushevatz and Alexinatz; German submarine base at Ostend captured by land and sea forces; other Allied victories at Lille, Douai, and the Côte de Chatillon. Army commander Horne is among the victors with his British 1st Army (other contingents include 5th British Army and 1st American Army); the Ostend victory is, in large measure, the work of British naval forces under Sir Roger Keyes.
October 18	Czechoslovak council declares independence; Allied successes at Blankengerghe, Wassigny, Ribeaufille, and Bantheville (which the 1st American Army loses and regains).
October 19	Austrian request for armistice is denied; the *Lucia* is sunk; Italian General Diaz is ordered by Foch to attack Austro-Hungarian armies; Bulgarians completely evacuate Macedonia; Zeebrugge and Bruger are captured by Belgians and British; 1st British Army captures Denian.
October 20	Germans retreat from Dutch frontier; German submarines are recalled to their bases; French and Serbians reach the Danube.
October 21	Socialist newspapers in Germany demand the kaiser's abdication; 1st British Army enters Valenciennes.
October 22	Franco-Belgians attack La Fere salient and capture Chalandry and Grandlup.
October 23	Allied victories at Bruay, Bleharies, and Espain.
October 24	Italians capture Monte Solarolo; French seize Sisemol; British and Italian 10th Army, led by Lord Cavan, invade island of Grave di Papadopoli.
October 25	Marshall's forces take Kurkuk and the passage of the Sesser Zab, a branch of the Tigris; new Italian drive nets 50,000 prisoners in five days.
October 26	Serbians capture Kralievo; Aleppo is captured; British take Artes, Famars, and Englefontaine; 1st American Army uses 16-inch naval guns against the Meizieres-Metz supply railway.
October 27	The Chapans sunk; British occupy Kirkuk.
October 28	Marshall takes Kalat Shergat on Tigris; Austria-Hungary sends message accepting Allied terms, including independence for the Czechoslovaks.
October 29	Italian armies advance on a 30-mile front.
October 30	Turkey signs armistice; Turkish army on the Tigris surrenders (7000 prisoners); Turkey opens Black and Aegean Sea passages to Allies.
October 31	British 3rd Army and American 30th Division release several towns from Prgwyk to Winterkern.
November 1	American 1st Army captures Clery-le-Grand; the *Viribus* is sunk; Versailles conference opens; 3rd, 8th, 10th, and 12th Armies reach the Livenza.
November 2	British occupy Valenciennes.
November 3	Germans are in full retreat as American armies push on a 50-mile front above Verdun; official reports indicate that 362,350 Germans are captured since July 15; Serbians occupy Belgrade; Belgian army reaches Terneuzen and liberates 10 miles along the Dutch frontier; 1st American Army destroys Mezieres-Metz railway at Montmedy and Conflans; Italians defeat Austro-Hungarians decisively, taking 100,000 prisoners and 2200 guns.
November 4	Americans strike at Sedan; Serbians approach Bosnia; Allied armies advance on 30-mile front between the Scheldt and the Oise-Sambre Canal; Austria surrenders and accepts peace terms (surrender is to Italian General Diaz)—armistice goes into effect at 3 p.m.; Allies agree to and sign truce terms for Germany.
November 6	American 1st Army captures heights of the Woevre and Sedan.
November 7	"False Peace" day in New York; American Rainbow Division and parts of 1st Division enter Sedan suburbs; Germans retreat on a 70-mile front from the Scheldt to the Aisne.
November 8	Marshal Foch receives armistice delegates from Germany.
November 9	French occupy Mezieres. Rawlinson's 4th British Army seizes Maurbeuge; German kaiser abdicates; British battleship *Britannia* is torpedoed.
November 10	King Victor Immanuel III makes triumphal entry into Trieste; ex-kaiser flees to Holland.
November 11	German envoys sign armistice, which takes effect at 11 a.m. (eleventh hour of eleventh day of eleventh month).
November 12	Austro-Hungarian emperor Carl abdicates.

Part II: Details of War

Military Leaders

American

Name	Position/Significance
Brigadier General U. G. Mac Alexander	Commander of 90th Division in the Army of Occupation
Major General Robert Alexander	Commander of 77th "Liberty" Division at the Argonne battle
Major General Benjamin Alford	Adjutant to General Pershing on headquarters staff
Major General Henry T. Allen	Commander of 19th Division at St.-Mihiel and the Argonne
Major General Charles G. Ballou	Commander of 92nd Division, composed of black troops
Brigadier General Frank E. Bamford	Commanding officer of the 26th Division, 1st Army Corps
Major General George Barnett	Commandant of the United States Marine Corps
Brigadier General George C. Barnhart	Commander of 178th Infantry Brigade, 89th Division
Major General Thomas H. Barry	Succeeded J. Franklin Bell as Commander of the East, January 1919
Major General George Bell, Jr.	Commander of 33rd Division of 3rd Army Corps
Major General J. Franklin Bell	Commanded Department of the East at New York City
Admiral W. S. Benson	Chief of naval operations; directed operations in the North Sea and became one of the armistice delegates at Treves
Brigadier General William H. Black	Chief of the Corps of Engineers, U.S. Army

Major General Tasker H. Bliss	U.S. chief of staff at beginning of war; later a peace delegate
Major General E. E. Booth	Commander in 4th Division of the 2nd Army Corps
Major General Andrew W. Brewster	Inspector General's Department, American Expeditionary Forces
Brigadier General Preston Brown	Chief of staff of the 2nd Division
Brigadier General R. A. Brown	Commander of 84th Brigade, 42nd "Rainbow" Division
Major General Beaumont B. Buck	Commander of 3rd Division of the 5th Army Corps
Lt. General Robert L. Bullard	Commander of 2nd Army; fought at Meuse and Argonne
Major General Omar Bundy	Commander of 5th Army Corps; fought at Chateau-Thierry
Major General William P. Burnham	Commander of 82nd Division, 2nd Army Corps
Major General George H. Cameron	Commander in 5th Army Corps at Argonne battle
Rear Admiral William B. Caperton	Commanded the Pacific fleet
Rear Admiral Washington Capps	A worker behind the scenes in Washington
Brigadier General Marlborough Churchill	Chief of the Military Intelligence Division
Brigadier General Charles H. Cole	Commander of 52nd Brigade, 26th Division
Major General Adelbert Cronkhite	Commander of 80th Division in the Argonne-Meuse offensive
Major General Enoch H. Crowder	Provost marshal general in charge of the draft
Brigadier General William Crozier	Chief of Ordnance Department; invented the disappearing gun
Brigadier General Deakyne	Chief of Engineers of the 2nd Army
Major General Joseph T. Dickman	Commander of the 3rd American Army of Occupation
Brigadier General E. T. Donnelly	Commander of 164th Brigade, 89th Division
Brigadier General Charles A. Doyen	Commander of first marines sent to France; died October 6, 1917
Major General George B. Duncan	Commander of 77th division, and later, 82nd Division
Major General Clarence E. Edwards	Commander of 26th Division, composed chiefly of New England troops
Major General C. S. Farnsworth	Commander of 37th division, composed mainly of Ohio troops
Major General C. A. F. Flager	Commander of 42nd Division in the Army of Occupation
Rear Admiral Frank Friday Fletcher	Commander in the Atlantic fleet
Major General Frederick S. Foltz	Commander of 91st Division of 5th Army Corps
Brigadier General Benjamin D. Foulois	Chief of the Military Intelligence Division
Rear Admiral Albert Gleaves	Commanded the antisubmarine convoy and escort system that transported more than 2 million U.S. troops overseas
Major General Edwin F. Glenn	Commander of 83rd Division
General William C. Gorgas	Surgeon general of U.S. Army
Major General William S. Graves	Commander of American Expeditionary Forces in Siberia

Major General Edward S. J. Greble	Commander of 36th Division National Guard
Major General William G. Haan	Commander of 32nd Division, forming part of the Army of Occupation
Major General James G. Harbord	Chief of staff of the American Expeditionary Forces
Major General Peter C. Harris	Adjutant general of the Army, succeeding General H. P. McCain
Major General Harry J. Hatch	Commander of Coast Artillery Section of U.S. Army
Major General William H. Hay	Promoted from command of 134th Infantry Brigade
Major General Eli A. Helmick	In command of Embarkation Port at Brest, France
Major General John L. Hines	Commander of 4th Regular Army Division; later with Army of Occupation
Major General Harry F. Hodges	Commander of 76th Division of the 5th Army Corps
Major General W. A. Holbrook	In command of Southern Department of U.S. Army
Major General Robert L. Houze	Commander of 38th Division
Major General Grote Hutcheson	Administrator of service of embarking troops for overseas
General M. W. Ireland	Replaced Gorgas after the latter resigned
Brigadier General Evan M. Johnson	Commander of 154th Infantry Brigade of the 77th Division
Major General W. T. Johnston	Commander of 91st Division in Argonne Meuse offensive
Brigadier General William L. Kenley	Army chief of military aeronautics; active in development of wireless telephone
Major General Charles W. Kennedy	Commander of 85th Division of 5th Army Corps
Major General F. J. Kernan	Organizer of supply service for American troops abroad
Rear Admiral Austin M. Knight	Commanded the American fleet that operated in Asiatic waters
Major General Joseph E. Kuhn	Commander of 79th Division and later in American Army of Occupation
Major General G. W. Langfitt	Chief engineer of American forces
Major General John A. Lejeune	Commander of 2nd Division of U.S. Marines at Belleau Wood
Major General Edward M. Lewis	Commander of 30th Division, cooperating with the British
Lt. General Hunter Liggett	Commander of 1st Army Corps; fought at St.-Mihiel and the Argonne
Major General LeRoy S. Lyon	Commander of 31st Division in the final period of the war
Brigadier General Paul R. Malone	Commander of 10th Brigade, 5th Division
Major General William A. Mann	First Commander of the 42nd, or "Rainbow," Division
Major General Peyton C. March	Chief of staff
Major General Charles H. Martin	Commander of 86th Division
Rear Admiral Henry T. Mayo	Commander of the Atlantic fleet on its return to America
Brigadier General Douglas McArthur	Commander of 42nd Division on march into Germany
Brigadier General B. L. McCawley	Quartermaster of United States Marine Corps
Brigadier General Frank R. McCoy	Secretary, general staff, U.S. Army in France

Major General Edward F. McGlachlin	Commander of 1st Division in the Army of Occupation
Major General Frank McIntyre	Executive assistant to U.S. Army chief of staff
Major General John E. McMahon	Commander of 5th Regular Army Division of 3rd Corps
Major General J. H. McRae	Commander of 78th Division of the 3rd Army Corps
Major General Charles T. Menoher	Commander of 42nd ("Rainbow") Division of 1st Army Corps
Brigadier General Edward A. Millar	Commander of 6th Artillery Brigade, 6th Division
Major General John F. Morrison	Director of Military Training at U.S. War College
Major General C. G. Morton	Commander of 29th Division of the 4th Army Corps
Major General Charles H. Muir	Commander of 28th Division of Pennsylvania troops
Major General John F. O'Ryan	Commander of 27th Division of 3rd Army Corps
Brigadier General Frank Parker	Commander in 1st Division, 1st Army Corps
General John J. Pershing	Commander in chief of the American Expeditionary Forces
Major General George W. Read	Commander of 4th Army Corps; fought at Bellicourt
Major General John Riddle	Assigned to Engineer Corps and assistant chief of staff
Brigadier General D. S. Rockenback	Chief of Tank Corps, general Army headquarters
Rear Admiral Hugh Rodman	Present at the surrender of the German fleet, November 21, 1918
Major General John W. Ruckman	Commander of the Northeastern Department of U.S. Army
Major General Edgar Russell	Assigned to U.S. Signal Corps
Major General Hugh L. Scott	Former chief of staff in the U.S. Army
Brigadier General W. S. Scott	Commander of General Base Section No. 2
Major General Henry C. Sharpe	Quartermaster general of U.S. Army
Brigadier General J. A. Shipton	Commander of 55th Brigade of 33rd Division
Major General William L. Sibert	Organizer and administrator, Chemical Warfare Service
Rear Admiral William S. Sims	Commander of United States fleet in European waters during the war
Brigadier General Harvey A. Smith	Commandant of the Army school at Langres, France
Major General William R. Smith	Commander of 36th Division of 5th Army Corps
Major General Frederick S. Strong	Commander of 40th Division in the last days of the war
Major General Samuel D. Sturgis	Took command of 80th Division on November 18, 1918
Major General Charles P. Summerall	Commander of 5th U.S. Army Corps
Brigadier General L. D. Tyson	Commander of 59th Brigade of 30th Division
Brigadier General M. L. Walker	Director, military training schools, Tours, France
Major General E. M. Weaver	Commander of United States Coast Artillery
Major General Charles B. Wheeler	Chief ordnance officer of U.S. Army in France
Brigadier General Roger D. Williams	Commander of 75th Brigade of the 38th Division
Rear Admiral Wilson	Commanded the part of the U.S. fleet that operated in French waters
Brigadier General E. B. Winans	Commander of 64th Brigade of the 32nd Division
Brigadier General Charles D. Winn	Commander of 305th Field Artillery of 77th Division
Major General Frank L. Winn	Commander of 89th Division
Major General William M. Wright	Commander of 85th Division and 3rd Army Corps

Austro-Hungarian

Name	Position/Significance
General Victor Dankl	One of the most popular leaders; commander of the Austrian army in the Galatian battles early in the war
Archduke Eugen	
Archduke Frederick	Commander in chief of Austrian armies; active in campaigns against Russians
Field Marshal Alfred Krauss	
Admiral Montecuculi	
Moritz Ritter von Auffenberg	A corps commander at the start of the war; eventually became Army inspector
Baron Conrad von Hötzendorff	Chief of the general staff and director of the 1918 advance against the Italians; a proponent of first-strike tactics who often disagreed with Emperor Karl
General Alexander Ritter von Krobatin	Austro-Hungarian minister of war, said to have wide experience in military affairs

Belgian

Name	Position/Significance
Baron de Brocqueville	Minister of war
General Gillain	A distinguished Belgian commander who received the Cross of the Legion of Honor from the French government
General Leman	Defender of Liège
General Rucquoy	Became commander in chief of the Belgian army after the death of General Wielmans

British and Colonials

Name	Position/Significance
General Sir Edmund Allenby	Led Palestinian campaign that crushed the Arabs
Admiral Sir David Beatty	Victor at Battle of Jutland; selected to receive surrender of German fleet on November 21, 1918
General Sir W. R. Birdwood	Called "the soul of Anzac"; leader in the Gallipoli campaign who later saw service in Belgium
General Botha	One of Britain's fiercest enemies during the Boer War, and among the first to volunteer his services at the outbreak of hostilities; became the premier of South Africa and the director of operations that won German East Africa for the Allies

Admiral Sir Cyrian Bridge	Present at the attack on Zeebrugge, a feat which has been called the "most daring adventure in naval history"
General Sir Julian Byng	Victor at Cambrai over German forces
Winston Churchill	Minister of War and Air Service, First Lord of the Admiralty
Admiral Sir Christopher Cradock	Went down with his vessel, the *Good Hope*, rather than desert
General Sir Arthur Currie	Commander of the Canadian forces in France
Admiral Sir John "Jacky" Fisher	Head of the British Admiralty at the beginning of the war, who later resigned into retirement over policy decisions
General Sir John French	Led the "honorable" retreat from Mons to the Marne
General (later Field Marshal) Douglas Haig	Commander in chief of the British forces in France
General Sir Ian Hamilton	1st Commander at Gallipoli
General H. S. Horne	Known for his pluck and decisiveness on the Western front
Admiral Sir Herbert B. Jackson	Assisted Allenby in the Palestinian campaign
Admiral Sir J. R. Jellicoe	Commanded the British fleet at the Battle of Jutland
Field Marshal Horatio Herbert Kitchener	British secretary of state for war; drowned when the *Hampshire,* on which he was sailing, was sunk by a mine on June 5, 1916
General Lawrence	In command under Sir Archibald Murray
General Sir W. R. Marshall	Concluded the Mesopotamian campaign in victory in 1918
General F. Stanley Maude	Had a victorious career in Mesopotamia that was terminated by his death in 1917
General Sir Frederick Maurice	British director of war operations until the spring of 1918; Maurice was removed from his command for not respecting the appointment of Foch as supreme Allied commander
General Sir John Monash	Australian commander present at Gallipoli
General Sir Archibald Murray	First commander of the 3rd Army in Egypt; later recalled and replaced by General Allenby
General Sir Herbert C. O. Plumer	Commanded the Army of Occupation at Cologne
General Sir Henry Rawlinson	Led American forces in Foch's counteroffensive
General Sir W. R. Robertson	British chief of staff
Vice Admiral Frederik Sturdee	Destroyed von Spee's German fleet in 1914
General Townshend	Was forced to surrender Kut-el-Amara to the Turks after a siege that nearly starved his men to death
Admiral Sir Reginald Tyrwhitt	Received the surrender of the German submarines
Lt. H. T. C. Walker	Naval hero of the British attack on Zeebrugge
Admiral Sir Rosslyn E. Wemyss	First sea lord of the admiralty; delegate at signing of the armistice
Sir Henry Wilson	A leading British staff member directing operations in France

French

Name	Position/Significance
General Henri Berthelot	Led the mission to Rumania in 1916
General D'Aumade	Fought with distinction in the early campaigns
General Debeney	Recaptured Roye in Foch's counteroffensive
General de Langle de Cary	Commanded at Verdun before Pétain assumed control
General Henri de Castelnau	Called the "Savior of Nancy," he commanded the French 2nd Army
General Franchet D'Esperey	Commander of the Balkan Armies that defeated the Bulgarians
General Dubail	Awarded the Grand Cross of the Legion of Honor for his services
General Fayolle	A hard fighter during the German Spring Offensive who refused to retreat beyond a certain point
General (later Marshal) Ferdinand Foch	Second leader of Allied armies, replacing Joffre
General Galleini	French minister of war whose mustering of the "Taxi Cab Brigade" very likely saved Paris from falling into the hands of the German Army
General Gouraud	"Lame Lion of Africa"; aided the Americans in Argonne fighting
General Humbert	Effective in the Picardy offensive in 1918
General Maud 'Huy	Commanded from Arras to the Aisne in 1914
General (later Marshal) Joseph Joffre	First leader of the Allied armies in France
General Charles Mangin	"Hero of the Marne" who withstood all the might of the German crown prince's army
General Manoury	"Hero of the Ourcq" in 1918
General Robert Nivelle	Commanded in the 1917 offensive on the Aisne
Lt. Colonel A. J. Paegelow	In charge of balloons
General (later Marshal) Henri Pétain	Rose from the rank of colonel to that of commander in chief of all the French armies in France by April 1917
General Sarrail	Commanded Allied forces in Greece
General Sordet	Commanded Cavalry Corps
Other French Leaders:	
General Belin	Said to be Joffre's right-hand man
General Galopin	
General Guacher	
Rear Admiral Lacaze	French minister of marine who was effective against enemy subs
General Pau	
General Pelletier	

German

Name	Position/Significance
Duke Albrecht	Of Wurttenberg; commanded forces on both Eastern and Western fronts

Admiral Hipper	Conducted negotiations with Sir David Beatty for the surrender of the German fleet, November 21, 1918
Prince Leopold	Of Bavaria, whose army had successes in both Russia and Eastern Europe
Count Paul Lettow-Vorbeck	Commander of German army in East Africa
General Erich Ludendorff	Chief quartermaster general and chief of staff the last two years of the war who, it has been suggested, was a better strategist and tactician than Hindenburg himself
Crown Prince Rupprecht	Of Bavaria—along with Prince Leopold, the shining star of royalty who wore military cloth; credited with battlefield successes that were remembered by Germans only too glad to rid themselves of other royal figures after the war was completed
Vice Admiral Scheer	Commanded the German fleet at the Battle of Jutland, May 31, 1916; appointed Imperial naval chief of staff, August, 1918
General Sixt von Arnim	Best known for his defeat in the fighting before Ypres, April 29, 1918
General von Below	Responsible for the Austro-German defeat of the Italians at Caporetto in 1917
Major General Hans von Beseler	Occupied Antwerp in 1914 and became military governor of Warsaw in 1915 (after Russians were driven out)
General von Bissing	Military governor of Belgium at the time of Edith Cavell's assassination
General von Boehn	Known as the "Organizer of Retreat" because of his ability in this area of operations
General von Bulow	Another distinguished commander on the Western Front whose historical destiny was decided by other military leaders, or rather by their actions (and in some cases, their lack of them)
Admiral von Capelle	German minister of marine at the time mutiny occurred in 1917; had succeeded von Tirpitz as chief of naval affairs after the latter's resignation over disagreements concerning his submarine warfare policy
General von der Goltz	Leader of turkish forces in Mesopotamian campaign at the time of the victory at Kut-el-Amara
General von Eichhorn	Another commander in the Ukrainian campaign; assassinated while pushing through Kiev in 1918
General von Einem	Fought against Foch in the latter's counteroffensive
General von Emmich	A fierce fighter, small in stature, whose army followed on the heels of the Belgium invasion
General Eric von Falkenhayn	At one time, chief of staff; later led the Austro-German armies in the Balkan campaigns
Baron von Freytag-Loringhoven	Quartermaster general under von Falkenhayn and later deputy chief of the general staff
General Max von Gallwitz	One of Crown Prince Wilhelm's divisional commanders
General von Groener	Commander in Ukrainian fighting and later replacement for Ludendorff as commander in chief after Ludendorff's resignation
General von Hausen	Led a German army in the war's first year
General von Heeringen	Involved prominently in the early fighting at the Marne and the Aisne
Field Marshal Paul von Benckendorff und von Hindenburg	Victor at Tannenburg and Mazurin Lakes; rose in command to control the entire German Army
General Max von Hoffman	Said to play at least a minor role in German victories in Russia
General von Hutoer	Inventor of the tactics named after him, which aided in the capture of Riga
General von Kathen	Commanded a German army in the Great Offensive of March 21, 1918
General von Kluck	Led the right wing of the German army, seeking to envelop Paris, at the beginning of the war—when the Schlieffen Plan was still considered feasible (Von Kluck's lack of initiative and some fierce fighting by the French did not permit him to come any closer to Paris than 22 miles from the city, at which point he was thrown back to the Aisne. It is reported that the expression "dumb Kluck" had its origin here.)
General von Mackensen	Began as a cavalry officer and gained distinction as an infantry commander in his victories in Russia and Rumania
Count Helmuth J. L. von Moltke	Chief of staff of the German army who, unlike his more famous father, had neither the nerves nor the tactical genius to prosecute a war, and was permitted to resign from his position soon after the war began
General von Quast	Became famous for his daring while fighting on the Flanders front
General Otto Liman von Sanders	German advisor to the Turks; later commanded the Turkish troops in Palestine that were defeated by the British
Admiral Count von Spee	Battled the British in the Falkland Islands and went down with his vessel, December 8, 1914
General Alexander von Stein	Prussian minister of war; entrusted with the preparation of military news for publication (military operations)

Grand Admiral von Tirpitz	Head of the German Admiralty; originator and advocate of unrestricted submarine warfare; later resigned
General H. K. von Winterfield	One of the envoys signing the armistice at Rethondes, France, on November 11, 1918
Crown Prince Wilhelm	Not much of a military man, as his inglorious career proved (His losses at Verdun are perhaps the most lamentable, as the kaiser continued sending him reinforcements rather than having him suffer a setback in the field and, more fearfully, in the eyes of the German people.)
Other German Commanders:	
General Lowenfeldt	
Marshal von Bergmann	
Admiral Henning von Holtzendorff	Imperial Navy's chief of staff until August, 1918
General von Kuhl	

Italian

Name	Position/Significance
Duke of Abruzzi	Commander of the largest fleet Italy had ever had on the Mediterranean
General Albricci	
Duke of Aosta	A man who served in various positions throughout the war
General Badoglio	Second in command to Diaz; present at the armistice
General Luigi Cadorna	First commander in chief of the Italian armies, whose reverses at Caporetto led to his being replaced
General Armando Diaz	Later commander in chief of the Italian Army who recorded numerous victories
General Porro	Chief of staff of the Italian army during the offensive against Austria
Admiral Thaon di Revel	Commander in chief of the Italian navy
General Zupelli	Italian minister of war as the successor to Alfieri in March, 1918

Russian

Name	Position/Significance
General M. V. Alexeieff	Appointed commander in chief of Russian armies April 15, 1917; resigned June 5, 1917
Commandant Bachkarova	Leader of the Women's Death Battalion
General Alexei Brusiloff	Led a series of battles with mixed results; was appointed commander in chief of the Russian armies June 5, 1917; resigned August 2, 1917
General Ratko Dmitrieff	Acknowledged as one of the leaders responsible for the capture of Przemysl
General Jilinsky	Chief of the Russian general staff
General Kaledine	Leader of the Don Cossaks and a determined foe of the Bolsheviks
Admiral Kolchak	Commander of the Black Sea fleet; later succeeded General Harvath as head of government at Omsk
General Kuropatkin	A loser in the war with Japan in 1905; appears to have acquitted himself somewhat better during the World War
Grand Duke Nicholas	Commander in chief of the Russian armies from the war's outbreak until replaced by the czar himself
General Rennenkampf	Led the invasion into East Prussia at the beginning of the war, where he met initial success, but was later repulsed
General Semenoff	Commanded an army acting in concert with the Allies against the Bolshevik forces
General Skoropadski	Became an ally of Germany after the signing of the Brest-Litovsk treaty
General Sukhomlinov	Russian minister of war who suffered severe reverses under the Bolshevik government, which discovered his governmental thievery
Other Russian Military Leaders:	
General Kondrotonitch	
General Russky	
General Shadorfsky	

Other Military Leaders

Origin/Name	Position/Significance
Boer	
General Beyers	
General Louis Botha	Fought for Britain
General Cronje	Fought for Britain
General De Wet	
General Kemp	Fought for Britain
General Smuts	Fought for Britain
Bulgarian	
General Yankoff	
Polish	
General Haller	
General Joseph Pilsudski	Commander in chief of the Polish armies; once escaped from German captivity
Portugese	
General Fernando	
General Garcia Rosado	Commander of the Portuguese troops in France in 1918
Rumanian	
General Averescu	Commander in chief of the Rumanian army
General Zottu	Chief of the Rumanian general staff in 1916
Serbian	
Marshal Putnik	
General Vassitch	Commander of 2nd Army
Turkish	
Enver Pascha	Turkish minister of war; an ally of the Central Powers

A Few Heroes

Captain Albert Ball (British). Had 44 victories between 1916 and 1917; was eventually shot down by a German infantryman hiding in a church tower.

Victor Chapman (American). First American to die in the air (June 17, 1916), which happened as a result of fighting five Fokker pilots simultaneously. Some suggest that Chapman fainted because of a previous head injury and crashed, rather than that he was actually shot down.

Major Raymond Collishaw (British). Leader of the famous Black Triplane flight in which 87 enemy planes were downed. Personally responsible for at least 60 kills, Collishaw fought against the Red Russian revolutionaries after the war, where he destroyed another 20 enemy planes. He also commanded a fighter group during World War II.

Major Christopher Draper (British). Both daring and reckless, Draper seemed only to fear being afraid and, consequently, gained a reputation for courting death.

Roland Garros (French). He is considered by many to have been the greatest French aviator.

Herman Göring (German). The famous Nazi of World War II fame, Göring was an ace given command of Richthofen's squadron after the latter's death.

Georges Guynemer (French). Arguably the best fighter pilot France produced, Guynemer, originally a mechanic, decided early that he wanted to be a flyer. Always a bit reckless and his behavior somewhat compulsive, Guynemer was at his best only when he had an enemy plane in his gun sights and he was attacking it in his favorite style: head-on. He was actually precise and well organized, but his enthusiasm and determination led to a few disagreements with superiors. Said to be fatalistic and extremely nervous the last few months of his life, Guynemer was last sighted flying into cloud cover after being hit by a German plane. The report of his death left sadness and disbelief; France had lost as determined a pilot as she was ever to see.

Dudley Hill (French). Another well-known pilot with the Lafayette Escadrille.

Major Raoul Lufberry (American). Born in France, Lufbery spent part of his youth in Connecticut. After serving in the U.S. Army during peacetime, he joined the Foreign Legion and then transferred to aviation. He lived long enough to shoot down 17 enemy planes.

Major McKelvie (British). A well-received English fighter pilot.

Jean Marie Navarre (French). A pilot with the kind of derring-do that led to his death: He died after the war while attempting to fly his plane through the Arc de Triomphe.

2nd Lieutenant William B. Rhodes-Moorehouse (British). Air hero who was first gunner of Air V.C. (Victoria Cross). After the bombing of Coutrai station, during which he was wounded, he decided to fly to headquarters to give his reconnaissance report rather than seek medical assistance beforehand; he died as a result.

W. J. Tampest (British). Shot down the dirigible L-31, which was carrying Germany's airship commander, Captain Heinrich Mathy.

Baron (Captain) Manfred von Richthofen (German). The "Red Baron," who scored over 80 hits, Richthofen was trained by famous pilot Oswald Boelcke after starting his war career as a cavalry officer and supply clerk. Transferring to the Aviation Service, the Red Baron quickly made his presence felt once he found himself under Boelcke's command and, after Boelcke's death in 1916, found the chance to prove himself. Known for his courageousness, Richthofen had taken his master's advice seriously and seldom took unnecessary chances. Finally brought down in what has become a matter of controversy, the Red Baron was accorded every respect, receiving over his casket a gun salute fired by the Australians who buried him.

Other Heroes

Major Paul Armengaud
Major Baracca
Lt. Reed Chambers
Colonel Halsey Dunwoody
Lt. Joseph Eastman
Captain James Meissner
Colonel T. D. Milling
General Mitchell
Lt. Thorne Taylor
Lt. Vosse

World War I Air-Related Details

World War I Airplane Aces

Country	Ace	Scores
Austria-Hungary	J. Arigi	32
	G. Brumowski	40
	B. Fiala	29
	J. Kiss	19
	F. Linke-Crawford	30
Belgium	Lt. Willy Coppens	37
	Adjutant Andre de Meulemeester	11
	2nd Lt. Edmund Thieffry	10
Britain	Captain Albert Ball	44
	Major William G. Barker	53
	Captain Anthony W. Beauchamp-Proctor	54
	Lt. Colonel William Bishop	72
	Lt. Colonel Raymond Collishaw	60
	Captain Phillip F. Fullard	46
	Captain Tom F. Hazell	41
	Captain J. Ira T. Jones	40
	Captain Robert A. Little	47
	Major Donald R. MacLaren	54
	Major Edward Mannock	73
	Major James T. B. McCudden	57
	Captain George E. H. McElroy	46
France	Lt. Jean Bourjade	28
	Lt. Maurice Boyau	35
	Lt. Michel Coiffard	34
	Captaine Albert Deullin	20
	Sous Lt. Rene Dorme	23
	Captaine Rene Paul Fonck	75
	Lt. Gabriel Guerin	23

French Women Volunteer Flyers
Mademoiselle Valentine Ducisg
Mademoiselle Marvingh
Mademoiselle Mathilde Moisant
Madame Niel

Country	Ace	Scores
	Captaine Georges Guynemer	53 or 54
	Sous Lt. Claude M. Haegelen	23
	Captaine Alfred Heurtaux	21
	Captaine Georges F. Madon	41
	Sous Lt. Pierre Marinovitch	22
	Lt. Charles Nungesser	45
	Captaine Armand Pinsard	27
Germany	Paul Baumer	43
	Hauptmann Rudolf Berthold	44
	Hauptmann Oswald Boelcke	40
	Leutnant Franz Buchner	40
	Leutnant Julius Buckler	35
	Leutnant Gustav Dorr	35
	Leutnant Heinrich Gontermann	39
	Leutnant Josef Jacobs	41
	Hauptmann Bruno Loerzer	41
	Oberleutnant Erich Loewenhardt	53
	Leutnant Karl Menckhoff	39
	Leutnant Max Muller	36
	Leutnant Fritz Rumey	45
	Oberleutnant Ernst Udet	62
	Oberleutnant Lothar von Richthofen	40
	Rittmeister Manfred von Richthofen ("Red Baron")	80
	Hauptmann Eduard von Schleich	35
	Leutnant Werner Voss	48
Italy	Baracca	34
	F. T. Baracchini	21
	M. Cerutti	17
	F. R. di Calabria	20
	P. R. Piccio	24
	F. Ranza	17
	S. Scaroni	26
Russia	A. A. Kazakov	17
Serbia	Sava Mikitch	?
United States	F. Gillette	20
	F. Hale	18
	A. Iaccaci	18
	Captain Field E. Kindley	12
	W. Lambert	22
	Major Reed G. Landis	10
	Major Raoul Lufbery	17
	2nd Lt. Frank Luke, Jr.	21
	J. Malone	20
	1st Lt. David E. Putnam	12
	Captain Edward V. Rickenbacker	26
	Captain Elliot W. Springs	12
	Captain Jacques Michael Swaab	10
	1st Lt. George A. Vaughn, Jr.	13

Types of Aircraft

Name	Description
B.E. 2C	British
Bristol Fighter	British
Bristol F 2B	British
Caproni CA 45	Italian bomber
D.H. 2	Royal Flying Corp's single-seater pusher biplane
F.E. 2B	Britain's first two-seater fighter
Fokker DR. 1	German triplane
Maurice Farman	French, reconnaissance
Morane Monoplane	French
Nieuport Scout	French
Sopwith F1 Camel	British fighting scout; destroyed more enemy aircraft than any other single type of allied plane
Spad 13	French, used by many of the Allies

Other Types of Aircraft

Albatros DI	Hansa-Brandenburg D.1
Albatros DII	H.F. 20
Albatros DIII	H-12
Antoinette Monoplane	Jasta 2
Aviatik	Jasta 5
Avro Trainer	Jasta 11
Bleriot Monoplane	Letord Three-Seater
Breguet 14. B2	M. 5K
Cody Biplane	Nieuport 17
D.H. 4	RNAS Seaplane
E. 1	S.E. 5
Fokker D. VI	Sopwith 1½ Strutter
Fokker D. VII	Sopwith Pup
Fokker DR. I	Taube Monoplane
Gotha Bomber	Voison Biplane
Gotha G IV	Wright Biplane
Handley Page 0/400	

Aircraft Numbers: Beginning of War and During Mobilization

Type	Number	Other Information
Austria		
Airplanes	350	All but 100 acquired at beginning of war
Dirigibles	8	Most less than 300 feet long
Belgium		
Airplanes	40	40 acquired at war's opening
Dirigibles	2	
Britain		
Airplanes	800	200 navy seaplanes 300 army planes 300 added during mobilization
France		
Airplanes	1200	500 added after mobilization
Dirigibles	31	12 about 400 feet long 14 less than 300 feet 5 privately owned
Germany		
Airplanes	600	400 added during mobilization
Dirigibles	35	12 zeppelins 23 other types
Russia		
Airplanes	800	150 added during mobilization
Dirigibles	16	16, most under 250 feet long
Serbia		
Airplanes	40	
Dirigibles	0	

Groups of Soldiers and Their Lands of Origin

Soldiers	Origin
Albanians	Albania
Annamites	Indochina (South)
Arabs	Arabia, and later, other areas
Armenians	Northeast Egypt
Australians	Australia
Austrians	Austria
Belgian Colonials	Belgian Congo
Belgians	Belgium
Bulgars	Bulgaria
Canadian Indians	Northern Canada
Canadians	Canada, general
Cossacks	Russia
English	England
French	France
Germans	Germany
Ghurkas	India (North)
Hungarians	Hungary
Italians	Italy
Japanese	Japan
Kalmuks	Northeast Africa
Kurda	Caucasus/South Russia
Madagascans	Madagascar
Maoris	New Zealand
Montenegrins	Montenegro
Moroccans	Morocco
Native South Africans	Southernmost Africa
Nigerians	Nigeria
Pathans	India
Poles	Poland
Portuguese	Portugal
Rumanians	Rumania
Russians	Russia
Senegalese	French West Africa
Sepoys	India (South)
Serbians	Serbia
Siberians	Siberia
Sikhs	India
Tonkinese	Indochina (North)
Turcos	Algeria
Turks	Turkey
West Africans	West Africa
West Indians	Jamaica

Unmentioned, but also to be included, are Americans from the United States, various groups with the Austro-Hungarian empire, various other colonial groups, and other nations that lent military assistance, if not troops (Brazil, Cuba, and others).

Part III: Postcards

Types and Categories

Type	Category
Advertising cards, various categories	R3–R5
Airplane aces:	
American	R2–R4
Austro-Hungarian	R4
Belgian	R4
British	R2–R3
French	R2–R4
German	R2–R3
Italian	R4
Russian	R5
Other	R5
Airplane crashes	R2–R3
Airplane encounters	R3–R4
Airplane-related, poster-type	R4–R5
Allegorical representations from mythology	R3
American Women's War Fund	R3
Armenian-related	R3–R4
Armistice-related	R2–R3
Armored trains	R3
Artillery-related cards	R2–R3
Attack on Zeebrugge	R3–R4
Bamforth song cards	R2
Battle cards	R2–R4
Beautiful women as symbols of patriotism	R3
Before/after cards of civilian/soldier	R1–R2
Before and after destruction of "pill boxes"	R2
Belgian atrocity-related	R3–R4
Belgian relief fund cards	R2
Bicycles	R3
"Big Bertha" (German monster cannon)	R3
Blue Cross cards (sold for Animal Medical Society)	R3
Bodies on the battlefield	
Bombing of civilian targets and locations	R2–R3
Bombs exploding	R2
Booklets of Louis Raemakers cartoons	R4
Other military booklets	R2–R4
Boxing and other non-war-related soldier activities	R2–R3
Boy Scout-related	R2–R3
Building bridges	R2
Building other fortifications	R2–R3
Camouflaged weapons	R2–R3
Cantonments (barracks) being erected	R1–R2
Captain Koenig and "Deutschland" cards	R3–R4
Captured spoils of war	R2–R3
Cardinal Mercier-related	R3–R4
Cards with a religious/battlefield allegorical scene or motif	R3–R5
Caricatures of Allies illustrating unity	R3
Caricatures of the Central Powers illustrating unity	R3–R4
Carrier pigeons	
Cavalry-related	R2–R3
Christmas cards:	
American	R2–R3
Austro-Hungarian	R3–R4
British	R2–R3
German	R3
All others	R3–R5
Commanders being awarded special honors	R2–R3

Concentration camps	R3–R4
Convoys of transports	R2–R3
Cutting wire entanglements that lead to enemy territory	R2–R3
Depictions of Allies and Central Powers on same card	R3–R4
Digging wells	R2–R3
Documents reproduced on postcards	R2–R3
Dog-related	R2–R3
Draft or draft board–related	R2–R3
Edith Cavell	
Woven silk	R4
Other	R2–R3
Embroidered silk cards, various categories	R2–R5
Executions	R4
Feeding the troops	R2
Field communications:	
Telegraph	R2
Telephone	R3
Other (including telegraph)	R3
Field hospitals	R3
Field kitchens	R2–R3
First American gun fired in war	R2
First American soldiers to die	R2
Flag-related	R1–R2
Flame throwers in action	R3
Foreign Legion–related	R4
Gargoyle-related	R2
"Gas" attacks	R2–R3
General Allenby in Jerusalem	R3–R4
German naval bombardment of land areas	R3
Other naval bombardments	R3–R4
German U-boat:	
In action	R3–R4
Interiors	R3
Stationary	R2
With crew	R3
Germany's Krupp works	R2–R3
Headquarters buildings	R1
Headquarters of commanders in the field	R2–R3
Hero-related	R3
Humorous training cards	R2
Important personages on inspection tours	R3
Installment cards:	
As a set	R5
Individually	R2
Japanese military operations	R4
Japanese patriotic cards	R4
Jewish Welfare Board cards	R3
Kitchener memorial cards	R2–R3
Knights of Columbus–related	R2–R3
Leaders who have both political and military power	R3–R4
League of Catholic Women–related	R3
Liberation-related cards	R3–R4
Lord Robert's memorial cards	R2–R3
Lusitania-related	R3–R4
Mail-related	R2–R3
Map cards	R3
Marine cards	R3–R4
Men in dugouts	R2–R3
Metamorphic cards	R4
Metamorphics	R3–R4
Military and national leaders visiting heroes' grave sites	R2–R3
Military and national leaders visiting hospitals	R2–R3
Military funerals	R3–R4
Military grave sites	R1–R2
Military insignia cards	R1–R3
Military leaders, formal or informal poses:	
American, real-photo or artist-drawn, major figures	R2–R4
American, all others	R3–R5
Austro-Hungarians, real-photo, major figures	R2–R3
Austro-Hungarians, real-photo, minor figures	R3–R4
Austro-Hungarians, artist-drawn, major figures	R2–R3
Austro-Hungarians, artist-drawn, minor figures	R3–R5
British, artist-drawn, major figures	R2–R3
British, artist-drawn, minor figures	R3–R4
British, real-photo, major figures	R2
British, real-photo, minor figures	R3
French, artist-drawn, major figures	R2–R3
French, artist-drawn, minor figures	R3–R4
French, real-photo, major figures	R2
French, real-photo, minor figures	R3
German, artist-drawn, major figures	R2–R3
German, artist-drawn, minor figures	R3–R4
German, real-photo, major figures	R2
German, real-photo, minor figures	R3
Russian, real-photo, major figures	R3
Russian, all others	R4–R5
All other countries	R3–R5
Military leaders, other scenics:	
American	R2–R4
Austro-Hungarian	R3–R5
British	R2–R3
French	R2–R4
German	R2–R4
Russian	R3–R5
All others	R3–R5
Military operations:	
In Eastern Europe	R3–R4
In Near East	R3–R4
Inside Russia	R3–R4
On Western Front	R2–R3
Military parades after the war	R2–R3
Military personnel on leave or furlough	R3
Military personnel with beautiful women	R2–R3
Military post offices	R4
Military reviews	R2–R3
Military vessels:	
In action	R3
Interiors	R2
Stationary	R1–R2
With crews	R2–R3
Mine- (to blow up sea vessels) related	R3
Miscellaneous cards:	
Celebrated posters	R3–R4
Destruction scenics	R1
Friendship between allies	R2–R3
Humorous cards making fun of various aspects of military life	R2–R3
Prepared messages	R2–R3
Remembrance cards	R2–R3
Romantic themes	R1–R3
Miscellaneous propaganda cards:	
American	R2–R3
British	R2–R3
French	R2–R3
German	R2–R3
Russian	R3–R5
All others	R3–R5
Montages of military leaders linked together	R3–R4
Motorcycle-related	R3
National Fund for Welsh Troops–related	R3
Newspaper headlines reproduced on postcards	R3
New Year's Day or other holiday cards, military-related	R2–R3
"No Man's Land" cards	R2–R3
Novelty types	
Mechanicals	R3–R5
Other novelty types	R3–R4
Nurses:	
As glamour girls	R3
In amorous situations with soldiers	R3
Tending the wounded	R2–R3

Observation balloons	R2
Observation posts	R2
Official cards for aiding the wounded	R2–R3
Official Soldier's Correspondence cards	R2–R4
Opening or dedicating war memorials after the war	R2–R4
Parades for departing soldiers	R3
Patriotic and sentimental types:	
American	R1–R2
Belgium	R3
British	R2
French	R1–R2
German	R2–R3
Italian	R3
All others	R3–R4
Payday-related	R2
Pilots in training	R3–R4
Planes being assembled or repaired	R4
Poem cards with military motif	R2
Quentin Roosevelt-related	R2–R3
Reconnaissance-related	R3
Recruitment-poster types	R3–R4
Red Cross cards:	
American	R2–R3
British	R2–R3
German	R2–R4
Swiss	R2–R4
All others	R3–R5
Refugee-related	R2
Regiments composed of Black soldiers	R3–R4
Ridicule of men not in uniform	R2
Royalty returning in triumph after the war	R3
Royal women as nurses	R2–R3
Salvation Army cards	R3
Scout and sentry cards	R2
"Scrap of Paper"–related	R2
Sergeant York- (Alvin C. York) related	R4
Ships' captains	R3–R4
Shipwrecks	R3
Silhouette types	R3
Smoke-pot-related	R3
Soldiers:	
Accoutrements (gas masks, rifles, grenades)	R2–R3
Acts of kindness to civilians	R2–R3
In basic training	R1–R2
Receiving medals and decorations	R3
Relaxing	R1–R3
Scaling mountains	R3
Special Christmas cards involving royalty	R3
Specially prepared cards with a place for photo of soldier	R3
Spy-related	R4
Superstition-related	R3
Supply ships with cargo	R2–R3
Surrender types	R3
Swiss Bundesfier cards	R3–R4
Tanks:	
American	R2
British	R2
French	R2–R3
German	R2
All others	R3
"The Whole Damn Family"	R2
Transporting wounded soldiers	R2
Trials	R3–R4
Unfavorable caricatures:	
Franz Joseph	R3–R4
Nicholas II	R3–R4
Wilhelm II	R2–R4
All others	R3–R5
Unknown Soldier–related	R2–R3
U.S. nurses arriving in England and France	R3
U.S. soldiers arriving in England	R3
U.S. soldiers arriving in France	R2
Various armies:	
In Russia during the Revolution	R4
Marching through open country	R1–R2
Marching through towns or cities	R2–R3
Various regiments:	
American	R2–R5
Austrian	R2–R3
British colonials	R2–R4
British regulars	R2–R3
French colonials	R3–R4
French regulars	R2–R3
Germans	R2–R3
All others	R3–R5
Views of training camps	R1–R2
Violation of Belgian neutrality	R2–R3
Violation of Luxembourg neutrality	R3–R4
Volunteers being inducted and outfitted	R1–R2
Wanton destruction of land by retreating armies	R1–R2
Wanton destruction of machinery by retreating armies	R2
War bond–related:	
Eastern European	R4–R5
Western European	R3
All others	R4–R5
War plants	R1–R2
War proclamations	R2–R3
Weekly Dispatch Tobacco Fund Campaign	R3
Welcome Home cards	R3
West Point–related	R2
Women civilians working for the war effort	R2–R3
Women in uniform:	
American	R3
British	R2–R3
German	R2–R3
All others	R3–R4
Woven silk cards of leaders (military and civilian)	R4
Y.M.C.A. cards used for correspondence	R2
Zeppelin-related	R3–R4

Sets and Series

It is hopefully demonstrated with this listing, which is in no way exhaustive, that the number of postcards published during, and relating to, World War I are at least equal in number to the total of all postcards produced for all other conflicts. The postcards of World War I make up an encompassing group that is historically informative, vastly interesting, and charged with messages for those attentive enough to decipher them.

Adolf Gohring. Published a numbered series of German military leaders. Other publishers to do series on German military leaders:

- ☆ Herman Wolff (#400 series)
- ☆ F. H. & S. (#100 series)
- ☆ Gerhard Stalling
- ☆ E. A. Seeman
- ☆ Gustav Liersch (with numbered royalty series)

A. E. Buck Private Marshall Semmelman. An army man, Semmelman privately produced a series titled *Overseas A. E. F.* (American Expeditionary Forces). These are comic cards that were hand-produced using yellow and white stock.

American Colortype Company. Published a series of colored view cards photographed by Underwood and Underwood, International Film Service, and Brown Brothers. Among the illustrations are pictures of early military vehicles, airplanes, submarines, and various army activities. Supposedly 36 cards in the series.

American Red Cross. Published a series of the Allied commanders, including the American commanders. Artist-drawn sketches are by J. F. Bouchor, the official French Army artist. Although most of the facial wrinkles have been removed and are replaced by alternate looks of leadership, persistence, and control, it is apparent that Bouchor added generous doses of realism to his paintings. This is a much-coveted set that is seldom totally assembled.

A. M. Simon. An American publisher who produced a series of photocards of Camp McClellan in Anniston, Alabama.

A. Noyer. This French firm produced many different kinds of war-related postcard material:

☆ A set of six artist-drawn (Xavier Sager) color cards—*Petites femmes pour poilus*—glamorous women identified with the war. As in other cards of this nature, the women are either pictured with some military accoutrement, in uniform, or with a soldier prominent on the cards. Series 43, #218–#223.

☆ An artist-drawn (Marcel Bloch) *Comique Militaire* series dealing with various Allied soldiers in situations of elation and humor.

☆ A set of six color artist-drawn (Xavier Sager) cards titled *Mode Amèricaine* (Series 126). Shown on these gorgeously painted cards are patriotic, romantic, and sentimental themes—glamor, women in uniform, soldiers with pretty women.

☆ Other sets by Xavier Sager with identical themes and similar illustrations:

La Guerre en Dentelles, series 36.
Attractions Parisiennes, series 127.
Drapeaux Alliès, series 66.
Proverbes Amèricains, series 84.

These cards are all actively sought by collectors and therefore infrequently offered for sale. The coloration, which seems to be both delicate and striking at the same time, is only one point of interest; also commending them is the artist, Xavier Sager, whose illustrations were classified even then as art, just as they are now. The business of finding various ways of linking beautiful women with the military in general or with war in particular isn't a new idea. One need look no further for evidence of this than the statuary residing in the world's museums. Sager is among the last in a long line of artisans promoting this identification of women and the military; the fact that this unison is neither wholesome nor valid does not detract from its beauty or appeal as an object of patriotism and allure.

Associated Newspapers, Ltd. A little-known British firm, Associated produced a series of numbered and lettered (for example, 9Y, 11A) photo-type cards of battlefield scenics and life at the front line of action. Cards number to 72 and are instructive, although not especially attractive.

A. Ternois. Published an artist-drawn series of sepia sketches (at least 24 sketches) about the effect of the war in Belgium. Shown are German atrocities, the German occupation of Belgium, kids playing tricks on German soldiers, altered family life as a result of the war, and the Occupation. Excellent social commentary. This set is most difficult to complete.

Bamforth. Produced several different card sets and series:

☆ Perhaps the best-known series of cards published by this firm is a group of song cards titled *It's a Long Way to Tipperary.* The numbered series includes sets #4742, #4781, #4787, #4788, and #4831, which contain four cards each. As with most Bamforth material, these cards are in color and contain elements of humor, sentiment, and patriotism in the pictures.

☆ Another song series is titled *Till the Boys Come Home* (three cards—#1, #2, #3); sentimental in nature; color. Views are of soldiers taking leave of their loved ones with appropriate song words.

☆ A song series (5053) titled *Friends Across the Sea* is about the Allies. Color; set of 3.

☆ *America's Mighty Army* is a sentimental, patriotic song series. Colored set of three cards (set 5063).

☆ In the numbered series (180–190s and 400s–500s) titled *Witty Comics,* many of the artist-drawn cards (color) depict British soldiers and sailors with their "ladies fair." The wording at the top of each card is sometimes a short poem or a literary quotation. As the title suggests, the cards are frequently comic in tone and nature.

☆ The set *Soldier Comics* was drawn by such artists as J. Collins, Joe Rankin, and Clare Ungel.

☆ An artist-drawn black-and-white numbered (#500s) set of cards feature unfavorable caricatures of Wilhelm II. Most, if not all, are humorous.

☆ Of the colored, artist-drawn set lampooning the German kaiser and the crown prince, at least four cards are known to exist. This set was reportedly aimed at America in an effort to enlist American aid in the war during the time before the United States declared war.

B & C. Published a *Savoy* series, which included some military themes in its offerings. The most famous ones show insets of Britain's wartime leaders (both civilian and military) in color. Overall, a nice group of cards.

Beagles. One of the most famous British publishers, J. Beagles was also involved with a number of military cards. Of special mention are a set of real photos of Britain's military leaders; photography is by Davidson Brothers. The various series include #100, #400, #600, and #1100.

Birn Brothers. Published a series *T* and a series *K* of colorful real-photo-inset cards displaying British leaders and territorial soldiers. Patriotic, poetic jingles appear at the bottom of each card. Also produced an #88 series.

Brunner & Company. Published a series of photographs of Italian leaders, military and civilian. On the front of each card is a photograph of the leader with a colored Italian flag at the bottom. Series 216. Difficult to acquire.

Bystander. Published a number of sets by artist Bruce Bairnsfather under the title *Fragments from France*; these sepia cards show life at the front in picturesque detail. Bairnsfather was in the trenches with the British soldiers and drew sketches of them showing their courage, dry wit, and persistence. All cards are at least nominally humorous. Nine sets of 6 cards were finally published and included two types: a standard print and a deluxe reproduction (higher price).

Chicago Daily News. Produced a series of cards that are also occasionally identified as *Kavanaugh War Postals.* The black-and-white photo-type cards are believed to number as high as 70. Reportedly, 16 of the cards were originally in envelopes priced at 25 cents. The envelope's reverse states that the newspaper gives "smokes" to the boys in France. The photographs should be credited to Underwood and Underwood and International News Service. The cards cover such diverse topics as life at camp, humorous military-occasioned activities, soldiers arriving or parading in France, infantry movements, weaponry, artillery action, trench activity, gas attacks, reconnaissance, wounded soldiers, prisoners, and other scenics.

Christoph Reisser's Sohne. An Austrian firm that published a beautifully colored artist-drawn (Bruch) set of cards on Austrian and German military leaders. Coloration is delicate on these stylized mini-paintings.

Cranford Press. Published a set of six cards dealing with the execution of nurse Edith Cavell. Cards are artist-drawn by T. Corbella. Scarce set.

C. T. American Art. This American publisher (Curt Teich) produced a *U.S. Army* series. These colored, photo-type cards illustrate many activities related to the military, including basic training, military bases, weapons, military units, and more. Also produced a *Cantonment* series dealing with similar themes. Rather bland, but certainly an educative series.

Curtice S. McCain. Published a numbered series (#100–#118) depicting different types of flowers that represent each of the Allies. A very picturesque set that also has flowered vignettes surrounding each card.

Daily Mail. Considered by some to be among the most thorough of sets dealing with the British army are the sepia real-photo cards published as *Official War Photographs* by British publisher Daily Mail. The numbered cards came in series of 8 and eventually ran into the hundreds. Even during wartime, their popularity was so great as to prompt the issuer to produce (in 1916) an album into which 240 could be placed. A few (including one of King Goerge at the Front) are in color. The real appeal for them was the fact that (even when the photographs were posed) these were viewed as authentic pictures of the boys at the Western Front as they went about their sometimes serious, sometimes humorous business of prosecuting the war to what everyone was certain would be a "winning" conclusion. It is little to be wondered why the Daily Mail postcards of World War I have such universal and enduring value.

Davidson Brothers. Produced an artist-drawn group of cards titled *Illustrated Song Series.* Artists include Tom Browne, Will Owen, and Dudley Harvey.

Dobson Molle & Company Ltd. Produced a *St. Clair* war series of artist-drawn cards for the British and colonial public. The ever-popular artist Larson Wood was one of those commissioned for this series. It may be recalled that Wood saw active service in the Royal Flying Corps, where he eventually received a decoration (from the French rather than the British). Sentimental and patriotic, these are the sorts of cards (scenes of brave, determined men; romantically inclined men; men with an overweening desire to preserve French honor) that France produced in abundance to a public who was, at least initially, captivated by pictures that didn't require the embellishment of language to transmit their messages. However, the sobering existence of trench warfare blunted their impact, and millions were discarded—one reason why so few survive today.

Fatherland Magazine. This magazine for Germans published a series of cards to commemorate the visit of the German merchant marine submarine *Deutschland* to America—a very popular event which involved the spirits and good will of the American people. Twelve cards.

Faulkner. Produced a #1476 series.

F. McG, Ltd. Produced a set of Correspondence Cards that were essentially song cards. *It's a Long Way to Tipperary* was the title of one set. The cards came in packets of 6 and the price per packet was one penny. With nothing more on the cards than the words of the song, the packet admonished the purchaser to "send these to your sailor and soldier friends."

Fordham and Company. Published a *Regal* series (4802) of British military leaders.

Gale and Polden. A well-known postcard producer during this time, G & P published one of the largest, if not best, sets of military cards, under the simple heading *History and Traditions.* The history and traditions referred to belonged to the British military. Authorized by the War Office (the only set so honored at the time), it shows every regiment of the British Army. The total set comprises 120 cards, and it is no small undertaking to assemble them all. Educative, historical, and highly recommended.

The German Red Cross. Produced at least four numbered series of colored, artist-drawn battle scenes and soldiers (and leaders). Descriptions are on the reverse. The cards themselves are titled *Official* cards.

G.G.W. II. Artist J. Jaunbers painted a masterful set of cards dealing with Austrian and Hungarian military leaders for this company, numbered in a #100 series.

Also produced a second set of Austrian and Hungarian military leaders that are sepia-toned photo-type cards.

Gilbert Post Card Company. A Chicago firm that produced a numbered set (1 through ??) related to war scenics, particularly from an American perspective. Card #8 shows General Pershing at the grave of Lafayette in France.

Gloria Vittoria. Published a numbered series of sepia-toned cards of both royal and military figures in Austria and Germany. Since most royal figures in these countries had strong military connections, it was common to be both royal and military at the same time. Many of these cards are rare.

G. Piprot. Produced a series (#300) of colored French sentimentals and patriotics.

G. Savigny. French producer who published a lightly colored series of artist-drawn sketches (F. MacKain) titled appropriately *Sketches of Tommy's life* and dealing with scenes and situations in the wartime life of the British soldier. These vignettes, humorous and occasionally ironic in nature, are thus some reflection of the French mind set regarding the war.

H. H. & Co. American firm that published a set of artist-drawn sketches of German military leaders. Considering that the United States was neither anti- nor pro-German at the war's outset, and that many American citizens were of German extraction, it is not surprising that a few cards favorable to the Central Powers were produced in the U.S. at an early date.

Illustrated Postal Card Company. Produced a numbered series (#1368) depicting soldiers with girls, leaving home, and making friends. These are artist-drawn cards by the popular illustrator Archie Gunn. At least 6 cards (could be 12).

Other sets by the Illustrated Postal Card Company:

- ☆ 1364: similar to series 1368; patriotic, sentimental, romantic; six cards.
- ☆ 1366: Navy rather than Army, but similar to the above.
- ☆ 1371: similar to the above.
- ☆ Series of U.S. battleships.

Inter Art Company. Published several different sets and series:

- ☆ #828–#833: set of artist-drawn cards (A. A. Nash) dealing with the Allies; humorously patriotic in tone; children are central figures.
- ☆ #209–#220: a separate set similar to the above—patriotic and sentimental, child figures.
- ☆ #2300: series similar to the above.
- ☆ Patriotic series of artist-drawn (Fred Spurgin among others) cards about Britain's "Tommy." Depicted are his exploits, equipment, surroundings, and perceptions of military reality, often with a touch of humor.
- ☆ At least two separately numbered series (#1600 and #2300) titled *Comique.* Artist-drawn (some by Donald McGill), frequently humorous, and displaying wartime conditions both at home and at the front.
- ☆ An artist-drawn (Arthur Butcher) *United Six Series* showing human representations of each of the Allies; at least six cards in this unnumbered set.
- ☆ A *British* series and a *Bulldog* series.

Of the following sets, some are published under the *Comique* title; all are artist-drawn:

- ☆ #1104–#1109
- ☆ #1256–#1261
- ☆ #1669–#1674
- ☆ #1901–#196
- ☆ #2101–#2106
- ☆ #2485–#2490

James Henderson. Very similar to the Vivian Mansell series (see Vivian Mansell). Hard to find.

Jarrold & Sons. Among the most eagerly collected of all World War I postcards are the *Punch* cartoon sketches drawn by artists L. Raven-Hill and Bernard Partridge. The drawings range from illustrations of British troops in action to unfavorable caricatures of the kaiser and Franz Joseph and other sorts of anti-German sketches and pictures whose purposes are clearly propaganda. Reproduced on light yellowish stock, the drawings are dark brown. Among the phrases at the bottom of each sketch are the following: *Take Courage, My Brave Germans. Your Kaiser Is Prepared to Sacrifice a Million of You*; (Wilhelm II) *What Is This Distant Rumbling That I Hear? Doubtless the Plaudits of My People*; (under the drawing of a German soldier brandishing a gun over the bodies of a murdered woman and child) *The Triumph of "Culture."* A most intriguing, if somewhat biased, set of cards by this British publisher, they were originally offered in packets of 12.

Joseph Piludski. Produced a seldom-seen set of cards about the Polish army; rare.

J.P. French publisher who produced a numbered set (#94–99) portraying French army uniforms; artist-drawn (by Edy).

J. Salmon. Produced a numbered set of colored cards dealing with British regimental badges. Nice group, detail-oriented.

J.S.M. & Co. Produced a set of artist-drawn color cards on both Austrian and German royalty.

Lawrence & Jellicoe. Produced a humorous set of artist-drawn cards titled *Told to the Marines* (British marines). Each of the cards has a colored illustration and one of the following lines:

The Admiral Told a Story
The Ward Room Approved It
The Gun Room Adorned It
The Petty Officer's Mess Expanded It
The Lower Deck Elaborated It
The Marines Swallowed It

L.L. (Levy Fils Cie). Produced many series, including *Areas After Bombardment by Germany; Battle Views; Victory March Through Paris;* and others. L.L.'s material ranges from real-photo cards to sepia prints. This most prolific of all French publishers presented the war from various perspectives, all accurate and straightforward.

McLagan & Cumming. This Scottish publisher produced a numbered set of six artist-drawn color cards whose purpose was "To Assist Soldiers Disabled and Invalided at the Front." These cards were produced for the Lowland Regiments Badge Day (June 19, 1915) and show various uniformed regimental soldiers. A beautiful set.

Meissner & Buch. Published a #2100 series of German and Austrian military leaders.

Merval Corporation. This American company produced a set of 20 artist-drawn cards that are primarily patriotic in nature. Inside the periphery of stars are illustrations depicting Uncle Sam, soldiers displaying bravery, women maintaining the home front, unity scenics, nursing scenes, wistful scenes, and others. A dated, attention-getting set featuring propaganda in its purest form at a time when the term *naïve* had less meaning.

Millar & Lang. Produced a numbered series of artist-drawn (Glanville) comic cards about various aspects of military life and military personnel.

Also produced a *National Series* of patriotic and sentimentals including some of the *Hands Across the Sea* types.

M. Munk. Viennese publisher; produced a set of cards on Austria's military leaders. A cameo of each leader is superimposed on a sword that runs the length of the card's left side; a poem is on the right. These numbered cards have *1041* printed on them and are in color.

Musée de L'Armée (Museum of the Army). Produced a numbered series consisting of black-and-white pictures of war-related items. The main concentration seems to be on captured enemy equipment, armaments, and means of transportation (tanks, airplanes, and so on). A highly recommended set that combines history and visual imagery of the engines and wherewithal that made war both possible and frightening.

Nash. Published a set of six patriotic song cards with accompanying scenics. Songs include "Star Spangled Banner," "Yankee Doodle," "America," "Columbia," "Battle Hymn of the Republic," and "Flag of the Free." Cards are in color and are embossed; not rare, but certainly desirable.

National Catholic War Council of the United States. Produced a little-known series of black-and-white cards, the sale proceeds of which were devoted to war children in France.

New Haven Illustrating Company. Published a set of sketched caricatures unfavorable to Kaiser Wilhelm II.

Offizielle Karate Fur: Rotes Kruez. German Red Cross cards; numbered (#1 to ??), artist-drawn, and in color; depicting various armies and activities. Green border and green printing on reverse.

Philco Publishing Company. Published a *Patriotic Series* set of cards similar to the Millar and Lang *National Series* and including patriotics and sentimentals that have a decidedly strong flavor of old-style romanticism in their makeup.

Photochrom. This British publisher produced many sets and series of military postcards:

- ☆ A 48-card set titled *On Active Service*, one of the most popular. All cards have an orangish-colored border. Cards depict weapons, machines, soldiers at the front, royalty visiting the troops, army commanders, soldiers in action, naval vessels in action, various regiments, and more. A highly illustrative set.
- ☆ A numbered series titled *Britain Prepared.* Colored cards show weapons, ships, and military personnel. Pictures either depict a state of readiness, or they serve as helpful, informative material.
- ☆ An excellent series identified with the words *On Active Service by Air, Land, and Sea.* Cards depict Britian's multifaceted military and include the various branches and the activities in which they engaged, as well as their vehicles, armaments, and weaponry. Like their many other offerings, these cards aptly demonstrate how the war appeared to those closest to it, the military personnel.
- ☆ *Camp Silhouette* series of the shadows or silhouettes of British soldiers engaged in both military and nonmilitary activities. Ever present is the humor of any given situation, although it must be admitted that the views often have an added element to ensure a laugh from the card's recipient. For example, a card titled *The Flying Corps* illustrates a group of airmen silhouettes fleeing from a horde of attacking bees. All cards are numbered and signed with a G.E.S.
- ☆ A numbered series similar to *Camp Silhouette,* titled *American Silhouette Series.* This group, which seems to number to at least 40, is cut from the same cloth as the *Camp Silhouette* cards, meaning the humor ranges from unobtrusive to outrageous, but is always understandable.
- ☆ A set of six artist-drawn (Algernon Black) cards of airplanes either in action or in flight. An educational group of colored cards.
- ☆ A *Red, White and Blue* series.

Pictorial Newspaper Co. Canadian company; demonstrated that quality material could also be produced by "colonials." At least two sets of cards were identified as *The Daily Mirror Canadian Official Series.* The first group consisted of real photos of people and battle areas, and scenics. Without being gruesome, these numbered specimens managed nonetheless to illustrate many aspects of the war. Not least was the determination and sense of camaraderie World War I fostered among people who might otherwise have never come to know one another. The second series appears to be very much the same types, if not the same cards, as in the first group, two differences being that the latter group is sepia and unnumbered. An interesting series of cards, many seem to focus on the human element or to otherwise inject it.

Pictorial News Company. Produced a souvenir folder containing 20 view cards of "Uncle Sam's Army in Training." Scenes in black-and-white; the U.S. flag in color to the left and right.

P. J. Gallais et Cie. This French publisher produced artistic sketches (Frain) demonstrating German atrocities, French bravery, and French sacrifice. The effect of German insensitivity is clearly depicted.

P. Schneider. Published a set titled *At the Front.* At least ten cards are reported to exist.

Raffaelli. Published various artist-drawn cartoon types relating to life in the British navy and to naval activities generally. Gervese was the artist used in this numbered set.

Raphael Tuck. This fine British publisher is without doubt the premier producer of World War I postcards.

☆ One artist-drawn (Sancha) set uses Aesop's *Fables* allegorically; various characters are portrayed as Germans (foxes, dogs, wolves, birds) in negative situations. Titles include
The Tortoise and the Eagle
The Hen That Laid the Golden Egg
The Hare and the Tortoise
The Wolf and the Stork
The Dog and the Shadow
The Fox and the Grapes

☆ #115 A set of colored cards dealing with World War I aircraft.

☆ #116 This set is an addendum to the above and shows the planes in action. Artist is G. T. Clarkson.

☆ #3100 A set of six cards drawn by Harry Payne that depicts military engagements by British troops, 1916–1917; also some prisoner-related.

☆ #3101 Six cards of airplanes.

☆ #3105 Harry Payne–drawn cards dealing with mainly pre–World War I battles (one exception is a card on the Battle of Maine). Six cards.

☆ #3160 A series of six Oilette cards titled *Colonial Badges and Their Wearers* (Canada, Australia, New Zealand, Newfoundland, South Africa). Artist is Harry Payne.

☆ #3163 Another Oilette series of six artist-drawn cards titled *Our Fighting Regiments.*

☆ #3165 An Oilette series similar to the above and titled *Our Fighting Regiments.* Six Cards.

☆ #4309, #4310, #4314 Three sets of six cards each relating to types of Allied armies. Russian Infantry, French regulars and colonials, Belgian Infantry, and Australian armies are among those depicted.

☆ #4318 Six cards of various front-line scenics. Artillery, infantry, parades, and even the King are among those subjects depicted.

☆ #4319 Cards on the Indian Contingent of the British Army; six cards.

☆ #4339 Photogravure series of six cards titled *At the Front.*

☆ #4340 Six-card continuation of #4339.

☆ #7312 Set of six cards on Aix-la-Chappelle.

☆ #8400 Beautifully colored set titled *Regimental Badges and Their Wearers.*

☆ #8600 Set of artist-drawn colored cards of English troops, colonial troops, and England's allies.

☆ #8700 Set of six cards related to the Allies, territorial regiments, and more; Oilette; six cards.

☆ #8721-22-23-36-37-41, #8811 Sets and series showing portraits of war notables (Kitchener, John French, Lord Roberts, and others) along with other types.

☆ #8729 An Oilette series of six Allied flag cards.

☆ #8733 Set of six cards about various Indian colonials who constitute the Indian/British army.

☆ #8735 Set of six artist-drawn (B. G. Baker) cards dealing with Britain's allies in action scenics (French, Russian, Belgian, and so forth).

☆ #8744 Series titled *Fighting Regiments.* Six cards; Oilette.

☆ #8754 Set of six cards dealing with General Joffre and others; Oilette.

☆ #8756 An artist-drawn set of cards titled *History in the Making.* Artist is F. Gribble; Oilette.

☆ #8799 Six cards drawn by F. E. M. The set is captioned *An Air Raid.*

☆ #8800 Similar to #8600.

☆ #8818 Set of six cards dealing with vehicles and artillery at the front.

☆ #8818 As above, but includes telegraph corps, infantry, and field kitchens as well as artillery.

☆ #8821 Six cards dealing with the medical corps. Depicted are medical personnel giving service in various ways to the wounded.

☆ #8822 Set of six cards related to the Italian army and its various troops. Artist is A. Pearse.

☆ #8842 Set of six cards dealing with various actions and also prisoners.

☆ #9080 An Oilette set of six naval-related cards.

☆ #9100 A set titled *The Rise of Our Empire Beyond the Seas*; artist-drawn color scenics of Britain's former glory days and her conquests.

☆ #9120 A set titled *Military Life—The Volunteers*; Oilette.

☆ #9162 An Oilette series on the Royal Welsh Fusiliers.

☆ #9200 A beautiful color set showing acts of heroism and titled *How We Won the Victoria Cross.*

☆ #9425 A set titled *The Royal Horse Artillery.*

☆ #9495 A set of airship cards.

☆ #9857 A set of Oilette cards on airplanes and airships. Six cards.

☆ #9883 A set of artist-drawn (Harry Payne) cards titled *The Queen's Own Cameron Highlanders.* Six cards.

☆ #9900 A set on territorial regiments.

☆ #9998 Another colorful set of airship cards.

Raphael Tuck miscellaneous sets:

#990	#8743
#4320	#8743
#4332	#8750
#4333	#8811
#4484	#8831
#8491	#8871
#8666	#9237
#8736	#9300
#8737	#9367
#8741	#9400

- ☆ Series #3105 and #8744: Oilettes of fighting regiments. Six cards to each set.
- ☆ Series #8831: An Oilette on First Royal Dragoons.
- ☆ Series #8666 and #8669: Two Oilette series on the French army.
- ☆ Series #8750: An Oilette on French Zouaves; six cards.
- ☆ Series #9367: An Oilette on Fifth Royal Irish Lancers; six cards.

It should not go unmentioned in reference to the cards of Raphael Tuck that the above-mentioned sets are not all the World War I cards of this firm; neither was this listing intended to be authoritative nor exhaustive. Most Tuck sets are in groups of 6 and most are colored. The photogravure series, which are not in color, are still very well executed and avidly collected. Not all of their sets are equally well done, but all are both historically informative and detail-oriented.

Rotary. Like Beagles, Rotary published a series (#1–#100) of real photos on military leaders of Britain. Both of these series (see "Beagles" entry as well) are well worth viewing and collecting as views of leaders in a war that is too little discussed.

Sackett & Wilhelms. Published two series of cards on different topics. Series #12 is on U.S. Aviation and series #24 is on U.S. recruits in training. The latter set includes postcards on weapons, training, and life at camp. Numbered cards; printed photos; sets are believed to number more than 20 in #24, with less in series #12.

Stengel & Company. Produced a set of portrait cards of German generals in its first 49,000 series (sepia). Beautifully and artistically rendered; an elusive set to collect in total.

Times Press (Bombay, India). This publisher produced what is arguably one of the scarcer sets of World War I postcards. Partly artist-drawn and partly printed phototypes, this series of unnumbered cards was given away by women of the Bombay branch as Christmas presents to the soldiers, probably for mailing to their friends and family in England or the colonies. Each card's salutation, "With Best Wishes for Xmas and the New Year," is printed in red on the card's cream-white background. To the left is a sketch of a British soldier in the parade-rest position, while an ovaled inset reveals a printed phototype of landmarks or people native to the Near Eastern area. Completing the montage are crossed Union Jacks above the inset.

Underwood & Underwood. Produced several sets of war-related cards:

- ☆ Either produced or coproduced a set with the International News Service. The numbered, colored cards dealt with the reality of World War I from several perspectives. Although the focus is almost totally military, the pictures themselves are obviously for the edification of the "folks back home" and are therefore ever so slightly censored in terms of portrayals. Pictures to be seen among the 48 cards composing the set are the damage of German guns and bombs; Allied army types; colonial types; normal routines, including eating and resting; leaders with their men; miscellaneous destruction scenics; soldiers on their way to the action; the wounded being ministered to; and even the Germans variously depicted. As accurate as most such types, these cards are priceless for their social comments, wealth of detail, and historical interest. Although not complete in how they picture the war's reality, they are to be commended for their inclusiveness. Highly recommended. (On the reverse of each card is one of two designations: *W. C. A. 145* or *W. C. A. 146*.)
- ☆ A numbered #100 series of sepia cards showing scenes of life at camp and of life in the field. An interesting, worthwhile group of postcards.
- ☆ An unnumbered, colored set of cards of a patriotic nature, illustrating various camp scenes; also, individual and group photos of military personnel demonstrating the army as prepared and willing to fight for liberty and justice. Each card has an American flag in the upper left-hand corner.
- ☆ Other sets and series were produced in conjunction with other publishers.

Visé. Published a beautifully colored numbered set of French commanders.

Vivian Mansel. This British firm published a series of artist-drawn cards of beautiful women's heads as representative of the Allies (except for Italy, which is depicted by the head of a young man wearing a plumed hat). Seldom seen and vigorously collected cards.

W. A. Keller Company. Published a series of unretouched news photos of the war. Little is known about these cards, which came from the photographs of Underwood and Underwood and are said to depict various aspects of the war.

W. H. Smith & Company. Published a "Kingsway Real Photo" series of British military leaders.

Y.M.C.A. Hut Fund. Like their American counterparts, the British Y.M.C.A.'s sought to lend assistance to their countries' soldiers and sailors. Many of these cards are legitimate pieces of the war and include a variety of themes. Total number of cards in the series is 312.

Anonymous. The following sets and series are by anonymous publishers. Origin is indicated if known.

- ☆ American. For a narrower view of the war, this publisher focuses on the occurrences of one naval vessel during a specified period of time. The six artist-drawn cards in this *Armed Guard Series* were titled "Ayres, U.S.N. 1918," and must be defined as humorous in nature. An interesting set.

☆ American. Produced a numbered (#2274) set of ten designs called *Flags of Victory.* Each colored flag is on a white background and is accompanied on the card by a patriotic or sentimental poem.

☆ British. Produced a six-card set on the sinking of the *Lusitania.* The set is reportedly a strong series of visual statements about this German atrocity.

☆ Czechoslovakian. Published a very rare set of artist-drawn, poster-type cards aimed at increasing recruitment among Czechs living in America. At least 15 cards; a magnificent set. Patriotic symbolism and military motifs are used to resounding effect.

☆ French. Offered a series of at least 14 cards titled *The Allies in the Orient.* These black-and-white cards dealt with the Oriental army and navy.

☆ French. Stated by many collectors to be the premier World War I set are a series of artist-drawn cards by French painter Emile Dupuis. His sketches of "heads" are painstakingly rendered. Each head represents a type of soldier from both Allied armies and those of the Central Powers. The three series (*Nos Allies, Nos Poilus,* and *Leurs Caboches*) are caricatures, and more than caricatures; sketches, and more than sketches; art, and all of art. Not only are the uniforms accurately displayed, but the demeanors, the very essence of the individual types appear to have been captured and immortalized by Dupuis's brush strokes. Whether it's a jaunty smile, forbearance, resignation, ennui, or determination, he seems to know each subject well; his artistry lets us know them, also.

☆ German. Produced a lettered and numbered set (F90s through at least F112) of artist-drawn (H. Heusser) cards concerned with German and Austrian naval vessels in action against the Allies. There are scenes of naval battles and of fleets from Germany and Austria bombarding Allied land positions. Although these are clearly propaganda pieces, they are nonetheless scarce historic representations of little-recorded events.

☆ German. Produced a set of six phototype cards related to German victories in Belgium in 1914, August–October.

☆ German. Produced a series titled *Children in Uniform.* Drawn by such artists as Diehl, Engelhardt, and Dondorf, these cards strike at the very core of both patriotism and propaganda, blurring the distinction between the two. Small children are seen imitating the warlike behavior of their adult counterparts as they parade about in their resplendent military attire replete with spiked helmets. Originally used for purposes of instilling pride, the cards exist as telling comments on the real nature of war.

☆ German. Produced a set of at least five cards that show a German soldier taking leave of his wife for his duties.

☆ German. Published a set of artist-drawn cards (A. Frohlich) of German and Austrian military leaders.

☆ Russian. Offered a set of artist-drawn cards that look to be wooden or mechanical soldiers going about their duties as ordered by an officer in charge. This may be an unfavorable representation of the German and Austrian soldier blindly following all orders from his superiors. In some situations, the normal order seems to be reversed (saluting with the left hand) while in others the soldiers are just bumbling incompetents. Whether viewed as propaganda or merely from a humorous perspective, it is obvious that this is a very rare set of postcards.

☆ Russian. Offered for sale at least two numbered sets (one with normal, black printed figures and another using green print) of artist sketches unfavorably portraying Kaiser Wilhelm II. The background is a very light brown. All Russian cards relating to World War I are at the least scarce; artist-drawn caricatures are rare and seldom seen.

☆ Russian (presumably the Russian government). Like the other Allies, Russia attempted to raise funds for the prosecution of the war through the sale of war bonds. One such set is particularly striking. Each of the unnumbered artist-drawn specimens is a colored illustration directly referring to the conflict. Cards are either battle types that show attacking soldiers or troops firing from behind barricades, or they illustrate Russian unity and symbols of Russian pride. This is a quite rare set of poster-type postcards.

☆ Unknown. Produced a set of artist-drawn color cards of Russian military types.

☆ Unknown. Produced a set of black-and-white artist-drawn (Forrest) cards, which are comic depictions of the American army overseas. At least nine in the set.

☆ Unknown. Produced a series of at least 15 black-and-white views of the American camp at St. Nazaire, France.

☆ Unknown. Copublished for English, American, and Japanese purchasers. The cards show scenes of the Allied armies in Siberia during the Russian revolution. These cards came in a packet containing the words *Memorial Post Cards of Victorious Allied Military Developments in Siberia.* Writing is also in Japanese. Black-and-white pictures depict arrivals of various armies (French, American, Japanese) in Vladivostok, the Imperial Japanese Navy, insets of various Allied commanders, Czechoslovakian troops and victims, cards dealing with the Bolsheviks, and others. A very nice set to own, but somewhat difficult to acquire.

☆ Unknown. Presented the world with what is undoubtedly the best series of British commanders printed during the conflict. Titled *Generals of the British Army,* these artist-drawn sketches are true-to-life representations of the men they portray. The creased uniforms, timeworn faces, and semi-relaxed poses all combine to create the impression that reality was artist Francis Dodd's ultimate goal. With these exquisite and lightly colored renditions, it is obvious that he succeeded. It is worthy of note that the cards were reproduced in at least one other language (Spanish), if not more than one. The printed information at the bottom of the cards increases their historical value. An identical set by the same artist is titled *Admirals of the British Navy.*

☆ Unknown. Produced a set of cards (#1031) devoted to Red Cross nurses. Each artist-drawn nurse represents an Allied country (France, Belgium, Russia, and others).

☆ Unknown. Produced a series (#558) called *Flags of the Allies.* A total of six colored cards.

☆ Unknown. Published a set of at least six artist-drawn cards on German generals. Excellent sketches.

☆ Unknown. Published a set of six cards showing the destruction of a zeppelin in six stages. Cards are numbered.

Publishers

Name	Origin
A	
A. Adlington	British
A. & C. Black	British
A. & G. Taylor	British
A. B. & Co.	Austrian
Abraham & Sons	British
A. Christensen	French
Acme Publishing Co.	British
Adolf Gohring	German
A. H. Katz	French
A. Hoffman	German
Albert Fink	German
Albertype	American
Alexander Manufacturing Co.	American
A. L. Hoste	French
Alpha	British
A. M. Davis	British
American Colortype	American
American News Co.	American
American Red Cross	American
A. M. Simon	American
Anglo Eastern Publishing Co.	British
A. Noyer	French
Art & Humor Co.	American
Art & Humorous Publishing Co.	British
Artistic Novelty Manufacturing Co.	American
A. T.	French
A. Ternois	French
A. Traldi	Italian
August Scherl	German
A. U. H. Brunotte	German
A. V. et M.	Belgian
B	
Ballerini and Fratini	Italian
Bamforth	British
B & C	British
Bardell	
Barty Publishing Co.	British
Batchelder Brothers	British
Baudiniere	French
Bayer	German
Bering	German
Birn Brothers	British
Bohlgemuth & Lissner	German
Boot's Cash Chemist Ltd.	British
Brown & Calder	British
Brunner & Co.	Italian
The Bystander	British
C	
C. A. Maschke	German
Cairo Postcard Trust	Egyptian
C. & A. G. Lewis	British
Carl A. E. Schmidt	German
Castle Studios	British
Caterham Fancy Stores	British
C. Cozens	British
C. D.	Belgian
Central Art Gallery	British
C. G. Roder	German
Ch. Fontane	
Chicago Daily News	American
City Postcard Company	British
Commercial Colortype	American
Committee on Public Information	
Coquemer	French
Corte-Scope Company	
C. Pietsch	Austrian
Cranford Press	
C. T. American Art	American
D	
Daily Mirror	British
Daily Sketch	British
David Allen & Sons	British
Davidson Brothers	British
Davis, Allen & Sons	British
Delta Fine Art Company	British
Detroit Publishing Co.	American
Dobson Molle & Co.	British
Doring & Huning	German
Dr. Eysler & Co.	German
Dr. S. & Co.	German
Dr. Trenkler Co.	German
E	
E. A. Seeman	German
East London Printing Company	British
E. C. Kropp	American
E. Deffrene	French
E. F. A.	
E. J. Hey & Company	British
E. Le Deley	French
Elizabeth Banks	British
E. Mack	British
E. Milner	British
Em Thill	
The English Pharmacy, Khartoum	Egyptian
E. P. & Co.	German
F	
F. A. Brockhaus	German
Fatherland Magazine	American, but about Germany
F. Braun	French
F. Bruckmamm	German
F. Buchmann	German
Feige & Parreyss	Austrian
F. G. O. Stuart	British
F. H. & S.	German
F. H. Leslie, Ltd.	American
Fine Arts Publishing Co.	British
Fischer and Uninger	German
F. Ladendorf	German
Flag of Peace Co.	American
F. McG. Ltd.	
Fordham & Co.	British
Franz Huld	American

Frederick Garnett	British
Friends of the Army Museum	French
F. W. Woolworth	British
G	
Gale & Polden	British
G. Cailliau	Belgian
Gebruber Dietrich	German
Gehard Stalling	German
George Faulkner & Sons	British
G. G. W. II	Austrian
Gilbert Post Card Company	American
Gloria-Vittoria	German
G. Pipbot	French
G. Pirot	French
G. Pulman & Sons Ltd.	British
G. Sagigny	
G. Stalling	German
Guggenheim	
Gustav Liersch	German
G. W. Jones	British
H	
H. & C. H.	British
Hannaford & Nasser	American
Harold H. Camburn	British
Harris Bros. Co.	Cuban
H. C. Dollison	American
Hemine	French
Henry Heininger	American
Hermes Druckerel	Austrian
H. H. Co.	American
H. H. I. W.	Austria
H. Rathjen	German
H. T. Cook	
Hugo J. Thiede	American
Husnik & Hausler	Hungarian
Hutson Brothers	British
H. W. Speyer	
I	
I. & M. Ottenheimer	
I. F. S.	American
I. Lapina	French
Illustrated Post Card & Novelty	American
Imberg and Lefson	German
Imperial War Museum	British
Inter-Art Company	British
Italian Aeronautical Command	Italian
J	
J. A. Goossens	Belgian
James Henderson	British
Jane & Gentry	British
Jarrold & Sons	British
J. Ashworth	British
Jay Em Jay	
J. B. Hoffman	American
J. Cussac	French
J. Deil	Austrian
J. Mat.	Belgian
J. M. P.	American
John Paddington	British
Jones Sewing Machines	British
Josef Eberle	German
Joseph Clarkson	British
J. Salmon	British
J. S. M. & Co.	German
Judges, Ltd.	British
Jullien Brothers	

K	
Karl Harbauer	German
K. B. & Co.	German
Kilophot	Austrian
Knackstedt & Co.	German
Kriegskarten Verlag	American, meaning "War Card Publishing"
L	
L. & P.	German
Laureys	French
Lawrence & Jellicoe	British
L. Dobrecourt	Belgian
Life Publishing Co.	American
L. L. (Levy Fils et Cie)	French
Louis Kaufman & Sons	American
M	
Marcus Munk	Austrian
Marshall Semmelman	American
Max Ettlinger & Co.	
Max Rigot Selling Company	American
May & Co.	British
McLagan & Cumming	British
Meissner & Buch	
Merval Corporation	American
Millar & Lang	British
M. L. M.	German
M. M. & F.	Belgian
M. M. S.	Austrian
M. Pikowsky	Russian
M. Schulz	Prague, still Austrian
N	
NAPCo	
Nash	
Neurdein Frères	French
New Haven Illustrating Company	American
Newspaper Illustrations, Ltd.	British
Niedersedlitz	German
Nodher	German
Noever & Co.	German
Nossi-Lespinne	French
N. P. G.	German
O	
Odhams	British
The Official War Committee	American
O. K. Liga	Austrian
Ostdick	
Ottmar Zieher	German
Otto Elsner	German
P	
Pacific Novelty Co.	American
Palmer Publishing Co.	American
Paul Vondrann	German
Peter Luhn	German
Philco Publishing Company	British
Phillip Rubel	Austrian
Photo Roto	
Photochemie	German
Photochrome	British
Pictorial News Company	British
P. J. Gallois et Cie	French
Postal Card & Novelty Company	British
R	
Radermacher, Aldous & Co., Ltd.	British
Raffailli	
R. & K. L.	German
Raphael Tuck	British

Publishers, cont.

Real Photos	British
Red Cross	Various countries under different designations
Regent Publishing Co.	British
Reinthal & Newman	American
Reynolds & Branson, Ltd.	British
Rood Brothers	
Rossi-Lespinne	French
Rotary	British
Rotophot	German
R. Sennecke	German
S	
Sackett and Wilhelms Corporation	American
Samuels Ltd.	British
Schrader-Kellogg Co.	
Scopes and Co.	British
Sevampez	French
S. Gold	U.S. naval station photographer, Great Lakes
Shamrock and Company	
S. H. & Co.	British
S. I. P.	French
S. K. Simon	American
Smith Brothers	British
Solomon Brothers	British
South African Garrison Institutes	South African
Souvenir Post Card Co.	American
Stengel & Co.	German
Stephen Cribb	British
Stevens and Grant	British
S. V. D.	
T	
T. & G. Allan	British
Tichnor Brothers	
Tilley & Son	British
Times Press	Indian
Trau & Schwab	German
U	
Underwood and Underwood	American
U.S. Signal Corps	American
V	
Valentine	British
Vaugirard	French
Visé	French
Vivian Mansell	British
V. K. K. W.	German
V. O. Hammond Publishing Co.	American
von Christoph Reisser's Sohne	Austrian
von Walter Müller	German
W	
Wallace	American
W. & D. Downey	British
The War Cartoon Studios	British
War Photogravure Publications	British
Wayne Paper Box & Printing	
W. E. Hardison	Hungarian
W. H. Bechtel	American
W. H. Smith & Co.	British
Wildt & Kray	British
Wilhelm Hannemann	German
Wirth & Co.	
W. N. Sharpe	British
Woodland Card Co.	British
Woolstone Brothers	British
Y	
Y.M.C.A. Hut Fund	British
Z	
Zerreis & Co.	German

Artists

This list is included to help acquaint both novice and seasoned postcard collectors with some of the artists who were plying their trade during the World War I years. To stop with this enumeration, however, would be to do a disservice to the handful of artists whose work continues to attract the attention and interest of ongoing generations. With that thought in mind, the following are given only as brief profiles of the particular artists mentioned—real appreciation comes from viewing the artists' offerings with a practiced eye. An alphabetical listing of postcard artists follows.

Bruce Bairnsfather. Few caricaturists have been able to stir the public imagination as much as Bruce Bairnsfather. An Englishman with a penchant for the type of wry humor identified with the British, Bairnsfather was in an excellent location to observe and record the war firsthand—in a trench. As he was a captain in the British army, his drawings about life for the British soldier, while humorous, contained generous amounts of underlying reality. For example, his "Old Bill" creation in the *Fragments from France* series dealt mainly with how the English "Tommy" experienced the war. These sepia sketches poked fun at everything from life in the mud and never-ending shell barrages to inherently humorous everyday situations faced by soldiers in the war. Of course, it was always easier to appreciate the humor more after the war than during it.

The various Bairnsfather sketches portray old soldiers and young, the discomfort of both cold weather and hot, before- and after-attack scenics, and more; all are accompanied by the pithy, wry remark or explanation. Captain Bruce knew his subjects well and, through his incomparable art, passed the information along to all who viewed his cards.

Howard Chandler Christy. Known primarily for his paintings of beautiful American girls, Howard Christy deserves special mention because of his recruiting posters, which were reprinted on postcards. His full-color illustrations utilized the sort of gorgeous women who came to be known as "Christy girls." Among the better known is a card that pictures a smiling young lady in naval uniform, with the exclamation, "Gee!! I wish I were a Man, I'd Join the Navy." A similar postcard shows a woman in Marine Corps garb and the comment "If You Want To Fight, Join the Marines." Both examples have been reproduced on modern cards and posters. Other popular Christy offerings include "Fight or Buy Bonds" and "American All." The reproduction of these cards points to the enduring appeal and esteem held for one of America's premier artists. It is to be regretted, on the one hand, that Christy's earlier work (including sketches of the Spanish-American War, in which he was commissioned as scene illustrator) was not placed on postcards; on the other hand, it is to be appreciated that the collecting public has such material as is available from the pen of so exceptional an illustrator.

Archie Gunn. A Britisher transplanted to America at the age of 25, Archie Gunn was early inclined to a career in art. Working for both individuals and magazines, Gunn also drew sketches for postcard publishers, including the Illustrated Postal Card Company and the National Art Company. His World War I offerings included patriotics and sentimentals relating to both America and America and her allies. One of the very popular sets is a group of 12 cards depicting a soldier in various stages of his military life. A true romantic at heart, Gunn filled his military drawings with images of unity, wistfulness, camaraderie, and occasionally a lovely woman either dominant on the card or decorating the background to heighten the overall effect.

Donald McGill. Unable to join the ranks of the military during World War I because of an amputated foot, English cartoonist Donald McGill used his considerable talent for the war effort nonetheless. McGill occasionally used caricatures of chubby-cheeked children in military uniforms to make his observations regarding different aspects of the war: little boys with expanded chests in military attire; sentimental cards of boys waving goodbye to their little-girl sweethearts; comic situations linking children with the war. In fact, humor was McGill's strong suit, and he used it often to striking effect. His colored cartoon drawings varied, depicting sometimes the drudgery, sometimes the ridiculousness of military life; British soldiers outwitting their German counterparts, frequently to the latter's discomfort; and themes designed to instill patriotism and increase the enlistment ranks as well.

McGill had neither the subtlety nor the deeper and ultimate understandings of World War I that Raemakers possessed, but he did share the Dutchman's desire to see the war end with honor and with as little loss of life as possible. His humor was pointed, but always in the right direction and at the right target.

Harry Payne. For the British—and many others as well—the sight of a Harry Payne–drawn postcard is an exercise in wonder and delight. Although some of Payne's work is pre–World War I (and all of it eagerly sought), he will always be best remembered for his many colorful paintings commissioned during the first world conflict—of regiments, action scenics, heros, and individual types of soldiers within the British Empire. Two of his most popular series, *Colonial Badges and Their Wearers* and *Defenders of the Empire*, were, like most of his artistic efforts, produced under the aegis of the well-known postcard publisher Raphael Tuck and Sons. From the looks of determination and commitment on the faces of his subjects to his exactness of detail in weaponry and uniforms, Payne's renditions are justifiably and proudly displayed by their owners.

Louis Raemakers. Popular sketch artist Louis Raemakers was a native Dutchman who went in 1916 to reside in England, where he drew his timeless masterpieces. The decades since have seen these masterpieces rise to the level of universal and always-accurate social comment. As long as history texts continue to factually describe the occurrences of World War I, Raemaker's art will continue to punctuate and illustrate the language with vitality and panache. His lightly colored sketches often choose as their principal figures the leaders of the Central Powers carrying on their callous routine with relish and great dispatch, and without remorse or regret.

There is Kaiser Wilhelm II standing on a pile of bodies, examining the territory he acquired through the death of his soldiers, and looking for even more territory as he peers ahead; Wilhelm as a savage, replete with a leopard-skin cloth and club in hand, preparing to bludgeon the helpless form of a subdued female, who represents Belgium; and then Emperor Franz Joseph and Wilhelm plotting together for ways to painfully and completely crush their enemies.

Raemakers was equally adept at displaying the consequences of their behavior: One might see a picture of the kaiser being slowly squeezed beneath the "hydraulic press" of public opinion because of his unrestricted submarine warfare policy; or the kaiser in wolf's clothing with the bleeding "sheep" of Serbia, Belgium, and Luxembourg at his feet as weapon-bearing citizens from around the world approach him; or a sketch of a semiconscious Franz Joseph being alternately pummeled by an Italian and a Frenchman.

Raemakers' caricatures are allegory in its highest form, approaching the pinnacle of enlightenment and reflecting the widest range of understanding possible. Each scenic is different, yet somehow the same; each lesson repeatedly inculcated, but never tiresome. Raemakers' mastery of the sketch pad and drawing pencil could only be possible as part of a mind and eye capable of seeing and reasoning with clarity. More than mere artist, Louis Raemakers produced sketches which are the stuff of prophecy. They are eternally valid statements about what the modern world is pleased to call "the human condition." It is not to be wondered why such a man is remembered or respected.

Other Artists. Among the others whose names must be included are the noted American illustrator Norman Rockwell, who painted some fascinating posters, including *Fatherless Children of France* and a Knights of Columbus–produced soldier's greeting. Cartoonist Mabel Lucie Atwell, with her drawings of cute children reacting to the war with impatience, chagrin, determination, and overall humor, did much to contribute to our understanding of the social impact of war. Glamour artist Phillip Boileau gave the world a vision of beauty (beautiful women) which, although somewhat incongruous with war's destruction and ugliness, was a welcome respite to both soldiers and civilians. Emile Dupuis's colored series *Heads* presented various of the Allies so lifelike and exacting in detail as almost to defy description.

All these artists have furnished posterity a multiplicity of views that are less disparate than they are enlightening. Whether through humor, gruesomeness, or romanticism, they were all united in sending the messages that defined war in terms of the human element, and in so doing, they reminded us that war is the most single-minded, absorbing, and final of all human activities.

Artists

Name	Origin
A	
A. E.	British
G. D. Amour*	British
A. R. Dutch	
Arlent	French
William Armitage	British
William Armstrong	British
Raoul Arus	French
Mabel Lucie Atwell*	British
Joyce Averell	British
B	
Bruce Bairnsfather*	British
René Barbier*	French
W. Barribal*	British
Bartos	
A. Bastien*	French
Baumgarten	German
C. Becker	British
P. A. Becker	
Albert Beerts	French
Benesch*	
Bergen	German
Berndsen	Dutch
Bertiglia*	Italian
S. E. Beurmann	German
Albert Bianchi	Italian
J. L. Biggar	British
Algernon Black	British
Marcel Bloch	French
Hans Bohrdt	German
Phillip Boileau*	American
Luigi Bompard	Italian
Borgoni	Italian
Boschini	Italian
J. F. Bouchor	
M. Boulanger	French
F. M. Brendt	
E. C. Brinsley	British
O. Brush*	German
Herbert Bryant	British
Fred Buchanan	British
Burger	
E. Burnand	
Adolfo Busi	Italian
Dudley Buston	British
Arthur Butcher	British
C	
C. B. German	
C. K. Austrian	
Canivet	
H. Canivet	British
Capello	French
Ouillon Carrere	French
Carrey	
Reg Carter	British
T. Cartiel	French
J. R. Cattley	British
Chabaud	
J. Charmer	French
G. F. Christie*	British
Howard Christy*	American
G. T. Clarkson	British
Haskell Coffin	American
J. Collins	
E. Colombo	French
Pierre Comba	French
Corbella*	French
T. Corbella	Italian
Hilda Cowham	British
M. Crete	
Cyrus Cuneo	
D	
H. Delalian	French
Walter de Maris	
Dhuzmer	French
Carl Diehl	
M. Zeno Diemer	
Dinah	British
Diveky	
Francis Dodd*	British
Dohnalek	
B. Dondorf	
d'Ostoya	French
Drieux	
Emile Dupuis*	French
E	
Harold Earnshaw	British
Kay Edmunds	
Edy	French
P. O. Englehardt*	German
Archibald English	British
Erlich	
F	
F. Fabiano	
Fahringer	German
Fasche*	German
R. Feld	German
Fercham	
Alice Luella Fidler	American
U. Finozzi	Italian
Otto Flechiner	German
Folexondy	
Leo Fontan*	French
C. Fouqueray	
B. V. Francken*	German
Frohloch*	German
R. Fuchs	German
G	
Gabard	French
Gassner	
Genni	Italian
W. Georgi	
H. Gervese	French
G. E. S.	
T. Gilson	British
Godia	
V. Goland	
Gordon Grant	
Bernard Gribble	British
Grimes	
Archie Gunn	British

H

Dudley Hardy*	British
John Hassell	British
Hassenkamp	German
Georges Henri Hautot*	French
Dora Heckel	German
P. Henn	
Herouard	French
Hesse	German
H. H. American	
Hirlemann	
A. Hoffer	French
Hoffman	German
L. Hohlwein	German
F. Hollart	Hungarian
E. A. Holloway*	British
Honer	
Hornert	
Mary Horsfall	British
H. Huesser	German
Hal Hurst	American

I

Ernest Ibbotson	British
Ibels	

J

A. Jarach	
A. P. Jarry	French
J. Jaunbersin	Austrian
Fr. Jung*	German

K

J. Kalous	
Kargl	
A. H. Karlinsky	
Kaskeline	German
S. Kircher	Austrian
Raphael Kirchner*	Austrian
Klaber	Austrian
R. Klein	German
Ludwig Koch	German
W. Kossaka	Polish
R. Krause	
William Krause*	German
Kraus-Wichmann	German
Kristen	
F. Kudherna	Austrian

L

H. Landgrebe	German
Hans Larwin	Austrian
Lassar	
Lenhard	
Lenz	German
Leonnec	French
G. Leonnec	
Leroy	
Lienz	Austrian
Ludgate*	British

M

F. Mackain*	British
Harry A. Maden	British
Mailik*	German
Marienrux	French
G. Marr	Austrian
Marussig	Austrian
Armand Massonet	French
Mastroianni	Italian
Reg Maurice*	British
A. Mauzan*	Italian
Donald McGill	British
J. McNeill	British
I. Mermagen	German
G. Mescine	Italian
G. Metz	
Suzanne Meunier	French
R. C. Miller	British
Maurice Milliere*	French
Maggy Monier	
Willy Moralt	German
J. Morgan*	American
E. Muller	

N

G. Nanni	Italian
A. A. Nash*	British
Henry Newbolt	British
F. Nockher	German
G. Nogel	
Robert Nosak	Austrian
E. H. Nunes	German

O

F. O'Beirne	
Ostoya*	
Will Owen*	British

P

Paco	
Bernard Partridge	
Emil Pastien	
Arthur Payne*	British
Harry Payne*	British (Brother of Arthur)
A. Pearse*	British
L. Peltier	
A. Penot*	French
Maurice Pepin	
Poulbot*	French
Lyman Powell	British

R

Max Rabes	
M. Radiguet	
Louis Raemakers*	Dutch
Ramberg	German
Joe Rankin	
Ranzenhofer	Austrian
Rappini	Italian
L. Raven-Hill*	British
L. Ravenny	
R. B. L. German	
Regamey	French
Frederic Regamez	
Otto Renatus*	German
Fred Reynolds	British
Federico Ribas	
Right	British
Robinson	American
Norman Rockwell*	American
Roessler	
Ryan	

S

E. Sachetti	
Xavier Sager*	French
A. F. Sancha*	British
Tito Saubidet	
L. Sch.	Austrian
Ed. Schicki	Austrian
F. Schiegel	German
Schneider	
Curt Schulz	German

Hans Rudolf Schulze	German
Schwarz	German
Georges Scott	French
G. E. Shepheard	British
Sherie	
E. F. Skinner	British
Slimgo*	Belgian
Howard Smith	American
Snyder	American
Fred Spurgin*	British
Franz Stassen	
Stewart	British
Stockwell	American
W. Stower	German
George Studdy*	British
T	
Jean Tam	
Louis Tauzin	French
Arnold Taylor	British
Douglas Tempest	British
A. Terzi	(Italian)
J. Thiriar	
Bert Thomas*	British
A. Torello	
H. Torggler	
Maurice Toussaint	French
Treiber	German
C. H. Twelvetrees*	British
U	
Clare Ungel	British
Usabal*	German

V	
Piet Van der Hem	
F. Vecchi	Italian
Ventura	
René Vincent	
Vlcek	Hungarian
Hugo Voigt	German
R. Von Wichera	German
W	
Louis Wain*	British
Bernhardt Wall*	British
Weiss	German
Wennerberg*	German
W. W. Werestchaguine	
Flora White	British
L. Wilbur	
K. A. Wilke	Austrian
Oscar Wilson*	British
Witenski	
Witt*	American
Larson Wood*	British
Richard Caton-Woodville*	British
Y	
Hayward "Jotter" Young	British
Z	
H. Zahl	German
Th. Zahne	German
E. Mazzoni Zarini	Italian
K. Zinn	German

**most popular*

Prince Heinrich of Germany with von Hindenburg. N.P.G. R3

Wilhelm II pursued by Russian bear. Anonymous. R3

Prince Freidrich of Austria. B. K. W. I. (Brüder Kohn). R3

"With God for the Fatherland." Wilhelm II and six sons. N.P.G. R3

Prince von Holstein of Germany with his regiment; special cancellation. Anonymous. R4

German Prince Heinrich (Admiral). H. H. R3

Unflattering caricature of the Central Powers leadership. Russian card. Anonymous. R4

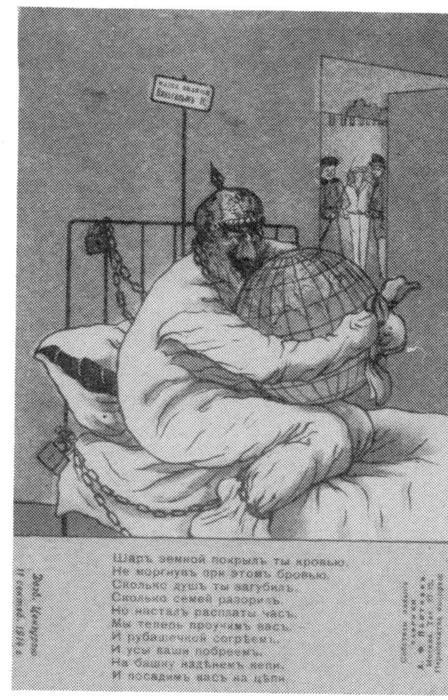

Wilhelm II as a chained lunatic clutching a globe of the world. Russian. Anonymous. R4

Unflattering caricature of Central Powers leadership. This one could be titled "Alexander's Ragtime Band." Russian card. Anonymous. R4

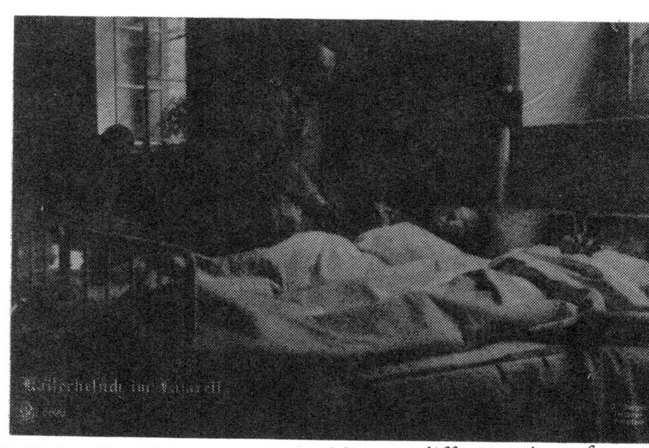

Wilhelm II visiting wounded soldiers; a different view of an unpredictable man. N.P.G. R3

Abbas Pasha Hilmi, Khedive of Egypt who opposed the Allies. Rotary. R3

Yoshihito, Emperor of Japan. Rotary. R3

"Two against Seven; Franz Joseph and Wilhelm II against Allies." Gustav Liersch. R4

Germany and Austria forging Central Powers unity. Von Knackstedt & Company. R3

British field marshal Earl Roberts. Beagles. R2

Earl Roberts; special handwritten message about Roberts' death and other war activities. Rademacher, Aldous & Company. R5

Leaders of Central Powers, 1916. N.P.G. R4

Field Marshal Roberts with his titles printed at the bottom. W. H. Smith & Sons. R2

German patriotic with appropriate symbols. Anonymous. R3

An overt German patriotic card. Anonymous. R2

Count of Dohna-Schlodien and officers. R4

Unveiling of war memorial in 1924. Anonymous. R4

Wilhelm II with six sons and son-in-law. N.P.G. R3

Wilhelm II inspecting a regiment. N.P.G. R3

Austria's prince Eugen. Ö.k. Liga. R3

General Linsingen. M. Munk. R3

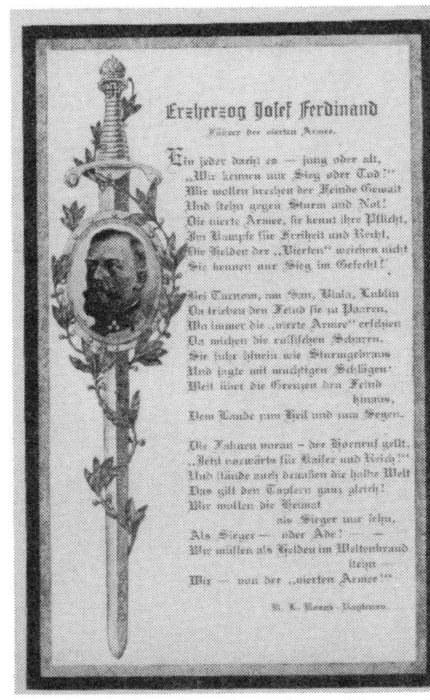

Austria's prince Ferdinand. M. Munk. R3

Wilhelm II with von Hindenburg. Red Cross card. R3

Austria's prince Eugen. Von Christoph Reisser's Sons. R3

Von Moltke, first German chief of staff at war's beginning. N.P.G. R3

German kaiser with crown prince and other notables. N.P.G. R4

German kaiser examining torpedo plant. Finka. R4

Artillery General von Scholtz. Anonymous. R3

War Minister von Falkenhayn (Austria). Gustav Liersch. R3

Von Raben, conquerer of Mora, Africa. N.P.G. R4

"General Congreve—Generals of the British Army." Anonymous. R2

"General Byng—Generals of the British Army." Anonymous. R2

"General Plumer—Generals of the British Army." Anonymous. R2

"Commander Paine—Admirals of the British Navy." Anonymous. R2

"Admiral Burney—Admirals of the British Navy." Anonymous. R2

"Admiral Halsey—Admirals of the British Navy." Anonymous. R2

"Admiral Napier—Admirals of the British Navy." Anonymous. R2

Prussian prince Adalbert, German naval officer. Gustav Liersch. R4

Prince Friedrich Leopold's son. N.P.G. R3

Kaiser with Red Cross nurses. N.P.G. R4

Wilhelm II with his general staff. N.P.G. R3

Montage of German and Austrian military leaders. W. R. B. & Company. R3

Caricature of Bismarck being thwarted. Punch *series; Jarrold and Sons, #7. R3*

Wilhelm II with von Plettenberg and von Friedeburg. Gustav Liersch. R3

British general Sir Charles Douglas. Fordham & Company Ltd. R3

Wilhelm II with von Hötzendorff. N.P.G. R4

Von Hötzendorff studying a map of Europe. M. M. S. R3

Austrian field marshal von Hötzendorff with Prince Friedrich and von Hindenburg. Anonymous. R4

German kaiser with his generals. Finke. R4

General Castelnau in 1919 Paris victory parade. E.L.D. R3

Wilhelm II with Generals Häseler and von der Goltz. Gustav Liersch. R4

Captain Koenig, commander of Deutschland. The Fatherland *magazine. R3*

General Wille with the general staff. G. Metz. R3

Marshal Foch. Musée de l'Armée (Museum of the Army). R2

Wilhelm II with von Mackensen. N.P.G. R4

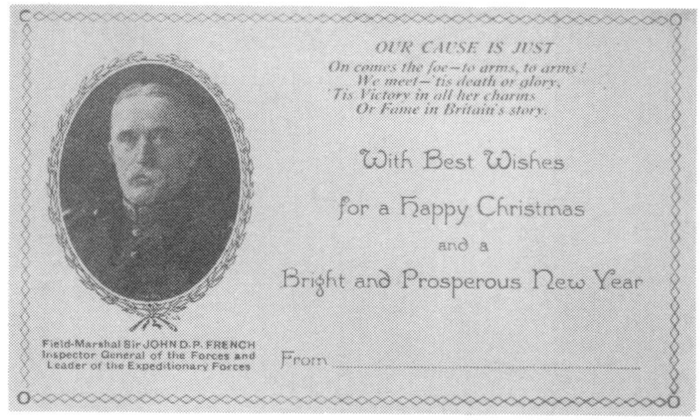

Christmas card with inset of General French. Anonymous. R2

German kaiser with King Ferdinand of Bulgaria. N.P.G. R4

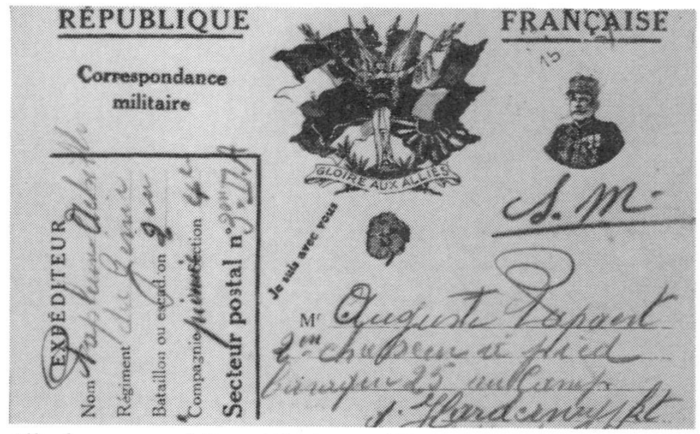

Allied war postal for soldier's use. R3

Marshal Foch portrait by Bouchor. American Red Cross. R2

General French, first commander of England's Expeditionary Corps. Underwood and Underwood. R2

Memorial card for Lord Kitchener. Anonymous. R2

The kaiser and his six sons. N.P.G. ***R3***

"Men of the Moment: Lord Kitchener." Valentine's Series. ***R2***

Postcard printed in memory of Lord Kitchener. Anonymous. ***R2***

General Foch and King Albert of Belgium. P. Houstraas. ***R3***

"The Sphinx Smiles—Lord Kitchener." Stephen Cribb. ***R3***

Von Hindenburg with the Kaiser. N.P.G. ***R4***

Von Hindenburg; facsimile signature. Anonymous. ***R4***

Von Hindenburg in Napoleonic pose. Wirth & Company. ***R3***

King of Italy and war leaders. *Anonymous.* R4

King of Italy (Victor Emmanuel III) with political and military leaders. Anonymous. R4

Wilhelm II with von Below. N.P.G. R4

Von Hindenburg with his staff on the Eastern Front. Gustav Liersch. R4

Von Hindenburg in conversation. E.A.S. R4

King George V reviewing Canadians at the Front. Daily Mirror *series. Pictorial Newspaper Company.* R2

George V at Ypres. Marco Marcovici. R3

French colonel Raynal, defender of Fort Vaux. Anonymous. R3

Wilhelm II deluding himself. Punch *series; Jarrold and Sons, #8. R3*

The kaiser foolishly exhorting his troops. Punch *series; Jarrold and Sons, #1. R3*

Germany's top military commanders (kaiser, von Hindenburg, and others). Gustav Liersch. R4

Kaiser with Admiral von Köster and Prince Heinrich. N.P.G. R4

General von Mackensen. Stengel and Company. R3

Von Mackensen and Prince Friedrich in Carpathian campaign. N.P.G. R4

The soldier-king, Albert I of Belgium. Anonymous. R3

Sketches of Tommy's life. *Visé; #7. R2*

Sketches of Tommy's life. *Visé; #8. R2*

Albert I of Belgium. J. Mat. R3

German captain Meyer-Waldech, governor of Kiautschow, China. N.P.G. R4

Meyer-Waldech, governor of Kiautschow, A.R. & C.I.B. R4

Austro-German unity. P. Vondrann. R3

Vice admiral Sir David Beatty, Commander of the 1st Squadron (Cruisers) of the British navy. Underwood and Underwood. R2

British admiral Lord Charles Beresford. Rotary. R2

German-Austrian unity propaganda. M. M. S. R3

King Albert at the Front. M. M. & F. R3

Unflattering caricature of Wilhelm II. A. U. & F. M. R3

British admiral Jellicoe. Russell and Sons. R2

Britain's Admiral Sir John Jellicoe, a man of controversy. Beagles. R2

U.S. Army and Navy injuring the kaiser. Anonymous. R3

British general Sir Smith-Dorrien. Fordham & Company. R2

French General Leman, heroic defender at Liége. Anonymous. R3

"Insulting caricature of Wilhelm II saying Degenerate German." Italian publisher. R4

Marshal Joffre manhandling Wilhelm II and Franz Joseph, obviously an early issue. Visé. R3

Marshal Joffre, Bouchor portrait. American Red Cross. R2

General Joffre. Anonymous. R2

Russian card caricaturing German kaiser. Anonymous. R4

Field Marshal Sir Douglas Haig. Beagles. R2

Franz Joseph in prayer. J. Deil. R3

Kaiser getting the boot. Russian card. Anonymous. R4

Douglas Haig with General Pershing and other officers. Anonymous. R4

Joffre, Haig, and Sir Pertab Singh. Daily Mail Series VII; #49. R2

"Funeral of 'The Unknown Warrior.'" Beagles. R3

Wilhelm II "before and after." Russian card. Anonymous. R4

Prince Leopold entering Warsaw after capturing it August 9, 1915. Anonymous. R4

Russian Czar reviewing his troops. Underwood and Underwood; W.C.A. 145 series, #22. R3

"Czar Samples Food of Russian Soldiers." Underwood and Underwood; W. C. A. 145 series, #21. R3

A message from the kaiser to the German people. Rotophot. R2

Franz Joseph. N.P.G. R2

Prince Leopold of Bavaria. N.P.G. R3

Franz Joseph and Wilhelm II beaten and abused. Russian card. Anonymous. R4

A fake Wilhelm II indicating that Russia will soon be his. Russian card. R4

Field Marshal von Haeseler, World War I's oldest general. Anonymous. R3

General von Krobatin, first Austro-Hungarian minister of war. Anonymous. R3

Franz Joseph handling his paperwork. Anonymous. R3

Franz Joseph in Hungarian royal attire. Official card for Red Cross. R3

British general Ian Hamilton. Beagles. R2

Ian Hamilton in stilted pose. Fordham & Company. R2

King and crown prince of Bavaria displaying unity. N.P.G. R3

Crown Prince Rupprecht of Bavaria with other generals. Wilhelm Wissman. R4

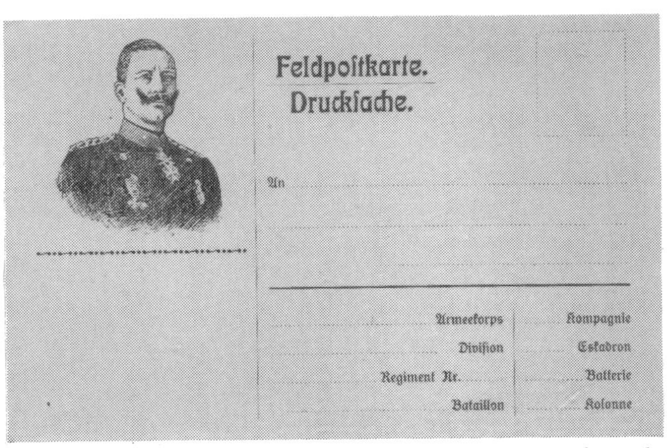

A special soldier's correspondence card; inside is a song from the Franco-Prussian War. R4

Emperor Karl of Austria-Hungary conversing with wounded soldiers on the Isonzo. B. K. W. I. R4

Emperor Karl with Wilhelm II. B. K. W. I. R4

Emperor Karl reviewing troops with General Rohr. Gloria-Viktoria-Album. R4

German general von Beseler. Anonymous. R3

General von Kluck, who lost his courage before Paris. H. H. Company. R3

Crown Prince Karl of Austria-Hungary with von Hötzendorff in the field, 1914. B. K. W. I. R4

General von Emmich with award winners and other special officers. Photochemie. R4

Von Emmich's funeral, December 25, 1915. E.P. & Company. R4

Emperor Karl with von Hötzendorff greeting troops, March 1918. Anonymous. **R4**

Emperor Karl with Empress Zita on the Isonzo. Hermes. **R4**

General Pershing smiling to French people. Red Cross. **R3**

Pershing with General Bliss. Anonymous. **R4**

Generals Haig and Pershing on a 1917 Christmas card. J. Russell & Sons. **R2**

"Pershing at the Grave of Lafayette." Gilbert Post Card Company. **R2**

Pershing with Joffre, Foch, Haig, Pétain, and Diaz. Le Printemps. **R3**

Pershing at victory parade in Paris, July 1919. L.L. **R2**

Pershing with Secretary of State Lansing, French ambassador to the United States Jules Jusserand, Admiral Benson, General Bliss, and others. U.S. Signal Corps. R3

Turkish navy at Constantinople; inset of Sultan Mohammed V. N.P.G. R4

"Wilhelm II, Destroyer of Culture." Russian card. Anonymous. R4

Pershing with Foch and Haig. Beagles. R3

Edith Cavell, the war's foremost heroine. R. Ringoet. R3

Edith Cavell's cell room. F. Mat. R2

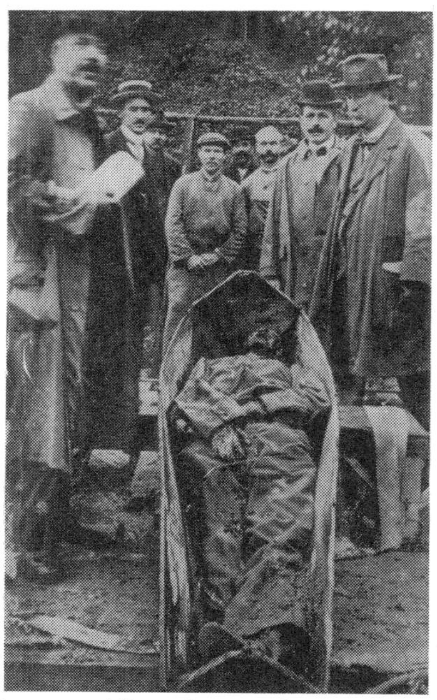

German soldier who was shot without a trial for refusing to fire on Nurse Cavell. R. Ringoet. R3

Christ ministering to wounded French soldier. Anonymous. R3

Removal of Edith Cavell's body from the "Tir National." R. Ringoet. R3

Monument to Nurse Cavell. R. Ringoet. R2

Another monument to Nurse Cavell. Ern. Thill. R2

Christmas 1916, Royal Medical Corps. Anonymous. R3

Highlanders piping back from the trenches. Daily Mail *Series 5; #37.* ***R2***

Australians heading for the trenches. Daily Mail *Series 5; #40.* ***R2***

American Red Cross card for soldier's use. R2

German feld postkarte *with message. Anonymous. R3*

"The Wiltshires cheering during the great advance." Daily Mail *Series 6, #42.*

Northumberland Fusiliers after the battle of St. Eloi. Daily Mail *Series 6, #40. R2*

"Happy 'Tommies' wearing Hun helmets." Daily Mail *Series 4, #27. R2*

British "Tommies" in German dugouts. Daily Mail *Series 4, #29. R2*

"Typical" German soldier standing with gun in hand over the bodies of a mother and child. Punch *series; Jarrold and Sons, #12. R3*

"India for the King!" Punch *series; Jarrold and Sons, #3. R3*

"The king at the front." Daily Mail *Series XII, #95. R2*

"Decorating a Canadian on the field of battle." Daily Mail *Series 4, #25. R3*

American sailors parading in Paris, July 14, 1919 (July 14 is France's day of liberation). L.L. R2

American troops in Paris, July 4, 1918. J. Cussac. R2

Gotha's raid on Paris, June 1918. Anonymous. R2

Sailors bedding down at Royal Courts of Justice, London. American Red Cross. R2

Target practice at Camp Travis, Texas. Dahrooge Company. R2

The Awkward Squad at Camp Dix, New Jersey. Underwood and Underwood, Y.M.C.A. R1

Salvation Army making doughnuts at the Front Line in France. Chicago Daily News. *R2*

American General Headquarters in Germany. L.F.D. R1

"On with the new." American Silhouette Series, No. 38. Photochrom. R3

Russian War Bond card. R4

A single German putting a group of Russians to flight. Meggendorfer-Blätter. R3

Russian War Bond card. R4

Russian War Bond card. R4

Austrians fighting in the mountains. Von R. Kargl. R3

Austrian troops building fortifications. Anonymous. R3

American Army Post Office. H. H. Stratton. R3

"Kaiser Wilhelm bread" feldpostkarte. *R3*

Soldier watching an airplane, "You must make yourself thinner!," feldpostkarte. *R3*

"The Tactless Teuton." Bystander; Fragments from France, series #3. R2

"That Evening Star-Shell." Bystander; Fragments from France, series #3. R2

"A.D. Nineteen Fifty" (a chilling comment on war). Bystander; Fragments from France, series #4. R2

Before, during, and after an attack. Bystander; Fragments from France, series #4. R2

American Red Cross ambulance. Anonymous. R3

U.S. troops marching through liberated Luxembourg, November 21, 1918. Anonymous. R3

"After the Hike." Illustrated Postal Card Company. R1

Recreational boxing at Camp McClellan. A. M. Simon. R2

Captured German tank exposed at Paris. Anonymous. R3

French tank going into action. Anonymous. R2

"American Tank in Action." Anonymous. R2

German crown prince's observatory; special cancellation. Anonymous. R2

Dinner at an American camp. Anonymous. R2

"Repairing U.S. Army field gun." C. T. American Art. R2

Life in the dugout with poetry. Bystander; Fragments from France, series #4. R2

"Situation Shortly Vacant." Bystander; Fragments from France, series #4. R2

A "pill box" before and after bombardment. Anonymous. R2

Austrian 30.5cm cannon, a substantial weapon; special cancellation and K.u.k. stamp. Karl Harbauer. R3

Soldier's Free Mail card promoting war bonds. R2

Americans setting off a smoke-pot. U.S. Signal Corps. R3

S.S. Lucia *torpedoed in 1918. Anonymous. R3*

"City of Glascow sinking; torpedoed September 1, 1918." Anonymous. R3

S.M.S. Leipzig, *sunk by British in 1916. Anonymous. R3*

"Inflating a French 'sausage.'" Anonymous. R3

"Clemenceau visiting French aviation camp near front." Anonymous. R4

French "Caudron" plane with airmen aboard. Anonymous. R3

Americans creeping with hand grenades. Chicago Daily News. *R2*

German cannons captured by British 4th Army. Anonymous. R3

German Taube plane on display. Museum of the Army in Paris, #3. R3

German 155mm cannon. Museum of the Army in Paris, #19. R2

"Round the Camp Fire," from the "Tipperary" song series. Anonymous. R2

"Surrender—On the Rhine," from the "Tipperary" song series. Anonymous. R2

"A Refresher—On the Way to Ypres," from the "Tipperary" song series. Anonymous. R2

A U.S. soldier posing for the home folks. Anonymous. R2

A U.S. soldier in a posed setting. Anonymous. R2

"Austrian, German, and Turkish prisoners put to work in Italian streets." Y.M.C.A. Hut Fund. R2

Pay day, always a popular time. Anonymous. R2

A furry "prisoner of war." Daily Mirror *Canadian Official Series; Pictorial Newspaper Company. R2*

"First Line Hospital"; real photo. Daily Mirror *Canadian Official Series; Pictorial Newspaper Company. R2*

From civilian to soldier. J.M.P., series #546. R2

1914 Austrian war medal: Franz Joseph on obverse, with Austrian artillerymen and winged Victory on reverse. Anonymous. R4

Scottish war prisoners at the station in Westfalen, 1914. Von Walter Müller. R3

Eating in the field. U.S.P.B. R2

Shaving the hard way. Underwood and Underwood, series #100. R2

A card sold with an empty slot into which a picture or view could be inserted. A photo is used here. R3

"Singing Sammies," U.S. soldiers. Y.M.C.A. R2

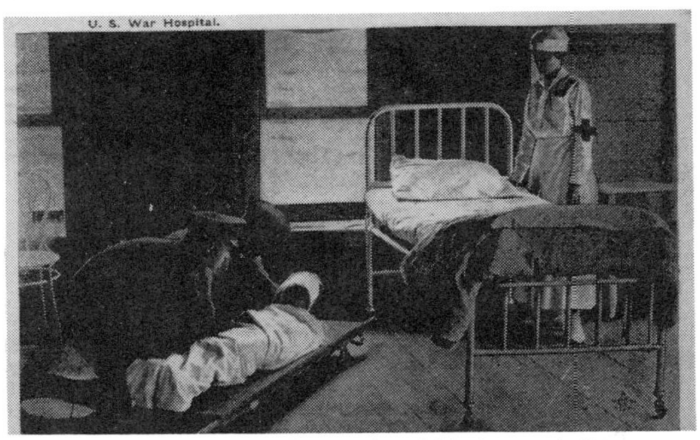

"U.S. War Hospital." Underwood and Underwood. R2

Attacking Italians, ready for action; sold for soldiers' assistance. G. Ricordi. R2

On a drill ground at West Point, Kentucky. Anonymous. R2

"A shot in the arm." Underwood and Underwood, series #100. R2

Principals at signing of armistice; special cancellation on reverse. A. L'Hoste. R4

Sentimental scenic. Merval Corporation. R1

Civilians arriving at training camp. I.F.S. R2

Y.M.C.A. soldier's correspondence card. R2

Scottish American war memorial, Edinburgh. Judges Ltd. R2

"In Honoured Memory of the Little British Force of 1914; Ypres." Anonymous. R3

"Belgian Soldiers in the Trenches near Malines." Underwood and Underwood; W. C. A. series, #11. R2

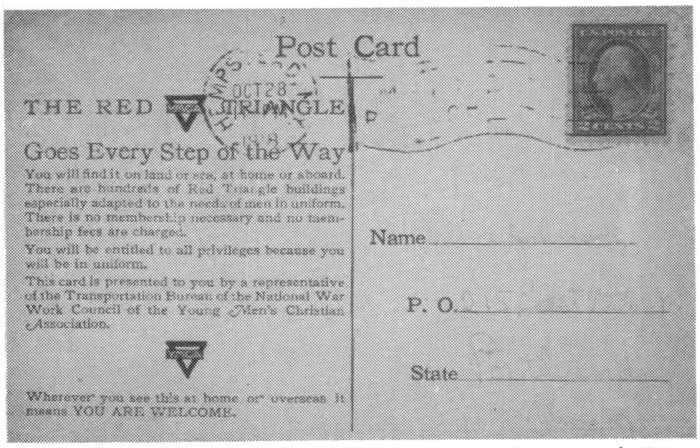

A second type of Y.M.C.A. soldier's correspondence card. R2

Germans in the trenches. Shaffer. R3

An already-destroyed street is also mined by the Germans. Anonymous. R3

British practicing with dogs in trenches at the Marne. Anonymous. R3

Wiring an Allied communication trench with barbed wire above. Anonymous. R3

Battered and wounded, but still determined. Anonymous. R3

"Naval Base Training Station, Hampton Roads, Va.; Sham Battle." Louis Kaufmann & Sons. R2

Secretary of the U.S. Navy, Josephus Daniels, addressing Bluejackets on October 22, 1917. S. Gold. R3

Russian propaganda card caricaturing army activities. Observe the left-handed salute. Anonymous. R4

Russian propaganda card, probably meant as an insult to the Germans and Austrians. R4

"A Zeppelin Bomb Explosion at Antwerp." Underwood and Underwood; W. C. A. 145 series, #1. R2

"Belgium's Scattered Army Reassembled." Underwood and Underwood; W. C. A. series, #2. R2

"French Infantry Advancing on the Double Quick." Underwood and Underwood; W. C. A. series, #10. R2

"Belgian Troops in Action 'Round Louvain." Underwood and Underwood; W. C. A. series, #14. R2

"London Scotties March to the Highlanders." Underwood and Underwood; W. C. A. series, #15. R2

"French Cavalry Crossing the Marne on Pontoon Bridge." Underwood and Underwood; W. C. A. series, #19. R2

"German Uhlans Captured by French Dragoons." Underwood and Underwood; W. C. A. series, #20. R2

"French Moving on the Enemy's Flank." Underwood and Underwood; W. C. A. series, #25. R2

"The Battle of the Marne." Underwood and Underwood; W. C. A. series, #28. R2

"British Highlanders Crossing a Square in Boulogne, France." Underwood and Underwood; W. C. A. series, #33. R2

"Charge of Heroic Scotch Highlanders." Underwood and Underwood; W. C. A. series, #36. R2

"Artillery of German Army Passing Through Brussels." Underwood and Underwood; W. C. A. series, #39. R2

"Belgian Soldiers Behind the Entrenchments on the Road to Malines." Underwood and Underwood; W. C. A. series, #41. R2

"Germans Search Ruins of City of Visé Devastated by Them." Underwood and Underwood; W. C. A. series, #42. R2

"The Coldstream Guards, the Crack Infantrymen of Great Britain, passing through Hyde Park in Heavy Marching Order, on their way to Paddington and the Front." Underwood and Underwood; W. C. A. series, #46. R2

"German Mobilization—Reservists on Way to Railroad Station, Berlin." Underwood and Underwood; W. C. A. series, #47. R2

The Serbian army in the field. Official card for Red Cross. R3

German bombardment of Rheims, September 1914. Official card for Red Cross. R3

Indian Allied army marching through Paris, 1916. Visé. R2

Hindus marching in Paris victory parade, July 14, 1919. N.D. Phot. R2

"Germany in all her beauty!!"—sausages, beer, vulgarity, and militarism. A. Noyer. R3

"Camping Scene—Awaiting Our Country's Call." Underwood and Underwood. R2

"You shall not pass!" (determined French soldier). A. Noyer. R3

"Ach! . . . Dirty Belgium! . . . raining again!"; anti-German card. A. Ternois; Poulbot *series, #12. R2*

Unity and aggressiveness of German and Austrian armies. C. A. & Company. R3

"Always unity, in war and peace"; figures representing Italy, Russia, and France. D.M. R3

German empress greeting officers of the 1st Honor Guard Regiment on their farewell departure. Gustav Liersch. R4

Germania's infantry regiment #113 going to glorious battle, August 4, 1914; feldpostkarte. *R3*

German empress visiting the war wounded. Anonymous. R4

French infantry unloading bread. L.V. & Company. R3

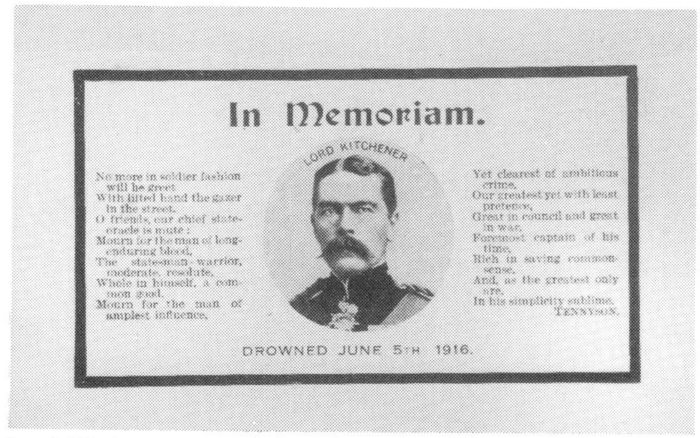

Lord Kitchener memorial card; Kitchener's death helped him retain his honorable reputation, which had begun to slip after the Dardanelles debacle. Philco. R2

Lord Earl Kitchener. Rotary. R3

"Sgt. A. Charman—Hero of Mons Retreat." Anonymous. R3

Lt. William Robinson, R.F.C., hero "who brought down the Zeppelin at Cuffley." St. James' Press. R3

Bulgarian field postcard, souvenir of Monastir. Anonymous. R4

"Belgians searching a haycart for spies." Ward, Lock & Company. R3

"French artillery in action at Verdun." Newspaper Illustrations Ltd. R3

Austrian army in battle at Rudnik, 1916. Kilophot. R3

German infantry forces a bridge at Antwerp. Anonymous. R3

Italian soldier having a vision of glory. Anonymous. R3

Christmas greetings from British soldiers in the Near and Middle East; special stamp. Times Press. R4

"Recruits on spud duty." Sackett & Wilhelms Corporation. R1

"A Happy Christmas from the Balkans." Anonymous. R4

Military Silhouettes. G. Savigny. R3

Military Silhouettes. G. Savigny. R3

German crown prince's heliographer sending dispatches. Underwood and Underwood; W. C. A. 145 series, #17. R3

"Rounding Them Up"; flags of Allies surround flags of the Central Powers. Illustrated Postal Card Company. R2

"12-inch Mortars at Fort Wright." American Colortype Company. R2

"Carrying Wounded to a U.S. Army Ambulance." A. C. Bosselman and Company. R2

Russian war bond card. Anonymous. R4

A German iron cross with the four H's: Hohenzollern, Habsburg, Hindenburg, and Hötzendorf. Anonymous. R2

Russian war bond card. Anonymous. R4

Peace Flag. Flag of Peace Company. R2

German kaiser and his army being lampooned. Russian card. R4

Christmas greetings from the British Foot Guards. George Falkner & Sons. R2

First Aid nurses of the Yeomanry Corps busy in the trenches. Underwood and Underwood; W. C. A. series 146, #146. R2

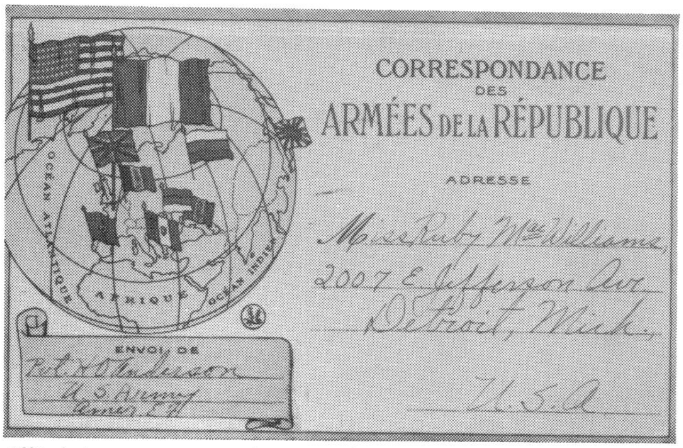

Allied Army correspondence card. R2

Two kaisers on horseback, 1914–1915. Anonymous. R3

Crown Prince Karl of Austria-Hungary sending holiday greetings. Official card for Red Cross. R4

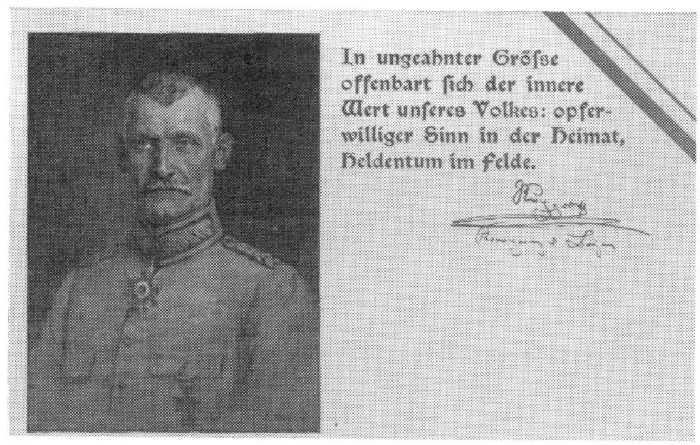

Crown Prince Rupprecht of Bavaria issuing a war message; special stamp. S. V. D. R4

"Friendship Ever," an Allied holiday card. Solomon Brothers Ltd. R2

Winston Churchill, first lord of the British admiralty. Valentine's Series. R3

"Lord Kitchener, Great Britain's Minister of War." Underwood and Underwood; W. C. A. series 146, #71. R2

German crown prince during World War I and his status after the war. W. den Boer. R4

German and Austrian war leaders. B. K. W. I. (Brüder Kohn). R4

German general von Emmich and his staff. Gustav Liersch. R4

U.S. light field artillery. American Colortype Company. R2

U.S. Army foraging party. Anonymous. R2

Allied Armies in Siberia *series; Allied naval fleet in Vladivostock with insets of commanders. R4*

Allied Armies in Siberia *series; "American Army landing at Vladivostock." Anonymous. R4*

Allied Armies in Siberia *series; Imperial Japanese Expedition in Vladivostock. Anonymous. R4*

Allied Armies in Siberia *series. Japanese Vanguard relieving Imperial Japanese Naval Party. Anonymous. R4*

Allied Armies in Siberia *series. "British army landing at Vladivostock." Anonymous. R4*

10
World War II

Part I: History and Chronology

What Is Left to Say?

After more than 40 years, innumerable motion pictures and television docu-dramas, books beyond counting, and words beyond number, what is there left to say about World War II? We could retell the story of a World War I corporal who rose from obscurity to near-demigod status. We could recount the deeds glorious, the deeds infamous, the heroism, and the shame, and we would surely be remiss if we dared omit the treatment which some men afforded to their fellow men because of their race, punishing them for being unable to control the circumstances of their birth, for having the effrontery to be born Jewish. Would we dare ignore the splendid military successes or their corollaries, the occasional ignoble defeats?

The good and the bad, the beautiful, the pathetic—as this war generously demonstrates, war is both wistful memories and the closest thing that man may know to hell on Earth.

The Locarno Conference: Prelude to Disaster

After Germany's crushing defeat in World War I, the Allied powers began the lengthy process of assessing indebtedness and deciding territorial boundaries. Although much disagreement ensued and more than one conference was needed to resolve the issues, there was an understanding by all on one particular point: Germany should never be in a position of military might from which she could wage war. As might have been expected, it was Clemenceau who spearheaded the effort to reduce the German army to naught. Regarding other matters, many hours were spent arguing about various treaty articles, creating an atmosphere in which uniformity of opinion became a rare commodity. In the final scrutiny, the newly initiated League of Nations (its creation was the first order of business at Versailles) proved to be an ineffective vehicle for fruitful negotiations, but it did render assistance in that it was recognized as an umbrella under which the Allies might pursue their task.

The finally agreed-upon Versailles Treaty of 1919 dictated severe terms to Germany. Had she been forced to meet all the tenets, it would have reduced her to a weak position both militarily and economically—bankrupt on paper and in fact. And although the former condition was certainly desirable, the latter would be troublesome for those countries obliged to rescue and revitalize a debilitated German economy.

Fortunately for all involved, Germany's treatment at her victors' hands was not as severe nor distressing as some historians have suggested. Compared with the last two years of the war, when the citizenry of Deutschland were forced to survive on an unpalatable vitamin-deficient diet of cabbage and dark bread, the war's termination at least meant that all the earth's produce would not be used to maintain an army in the field while a good deal of suffering continued on the home front. As for many of the Versailles treaty demands, especially some of the more unsavory ones, Germany refused to comply. In the matter of prosecuting war criminals, Germany became so indignant that a group of pliable Allies backed down. The final outcome witnessed the trials of a mere handful of men who were given minimal sentences and interned within Germany itself. The monetary debt became the cause for yet another miscarriage of justice—originally set at 269 billion gold marks, it was cut in half barely a year after the initial assessment; by 1932, the Allies had promised to absolve Germany of further payment should she agree to pay the greatly reduced sum of 3 billion marks. Hitler came to power the next year and the money was never seen. Moreover, as shall be seen later, Germany successfully evaded the demand to surrender all her weapons as well as the further proviso forbidding any attempt at rearmament.

As is often the case in such matters, it was the perception more than the reality that was to create so many problems. Most of Germany's citizens knew only too well about the treaty's prescribed harshness and they chafed at the vindictive attitude of some of the victors. The hatred this engendered was not soon forgotten, and neither was the Allied occupation of the frontier provinces, a provision used to ensure acquiescence. France was especially notorious for cruel, if spotty, treatment of selected Germans who were not quick enough with their compliance of any French soldier's orders. Still, it is clear that conditions could have been infinitely worse.

Within a few years, the furor fostered by the war's atrocities had abated somewhat and Germany encountered sympathetic ears as she began discussing matters of concern with other governments. International diplomacy was beginning anew. The conference which was to prove the most meaningful occurred at Locarno, Switzerland, October 5–16, 1925. Things, from the Teutonic point of view, were looking up.

The German government had convinced the bulk of the Allies that her intentions were the result of honorable aspirations. She agreed to repay all debts and to respect the territorial integrity and security of the Rhineland. It may never be known whether Germany was acting from a position of idealism or seeking an opportunity to pursue some as yet unknown objective.

In either case, the Locarno Conference represented the first time since the Napoleonic threat that the world's great military powers openly sought to deal with an international community of interests. The old antagonisms, especially those regarding Germany, had not been forgotten, but it was agreed to place them in the background and work instead for the universal good. It was hoped that Germany's posture as a promoter of peace would bring into effect some lasting, positive results.

Expectations were high at Locarno, even taking into account that France would be the only country voicing an objection to the extension of unbiased friendship to Germany. However, even the French managed to hold their Gallic tongue in abeyance to the general mood of conviviality. The following agreements were reached:

☆ Respect for the French-German-Belgian borders was guaranteed.
☆ Promises were made by Germany, France, and Belgium not to resort to war with each other except in defense against an act of flagrant aggression.
☆ Any disputes between the three powers that they could not settle among themselves would be referred to some sort of judicial decision.
☆ All or any of the three would immediately report any violation of the terms of the League of Nations.
☆ All signatories pledged themselves to immediate support of the aggrieved party if the league confirmed the charge.
☆ France, Poland, and Czechoslovakia consented to two treaties mutually guaranteeing frontiers.

Unfortunately, it is often true that treaties and agreements are often made to be broken or modified and reinterpreted to the point of absurdity. Locarno was no exception. One of the arbitration arrangements between Germany and Czechoslovakia, and another involving Germany and Poland, left open the possibility of future frontier modifications. Once the League of Nations, from whom the conference had gained authority and respectability, fell apart, the way was clear for Germany to reconsider her position.

It may be worth noting that Chamberlain of Britain, Stressemann of Germany, and Briand of France all received the Nobel Prize for Peace as a result of the treaties reached at Locarno and for their efforts in getting Germany admitted into the League of Nations the following year. One is led to conclude, however regretfully, that Locarno is but another in a long line of examples illustrating how the best of gestures may be unwittingly used to promote the most insidious—and in this instance, militaristic—of goals.

By seeming to align herself with the interests of Poland and Czechoslovakia, Germany was—perhaps unknowingly at this time—laying the groundwork for Adolf Hitler's schemes of the 1930s. The key to his success, both economically and militarily, lay in rearmament. As the history books inform us, he wasted precious little time getting started with his plans. Refusing to repudiate the spirit of Locarno, the bulk of the Allies turned a deaf ear to a still-skeptical France and the repeated protests of Winston Churchill. Indeed, the all-too-passive British government was too eager to trust Hitler when he claimed that universal disarmament, world peace, and mutual pacts were his fundamental aims.

In 1933, Hitler withdrew from a conference on disarmament in Geneva on the grounds that not all of the participants had renounced offensive weapons. On this pretext alone, the man only interested in universal disarmament began, with minor opposition, to increase German military might geometrically. In January of 1934, he signed a nonaggression pact with Poland—an agreement made possible because of the loopholes created at Locarno. What happened next is a pitiable matter of public record.

The year 1935 witnessed a complacent group of Allies (France excepted, of course) who continued to permit Hitler to rearm. The British government, as yet unskeptical, allowed him through yet another ill-advised and hastily prepared treaty to increase German naval strength to 35 percent of that of the Royal Navy. Stuck in the middle of his "Wilderness Years," Churchill's cries of anguish were worse than ineffectual—they were considered by many to be a war-mongering posture.

Normally distrustful where Germans were concerned, France had no such gap of gullibility. Their apprehensiveness was elevated to alarm over the complicity of the Nazis in the murder of Austrian Chancellor Engelbert Dollfuss. As a safety measure, France concluded an alliance with Russia in 1935. The next step was predictable: Complaining that France's arrangement invalidated the treaties of Locarno, Hitler proceeded to march German troops into the Rhineland. World War II was a mere breath away.

It would be easy, perhaps accurate, to believe that the Allied policies of appeasement helped make the Second World War a reality, but it should be understood that the conference at Locarno did much toward making Hitler's decisions politically feasible. Locarno supported an atmosphere that, although neither totally nor universally accepted, passed for goodwill and increased international accord. Without it, the Allies may forever have been casting skeptical eyes at any potential German military buildup. Even more, the abstract nature of the provisos at Locarno made possible further territorial discussions. Adolf Hitler used the clauses for all they were worth; the major powers (France being the exception again) hardly blinked an eye.

The lessons for our own world are clear-cut, chief among these being that treaties and agreements between nations, however detailed or carefully penciled, must be reviewed and carefully searched for clarity. Moreover, it must be ascertained that treaties always ensure mutual verification and contain no escape clauses. Without these safeguards, treaties are, as the old saw would have it, not worth the paper they are written on.

A War Like No Other

World War II was the last truly international war. It has been further described as the last war to thrust unrestrained militarism against the ideals of democracy.

All may agree that the destructiveness of the Second World War was without parallel. The same applies to the body count. Even minus the concentration camp victims, the numbers far exceeded those of World War I, which ran into the millions. However, the Jews, Poles, Slavs, Russians, and others who did constitute the inmate populations of these camps represented the most piteous and lamentable of World War II's victims. Without the benefit of a gun or the fragile protection of a foxhole, they were unwittingly and unwillingly recruited as human test studies in deprivation, disease, and medical experimentation. Their certain fate was a sometimes swift, but often painful, death. Equally inexcusable were those multitudes required to dig their own graves before being summarily executed, without even the hope of surviving that at least came with concentration camp existence. Camp inmates experienced the reality of implementing Herr Hitler's "Final Solution," and the number of lives lost to this experiment exceeded 13 million (a figure that humiliates neo-Nazis even as they deny its validity).

On the battleground itself, the overwhelming initial activity was the German blitzkrieg. Images of artillery and aerial bombardment of targeted areas, followed by the dreaded panzer tanks, followed in turn by smartly dressed and sharply drilled infantry divisions—these linger in the minds of all who lived through the war and of those who study it. Long after Chamberlain's ineptness and Churchill's pleas are forgotten, the lightning rapidity of the blitzkrieg will clearly and poignantly be remembered. Neither victory nor the passage of four decades have erased these memories, the horror of which has been forever immortalized on film.

Unlike World War I heroes, who have been all too often forgotten, the legendary figures of World War II are still very much with us, the United States and Germany presenting us with the bulk of these figures. That Germany was the aggressor and her motivations less than altruistic, and that the actions of not a few of her soldiers were cruel when measured by any standards of decency, does not detract from the fact that several of Germany's generals were men of exceptional ability. In this sense, it should be noted that Corporal Hitler himself proved again and again to be a brilliant tactician as long as his mind retained some semblance of sanity. Had his goals been less ambitious, it is likely that success would have preceded and followed success.

Chronology: World War II

Date	Event
1934	
August 2	President Hindenburg dies.
1935	
June 30	"Night of Long Knives," S. A. purged, Rohm assassinated.
1936	Hitler denounces Versailles Treaty in Reichstag.
1938	
September 30	Agreement reached at Munich paving the way for Nazis to occupy Sudetenland in Czechoslovakia. Signers are Hitler, Mussolini, Chamberlain, and Daladier.
October 30	Germany occupies Sudetenland.
1939	
March 14	Hitler invades Czechoslovakia, taking Bohemia and Moravia.
August 23	Russia and Germany sign nonaggression pact at Moscow.
August 24	President Roosevelt cables king of Italy, Hitler, and President Moszicki, urging arbitration, conciliation, or negotiation to avoid war.
September 1	German troops enter Poland at dawn on pretext of responding to Polish hostile activities without declaration of war. Poland resists fiercely with its 2-million-man army (mostly cavalry). First full-scale blitzkrieg.
September 3	President Roosevelt declares American neutrality in fireside chat; Great Britain declares war on Germany; British passenger ship *Athenia* torpedoed without warning—more than two dozen Americans drown when ship sinks the next day off the Hebrides.

September 4	After initial hesitation, France declares war on Germany.
September 5	U.S. proclaims neutrality as official policy.
September 17	Russia invades Poland.
September 27	Warsaw surrenders.
September 28	Poland is partitioned between U.S.S.R. and Germany.
October 9	U.S. ship *City of Flint* captured by Germans, released October 26.
October 18	American ports closed to belligerents.
November 4	Fourth Neutrality Act legalizes sale of munitions.
November 30–March 12	Russo-Finnish War.

1940

February 16	British naval vessels enter Norwegian waters to rescue 299 prisoners of war from the German ship *Altmark*; Norway protests.
April 8–9	French and British announce the mining of Norwegian waters to prevent German attacks; Germany attacks Norway from sea and air without physical resistance.
April 10	President Roosevelt freezes Danish and Norwegian assets in U.S. to prevent Germany from obtaining them.
April 11–30	Norwegian resistance appears and grows; Anglo-French expeditionary forces land in southern Norway, but are forced to withdraw by May 3.
April 29–May 30	Roosevelt appeals to Mussolini four times and asks him to exert influence for peace.
May 10	Germany invades Belgium, Luxembourg, and Netherlands in "lightning" fashion; President Roosevelt freezes latter countries' assets in the U.S.
May 13–26	Rotterdam surrenders; Queen Wilhelmina flees to London; German panzers overwhelm and divide British and French forces sent to aid Belgium; Boulogne falls.
May 28	President Roosevelt appoints National Defense Commission.
May 28–June 4	Forced to the shores of Dunkirk, British expeditionary forces and part of French army are rescued under a fog cover—every British ship, including dinghies, are commissioned for the rescue; result is that 200,000 British and 140,000 French soldiers saved; British losses total 30,000, including P.O.W.'s.
May 31	Roosevelt requests additional defense appropriation of $1,275,000,000.
June 5	Germany launches attack on French from Sedan to Abbeville.
June 10	Italy declares war against Britain and France and invades Southern France.
June 11–13	In U.S., Naval Supply Act authorizes appropriation of $1,490,000,000; Military Supply Act authorizes appropriation of $1,800,000,000.
June 13–15	Paris evacuated; Germans enter Paris unopposed; French fortress of Verdun captured.
June 17	All French assets in U.S. ordered frozen by President Roosevelt; Pétain asks Germans for an armistice.
June 22	French armistice signed at Compiègne.
June 23–24	General de Gaulle pledges resistance; British support de Gaulle and sever relations with regime of Marshal Petain; armistice between Italy and France occurs.
July 3	Battle of Oran; Britain destroys part of French fleet at Oran when French crews refuse to surrender (Britain does not want French navy to be used by Germany).
July 4–5	England seizes all French ships in ports under British control; French government at Vichy breaks relations with Great Britain.
July 10	Battle of Britain begins (first large-scale German air attack).
July 20	U.S. Congress authorizes $4,000,000,000 for two-ocean navy.
August 6	Italian army invades British Somaliland.
August 15	German planes (1000) attack select locations, especially Croydon Airfield.
August 17	Germany announces total blockade of all waters around England.
August 21	To avoid German air raids, English children begin leaving for America.
September 2	Britain and U.S. complete a deal whereby 50 American destroyers are exchanged for the right to build naval and air bases and possess them for 99 years. Areas for bases include Bermuda, Trinidad, Antigua, Newfoundland, Jamaica, and elsewhere.
September 6	U.S. Congress appropriates $5,246,000,000 for defense, providing for 201 naval war vessels, 7 to be battleships (55,000 tons each); King Carol of Rumania flees and is replaced by his son Michael V.
September 7	London bombing results in hundreds of daily casualties (as many as 500 killed each day, 1000–3000 injured).
September 11	Britain bombs continental parts of Antwerp, Calais, Dunkirk, and others to thwart German invasion plans.
September 13–15	Italian army invades Egypt from its position in Libya.
September 16	In U.S., Burke-Wadsworth Selective Training and Service Act; Britain downs 185 German planes invading the island in one 24-hour period.
September 17	German-Italian-Japanese ten-year military/economic alliance signed at Berlin.
October 8	Third supplemental Defense Appropriations Act authorizes $1,482,693,636 for defense; on pretext of defending her oil fields, Germany invades Rumania.
October 9	Troops under de Gaulle capture Duala, West Africa.
October 10	Russia and Lithuania sign mutual agreement pact; German Luftwaffe, aided by Italian aircraft, attacks London (bad weather and British defenses cause them to retire with nominal success).
October 16	Selective Service Registration Day; approximately 16,400,000 men ages 21–36 register.
October 28	After Greece refuses Italian demands for use of the former's bases, Italy invades Greece.
October 29	Drawing of serial number 158 by Secretary of War Stimson inaugurates America's first peacetime military draft.
October 30	British forces land at Crete and other Greek Islands; Russians give 134 aircraft to Greece.
November 10	Coventry, England, bombed by Germany; total aerial war results are 2375 German aircraft destroyed, 800 British aircraft destroyed, 14,000 civilians killed in London alone.
November 20	Stimson-Layton agreement coordinating military technology between U.S. and Great Britain; Hungary joins the Axis powers.
November 23	Rumania joins the Axis.
December 8	British begin a surprise attack against Italians in North Africa; by December 12, capture 1000 prisoners and open an invasion of Libya.
December 17	President Roosevelt suggests lend lease for supplying Great Britain with armaments.

December 29	In fireside chat, Roosevelt states, "We must be the great arsenal of democracy."
1941	
January 5	British forces defeat Italians at Bardia, North Africa, taking 25,000 prisoners.
January 6	President Roosevelt goes before Congress to recommend lend lease to the Allies; outlines the four freedoms—Freedom of Speech and Expression, Freedom of Religion, Freedom from Want, and Freedom from Fear.
January 10	Lend lease proposal before Congress to become law March 11; German Luftwaffe attacks British naval positions off Sicily.
January 15–February 26	British forces under command of General Sir Archibald Wavell capture more than 114,000 prisoners, from Ethiopia to El Argheila, within two months; British losses total 3000.
March 1	Bulgaria joins Axis after being deserted by Russia and Great Britain.
March 19	National Defense Mediation Board created to cope with strikes in defense industries.
March 25	Yugoslavia joins Axis.
March 26–28	Prince Paul overthrown in Belgrade, Peter II becomes king; new cabinet, under General Dushan Simovitch, declares Yugoslavia a neutral country.
March 27	U.S. Congress authorizes $7,000,000,000 for lend lease.
March 30	U.S. Coast Guard seizes 28 Italian ships, 2 German merchant ships, and 35 Danish freighters in American harbors; 3 Italian cruisers and 2 destroyers sunk by British in Eastern Mediterranean.
April 3	Reinforced with German help from Rommel, the British, reduced in number because of troops dispatched to Greece, give up their African conquests in a costly retreat.
April 6	German army invades Yugoslavia and Greece.
April 8	President Roosevelt cables aid to Yugoslavia.
April 9	U.S. and Denmark sign agreement permitting American air bases in Greenland.
April 10	U.S. declares Greenland under its protection.
April 13	Russia and Japan sign nonaggression pact.
April 14	Germans reoccupy Sollum and Bardia.
April 17	Yugoslavia surrenders after 12 days of fighting.
April 20	Germans advance in North Africa, stopping only at Egyptian frontier.
April 23	Greeks sign armistice; King George flees to Crete.
May 10	German air assault on London; British museum and British Parliament damaged.
May 20	German parachutists invade Crete and the Luftwaffe greatly damages British warships in Cretan waters.
May 21–June 6	German submarine sinks U.S. merchant vessel *Robin Moore* en route to Capetown; Congress authorizes seizure of all foreign ships in U.S. ports for needs of commerce and national defense.
May 24	Gigantic German battleship *Bismarck* destroyed by combined British air and naval attack after having sunk the British dreadnought *Hood.*
May 31	Remaining British forces evacuated from Crete.
June 14	President Roosevelt orders seizure of all Axis funds in U.S.
June 16	U.S. orders all German consulates closed by July 10.
June 19	Germany and Italy expel U.S. consular officials.
June 20	U.S. orders Italian consulate closed.
June 22	Germany invades Russia, violating their nonaggression pact; Battle of Britain.
June 24	President Roosevelt promises aid to U.S.S.R.
July 1–2	Capital of Latvia occupied by Germans; Russians retreat.
July 7	U.S. Marines occupy Iceland and relieve British troops.
July 12	British occupy Syria and Lebanon and terminate Vichy French government in those countries.
July 13–16	Mutual Aid Pact between Great Britain and Russia; Germans occupy Smolensk.
July 24	U.S. denounces Japan's invasion of Indochina.
July 25	Japanese assets in U.S. frozen.
July 30	U.S. gunboat *Tutuila* bombed by Japanese at Chunking, China.
August 1	Export of aviation oil to Japan banned by U.S.; Great Britain severs relations with German-occupied Finland.
August 9–10	Charter of the Atlantic drawn up by Roosevelt and Churchill.
August 17	U.S. ship *Sessa* torpedoed by German submarine near Greenland.
August 25–29	British and Soviet troops invade Iran (Persia).
August 28	Japanese ambassador presents note for peace from his government to the U.S.
September 4	Germans lay siege to Leningrad.
September 4–7	U.S. destroyer *Greer* attacked by German submarine off Iceland; U.S. offers lend lease to Poland; U.S. freighter *Steel Seafarer* sunk in Red Sea by German aircraft.
September 11	U.S. ship *Montana* torpedoed near Iceland; Roosevelt announces order to shoot on sight to U.S. Navy in American defense waters.
September 15–16	U.S. attorney general declares that U.S. ships may carry war material to British possessions in Near and Far East and Western Hemisphere under Neutrality Act; U.S. Navy assumes protection for all shipping as far as Iceland.
September 19–October 30	Axis forces push further into U.S.S.R. and by last of October are laying siege to Moscow (Russian government transferred to Kuibyshev).
October 1	First Soviet Protocol, whereby the U.S. and Great Britain agree to supply material to Russia; U.S. extends Soviet government 1 billion dollars' credit (October 30).
October 17	U.S. destroyer *Kearney* torpedoed by German submarine off Iceland, not sunk.
October 18	General Hideki Tojo becomes premier of Japan; new anti-American government joins him.
October 28	Second Supplemental Defense Appropriation Act adds $6,000,000,000 to lend lease; office of lend-lease administrator established.
October 30	U.S. destroyer *Reuben James* torpedoed near Iceland, 100 crew members lost; Roosevelt offers $1,000,000,000 in lend lease to U.S.S.R.
November 3	Ambassador Joseph C. Grew warns U.S. of possible sudden attack by Japan.
November 15	Siege of Sevastopol.
November 16	Germans capture Kerch.
November 17	Ambassador Grew warns that Japanese embassy may be unable to give advance notice of possible attack by Japan; Neutrality Act amended to allow arming of merchant vessels.
November 29	Premier Tojo states that American and British exploitation of the Orient must be purged with vengeance.
December 1	Russians retake Rostov.
December 3	Japanese consulates in U.S. begin burning secret documents.
December 6	President Roosevelt cables appeal to Japanese emperor to avoid conflict in the Pacific.

December 7 Japanese attack Pearl Harbor, the Philippines, and the British in Hong Kong and Manila. Casualties at Pearl Harbor are five battleships and three cruisers sunk or seriously damaged, three battleships less seriously damaged, several smaller vessels sunk or damaged, and 177 aircraft destroyed; 2343 dead, 876 missing, and 1272 injured (Thailand and Shanghai also attacked).

December 8 U.S. declares war on Japan—Senate vote is 82–0, House vote is 388–1; Japan attacks and occupies Guam and Wake Island (by December 11); Great Britain declares war on Japan.

December 10 Japanese land at Luzon, Philippines; British battleship *Prince of Wales* and battle cruiser *Repulse*, en route to Singapore, are sunk by Japanese aircraft.

December 11 Germany and Italy declare war on U.S.; U.S. declares war against Germany and Italy; second British drive into Libya.

December 12 Rumania declares war on U.S.

December 13 Bulgaria declares war against the U.S.

December 15 Third Supplemental Defense Appropriation Act authorizes $10,000,000,000 for armed services and lend lease.

December 16 French steamship *Normandie* requisitioned by U.S. Navy Department while docked in New York Harbor; Russians retake Kalinin.

December 17 Admiral Chester W. Nimitz succeeds Admiral H. E. Kimmel as commander of Pacific fleet.

December 18 First War Powers Act authorizes president to redistribute duties of executive boards and agencies.

December 19 Lt. General Douglas MacArthur made full general; Admiral Ernest Joseph King made commander in chief of U.S. fleet (December 20).

December 20 Draft Act mandates registration of all men ages 18–65, with liability for military service for all of ages 20–45.

December 21 Ten-year alliance treaty signed by Japan and Hong Kong.

December 22 Japanese begin full-scale attack on Philippines.

December 23 Wake Island falls to Japanese.

December 25 British troops in Africa reach Benghasi; British troops surrender Hong Kong to Japanese.

1942

January 2–3 Manila captured by Japanese; General MacArthur withdraws to Bataan; Southwest Pacific command given to General Archibald Wavell by Roosevelt and Churchill.

January 11 Japan begins attacks on Netherlands East Indies (Celebes, Rabaul, New Ireland, the Solomon Islands, and Amborna).

January 14 German submarines patrol U.S. Atlantic Coast; alien registration ordered by President Roosevelt.

January 20–May 12 In winter offensive, Russians recapture part of their territory from Mozhaisk to Kharkov.

January 23–28 Battle of Macassar Straits between U.S. and Dutch against Japanese; five Japanese transports sunk.

January 25 Thailand declares war on U.S.

February 1 Naval and air raid by U.S. on Japanese naval bases in Marshal and Gilbert Islands.

February 2 U.S. war cost since June 1940 equals $116,000,000,000.

February 6 U.S. and Britain establish combined chiefs of staff.

February 9 French ship *Normandie* burns and sinks in U.S. harbor at New York.

February 15 Japan captures Singapore, taking 60,000 prisoners.

February 20 Out of fear, President Roosevelt orders relocation of West Coast Japanese-Americans to concentration camps.

February 27–March 1 Battle of Java Sea results in Japanese victory and loss of an Allied squadron.

March 7 British evacuate Rangoon as Japanese occupy Burma. Japanese capture Lashio and Mandalay by May 2.

March 9 Japanese virtually secure Java.

March 10 General Joseph Stillwell made chief of staff of Allied armies in Chinese theater of operations.

March 12 American forces land on New Caledonia en route to Australia.

March 13 Japanese occupy Solomon Islands, threatening route to Australia.

March 17 General MacArthur arrives from Philippines to assume command of Allied forces in Southwest Pacific.

March 27 President Roosevelt activates Second War Powers Act, which allows him to allocate materials and facilities for defense.

April 8 U.S. War Production Board stops all nonessential building to conserve material.

April 9 After three months of heavy fighting, Bataan (Philippines) is captured by Japanese; General Wainwright, with his few remaining troops, escapes to Corregidor.

April 18 Major General James H. Doolittle, taking off from the deck of the *Hornet,* bombs Tokyo, Kobe, Nagoya, Yokohama.

April 29 After cutting off Burma Road, Japanese drive American forces toward India.

May 1 Air routes from India to China, called *Himalayan Hump,* opened by U.S. Transport Command.

May 4–8 Battle of the Coral Sea; U.S. naval and air powers defeat Japanese fleet and prevent it from attacking Australia; U.S. loses carrier *Lexington,* Japanese lose 100,000 tons of shipping.

May 6 General Wainwright surrenders Corregidor to Japanese.

May 14 W.A.A.C. (Women's Auxiliary Army Corps) established by Congress; Mrs. W. P. Hobby becomes director.

May 27 Second Axis drive toward Egypt; with reinforcements, Rommel recaptures Tobruk (June 21).

June 2 U.S. lend lease agreement for China signed at Washington.

June 3–6 Battle of Midway; carrier-borne planes inflict heavy losses on Japanese, halting their advance in the Pacific.

June 5–7 U.S. declares war on Bulgaria, Hungary, and Roumania; Japanese seize Attu and Kiska in Aleutian Islands.

June 13–17 Eight German saboteurs land by submarine at Long Island and Florida and all are captured; six are electrocuted, two imprisoned; army newspaper *Yank* is first published.

June 24 Royal family of Netherlands arrives in U.S.

June 25 Major General Dwight David Eisenhower appointed commander of U.S. forces in European theater.

June 30 U.S. Army appropriations reach $42,800,000,000.

July 2 German summer offensive in Russia captures Sevastopol, which had been under siege for eight months; pushing toward Caucasus, Germans capture Voronezh, Millerovo, and Rostov by July 24.

July 4 U.S. fliers join R.A.F. in assaulting Nazi targets on continental Europe.

July 30	Women accepted for Voluntary Emergency Services (W.A.V.E.S.); Naval Reserves authorized by Congress; Lt. Commander Mildred McAfee placed in charge.
August 7–8	U.S. forces land at Guadalcanal in first invasion of Solomon Islands; General Mark W. Clark, commander of U.S. Ground Forces, establishes headquarters in England.
August 9	Germans capture Maikop and open offensive against Stalingrad (August 22).
August 17	U.S. Marines attack Makin Island in the Gilberts; American bombing raid on Nazi arsenals in occupied France.
September 1	Germans cross Kerch Straits and capture Novorossusk (September 6), pushing into city of Stalingrad; Soviets counterattack northeast, then southeast of the city (October 1).
September 14	U.S. fliers raid Kiska.
October 10–20	General Clark and a group of commanders arrive secretly on North African coast to plan invasion.
October 23	Third British offensive in North Africa; General Bernard Montgomery's 8th British Army dislodges Rommel from El Alamein, driving him from Egypt by November 12 (expulsion starting November 2).
October 24	Vice Admiral William F. Halsey made Allied Commander in Pacific (South Pacific).
October 26	Battle of Santa Cruz Island in the Solomons witnesses sinking of U.S. aircraft carrier *Hornet,* but heavy losses are inflicted on Japanese.
November 7–8	Allies land in French North Africa with 500 British and U.S. transports, convoyed by 350 naval vessels; 400,000 men land at Casablanca, Oran, and Algiers; after brief struggle, French resistance is overcome (November 11).
November 11	Germans seize control of unoccupied France.
November 13–15	U.S. fleet under Admiral Halsey defeats Japanese efforts to recapture Solomons; Japanese losses are 28 warships and transports.
November 19	Russians apply pressure at Stalingrad and open new fronts through December.
November 23	Women's Division of Coast Guard Reserve (S.P.A.R.S.) created by Congress.
November 27	French fleet is scuttled at Toulon by its crews to prevent German use.
November 30	Third naval battle of Solomons, complete American victory.
December 17	U.S. Army and Navy announce plans to take 200–300 colleges and universities as training locations for armed services personnel.
January 1–18	Russians recapture territory including Stalingrad, which endured 17-month siege; by March 12, Germany and her allies in U.S.S.R. have suffered more than 500,000 casualties in three months.
January 5	General Clark's 5th U.S. Army constituted at Tunisia.
January 11	President Roosevelt submits budget to Congress—$108,903,047,923—of which $100,000,000,000 is for war effort.
January 14–24	Casablanca Conference (Roosevelt, Churchill, de Gaulle, and General Giraud); Eisenhower takes command of unified North African operation; Casablanca Conference agrees on plans for "unconditional surrender" of Germany.
January 22	Combined forces of Americans and Australians complete conquest of New Guinea.
January 27	American daylight attack on Wilhelmshaven.
January–December	Army Specialized Training Program (A.S.T.P.) and Navy college programs have 100,000 uniformed students on American college campuses by end of year.
February 6	General Eisenhower appointed commander in chief of Allied Expeditionary Forces in North Africa.
February 8	Americans complete capture of Guadalcanal.
February 25	Tunisia's Kasserine Pass recaptured by Allies.
March 2–4	Battle of Bismarck Sea; as many as 21 Japanese ships, with 15,000 troops bound for New Guinea, sunk by Liberators and Flying Fortresses.
March 11	Lend lease extended for one year.
March 15–July	Germans mount another offensive in Russia, retaking Kharkov and Belgorod (March 21)—summer offensive (begun in July) fails as the U.S.S.R.is continually resupplied by the Allies; although division numbers about the same (240–260 for Germany, 250–275 Russian), combination of Allied bombing in Germany's industrial centers and the replenishment of Russian material is too much for the formerly invincible Third Reich.
March 19	U.S. forces capture El Guettar in Tunisia.
March 30	British 8th Army transgresses the Mareth Line and meets the U.S. 2nd Army Corps in Southern Tunisia (April 7).
May 7–12	Bizerte taken by General Bradley's U.S. 2nd Corps; Tunis captured by British 1st Army; German General Arnim taken prisoner by Allies in North Africa; after defeat of the Axis in North Africa, the Ally-inflicted damage to Axis Powers is 950,000 men killed or captured, 8000 airplanes, and 2,400,000 tons of shipping.
May 11–31	American forces occupy and destroy Japanese resistance on Attu in Aleutians.
May 27	U.S. Office of War Mobilization created by executive order.
June 11	Pantelleria Island, off Sicily, surrenders to Allies after two weeks of aerial bombardment.
July 6	Naval battle in Kula Gulf spells defeat for Japanese.
July 9–10	U.S. and British paratroopers begin invasion of Sicily.
July 16	In a joint effort between Roosevelt and Churchill, the Italian people—by means of millions of leaflets dropped from airplanes—are asked to surrender.
July 19	Rome attacked by more than 500 U.S. bombers; Naples also bombed; half of Sicily occupied by July 22.
July 25	Mussolini to resign, antifascist government installed, which immediately seeks armistice with Allies (July 28).
August 5	Japanese air base on New Georgia, in Solomons, captured by U.S. troops.
August 15–17	Allies recapture Kiska, find it unoccupied; New Guinea bombed, destroying more than 300 Japanese aircraft (August 21); Messina captured, completing Sicilian campaign.
August 23	Russians continue to recapture their territory; by December 31, they reach Zhtomir.
August 29	Danish crews destroy 29 of the 48 ships in Copenhagen harbor rather than let them fall into the hands of the Germans.
September 3	Allies cross Messinian Straits and land in southern Italy; Italy signs armistice.

September 8–9	General Eisenhower announces Italian unconditional surrender; General Clark establishes 5th U.S. Army beachhead at Salerno.
September 11–16	New Guinea taken by American and Australian forces.
September 12	Most of Italian fleet escapes to the Allies.
September 15	Supported by German troops, Mussolini seizes leading Italian cities.
October 1	Naples captured by Clark's 5th Army; winter weather and stout German resistance stall American advance.
October 13	Italy declares war on Germany.
November 1	American forces land at Bougainville, in Solomons.
November 20–24	Tarawa and Makin Islands captured by U.S. troops; casualties are 3,772.
November 22–26	Cairo Conference between Roosevelt, Churchill, and Generalissimo Chiang Kai-Shek brings agreement about defeat of Japan and a free Korea.
November 28–December 1	Tehran Conference with Roosevelt, Churchill, and Stalin; date of Western Europe invasion discussed.
December 4–6	Second Cairo Conference with Roosevelt, Churchill, and president of Turkey; Turkey's entry into the war discussed.
December 24	In Christmas radio message, Roosevelt announces that Eisenhower will lead U.S. and British forces in Western Europe, and General Carl D. Spaatz will command American bombing against Germany; 3000 allied planes (1300 U.S. 8th Air Force planes) attack Pas de Calais area.
December 26	Allied landing on Cape Gloucester, New Britain.

1944

January 16–17	Eisenhower arrives in England as supreme commander of Allied Expeditionary Forces; General Omar Bradley appointed to command U.S. Armies in the field under Eisenhower.
January 22	Allied forces land on beach at Anzio 25 miles south of Rome; this proves to be a difficult beachhead to maintain.
January–February	Russian push reaches Estonia near Polish border.
January 26	U.S.S.R. refuses U.S. offer of mediation between Russia and Poland.
January 31	U.S. launches amphibious attack on Marshall Islands.
February 2	American troops invade Solomon Islands.
February 3	First attack on Japanese home territory by U.S. is shelling of Paramushirn Kuriles.
February 11	Sicily, Sardinia, and part of southern Italy returned to Italian jurisdiction.
February 16–17	U.S. Navy attacks Carolines, with 201 Japanese planes and 26 ships destroyed; U.S. loses 17 planes.
February 17	Russians defeat German divisions (ten of them) trapped near Cherkassy; U.S. troops land on Japanese air base at Eniwetok.
March	U.S. troops in Burma.
March 6	Beginning of round-the-clock bombing of Berlin by 800 U.S. planes.
March 15	Assault against Cassino by Allies (Cassino captured May 18).
March 22	General Tojo informs Japanese Diet that war situation is "truly grave."
March 26	Russians capture Odessa (April 10) and Sevastopol (May 9), and clear Axis Powers from the Crimea.
March 30	U.S. aircraft begin heavy bombing in Balkans.
April 22	Allies land at Hallandia in New Guinea.
April 26	Montgomery Ward and Company is seized by U.S. troops after defying orders of national labor relations board.
April 30	General MacArthur declares that he would refuse presidential nomination if it were offered to him.
May 1	"General" Jacob S. Coxey, age 90, delivers speech from Capitol steps in Washington, saying he was barred from giving it 50 years earlier as the leader of Coxey's Army.
May 10	Secretary of Navy, Frank Knox, who died April 28, is succeeded by James Forrestal.
May 18	Town and monastery of Cassino captured by Allies.
June 4	U.S. 5th Army captures Rome.
June 5–6	Using more than 1000 aircraft, Allied paratroopers land, under cover of darkness, behind German lines in Normandy.
June 6	D-Day; with strong naval presence of 4000 ships, and air protection from more than 10,000 aircraft, the major Allied counteroffensive begins at various points along the Normandy coastline.
June 9	General George C. Marshall (U.S. Army chief of staff), Admiral Ernest J. King (chief of naval operations, U.S.) and General Henry H. Arnold (commander of U.S. Army Air Forces) arrive in London.
June 13	First German flying bombs land in England.
June 15	B-29s bomb Yawata on Kyusha Island; first superfortress raid on Japan; Admiral Nimitz lands in the Marianas, with conquest by July 8.
June 19	Battle of Philippine Sea; Japanese lose 402 planes, Americans lose 27.
June 26	Cherbourg captured by American troops.
July 20	Attempt by German generals to assassinate Hitler; Americans land on Guam after 17-day aerial attack; 20 more days necessary to subdue the island.
July 25	Allied offensive from Normandy beachhead launched between St. Lô and Lessay; General Bradley is in charge of U.S. forces.
July 28	General George Patton placed in command of U.S. 3rd Army.
August 11–12	American Army crosses Loire River; Germans begin retreat from Normandy; Florence captured by Allies.
August 15	General Patch's U.S. 7th Army lands in southern France to proceed up Rhône Valley.
August 19	Patton's 3rd Army reaches Seine river.
August 23–25	After accepting Russian armistice terms, Rumania declares war on Germany; French troops retake Marseilles; Paris liberated by U.S. and French forces; unconditional surrender signed by German General Dietrich von Scholtitz.
August 28–29	Patton's army crosses Marne, captures Château-Thierry, takes Soissons.
August 30	U.S. 1st Army crosses Marne.
August 31	Amiens and Verdun taken by Allies.
September	Pisa taken by U.S. 5th Army; Belgium reached and Brussels liberated (September 3).
September 5	U.S.S.R. declares war on Bulgaria.
September 8	U.S. 1st Army captures Liege, pushes toward Germany.
September 9	Bulgaria surrenders to Allies.
September 10	U.S. 1st Army enters Luxembourg.
September 11	Patton's 3rd Army and Patch's 7th Army meet near Dijon; U.S. 1st Army crosses into Germany north of Trier.
September 15–October 13	U.S. Marines occupy and defeat Japanese on Pelelieu Island; American 7th and 3rd Armies meet French 1st Army at Dijon.

September 17	Allied paratroopers land behind enemy lines at Arnhem, Holland.
October 12	U.S. begins raid on Formosa (to last three days); more than 300 Japanese planes destroyed first day.
October 20	MacArthur's Philippine invasion begins; series of naval and air battles over next few days result in American victories; Russians enter Belgrade.
October 21	U.S. 1st Army captures Aachen.
October 23	General de Gaulle's provisional government recognized by Allies.
November 24	Air raids on Tokyo from Marianas.
December 16–25	Battle of the Bulge; Germans launch a counter-offensive in the Ardennes Forest.
December 26	Allies attack German Ardennes offensive and end the threat in January 1945; U.S. 3rd Army relieves 101st Airborne Division at Bastogne; General Anthony C. McAuliffe responds to German demand for surrender with the single word *Nuts* (December 22).

1945

January 9	Luzon attacked by U.S. forces; 60,000 men establish themselves along 15 miles of beach.
January 17	Russians capture Warsaw, forcing the Germans across the Polish border.
January 20	Hungary signs surrender to Allies.
February 1	500 prisoners liberated by U.S. Rangers from Japanese camp at Bataan.
February 3	U.S. air raid on Berlin, 1000 planes used.
February 4–11	Yalta (Crimea) Conference with Roosevelt, Churchill, and Stalin to decide final battle plans and occupations; U.S. troops enter Manila (February 4), secure it by February 24.
February 19–March 17	U.S. forces suffer 19,938 casualties in taking Iwo Jima.
February 23	River Roer line broken by U.S. 1st and 9th Armies.
March 2–7	Rhine reached by U.S. 9th Army; U.S. 1st Army occupies Cologne; Rhine crossed by U.S. 1st Army.
March 10	U.S. B-29s start incendiary raids on Tokyo; Mindanao, in Philippines, reached by U.S. troops.
March 15	U.S. 3rd and 7th Armies attach Saar Basin; last German troops retreat beyond Rhine (March 25).
March 21	U.S. aircraft carriers attack Japanese fleet in Japanese waters; Japan suffers destruction of 475 planes; 15 warships damaged; U.S. loses no ships.
March 27	Argentina declares war on Germany and Japan.
April 1–June 21	Okinawa invaded by U.S. 10th Army and U.S. Marines; Japanese losses included two cruisers, three destroyers, and the battleship *Yamato*; casualties are 79,000 for U.S., and nearly 120,000 for Japan.
April 1–18	Battle of the Ruhr as U.S. 1st and 9th Armies encircle Ruhr pocket and take 325,000 German prisoners.
April 12	Death of President Roosevelt; U.S. 9th Army crosses Elbe.
April 13	U.S. 3rd Army liberates Buchenwald concentration camp.
April 21	Russians reach Berlin suburbs; U.S. 7th Army captures Nurenburg.
April 24	Dachau liberated.
April 25	U.S. and Russian patrols meet at Torgau on the Elbe.
April 30	Under Lord Mountbatten, 14th British Army, with U.S. and Chinese troop support, destroys (in 15 months) the Japanese 15th, 28th, and 33rd Armies; Japanese casualties are 347,000; Hitler commits suicide with Eva Braun in Reich Chancellery.
April 28–30	While attempting to escape to Switzerland, Mussolini is captured and shot by Italian antifascists at Lake Como; the next day he is hung upside down alongside his mistress in Milan Square; German Armies in Italy surrender unconditionally (effective May 2).
May 1	Admiral Karl Doenitz, assuming the German command, announces Hitler's death; a million German and Italian soldiers in Italy and Austria lay down their weapons.
May 2	Berlin surrenders to Russian and Ukrainian Armies.
May 4–6	Surrender of German forces in Denmark, Holland, and northwest Germany; German forces surrender in Austria (May 6).
May 7	Germany makes an unconditional surrender at 2:41 a.m. in General Eisenhower's headquarters at Rheims.
May 8	V-E Day (Victory in Europe); Churchill and Truman announce end of war in Europe.
June 5	Germany divided into four zones of occupation (American, British, French, Soviet).
May–August	U.S. submarines, battleships, and aircraft bomb, torpedo, and shell the Japanese navy and industrial positions; aircraft destruction makes this the greatest air offensive in history (20th U.S. Air Force dropped 40,000 tons of bombs in one month).
July 5	With 60,628 killed, wounded, or missing, General MacArthur announces reconquest of Philippines; Polish provisional government recognized by U.S. and Great Britain.
July 16	First atom bomb tested in desert of New Mexico.
July 17–August 2	Potsdam Conference with Truman, Churchill, and Stalin; treatment of Germany topic of conversation; British carrier forces join U.S. 3rd Fleet in an air attack on Tokyo.
August 2	King George visits President Truman on board U.S. cruiser *Augusta.*
August 6	First atomic bomb used on a populated target is dropped by a B-29 *(Enola Gay)* on Hiroshima; estimated casualties exceed 180,000.
August 8	After declaring war on Japan, Russia invades Manchuria; War Crimes Tribunal created by U.S., France, Great Britain, and U.S.S.R.; Austria divided into four zones acceptable to U.S., Great Britain, France, and U.S.S.R.
August 9	After leaflets fail to bring capitulation, a second atomic bomb is dropped on Nagasaki.
August 10	Japanese cabinet sues for peace.
August 14	V-J day (Victory in Japan).
August 26	Surrender documents are signed by Japanese political and military leaders aboard U.S.S. *Missouri* in Tokyo Bay; General MacArthur in charge.
September 8	Tokyo entered by General MacArthur.
September 9	U.S. General John R. Hodge accepts surrender of Japanese troops in Southern Zone in Korea.
December 21	Following an automobile accident, General George S. Patton dies.

Part II: Details of War

German Military Leaders

Martin Bormann (1900–1945). Hitler's private secretary and head of the Party Chancellery.

Rudolf Diels (1900–1957). Founder and chief of Gestapo. Constantly in trouble with his superiors, Diels had the good fortune to be related to Göring; he even held positions with the government after the war.

Grand Admiral Karl Doenitz (1891–1980). Chief of the German navy from 1943; said to be Hitler's personally selected successor.

Field Marshal Herman Göring (1893–1946). President of the Reichstag and commander of the Luftwaffe, Göring was said to be Hitler's designated successor.

General Heinz Guderian (1888–1954). Tank commander responsible for successful thrusts into Poland, France, and the Soviet Union. He was the most proficient and successful of all German tank commanders.

General Franz Halder (1884–1972). Chief of army general staff until 1942, when he was dismissed over a disagreement with Hitler's Russian Offensive.

Heinrich Himmler (1900–1945). Last head of Gestapo and Waffen SS. His racial theories paralleled Hitler's and he implemented the Fuhrer's "Final Solution" with pleasure and enthusiasm. It was known that Himmler's power was unparalleled—he kept a dossier of everyone in any position, which was intimidating.

Adolf Hitler (1889–1945). Founder of Nazi Party and its only leader. Reich chancellor, Führer of Third Reich, 1933–1945. Supreme German military leader.

Hans Jeschonnek (1899–1943). Air Force chief of staff. After a series of reverses on the Russian Front, he took his own life.

Field Marshal Wilhelm Keitel (1882–1946). A member of the German general staff by the end of World War I, Keitel rose to become head of the Wehrmacht in 1935. By 1938 he was given the position of high command of the armed forces. Keitel was a servile officer, completely subservient to Hitler. His attempts to justify acts of brutality and uncivilized behavior coupled with his own orders to seize and detain any citizen thought to be endangering German security resulted in a sentence of death by hanging at the Nuremburg Trials.

Field Marshal Albert Kesselring (1885–1960). A leader of undisputed genius, Kesselring had many commands. Beginning in artillery service, he moved into the Air Force in 1935, where he rose to command both Air Fleet I and Air Fleet II. He was responsible for the bombings of Poland, Holland, Dunkirk, and England. He was later commander in chief in the South, dealing with the Mediterranean area and that extending into North Africa. He was captured by U.S. troops while performing service as a replacement for Rundstadt in Northwest Europe. The death sentence he received was commuted to life imprisonment.

Field Marshal Erhard Milch (1892–1972). Armaments chief of the Luftwaffe.

Field Marshal Walther Model (1891–1945). A Nazi totally loyal to Hitler, Model was commander of the 4th Army Corps during the Polish invasion and subsequently chief of staff of the 16th Army. He commanded the 3rd Panzer Division and later the 9th Army during Operation Barbaeossa. He then commanded both Army Group North and Army Group South in 1944. After the July 1944 plot, he replaced the humiliated Kluge as commander and chief of the West. His Army Group Four was trapped in the Ruhr in April 1945, and Model shot himself rather than surrender.

Erich Raeder (1876–1960). Grand Admiral Raeder was commander in chief of the German navy until 1943. He was responsible for the unrestricted U-boat warfare, but his disagreement with Hitler about a two-front war led to his forced retirement in January 1943.

Field Marshal Erwin Rommel (1891–1944). Germany's most respected tank commander, called the "Desert Fox." After a series of successes in Africa, Rommel met reverses against Montgomery and Patton when the Allies put considerable energy into defeating him. He was eventually persuaded to end his life by taking poison because of what was considered his complicity in the July 1944 plot against Hitler's life.

Hermine Braunsteiner Ryan (1919–). SS Guard Supervisor in Nazi concentration camps; known for her excessive cruelty, which included savage acts against children and the aged. After successfully evading war tribunals, she was finally sentenced to life imprisonment in 1981.

Field Marshal Ferdinand Schoerner (1892–1953). Major general during Greek campaign; later commanded mountain regiments, a Panzer Corps, Army Group South, and Army Group North, and was supreme commander of the Silesian Front in 1945. In 1944 Schoerner was also chief of the National Socialist Political Guidance Staff of the Armed Forces. His last wartime act was to surrender to the Americans after abandoning his men.

Field Marshal Hugo Sperrle (1888–1953). Starting as an infantry officer before World War I, Sperrle performed service during that conflict with the new air force. He later served with the Luftwaffe during the Spanish Civil War and eventually became field marshal of the air force in 1940. He was acquitted of all charges at Nuremburg.

Field Marshal Werner von Blomberg (1878–1946). War minister 1935–38. Through the designs of Göring and Himmler, who coveted his position and power, Blomberg was dismissed by Hitler in 1938 because of his marriage to an exprostitute with a criminal record.

Field Marshal Fedor von Bock (1880–1945). Led 8th Army into Austria in 1938 and later commanded Army Group North into Poland. He then commanded Army Group B in 1940 and Army Group Centre during the Russian incursion in 1941. Dismissed when the Moscow offensive failed, but later recalled and subsequently dismissed again after being unable to secure Stalingrad. Killed in an Allied air raid in 1945.

Field Marshal Walter von Brauchitsch (1881–1948). Commander in chief of the Werhmacht until December of 1941, when he was retired because of ill health and Hitler's growing lack of confidence in him.

Field Marshal Ernest von Busch (1885–1945). Commander of 8th Army Corps, later the 16th Army, and then the Central Army Group in Russia, where he presided over a failed campaign.

Admiral Hans George von Friedeburg (1895–1945). Commander of the German navy at the end of the war. He signed the surrender in Berlin and committed suicide two weeks later (May 23, 1945).

Field Marshal Ewald von Kleist (1881–1954). Commander of North Rager Corps. Later commanded Panzergruppes for invasion of France in 1940, the invasion of Russia, and advances in 1942 into the Caucasus area. Kleist was dismissed by Hitler in 1944.

Field Marshal Gunther Hans von Kluge (1882–1944). Rising through the ranks under the Nazis, Kluge commanded the 4th Army at the war's outset. Transferred later to the Russian Offensive, von Kluge was replaced since, like Rundstedt before him, he was unable to hold off retreating in the face of continued Russian aggressiveness. He committed suicide the day after being removed.

Field Marshal Wilhelm Ritter von Leeb (1876–1956). Commander of Army Group North during the Russian Campaign. Although he was initially successful at pushing through East Prussia into the Soviet Union, the Russian winter and Soviet determination stalemated him. Hitler relieved him in early 1942.

Field Marshal Erich von Manstein (1887–1973). Thought to be the ablest German commander by many, Manstein was the epitome of a professional soldier. After serving on both the Eastern and Western Fronts during World War I, he held a number of positions, culminating in a job with operations on the general staff. Chief of staff to von Rundstedt at the beginning of World War II, he attained the command of the 38th Infantry Corps in 1940 and became general of infantry in June of that year. He later headed the 56th Panzer Corps in East Prussia. His successes in Russia where others had failed were nothing short of remarkable, but his disagreement with Hitler resulted in his compulsory retirement in 1944. He has been regarded by friend and foe alike as the most versatile, talented general of the Third Reich.

Field Marshal von Paulus (1890–1957). A career soldier, von Paulus was commander of the 6th Army, which was soundly defeated at Stalingrad. Forced to surrender to the Russians in January 1943, von Paulus was finally released in 1953.

Field Marshal Walter von Reichenau (1884–1942). Made a field marshal after 1940 as a result of his unflagging support of Adolf Hitler. Died in 1942 of a stroke.

Field Marshal Gerd von Rundstedt (1875–1953). Commander of all armed forces in the West, 1942–1945. Replaced more than once for battlefield reverses, Rundstedt was eventually captured by the British. His postwar trial was dropped because of his ill health.

Field Marshal Maximilian Freihers von Weichs. Held several commands—was commander in chief of 13th Army Corps that invaded Austria and the Sudetenland; held command in the Balkan Campaign and in duty at the Russian Front; and was leader of all German troops in Hungary.

Field Marshal Erwin von Witzleben (1881–1944). Another officer who saw service in World War I, Witzleben commanded the 3rd Army Corps in 1939 and 1940. Later he was commander of Army Gruppe D in France. Military head of the resistance against Hitler after the Führer retired him, Witzleben was apprehended and brutally executed following his trial at the People's Court.

General Kurt Zeitzler (1895–1963). Chief of the general staff 1942–1943. Disagreements with Hitler over the Russian campaigns led him to attempt resignation several times. After Zeitzler succeeded in resigning because of ill health, Hitler had him stripped of all military privileges, including the right to wear a uniform.

Part III: Postcards

Types and Categories

Type	Category
Aerial dog fights	R3
Air Defense League	R4
Airplane pilots	R3
Airplanes attacking ground positions	R3
Allied armies meeting in Berlin or elsewhere	
Real photo	R4
Other types	R3
Allied commanders	
Omar Bradley	R3–R4
Charles de Gaulle	R3–R4
Dwight Eisenhower	R2–R3
Douglas MacArthur	R2–R4
Bernard Montgomery	R2–R3
George Patton	R3–R4
All others	R2–R4
Allied headquarters, military	R2–R3
Armies administering conquered areas	R3–R4
Army Day (Tag Der Wehrmacht)	R3–R4
Artillery in action	R2–R3
Axis commanders	
German	R2–R3
Italian	R3–R4
Japanese	R2–R4
Battleships, not in action	R2
Bombing, aerial	R2–R3
Building bridges or fortifications	R2
Captured weapons, supplies, equipment, vehicles, and so on	R2–R3
Cartoontype propaganda cards	R2–R3
American	R2–R3
British	R2–R3
French	R3
German	R3
Italian	R3–R4
Japanese	R4
Russian	R4
All others	R3–R4
Children, artist-drawn, in military cloth	R3–R4
Humorous or whimsical	R2–R3
In action	R3–R4
Concentration camp–related	R3–R4
Establishing beachheads	R3
Field command posts	R3
Flag cards	R1–R2
Freedom Day cards	R3
Germany victory banners or insignia	R3
Government postals for soldiers' correspondence	R2–R3
Hitler	
Addressing the crowds	R2–R3
Examining battlefields or destruction	R2–R3
Formal poses	R2–R3
Pre-1925	R4–R5
Reviewing the troops	R2–R3
With his generals	R3
With Hindenburg	R3–R4
With medal winners	R3
With miscellaneous groups	R3–R4
With Mussolini	R3
With political leaders	R3–R4
With youth	R2–R3
Other cards	R3–R5
Hitler youth	R3
Horse cavalry (last of)	R3
Hospital- and nursing-related	R2–R3
Infantry in action	R3
Insignia and mascot cards (also all symbols)	R2–R3
Liberation of Paris	R2–R3
Life in training camps	
Humorous	R1–R2
Real photo	R2–R3
All others	R2–R3
Marching German P.O.W.'s	R3
Memorial cards	R2–R3
Military parades	R2–R3
Miscellaneous activities of soldiers in the field	R2–R3
Miscellaneous comic cards related to field activities	R2
Miscellaneous camp view cards	R1–R2
Mussolini	
Addressing the crowds	R3
Awarding medals	R4
Formal poses	R2–R3
Pre-1920	R4
Propaganda cards	R3–R4
Unfavorable caricatures	R2–R4
With Annuncio	R3
With early followers	R4
With his generals	R3
With Hitler	R3
With Italian cabinet	R3
With Victor Immanuel II	R3–R4
With other political leaders	R3–R4
All other cards	R3–R5
Naval battles	R3
Nazi party convention cards	R2–R3
Nazi party headquarters	R2
"One People, One State, One Leader" cards (German)	R3
Paratroopers	R3
Patriotic types	R2–R3
American	R2–R3
British	R2–R3
French	R3
German	R2–R3
Italian	R3
Japanese	R3–R4
Russian	R4
All others	R3–R4
PT boat–related	R2–R3
Real photos of weapons, vehicles, or other machinery	R2
Reconnaissance patrols	R3
Red Cross canteen–related	R2
Red Cross–related	R3–R4
Ruins of Berlin	R4–R3
Seabee-related	R2
Siege of Stalingrad–related	R3–R4
Soldiers assisting the wounded	R3
Soldiers departing for the war	R2–R3
Soldiers (sailors) on leave or furlough	R2–R3
Soldiers with pretty ladies, artist-drawn	R2–R3
Soldiers with their sweethearts	R2
Song or poem cards	R3
Special Nazi-related art cards	R3–R4
All other Nazi atrocities	R4
Tank-related	R2–R3

Unfavorable caricatures of political leaders	R2–R3
USO cards	R2
Victory parades and celebrations	R2–R3
WAAC-related	R3
WAC-related	R3
War bond posters	R3–R4
War Sacrifice Day (German)	R3
Weapons being demonstrated	R3
Winter Relief Campaign Cards (Kriegs W.H.W.)	R2–R3

Sets and Series

Academy Patriotic Publications. Published a set of postcards for the War Relief Fund. On each card portraying military and civilian leaders is a facsimile of a British penny to indicate that each of these "patriotic postcards" purchased represents a penny donated to the war effort. A nice group.

American Colortype Company. Produced a set of six *Bugle Call* cards that illustrate such things as reveille and first call. Each card has an illustration of a scantily clad woman. Most show a naïve-appearing soldier.

Asheville Post Card Company. One of the giant producers of U.S. military postcards, this company published series *C–N.* Among these are training scenics and views of various military bases, artillery weapons, field bivouacs, and soldiers' personal activities. Cards are in color and have white borders.

Also produced a #500–#600 series of colored cards showing tanks, planes, and naval vessels.

Associazione Nazionale Mutilati E. Invalidi Di Guerra. This organization for the war-wounded produced a set of 12 cards of sketches by artist A. G. Santagata. Illustrated are various battle activities which highlight the kinds of heroic efforts that led to the wounding and death of so many. Although its cards are clearly propaganda, this Italian publisher has offered some picturesque messages of how much of the world views war. A rare set.

A. V. F. Published a set of photo cards with the words *France Libre* to the left of the pictures. The photos are of ships, army and navy contingents, and leaders. An interesting group. Number of cards unknown. Scarce.

Bassons Dummy Products. Produced an unnumbered set of cards titled *Hex the Axis Comic.* The artist-drawn (Henry Major), brown-tone cards illustrate Hitler, Mussolini, and Hirohito either separately or together as they receive the rewards of their various actions.

Beals. This company offered a set of colored, artist-drawn, humorous cards similar in theme to those produced by Graycraft. Cards are lettered and numbered AC-1 and following. At least a few dozen cards.

C. A. P. Published a set of real-photo cards titled *Liberation of Paris.* Each card has explanatory wording on the back in both English and French. Scenes included are parades, former barricades, de Gaulle followed by crowds and addressing crowds, Allied generals, and various welcoming themes involving soldiers and civilians. Cards are numbered beginning with 1 and proceeding past 23. An excellent historic group.

C. Pahl and Company. Published a beautifully colored set of war decorations for bravery, gallantry, and so on. At least 12 cards to the much-sought set.

Curt Teich. Produced several series, some in a *C. T. Art Colortone* group. Series include the following:

- ☆ U.S. Army series (C. T. Art Colortone group) of colored cards related to weaponry, vehicles, and military men (both Army and Navy) preparing for action. The numbering system begins with USA-1 and continues through 40 cards or more. Photos are credited to the U.S. Army Signal Corps. Titles include *U.S. Coast Artillery, U.S. Field Artillery, U.S. Armored Regiment,* and so forth. The higher-numbered cards are more muted in color and are captioned.
- ☆ In the C. T. Art Colortone group, a U.S. Navy series. Unlike the U.S. Army series, which has a few Navy types mixed in with the predominantly Army cards, these are strictly Navy cards, showing weaponry, training, naval vessels, and airplanes. Photos are from the U.S. Navy Recruiting Bureau. All cards are titled *U.S. Navy* and number USN-1 to probably 40 or higher.
- ☆ Series of colored sketches from the C. T. Army Comics group. Like the U.S. Army series (USA-1 to USA-?), these C.T. Art Colortone cards have a letter/number system. At least 24 cards are in the series. Some relate to an overbearing drill sergeant behaving in a free-roaming, haphazard fashion.
- ☆ Series T, which consists of army comics, ten subjects. These artist-drawn, colored sketches show various scenes, including a group of unfavorable caricatures of Adolf Hitler. Popular with military personnel and civilians alike, they saw wide distribution.
- ☆ Series S, similar to Series T. Artist-drawn sketches include pictures of soldiers and airmen in humorous situations or making humorous statements.
- ☆ An unnumbered series of *Keep 'Em Flying* color cards that picture different aircraft. At least ten U.S. aircraft corresponding to ten different cards are believed to exist. Also in the C. T. Art Colortone group.
- ☆ An unnumbered series of colored cards of military bases. Cards are identified by the words *Greetings from . . .*(various military locations). Obviously there are dozens of separate cards.
- ☆ A colored and numbered set (AS-1 to AS-?) in a *U.S. Action Series.* The U.S. Navy is credited with some of the pictures, which include various naval vessels as subjects.
- ☆ Series of cards with a dull orange border. Show military vehicles, installations, and various military activities and locations. Some cards are numbered at the top, some at the bottom. Most seem to be numbered at the bottom in 72,000 and 73,000 series. At least 20 cards.

☆ *V* (Victory) series; artist-drawn, colored cards show a giant *V* surrounded by patriotic scenics. Believed to be ten cards numbered V1–V10. Some examples are (V4) "Let's Pull Together," (V5) "Keep 'Em Flying," (V8) "Liberty and Justice for All," and (V10) "Defend Your Country."

D. Robbins and Company. Produced an artist-drawn series of six cards titled *Slam the Axis*—humorous cards depicting Hitler (also Hitler and Mussolini) being chased, attacked, flushed, or otherwise intimidated by Uncle Sam or other Allies. Card titles include "A Royal Flush," "Fortune Teller—I See a Bad Finish for You Rats," "How Did You Enjoy Your Trip To Russia?," "Adolf's Going Places," "Unconditional Surrender," and "Look! Uncle Sam Made Monkeys of 'Em."

Eastern Publishing Company. This Cairo firm published a numbered set (500 series) of artist-drawn (Saroukhan) colored postcards of life in Egypt for the British soldier. Women, romance, the camel, and miscellaneous desert activities are the themes. Cards are humorous in nature.

E. C. Kropp. Published a colored series of more than 40 cards, each one preceded by the letter O. Many of the cards are pre-1939 and may not be considered strictly World War II material. But the scenes of camps, military life, and so forth are of much the same vintage and are therefore included.

E. H. Wilkinson and Company. Canadian. Published a numbered set of printed real-photo cards dealing with Winston Churchill and his relation to the war effort. Each card contains a Churchill quote at the bottom, with the picture taking up the bulk of the card's surface. Scenics include Churchill on the deck of a ship, inspecting front-line defenses, and dealing with various military personnel. There are eight cards in this frequently overlooked, yet infrequently seen, set of historic postcards.

Erich Gutjahr. Produced a numbered series (100) of real-photo cards showing the German infantry in action, in charges, with artillery, victorious, and more. Very nice cards of the German infantry.

Esquire Magazine. Produced at least one set of six artist-drawn (Arthur Szyk) cards related to military and political leaders and their armies. Sketches are well done, very detailed.

German Army Headquarters. Produced a set of 12 artist-drawn hold-to-light cards for French soldiers serving on the Maginot Line. Cards are either patently insulting of the French soldier or they show them in awkward, grotesque, or frightening positions and situations. Death, pain, and perversions are among the themes. A scarce and provocative group.

Giraud-Rivoire. A French producer who introduced a set of combination photo/artist-drawn cards related to the French navy. Atop each picture of a French vessel is an artist-drawn (Paul Igert) sketch of the hero or famous French person after whom the ship is named. Duquesne, Volta, Montcalm, Pasteur, Jules Verne, and Joan of Arc are included in the group. At the bottom of each card is specific information about the vessel, including weight, armaments, and year of entry into service. A great set.

Government Issues. Published a set of eight postal stationary cards for the 1936 Nazi party convention (and later ones). Each sepia card has an imprinted six-mark stamp with Hitler's visage on it to the right. The left half of each card shows a muted green view. Included are marching soldiers, a party rally, an airplane in flight, motorcycle action, and a young boy blowing a bugle.

G. P. D. A British publisher who offered a group of beautifully colored postcards entitled *For Freedom.* Pictured are military and civilian leaders. Among the leaders thus illustrated are General de Gaulle, Generalissimo Chiang Kai-Shek, President Roosevelt, Admiral Louis Mountbatten, and Marshal Stalin. Also included among these offerings are a number of action scenics. It should be noted that this series, although infrequently seen, was also released in France, the United States, and the Arab countries. In each case, the wording is in the language native to the region.

Graphic Post Card Company. Published a numbered (50s–70s) series titled *Axis Series.* Black-and-white artist sketches by B. F. Long; these show unfavorable caricatures of Hitler, Mussolini, and Hirohito, or the same being chased or humiliated in another manner by Uncle Sam or another Ally.

Graycraft Card Company. Produced an artist-drawn, colored series of drawings that are primarily comic or comic/romantic. Cards are in a #200 series; apparently there are several dozen separate ones. Included are soldiers performing extra duty (washing dishes, peeling potatoes), splashing mud from an army truck onto a pedestrian sergeant, ogling pretty girls, in romantic situations, and more.

Also published a numbered set of colored, artist-drawn sketches titled *Private Breger.* (Sergeant) Breger was the artist of these humorous cards about life in the U.S. Army. These 300-numbered cards portray such activities as dining in the mess hall, artillery practice, romance, extra duty for rule infractions, bayonet practice, and more. Breger's central character was a rather homely, bespectacled, inoffensive G.I. who always managed to give as much grief as he experienced himself. Naturally, those on the receiving end were frequently his superiors.

Heinrich Hoffman. It would be altogether incorrect to prepare a book that touches on the visual military history of World War II and not include the name of photographer/publisher Heinrich Hoffman. Hitler's official photographer and the Führer's personal friend, Hoffman's photographs are among the most appealing of all military items and always have been. Included in his 2½ million pictures are countless thousands devoted to Hitler, and others of his generals, Nazi party rallies, Iron Cross winners, parades, and other political and military activities. Frequently employing a number system, Hoffman's cards are an admirable pictorial representation of Adolf Hitler and of Hitler's Germany. At one time a wealthy man, both because of the postcards and from the sale of his many picture books, Hoffman died in 1957 in near obscurity and near poverty; his property was confiscated at war's end. Hitler created the Third Reich; Heinrich Hoffman captured it on film.

Hilborn Novelty Advertising Company. Published a series of lettered and numbered (A-1 to A-?) artist-drawn black-and-white cards. Unflattering caricatures of Hitler, Mussolini, and Hirohito are pictured. Examples are Hitler's face in a toilet bowl; Hitler in jail; and Hitler, Mussolini, and Hirohito as choirboys. At least 32 cards.

J. Salmon Ltd. A British firm that published a set of at least 15 artist-drawn (A. F. D. Bannister) cards. These are representations of airplanes, 14 of which are British, and the others, American. Numbering is 4810–4899, which suggests many cards in this series.

King Features Syndicate. Produced a series of cards of various U.S. cartoon characters (Dick Tracy and Popeye, for example) promoting the war effort. A number of these were for the correspondence use of the military man and had printed messages with blank spots to be filled in. Printed in volume, they turn up most infrequently.

L. A. Gag/Joke Shop. Produced a set of cards showing a dog thumbing his nose and other, more derogatory gestures around pictures and memorabilia related to Hirohito or Hitler. Combination real-photo (the dog) and artist-drawn. Most cards are numbered higher than 37. Scarce.

Longshaw. Published a numbered series, *Keep 'Em Flying.* Various military aircraft. Numbered in the 950s; examples are (#951) Lockheed B-14 Hudson Bomber, (#954) North American B-25 Medium Bomber, and (#955) Vultee P66. Cards are in color and are artist-drawn (A. Jasmet).

L. W. Company. Produced a humorous set of color, artist-drawn cards about U.S. military life.

Mitteldeutsche Kunstanstalt. Published three separate series of black-and-white photo cards about life in Poland just before and during Nazi occupation. There are ten cards in each unnumbered set; each set is in its own envelope, marked by title *(Kriegsschauplatz in Polen)* along with other information, and priced. Pictures include civilian P.O.W.'s, artillery barrages, wagons stuck in the mud or overturned, horses dead, civilian work details, German temporary headquarters, civilians fleeing the city, and others. A truly revealing set of cards that is highly recommended, but seldom encountered as a full set.

Mutoscope. This well-known American publisher offered a series of six lightly colored (brown/yellow), artist-drawn comic cards. The theme, which is interesting and seldom portrayed on postcards, is *Women at War.*

M. W. M. Produced an unnumbered series of three colored sketches surrounded by typewritten minimessages by which the soldier, sailor, or aviator could place a check mark. The cards are identified at the bottom as "A Busy Soldier's Correspondence Card," "A Busy Sailor's Correspondence Card," or "A Busy Aviator's Correspondence Card." Each card instructs the sender to check the message desired. The real function of these cards, apart from the humor that they generated, was to let civilians know they had not been forgotten. Minimessages included:

I've Been	I Spend My Time
☐ Drilling	☐ Working
☐ On KP	☐ Soloing
☐ In the Clink	☐ Dancing
☐ On Guard Duty	☐ Loafing
☐ Caught Napping	☐ Kidding the Captain
☐ Flirting with the General's Daughter	☐ Shooting Craps
	☐ Thinking of You

Seven other categories include "I Just Got In . . .," "I Need . . .," "I Have My Meals . . .," "I Hate . . .," "Will Be Here for . . .," "Give My Regards to . . .," and "I'll Soon Be . . . ."

☆ Published an artist-drawn, numbered humorous set titled *Navy Comic Series* (NC 300 series).

☆ Also produced an *Army Comic Series* of both unnumbered and numbered colored, artist-drawn cards relating to soldiers and young women (or more infrequently, in comic situations in which soldiers occasionally found themselves). Most, but not all, are comical in nature. Cards are lettered and numbered beginning with AC-100.

NSDAP Central Office Publishing. Printed a beautifully colored set of the German army and navy insignia. The numbered set comprises 21 cards; some cards show flags or banners, others show insignia. Several have artist-drawn military scenes at the bottom. A very desirable, very elusive set to obtain. Cards are artist-signed (by Gottfried Klein).

Official Navy Postcards. Produced a set of ten cards of U.S. airplanes and ships. The set is in an envelope promoting Victory Bonds.

Oscar Tellgmann. Published a series of printed photo cards related to the German Army (including Wehrmacht infantry) in the field and in active campaigns. Cards appear to be numbered, but exact figures are unknown. Like the Erich Gutjahr set, these cards are good sources of information about uniforms, weaponry, and, to some extent, strategy and modus operandi.

Photochrom. Published a set of numbered postcards entitled *Home Guard Silhouettes.* Mostly humorous, they depict the British Home Guard in silhouette as it goes about its job of "protecting" the British. These cards go a long way toward showing that the British have a highly developed sense of humour. The jocular message is that, with these bunglers and senile old men, the English were ill-prepared for an invasion.

Photolumen. Another French publisher, Photolumen produced a numbered (1 to at least 24) series of black-and-white photo cards related to the Maginot Line. Both exterior and interior views are offered. Virtually every aspect of this extensive fortification is covered. Most of the cards feature French soldiers performing their various duties—or merely relaxing, eating, and so on—within the massive complex. An intriguing, worthwhile series to possess.

Printline. Published a set of sketches by Marshall Davis about the American GI and his daily life in the military. Called *Deep Etch,* these cards are similar to the sort of pencil drawings found in popular magazines. The GI is pictured usually in mundane activities (letter writing, smoking, and relaxing). At least eight cards to the set.

Steinbach. Produced a set of black-and-white artist-drawn comic cards of soldiers' life. The artist-drawn (W. Morgan) set contains eight cards. Related to soldiers' personal lives rather than to battles or weapons.

U.S. Navy. Produced a set of real-photo cards about the Seabees. The set is composed of ten cards numbered 1650–1659 and including (#1650) "Raising the Flag," (#1651) "Driving Instruction," (#1652) "Operating a Whale Boat," (#1656) "Original Seabee," and (#1659) "Obstacle Course."

Valentine's. Published a set of message cards urging the British to persevere, do their duty, and not be afraid. Each card has an overprinted *V,* doubtless representing victory.

W. R. Thompson. This American publisher produced what may be the largest series of World War II postcards, numbering over 3000 separate cards. They are real photos and cover multiple military themes. Included are infantry training, general camp views from several different camps, weaponry, vehicles, and much more. There are several types of backs to these realistic, very desirable postcards. The photos are to be credited to the U.S. Army Signal Corps, the U.S. Navy, and the U.S. Air Force.

Anonymous. The following sets and series are by anonymous publishers. Origin is indicated when known.

- ☆ Belgian. A set of artist-signed (Bizuth) anti-Nazi drawings of soldiers, including some unfavorable caricatures of German army personnel.
- ☆ Belgian. A set of colored, artist-drawn cards published by an unidentified firm. Included are both military and civilian leaders (de Gaulle, Churchill, George VI and the queen, and others). A seldom-seen set.
- ☆ Belgian. A set of at least 12 artist-drawn sketches depicting the German Army of Occupation in Belgium. A few are unfavorable caricatures, but most seem to be relatively straightforward representations of German soldiers.
- ☆ Dutch. A set of artist-drawn (Smits) cards of insulting caricatures of Hitler, Goebbels, and the German soldier in general. A very interesting group of cards that resemble cartoon sketches.
- ☆ French. A series of artist-drawn (Cass), colored cards relating to the social aspects of French army and navy personnel. Half-whimsical, half-humorous, the cards deal primarily with the two things uppermost in the military man's mind: the opposite sex and food. Each card is captioned in both French and English.
- ☆ French. A colored set of eight cards related to France's victory, enemies, and heros (especially de Gaulle). Beautiful color; rare.
- ☆ French. A set of artist-drawn (Cadore) cards. Prominent among them are American GIs rescuing girls or catching and punishing the enemy (one card illustrates two Allied soldiers administering a spanking to a captured German).
- ☆ French. Published a set of six beautifully colored sketches obviously designed for propaganda purposes. The following captions and pictures constitute the offerings:

A l'Est	A Russian bear squeezing Hitler.
Le Rouleau Compresfeux Est Passé	Stalin waving a finger of triumph.
Ainsi Passe la Gloire	Appears to be Hitler at three stages of his life.
Tout Va Très Bien, Mme. La Marquise	Women in uniform before a female representation of Victory—an obvious allegory.
Dernier Coup de Massue de l'Oncle Sam	Uncle Sam preparing his weapon, a club, while Hitler, in the background, shakes his fist.
Salut à la Belgique Libérée	A smiling Franklin Roosevelt raises his hat to a Belgian flag.

- ☆ German. A colored, artist-drawn set of specifically identified soldiers (Captain Delicia, Colonel Brauer, others). Superbly executed; numbers in the 460s. Each man pictured is a hero since each is shown wearing an Iron Cross.
- ☆ German. A set of 24 real-photo cards of Iron Cross winners. The photographer is the most famous of all German cameramen, Heinrich Hoffman, who probably published this interesting set of cards, as well. The historical importance of these cards is tied to what they reveal about the German army's military sensitivities—whether its militaristic tendencies began at the top and filtered down or whether they were feelings already existing in the German people. It is noteworthy that Germany produced more of these types of cards than did all other countries combined.
- ☆ German. A series of postal stationary cards titled *Kriegs WHW* (War Winter Relief Campaign). Each buff-colored card shows a dark brown sketch of the bust of a hero from Germany's past, including Martin Luther, Heinrich I, Carl Peters, Bismarck, Frederick the Great, and Ulrich V. Hutten. Each card has an imprinted six-mark stamp, also dark brown. Individual cards are relatively easy to locate; the entire set is somewhat difficult to find.

☆ German. Series 2 of *Kriegs WHW.* Cards have a patriotic orientation and include drawings that symbolize the unity of the German people and German military. There is a bit of coloration added to the brown of the first series, and this series is more difficult to locate.

☆ German. A third series of *Kriegs WHW,* but dissimilar to the other two. The German government, which is probably the publisher of these three series, proved itself more imaginative with this group. Each card states "Tag der Wehrmacht fur das KWHW." Artist-drawn pictures and sketches, including mother and daughter dropping coins into a can, marked *KWHW,* carried by a dog; a parachutist with a KWHW can swooping over a bench occupied by a soldier and his lady friend; a motorcycle soldier with children aboard, one of whom is carrying a KWHW donation can; a soldier at a grocery carrying a canteen, giving a spoonful of soup to a woman with two children in the background.

☆ Italian. A set of artist-drawn (Pergine) cards portraying children at war.

☆ Portuguese. A set of artists' renditions devoted to various German military leaders, with a statement from the leader beneath each portrait.

☆ Swiss. Among the most poignant of antiwar statements are these captioned scenics detailing the reality of war. Included are vignettes of a soldier's graveyard titled "The Field of Honor"; the bodies of countless civilian casualties in a large, freshly dug grave, with the caption "Extreme Unction"; a frightened wife and mother with her equally terrified child looking at a letter on the table facing them, titled "The Death Notice"; and others. Each of these numbered postcards is an indictment of war—an essay in itself on the ultimate cost that war engenders. A seldom-seen group of at least 12 cards. Highly recommended.

☆ Another group of the *Keep 'Em Flying* series, this one is marked "U.S. Air Corps Series," AC-1 through AC-10. Various military aircraft are depicted. This is probably an unidentified series from Curt Teich.

☆ A numbered (beginning with 1) set of cards titled *Nazi Nursery Rhymes.* These artist-drawn cards (by the famous caricaturist Will Owen) either have very strong propaganda orientations or are unfavorable caricatures. Each has a poem at the bottom; cards are red-and-black; total numbers unknown. Scarce.

☆ A numbered series of artist-drawn (Reg Manning) comic cards, some of which show Hitler, Mussolini, and Hirihito fleeing from approaching Americans.

☆ A series of artist-drawn sketches by the most famous German artist, W. Willrich. These cards depict various types of soldiers, sailors, and airmen within the German armed forces. Everyone—from generals to privates, from desert troops to tank personnel—is illustrated. Very realistic and desirable cards.

☆ A set of artist-drawn cards (Jack Watson) titled *Navykards,* which were inspected and approved by the Navy Department; ten cards in an envelope.

☆ A set of artist-drawn cards (Peter Lutz) illustrating various Allies in vehicles. Roosevelt, Eisenhower, Stalin, Churchill, and Prince Berhard are among those so pictured. Each card shows a large-head, small-body figure (of one of these men) operating a small vehicle (tank, steamroller, jeep, ship). An unusual and seldom-seen group of cards.

☆ A series of artist-drawn black-and-white sketches by Marshal Davis. Displayed are the artist's renditions of life in the United States Army in various settings: from wake-up to bedtime, from domestic activities to combat-related ones, from military preparedness to social life. Truly a compendium of army life as seen through the eyes of soldier Davis.

☆ A serviceman's *Kard Kit* series of humorous cards; 24 cards with cover; U.S. servicemen.

☆ A set of artist-drawn (Arthur Szyk) cards, published in 1939, related to the Polish-American Fraternity. Primarily military scenics; rare.

☆ A set of colored German war decorations, both beautiful and instructive.

☆ A set titled *V for Victory.* Cards show various Allied flags, each with a giant *V* followed by *for Victory.* Numbered E5339 and E5340, and possibly more.

Publishers

Academy Patriotic Publications	British
Acme	
A. Daehler	German
A. D. Steinbeck	American
A. H.	
Alfred Oemler	German
American Colortype Company	American
American News Company	American
American Red Cross	American
Andre Leconte	French
A. Noyer	French
Anstalt	
Asheville Post Card Company	American
Atlantic Photo	German
Bamforth	British
Beals	American
B. Mitschke	German
C. A. P.	French/American
Capitol Souvenir Company	American
Carl Werner	German
Cockayne & Company	British
Colorpicture	American
Colorprint	
Coopers News Agency	American
Corn Products Refining Company	American
C. Pahl & Company	German
Curt Teich	American
Dagblad	Dutch
D. Constance Ltd.	British
Dells Photo Service	American
D. R. & Co.	American
E. A. Schwerdtfeger and Company	German
Eastern Publishing Company	
E. C. Kropp	American
E. Landrock	
Erich Kaunghammer	German

Publishers, Cont.

Famous Artist Syndicate	
Film Toto	
Fleetway Press	British
Franckh	German
Frank C. Meyer Company	
Friends of Free France	French
G. Artaud	French
German Government	
Giraud-Rivore	French
Graycraft Company	American
H & K	British
H. B. Limited	British
H. Chipault	French
Heinrich Hoffman	German
Hermann Becker	German
Hilborn Novelty Company	American
Inter City News Company	American
Jack H. Bain	Canadian
J. E. Huber	German
J. Olsen	Dutch
Jon. Thordsen	
J. Salmon Ltd.	British
Keystone	
Mastercraft Pictures	
M. D.	French
Millar and Lang	British
M. Lescuyer	French
Mutoscope	American
M. W. M.	American
Nels	
Ogden News Company	American
Overseas League	British
P. C.	French
Pepsi-Cola	American
Photochrom	British
Printline	American
Raphael Tuck	
Red River News Company	American
Regent Publishing Company	British
Riffelmacher	German
Robert Frante	German
Santway Photo Craft Company	American
Seagrams	American
Service News Company	American
Signal Corps	American
Spagna	
Steinbach	German
Tichnor Brothers	American
T. Klem	German
Union Pacific Railroad Company	American
U. S. O.	American
U.S. Treasury	American
Valentine's	British
V. E. Boeri	Italian
Weiner News Company	American
Werner	
W. R. Thompson	American

Artists

A. E. C.	British
Albrecht	German
Mabel Lucie Atwell*	British
Axster-Heudtlass	German
Bannister	British
A. F. D. Bannister	American
Paul Barbier	French
Barlog	

Artists, Cont.

S. Bartoli	Italian
L. M. Bayle	French
Berdenier	French
Claus Bergen	German
Berthelet	Italian
Bertiglia*	Italian
Bizuth	
Rivo Blass	
Karl Blossfeld	German
Boccasile	Italian
Bob Bondart	
Len Borkowski	American
Fritz Brauner	German
Sgt. Dave Breger*	American
E. Burner	French
Buxton*	British
Cadore	
Leslie Carr	British
Cass	French
Cheneval	French
G. Christie	British
Bernard W. Church	British
Averardo Circello	Italian
Guilo Cisari	Italian
Erich Cleff	German
Harry Partlett, "Comicus"	British
Phyllis Cooper	British
Marshall Davis*	American
DeBarre	
Depiere	
D'Ercoli	
Dinah	British
E. F.	
Franz Eichhorst	German
Ernst Eigener	German
Marc Ely	French
E. M. C.	British
Erier	German
Willy Exner	German
Jacques Faizant	French
G. Filoginno	Italian
Kit Forres	British
W. Gemm	German
Vesper George	American
Guy Georget	French
Goff	American
Gotschke	German
Leslie Grimes	British
H. Gross	German
A. Halle	
Max Halverson	American
W. Hartman	German
Bill Havenstein	American
Joseph Hemard	British
A. Hensel	German
Ax Heu	
W. Hoeck	German
Conrad Hommel	German
Ingvar	Danish
Bruno Jacobs	German
A. Jaegy*	
A. Janesch	
Jung*	German
A. Jusmet*	American
Kaklo	
Morris Kellern	British
Gottfried Klein*	German
Kretschman	German
La Monaca	Italian
R. Langer	German

Artists, Cont.

Wilhelm Limpart	German
H. Liska	
B. F. Long	American
William Long	
Lotschke	German
R. Lupus	
Peter Lutz	
Beatrice Mallett*	British
Reg Manning	
Massonet	
Theodore Matejko	
Reg Maurice	British
Donald McGill*	British
K. Merten	
W. Morgan	American
V. Mundorff	German
O'Gallop	
Paul M. Padua	
Paris	American
Floriano Pepe	Italian
Pergine	Italian
J. Picot	
Paul Prien	German
V. Pryani	Italian
Virgilio Retrosi	Italian
Agnes Richardson	British
Cecil Rigby	British
Norman Rockwell*	American
A. G. Santagata	Italian
Saroukhan	
Sauter	German
Schickardt	German
Jean Schnebelen	French
A. Hermann Schneider	German
Rich Schreiber	German
Johann Schult	German
Raoul Serres	French
Stocker Shaw	British
Howard Smith	American
Smits	
Soldatini	Italian
Spear	American
F. Spoltora	Italian
G. L. Stampa	British
Steen	
George Studdy	British
Jarko Sumavsky	Czech
Arthur Szyk*	Polish/American
Taylor	British
Laurie Taylor	British
D. Tempest	British
Bert Thomas	British
Barney Tobey	American
Karl Truppe	German
Will Tschech	German
Tscheck	
J. Turner	British
A. Ventiorini	Italian
P. A. Vicary	British
Jack Watson	American
Bob Wilkin	British
Gilbert Wilkinson	British
W. Willrich*	German
Kurt Wolfram	German
Sikko Woude	Dutch
Gyula Zilzer	French

** most popular*

Hitler's birthday, 1938. Government postal. R2

Proud, boasting member of Waffen SS. Anonymous. R3

Recruitment poster-type card for Waffen SS. Anonymous. R3

Hitler's birthday, 1938. Government postal. R3

Hitler with Mussolini and Generals Göring, Hess, and Ciano. Jos. Huber. R4

An interesting recruitment poster for Waffen SS. Anonymous. R3

Iron Cross with Hitler's statement, "There can only be one victor and that is us." 1939 government postal. R3

German soldier as part of German rule in Poland, 1941. Government postal. R3

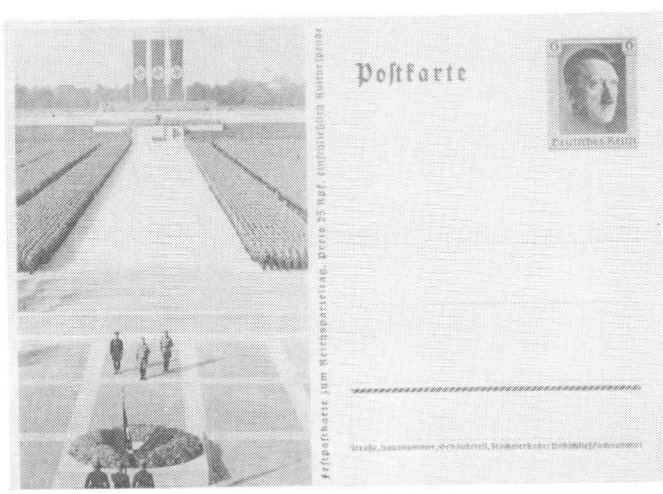

N.S. Party Convention; postal stationary, eight-card set, 1936. Each, R2

N.S. Party Convention, 1938. Central Office N.S.D.A.P. R3

N.S. Party Convention, 1939. Central Office N.S.D.A.P. R3

N.S. Party Convention, 1938. Georg Michel. R2

N.S. Party Convention, 1938. Hoffman Photo. R2

N.S. Party Convention, 1938. Hoffman Photo. R2

Belgium's King Leopold III, who earned his people's enmity by acquiescing to the Germans without a fight. Inter-Press. R3

War Winter Relief Campaign (K.W.H.W.). Government postal, series #1. R2

War Winter Relief Campaign (K.W.H.W.). Government postal, series #2. R2

German troops with their weapons. C. Pahl & Company. R2

German troops with their weapons. C. Pahl & Company. R2

German postal commemorative with a Nazi/military connection. R3

German feldpost on postal stationary. R2

Waffen SS in the role of protector. Photo by Hoffman. R3

German Red Cross card. R3

Hitler with facsimile signature. Anonymous. R3

Poster-type card for war bonds. U.S. Treasury Department. R3

Victory. Tichnor Brothers. R2

General Heydrich, head of Reich Main Security Office and organizational leader of the "Final Solution." Photo Hoffman. R3

Germans moving artillery across a recently constructed bridge. Photo by Hoffmann. R3

Victory and unity. Tichnor Brothers. R2

The Führer being greeted by Hitler Youth. Anonymous. R3

German soldier's song card. Robert Frante. R2

Adolf Hitler. Photo by Hoffmann. R2

The Supreme Nazi. Hermann Becker. R3

Introduction of a German rocket. Anonymous. R4

Hitler viewing his troops in Warsaw. Photo by Hoffmann. R3

Hitler with his generals at the Front. Photo by Hoffmann. R3

Nazi bridge building. Photo by Hoffmann. R3

Hitler saluting troops at the Front. Photo by Hoffmann. R3

German tank attacking a map of Europe. Feldpost. R2

The grim determination of the German army. Photo by Hoffmann. R2

Hitler in conquered Warsaw. Photo by Hoffmann. R3

German onslaught in Poland. Photo by Hoffmann. R3

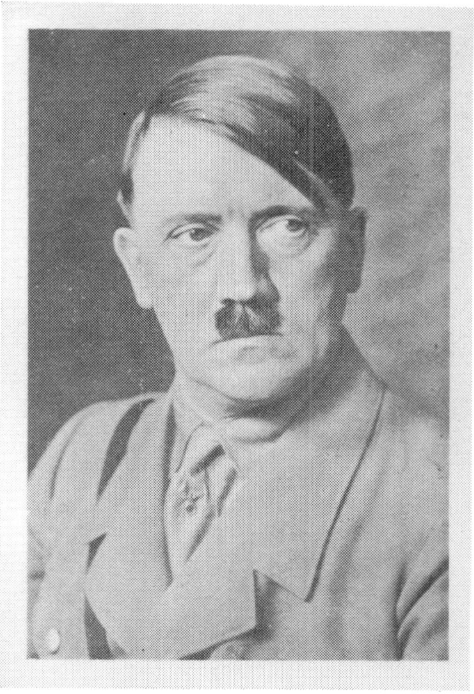

Adolf Hitler. Anonymous. R2

The SS in the East. Photo by Hoffmann. R4

Sketch of the Führer. K. Pechmann. R3

The German frontier police troops; poster-type. Anonymous. R3

General Adolf Golland, commander in chief of the Luftwaffe. Anonymous. R2

Field Marshal Rommel, the "Desert Fox." Photo by Hoffmann. R2

Hitler inspecting the conquered countryside. Photo by Hoffmann. R3

"Thanks for liberation from slavery" (a propaganda card that is more than insulting), canceled in Warsaw. Photo by Hoffmann. R3

Marseille Hauptmann, German aviator and hero of North Africa. Anonymous. R3

General Guderian. Photo by Hoffmann. R3

General Sepp Dietrich, Commander of 6th SS Panzer Army. Photo by Hoffmann. R3

Hitler with his troops in Warsaw. Photo by Hoffmann. R3

Waffen SS general Hausser. A. Daehler. R3

German infantry on the move. Albrecht & Meister. R2

German soldiers around their Führer. Photo by Hoffmann. R3

German infantry officer Meyer. Photo by Hoffmann. R4

Field marshal Hermann Göring. Photo by Hoffmann. R2

German infantrymen in action. C. Pahl & Company. R3

Nazi army in a 1936 parade. F. Brudmann. R3

Clearing away the rubble. Erich Gutjahr. R3

A German infantry charge. Erich Gutjahr. R3

Wermacht infantry preparing for battle. Oscar Tellgmann. R3

"German Destruction," The War in Poland *scenics. Mitteldeutsche Kunstanstalt. R3*

"Polish Work Detail," The War in Poland *scenics. Mitteldeutsche Kunstanstalt. R3*

"Polish Military Prisoners," The War in Poland *scenics. Mitteldeutsche Kunstanstalt. R3*

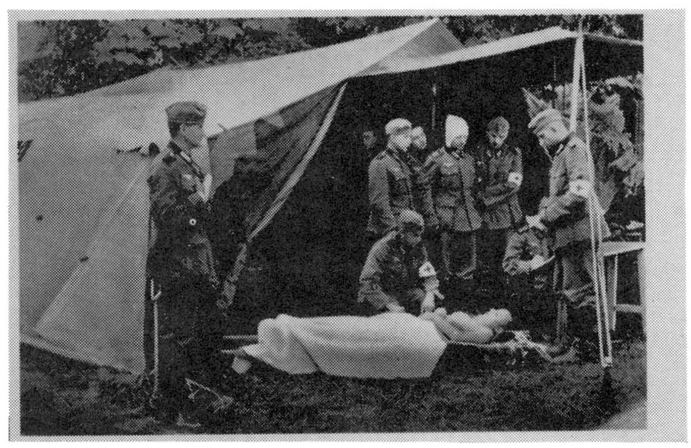

"Red Cross Station," The War in Poland *scenics. Mitteldeutsche Kunstanstalt. R3*

"Polish Women in Military Uniform," The War in Poland *scenics. Mitteldeutsche Kunstanstalt. R4*

"More German Destruction," The War in Poland *scenics. Mitteldeutsche Kunstanstalt. R3*

"Germans with Polish Prisoners," The War in Poland *scenics. Mitteldeutsche Kunstanstalt. R3*

"German Artillery Barrage," The War in Poland *scenics. Mitteldeutsche Kunstanstalt. R3*

"Fleeing Jews," The War in Poland *scenics. Mitteldeutsche Kunstanstalt. R4*

"Germans Burying a Fellow Soldier," The War in Poland *scenics. Mitteldeutsche Kunstanstalt. R4*

British general Bernard Montgomery. Raphael Tuck. R3

"The Barricades," Liberation of Paris *series. C.A.P., series #1. R3*

"The F. F. I. Parade," Liberation of Paris *series. C.A.P., series #13. R3*

British lt. general Sir Miles Dempsey; commanded the British and Canadian forces that landed at Gold, Juno, and Sword beaches at Normandy on D-Day. Raphael Tuck. R3

General George S. Patton with sultan Sidi Mohamed. Anonymous. R4

Camp Peary, Virginia. The parrot was a favorite naval symbol. U.S. Navy. R2

"Welcome to the 'Jeeps,'" Liberation of Paris *series. C.A.P., series #21. R3*

"General de Gaulle at the Triumphal Arch," Liberation of Paris *series. C.A.P., series #22. R3*

"U.S. Field Artillery," USA-2 (U.S. Army Series 2). Curt Teich. R1

"U.S. Armored Regiment." USA-4; Curt Teich. R1

"U.S. Navy." USN-4; Curt Teich. R1

"U.S. Navy," USN-5 (U.S. Navy Series 5). Curt Teich. R1

"Greetings from Fort Sill, Oklahoma." Curt Teich. R1

"A 37-Millimeter Gun in Action, U.S. Army Camp." Asheville Post Card Company. R1

"U.S. Planes and Tanks During Maneuvers." Asheville Post Card Company. R1

"U.S. Medium Tank with 75mm Gun." Asheville Post Card Company. R1

"Jeep in action at Fort Custer, Michigan." Tichnor Brothers. R1

An unpopular activity. Graycraft Card Company. R1

Generalissimo Chiang Kai-Shek—MacArthur eulogized him; President Truman considered him a thief. Graphic Post Card Company. R3

"Official Platform Place de la Concorde, Generals Koenig, de Gaulle, Bradley," Liberation of Paris *series. C.A.P., series #20. R4*

Busting suds (washing dishes). Graycraft Card Company. R1

"Infantry advances through smoke screen with tank support." W. R. Thompson. R2

Obstacle course training. W. R. Thompson. R2

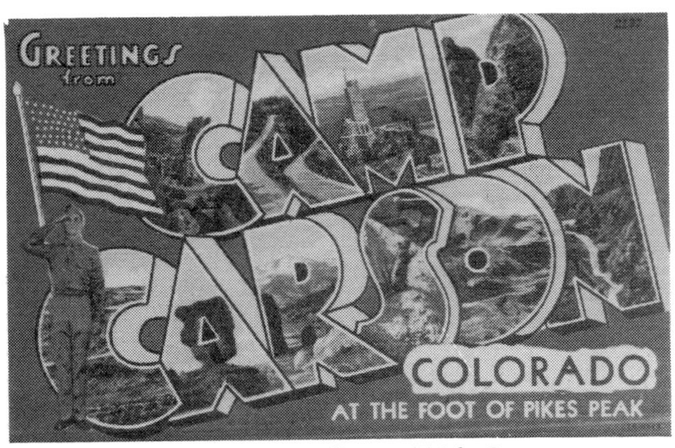

Greetings from Camp Carson." Curt Teich. R1

Greetings from Fort Bliss. Curt Teich. R1

"Keep 'em Flying." Curt Teich. R2

Rifle practice at a U.S. Army camp. Asheville Post Card Company. R1

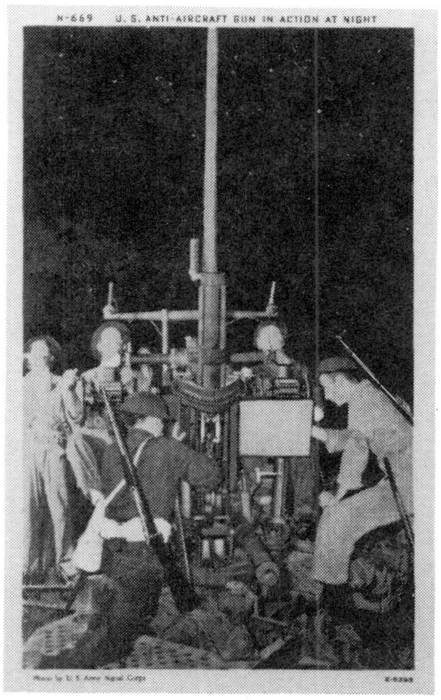

"U.S. Anti-Aircraft Gun in Action at Night." Asheville Post Card Company. R2

A sweater for the sergeant, Private Breger *series. Graycraft Card Company, #307. R2*

G.I. ingenuity, Private Breger *series. Graycraft Card Company, #311. R2*

Winston Churchill in classic pose. E.H. Wilkinson series. R3

American G.I.'s, typically in a hurry. Curt Teich. R1

Breger asking for a "military haircut," Private Breger *series. Graycraft Card Company, #312. R2*

Hard to hate a stuffed bag, Private Breger *series. Graycraft, #313. R2*

Winston Churchill addressing naval troops. E.H. Wilkinson series. R3

Winston Churchill. E.H. Wilkinson series. R3

Winston Churchill with the army. E.H. Wilkinson series. R3

Winston Churchill shaking hands with the youngest dockyard worker. E.H. Wilkinson series. R3

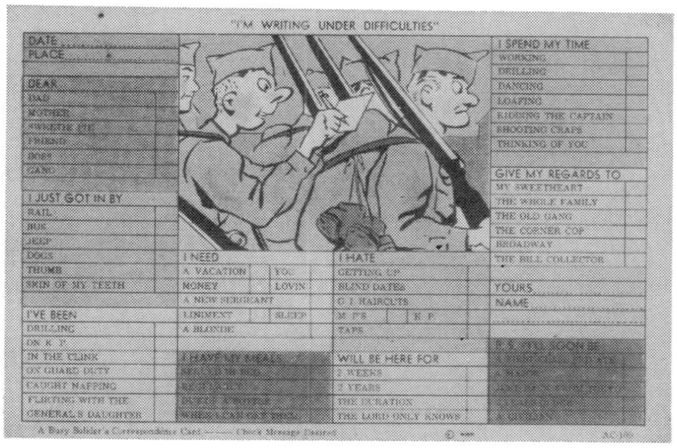

Busy Soldier's Correspondence Card. M.W.M. *R1*

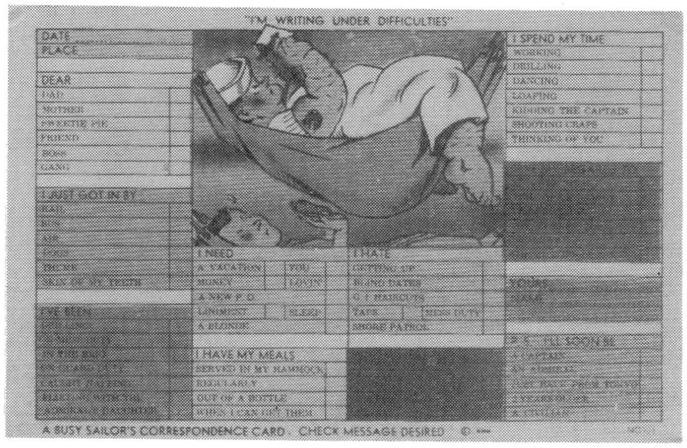

Busy Sailor's Correspondence Card. M.W.M. R1

Serving in the Tank Corps. Tichnor Bros. R1

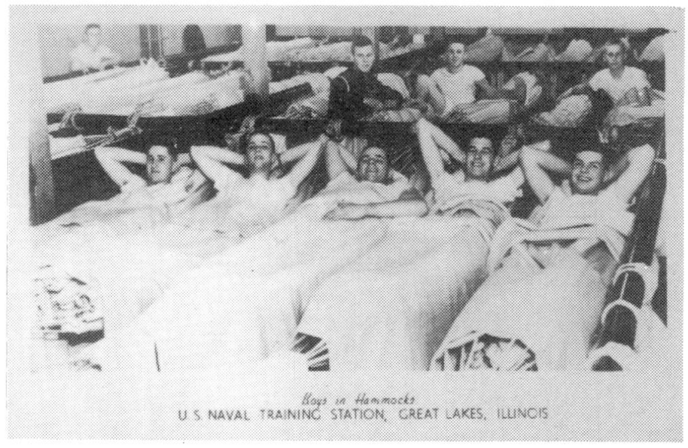

"Boys in Hammocks; U.S. Naval Training Station, Great Lakes, Illinois," 1942. Anonymous. R2

"Just Showing There's a Big Kick in This Outfit." Asheville Post Card Company. R2

"Machine Gun Nest; Camp Lejeune, Marine Base, New River, N.C." Curt Teich. R2

"The U.S.O. Buddies' Club, Boston, Mass." Frank C. Meyer. R2

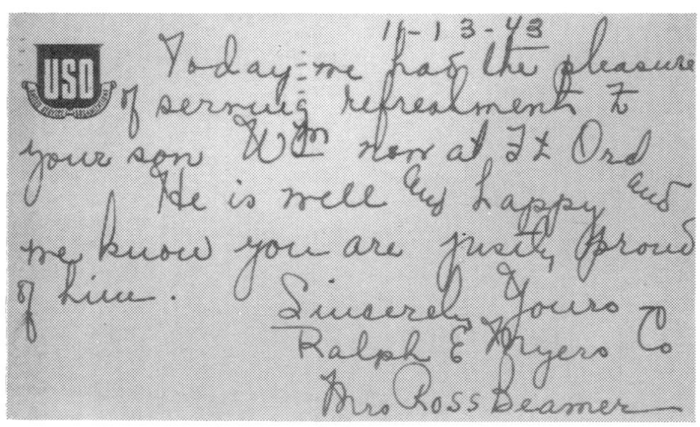

U.S.O. Correspondence card. R1

"Red Cross Canteen." Acme. R2

American Red Cross Canteen Service card. R1

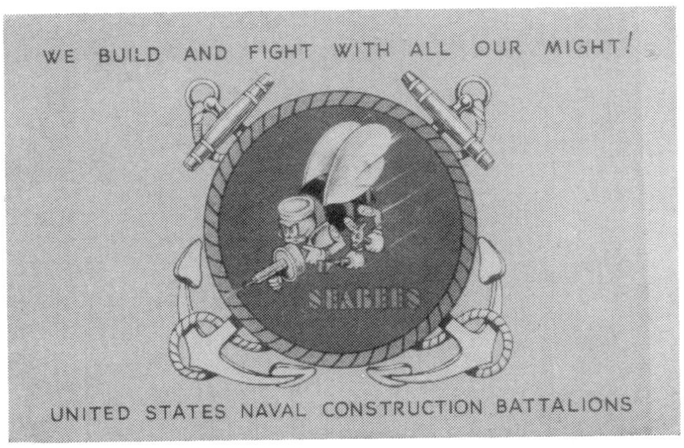

The Seabees; builders and fighters. U.S. Navy. R2

An American B-25 bomber. North American Aviation. R2

Keeping the press apprised. L. W. Company. R1

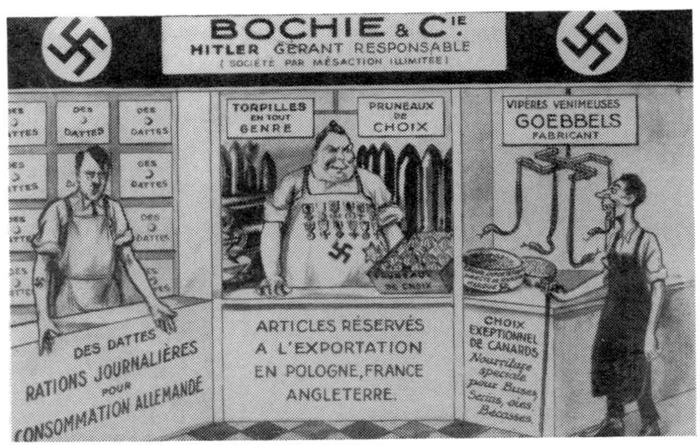

Hitler, Göring, and Goebbels as merchants of death and deceit. P.C. (Paris). R4

"Seabee Commando Trainees, Camp Peary, Va." U.S. Navy. R2

Even posed, Churchill looks deliberate. E.H. Wilkinson series. R3

The type of slander war encourages. Curt Teich. R2

The "little red school house" in Reims, France, where Germans signed the unconditional surrender to General Eisenhower. Floyd L. Purnell (sent by Purnell himself). R3

"His 'I've nothing more to ask'"—poignant reference to Hitler's prewar "requests." P.C. (Paris). R4

"The Boogie Man, Our Sargie." I. C. P. Comic Cards. R1

11 The Chino-Japanese War

Part I: Chronology

Although there are several wars in the "General" category, the one about which there were the fewest postcards and the least knowledge is the Chino-Japanese War of 1894–1895. The following information is therefore presented as a minor tonic to that historically unhealthy condition.

Chronology

Date	Event
1894	
June	Rebellion against the king (emperor) in southern Korea with what was believed to be Japanese connivance; Korean king asks Chinese emperor for assistance; Chinese troops are dispatched. Stating that this in violation of the treaty of April 18, 1885, whereby China is obliged to notify Japan of any incursions into Korea, Japan also takes the offensive by dispatching ships and troops to the area.
July	Japanese ships and troops arrive in Korea.
July 23	Japanese attack the palace at Seoul, later take the king captive.
July 25	Chinese transport vessel *Kowshing* sunk by Japanese cruiser *Namiwa* about 40 miles from Chemulpo.
July 29	Chinese defeated at Chanhon.
August 1	Japan declares war on China.
August 11	Japanese fleet fires on Chinese forts in the Straits of Pechili.
August 17	Chinese under General Tio rout Japanese at Ping Yang and the next day at Chungho.
September 6–13	Japanese capture Chinese entrenchments; Koreans defeat 2000 Japanese marching to Seoul.
September 15	Japanese army under Field Marshal Yamagata opens a cannonade under Ping Yang; Chinese return fire fiercely, but are defeated the next day and Japanese take possession.
September 16	Japanese attack Chinese fleet at mouth of Yalu river; determined fighting is on both sides. After sustaining considerable loss, Japanese prove victorious.
October 8	Japanese occupy Wi-Ju after a brief battle with the Chinese.
October 25	Japanese victory at Hoosan; the next day the Japanese army under Field Marshal Yamagata annihilates 16,000 Chinese in the command of General Sung at Kiu-lien-tcheng.
October 26	Japanese invade Manchuria and capture it in a few weeks.
November 3	Prince Kung asks the European powers to mediate and indicates that China is willing to relinquish suzerainty over Korea and even pay a war indemnity.
November 19–24	Port Arthur captured after several days of intense fighting on land and by naval bombardments. In retaliation for the alleged mutilation and decapitation of several Japanese prisoners by the Chinese, the Japanese show no mercy upon taking Port Arthur—shooting fleeing soldiers and pinioning, stripping, hacking with knives, disemboweling, and dismembering others.
December	Continued fighting, mainly Japanese victories. China increases the number of demotions of military personnel through court martials and investigations.
1895	
January 7	Independence of Korea proclaimed at Seoul; king and his cabinet declare themselves and their country to be free of outside influence (which means Japanese will thenceforth be exercising suzerainty over Korea).
January 10	Defeat of Chinese under General Seh at Kai-phing.
January 19	Defeat of Chinese at Teng-chou after Japanese bombardment of the fort there.
January 30	After repeatedly being repulsed, the Japanese finally capture all forts at Wei-hai-wei.
February 3–18	Japanese crush the back of the Chinese navy at We-hai-wei; Admiral Ting, General Chang, and Captain Liu commit suicide.
February 19	Taotai Kung and General Yeh-chi-cao are sentenced to imprisonment until the next autumn, when they are to be executed.
March 3	Chinese army in Manchuria twice attacks Japanese positions at Hai-tcheng, but is repulsed; Japanese under General Nodzu defeat 18,000 Chinese between the Liao Yang and Niu Chwang roads.
March 9	General Sung's army defeated by Japanese at Thien-chuang-thai; General Nodzu promoted to Field Marshal because of his successors in Manchuria.

March 19	Li Hung Chang (restored to honor after a series of political setbacks), the peace ambassador, arrives at Shimonoseki, Japan; on March 25 he is attacked by a young Japanese with a gun, and is shot in the cheek, but he quickly recovers. All of Japan, from the emperor down, expresses regret and outrage at the incident.
March 22–April 10	More Japanese successes on the Pexadore Islands, Yenkung Penninsula, Fisher Island, and the forts of Haichow.
April 16	Peace treaty signed.
August	In China, outrages are begun against Christian missionaries, a precursor to the Boxer Rebellion.

Part II: Details of War

Military Leaders

Chinese

Li Hung Chang	
General Kinlin	Taken prisoner after Ping Yang defeat
General Kirin	
General Lin-Kun-Yi	Originally viceroy of Nankin; appointed to command (December 1894) of all Chinese armies in the field
General Liu	Commited suicide after naval loss
General Ma	
General Neih	
General Seh	
General Shui	
General Sung	After the defeat at Ping Yang, assigned by Imperial decree to the command of the Manchu militia; all other Generals ordered to obey him totally
Admiral Ting	Commander of Chinese fleet (known as commander of the Peiyang Squadron)
General Tio	
General Tso Fonk Wai	Commander of the Chinese Manchurian army (mortally wounded and captured after defeat at Ping Yang)
Captain von Hanneken	Commander of the Kowshing
General Wei	Convicted of cowardice at Ping Yang and demoted (later beheaded)
General Tsa Paok Woi	Taken prisoner after Ping Yang defeat
General Wei Jink Woi	Taken prisoner after Ping Yang defeat
General Yeh	Beheaded for cowardice at Ping Yang

Japanese

Major General Hasegawa	
Viscount Ito	Naval commander in chief of the combined squadrons
General Katsura	
General Kawakami	Generalissimo of all Japanese armies
Captain Kawaraba	Commander of HJM *Yoshino*
Rear Admiral Tsuboi Kozo	
General Nodzu	
General Nozi	
General Oshima	
Count Oyama	Commander in chief of 2nd Army
Commander Sakamoto	Commander of HJM *Akagi*
Field Marshal Yamagata	
Commander Yamaji	Commander of 1st Provisional Army
Lt. Colonel Kimura Yuko	Officer in 3rd Regiments

Vessels

Chinese

Ting Yuen	Flagship
Kowshing	Transport, sunk July 25, 1894
Yang Wei	Cruiser, burned at Yalu river
Chao Yang	Cruiser, burned at Yalu river
King Yuen	Battleship, sunk at Yalu river
Chih Yuen	Battleship, sunk at Yalu river
Tsi Yuen	
Kwang Chia	
Chen Yuen	
Lai Yuen	
Ching Yuen	

Japanese

Naniwa, Yoshino, Takachicho, Akitsushima (formed the First Flying Squadron)
Chijoda
Itsukushima
Hashidate
Hiyei
Fuso
Matsushima
Akagi
Saikyo Maru

Major Incidences

☆ Engagement of the Yellow Sea
☆ Taking of Port Arthur
☆ Fall of Wei-hai-Wei
☆ Defeat of Chinese navy at Yalu river (first battle involving modern ironclads)

Peace Treaty Conditions (Peace of Shimonoseki)

☆ The independence of Korea.
☆ The retention of the conquered places by Japan.
☆ The cession of the Liaotung peninsula by China to Japan.
☆ The permanent cession of the islands of Formosa and the Pescadores by China to Japan.

☆ The payment of a war indemnity of 200 million taels in silver (100 million dollars) by China to Japan, in seven yearly installments, 5 percent interest being added each year on the amount remaining unpaid, the whole of the interest to be cancelled if China should pay the entire indemnity within three years.
☆ The opening of the ports of Çhingtu, Kai-fong, Huchou, and Shoaking, in China, to foreign commerce.

Because of European opposition to the treaty, Japan agreed to accept a money compensation in place of the cession of the Liaotung peninsula.

Afterward

In June 1896, Russia pressured Japan into an arrangement whereby both countries exercised control over Korea. In actuality, Russia's was much the greater role. Russia changed the Korean monarch's title from *king* to *emperor*.

12 General Potpourri

Other wars.

Part I: Background

Easily the broadest of all military categories is the one I shall call "General Potpourri." As the name suggests, it must be especially broad to encompass so many other categories. In fact, every conceivable type of military card not dealt with previously is to be placed under this heading. Briefly, these would fall under the following groupings:

☆ Pre-1870 cards
☆ Interwar cards
☆ Wars and conflicts not already covered

Under pre-1870 postcards, the types would include prepostcard-era wars and peoples (everything before 1869 for basic postcards and 1870 for all picture postcards). These, in turn, would be comprised of, but not limited to, the following: Napoleonic Wars, Austro-Prussian War, American Revolutionary War, American Civil War, and others. For all these conflicts, picture postcards exist, though not in abundant supply. Many are merely reproductions of paintings hanging in the world's museums, but not all. Some are copies of daguerreotypes; others, special artist-drawn creations. Still others, some rare ones among them, are anniversary or commemorative cards relating to these earlier conflicts. Not a few of those in these latter groups are excellent historical items in their own right—cards that may be placed with pride in anyone's collection. Incidentally, like most such treasures, the more appealing specimens are often the rarer ones and frequently have asking prices commensurate with their elusiveness.

The pre-1870 military people about whom postcards were produced could also fill several dozens of albums. Among them, the chief figure appears to be that of Napoleon Bonaparte, and picture postcards concerning him run into the dozens of individual specimens. A large number of firms have offered for sale postcards related to the general who would be emperor that are certainly worth preserving. Even the famous Raphael Tuck and Sons thus immortalized him. The ones that seem to be the most popular (as they were at the time of their manufacture) are the *Fantasy Heads* by P. F. B. and others, in which Napoleon's bust is composed of soldiers and weapons. There are more variations of this theme, including the use of nude female figures to constitute his facial parts, as well as an intricate map design that serves the same function. Another fascinating Napoleonic item (used with others as well) is the installment card. Installment cards are individual cards meant to be placed either alongside or atop one another to reveal Napoleon in a classic pose, surrounded by images of his exploits. Obviously a collection of Napoleonic postcards would be well worth the gathering, but the would-be researcher should be advised that this author knows of no completed checklist on him.

Although the "Little Corsican" is easily the winner for a number of cards devoted to one subject under this heading, it is equally true that his portrait did not exist in postcard isolation. Other persons to be so honored include a plethora of familiar visages: Otto von Bismarck, George Washington, Joan of Arc, Wilhelm I, Frederick the Great, Peter the Great, Catherine the Great—to name only a few. Again, not all are equally well done, nor are all of equal scarcity, but each is a miniature of history and a reminder of a world committed to memory, to books, to art objects, and to illustrations (in the form of postcards). The most inviting aspect of all this is that these cards are generally priced according to their scarcity. In other words, most are cheap, which makes them bargains in a market with plenty of room for expansion—a situation that common sense dictates will not remain forever.

The second grouping, the interwar cards, represents no small number of pasteboard types. Under this subcategory are special occasion cards; heroes and villains; U.S.O. cards; celebration types; monuments and national cemeteries; soldiers' and sailors' rest homes; camp cards; miscellaneous view cards of training or other soldier activities; song, verse, and story cards; reunion-related cards; heroes' statues, birthplaces, and grave sites; real photos of hometown boys in uniform; memorial cards; and others. Clearly, these types constitute many thousands of separate cards, totaling millions in the racks.

The final listing of the wars and conflicts not discussed in the text also contains dozens, if not hundreds, of individual picture postcards. Among these lesser-known campaigns are the Chino-Japanese War, 1894–1895; Chinese Civil War, 1911–1912; Italian Turkish War, 1911–1912; Italian Campaigns in Libya and Ethiopia, 1930–1936; Spanish Civil War, 1936–1939; Abyssinian War, 1939; Chino-Japanese War, 1937–1945.

Although these wars have not attracted the interest or attention of their better-known counterparts, it is to be understood that all the cards related to these conflicts are scarce to rare. None would be rated less than R3, with most of them deserving R4 and R5 designations. As postcard collecting becomes more sophisticated and research increases, deltiology will join numismatics and philately by pricing primarily according to rarity rather than strictly by popularity. When that happens, these types of cards will be sought for their uniqueness and historical value.

Napoleon and Bismarck: Military Geniuses

One of the truly absorbing things about studying events and people from the prepostcard era who have nonetheless been recorded with pasteboard representations is having these images to add to both the legends and our knowledge of those people. In this regard, the collector is doubly rewarded when it comes to analyzing the lives of Napoleon and Bismarck.

Arguably the two greatest military leaders of the past two centuries are Napoleon Bonaparte and the architect of the German Empire, Count Otto von Bismarck. It is significant that in each case, the leader not only had the command of field operations, but was active simultaneously with a relatively free hand in the political arena. That they succeeded where other men had failed testified to their genius; that both recognized the necessity of combining political ingenuity with tactical military expertise speaks of their intelligence. Being able to wield these sometimes separate components in an effective manner reveals their command of craftsmanship and cunning.

Unlike Hitler, Mussolini, and a host of other leaders great and small whose primary goals seemed to be ego gratification and emotional release, Napoleon and Bismarck were shrewd, farsighted men of the type that history will continue to love *and* hate, despise *and* praise. Postcard publishers, never remiss in furnishing their purchasing public with the items for which they clamor, produced many and varied cards on both men.

Napoleon

As mentioned earlier, no other prepostcard-era military figure has achieved the reproduction status of Napoleon Bonaparte. Card after innumerable card of the Little Corsican was produced and placed in racks the world over. Some depict the emperor/general leading his men into one of history's famous battles. Others showcase, in the most vivid colors, Napoleon in ermine robe, a crown upon his head, a sceptre in his hand. Some show him either being transported to or living in exile; others are character studies of a man about whom much has been written and much known, but somehow never fully understood. A man of intrigue, Bonaparte had the ability and charisma to lead men, conquer women, and structure society, from education and politics to religion—and all according to the dictates of a mind in continuous intellectual ferment. This is not to suggest that Napoleon did it all by himself. Indeed, he was astute enough to place competent men in key positions to assist him and to make recommendations, but it was his agenda to which these other men brought forward their ideas. He was multifaceted—fiery flashes of temper and spontaneous decision-making were only two parts of his engaging, incessantly thought-generating intellect. The image some historians have presented of a leader capable of drawing designs for a new school as he completed campaign preparations on the battlefield tell about a man with a restless nature and a quick mind.

No wonder there is a fascination with likenesses of him. Among the most beautiful Napoleon cards—and therefore those eagerly sought by collectors—are the ones executed by the renowned firm of Stengel and Company. The coloration and attention to detail exemplified by these artist-drawn cards make them excellent acquisitions.

Bismarck

Although Bismarck's life spanned the years both before and during the early postcard era, his reputation was made previous to it. Deltiologists may be thankful that Germany was the largest producer of picture postcards before 1918, for it was during the time frame of the 1890s through the end of the First World War that the bulk of cards referring to Count Bismarck were published, and those by a Germany grateful to the creator of its empire.

The man himself? Given both to forceful speech and direct approach, Bismarck was well suited to guide the fortunes of Prussia for his less aggressive master, Wilhelm I. Consolidating Prussia's position both politically and militarily with diplomacy and cannon, the Iron Chancellor seldom made the wrong move. When it suited his purposes, he opposed no less an institution than the Catholic Church; when it strengthened Prussia's status, he made an ally of his conquered foe, Austria. Balancing himself between statesmanship and war, Bismarck sought to guide first Prussia, then all of Germany under Prussian hegemony, onto the stable footing of political continuity with the Hohenzollerns of Prussia in control.

Unfortunately, Wilhelm II (the third Hohenzollern on the throne, he followed his father) wanted to devise his own counsel rather than follow that of his mentor. In fact, he insisted on it. Thus the old man's advice was at first ignored; following this, Wilhelm manipulated Bismarck into a no-win situation and gladly accepted his resignation. But neither Germany nor history forgot him, and it is interesting to observe that there were even postcards of him offered for sale during World War I, almost 20 years after his death. Germans who sought a wiser ruler than Wilhelm II knew exactly where to turn—to yesterday and to Bismarck.

For both Napoleon and Bismarck, the postcard arrived too late to contemporaneously record their actions and accomplishments, but when it did come along, it looked back long enough to take several images of them and transfer those onto pasteboard for posterity. Although military genius preceded the postcard, and political intelligence followed it, it typified both as well as, if not better than, any one person has done.

Part II: Postcards

Types and Categories

The types and categories that follow are included to indicate the many kinds of postcards that fall into this category. Moreover, in a number of cases, the listing represents as many as a dozen or more separate picture postcards.

There is much room for further research in all these areas, and ideally this book will stimulate such research.

Type	Category
Abyssinian War, 1939	R4
Admiral Nelson cards	R2–R3
Advertising cards with military motifs	R3
American Civil War cards	R1–R2
American Legion–related	R2–R3
American Revolutionary War cards	R1–R2
Army or Navy museums	R2
Austro-Prussian War	R3–R4
Bonus Army Incident, 1932 (Thousands of World War I veterans marched to Washington and camped out to demand bonuses they had been promised; they were driven out by the Army. George S. Patton was one of the officers in charge of dispersing them.)	R4
British National Antarctic Expedition, 1901, Commander Scott	R4–R5
British Wars, miscellaneous, artist-drawn	R3
Burial of national heroes	R2
Cards of little-known military events:	
Miscellaneous, real-photo	R3–R4
Other	R3–R4
Cards relating to military traditions, actions, or honors	R2–R3
Cards showing soldiers or other military types from ancient to medieval times	R1-R2
Chinese Civil War, 1912	R4
Chino-Japanese War, 1894–1895	R5
Chino-Japanese War, 1937–1945	R3–R4
Christmas and New Year's greetings, non–war-related	R3
Civilians entering the military, pre-1905	R3
Civilians entering the military, post-1905	R1–R2
Comic cards, non–war-related:	
American	R1–R2
British	R2
Others	R2–R3
D.A.R.–related	R2–R3
Decoration Day cards	R2–R3
Decoration Day cards featuring women in uniform	R3
Dedicating statues of national heroes	R2–R3
Dreyfus Trial–related	R3–R4
Flag cards	R1–R2
Forms of torture	R3–R4
G.A.R. meetings	R3
George Washington, military-related only	R2–R3
German lithographic types, 1890–1905:	
Good views of uniforms	R3–R4
Maneuvers	R3
Miscellaneous Gruss Aus types showing soldiers in various settings	R3
Mock battles	R3
Showing equipment or weapons	R3–R4
Soldiers enjoying themselves	R3
Special military units	R3–R4
300 days left in service	R3
Views of camp	R3
With insets of kaiser	R3–R4
All others	R3–R4
Group photos of various regiments, non–war-related	R2–R4
Hands-across-the-sea types	R2–R3
Heroes, military, non–war-related:	
Captain Philo Norton McGiffin	R4
Colonel Goethals	R3–R4
Commodores Peary and Scott	R2–R3
Major Burnham	R4
All others	R2–R4
Hold-to-light cards	R4–R5
Installments:	
As a set	R5
Each	R2
Interwar cards of military leaders:	
Common types	R2–R3
Scarcer types	R3–R4
Interwar humor cards	R1–R3
Italian campaigns in Libya and Ethiopia, 1900–1936	R3
Italian-Turkish War, 1911–1912	R3–R4
Joan of Arc:	
Artist-drawn, black-and-white or color	R2
Museum reproductions, black-and-white	R1
Museum reproductions, color	R2
Real-photo types with women dressed like Joan of Arc	R2
Statues	R1

Large-letter greetings from various camps	R1–R2
Lithographic types—American, British, French, Italian:	
Pre-1910	R3–R4
Post-1910	R2
Lithographic types—Japanese, Russian, all others:	
Pre-1910	R4–R5
Post-1910	R3–R4
Mechanicals	R4–R5
Metamorphics:	
Bismarck	R3–R4
Napoleon	R3
Others	R4
Military academies other than West Point:	
American	R2
British	R2
Others	R3–R4
Military air balloons	R2
Military booklets:	
Pre-1910	R4
Post-1910	R3–R4
Military camps, aerial views	R1
Military cards, close-ups	R1–R2
Military documents reproduced on postcards	R3
Military glamour cards, artist-drawn, pre–World War I	R3–R4
Military nurses	R3
Military parades and celebrations	R2–R3
Military personnel on leave	R2–R3
Military police–related	R3
Napoleonic Wars	R2–R3
Napoleon-related, miscellaneous	R1–R2
National Guard armories	R1–R2
National heroes from the past used as propaganda	R2–R3
National military headquarters buildings	R2
Naval fleets on tour or maneuvers:	
Pre-1914	R3–R4
Post-1914	R2–R3
Naval vessels during peacetime, stationary illustrations	R2
Otto von Bismarck:	
Commemoratives	R3–R4
Real-photo types	R2–R3
Undivided-back cards	R3–R4
Pay-day cards	R1–R2
Presentations of colors	R2
Prevention of war–related	R4
Raphael Tuck cards related to American Revolutionary War	R2–R3
Real photos of hometown boys in uniform	R1–R2
Red Cross–identified cards sold for benefit of wounded and disabled veterans	R3
Representations of past military heroes	R3
Romantic encounters between soldiers and women:	
Pre-1905	R3
Post-1905	R1–R2
Sam Houston–related	R2
Servicemen's clubs	R2
Ships in peacetime:	
Post-1905	R2
Pre-1905	R3
Ships woven in silk, non–war-related	R5
Soldiers' and sailors' rest homes	R2
Soldiers in training, non–war-related, post–World War I	R1–R2
Song, verse, and story cards	R1–R2
Spanish Civil War, 1936–1939	R4
Special cards to raise funds for wounded soldiers	R3–R4
Special military ceremonies relating to christenings, birthdays, anniversaries, inaugurations, and more:	
Real-photo	R3–R4
Other	R3–R4
Statues of military heroes by themselves	R1
Swastika "Good Luck" cards	R2
Testaments to the women behind the soldiers and sailors	R2
Trafalgar Day cards	R2
Treaty cards:	
Pre-1914	R3–R4
Post-1914	R3–R5
Troops being reviewed, non–war-related:	
Pre-1905	R3–R4
Post-1905	R2–R3
United States Indian Wars	R3
United States war with Mexico, 1840s	R3
U.S. Marine–related	R2–R3
U.S.O. cards	R2
U.S. patriotic cards related to:	
Civil War	R2–R3
Memorial Day, G.A.R.	R2–R3
Military leaders	R1–R3
Revolutionary War	R2
Veterans' parades	R3
Veterans Day cards	R2–R3
Veterans' hospitals	R1
Veterans' organization activities	R2–R4
Views of Tomb of the Unknown Soldier	R1–R2
Views of weaponry or equipment, not during wartime, post-WWI	R1–R2
War councils	R3–R4
War Department–related	R1–R2
West Point cards	R2–R3
Women in the military, non–war-related:	
Pre-1910	R4
Post-1910	R2–R3
Woven in silk, leaders, regiments, others	R3–R5

Sets and Series

A. & G. Black. Produced three numbered series of artist-drawn (L. V. Lovett) colored cards of British regiments. Also pre–World War I.

American News Company. Produced a set of cards, *How the U.S. Honors Its Naval Heroes;* six cards.

A. N. This French publisher offered a numbered series of colored cards that are reproductions of paintings in the museum at Versailles. Many are of Napoleon and/or the French Revolution.

Army & Navy Novelty Company. A Columbus, Ohio, firm that published an unnumbered set of postcards of pre–World War I military types. These artist-drawn colored cards have a shield insignia of the American flag; desirably set, well executed.

A. S. Company. Issued a #200 series of six cards dealing with a soldier's life from youth to old age.

Bamforth. Produced a song series (#5074) on Joan of Arc; three cards.

Birn Brothers. Produced at least three cards relating to the North Pole discovery; comical in nature, they show a man with a penguin.

Blum and Degen. This English firm published a set of pre–World War I artist-drawn (F. O'Beirne) cards of British regiments. A historic set.

Das Grosse Jahrhundert (The Great Century). A series of German Gruss Aus cards. The century is the nineteenth and the cards picture Germany's most noted personalities of that period. Each undivided-back card has an image of the individual on the left with details about his life at the bottom right. Some writing in green. An interesting, educational set.

Davidson Brothers. Published a humorous artist-drawn (British artist, Tom Browne) set titled *Yeomanry*. Cards are of the volunteer cavalry force that was organized in 1761 to serve as Home Guard and was later incorporated into the Territorial Army. Cards depict soldiers going through drills and exercises, and otherwise attempting to adjust to military life. A scarce set.

Decoration Day Series. The following are series, by various publishers, relating to Decoration Day:

☆ *A. S. B.* Series #283, set of six.
☆ *Fred Lounsbury.* Series #2083; artist is C. Bunnell; color; set of four.
☆ *Gabriel.* Produced a set for Decoration Day.
☆ *International Art.* Series #973, signed *Clapsaddle;* #973-1 to #973-6.
☆ *International Art.* Series #2444; set of six; Clapsaddle.
☆ *International Art.* Series #2935; Clapsaddle.
☆ *International Art.* Series #4397; Clapsaddle.
☆ *Langsdorf.* Various series (#100 through ?).
☆ *L. R. Conwell.* Series 376–381; six cards; colorful.
☆ *L. R. Conwell.* Series in 380s; six cards.
☆ *Nash.* Series D-6.
☆ *Nash.* Series #2, set of six.
☆ *Nash.* Series #3, set of six.
☆ *P. Sander.* Artist-drawn (W. F. Burger), titled *Honor the Brave 1861–65;* series #625.
☆ *Raphael Tuck.* Series #107 for Decoration Day; 12 cards.
☆ *Raphael Tuck.* Series #158 for Decoration Day; 12 cards.
☆ *Taggart.* Series #600.

D. Goldberg. Produced a black-and-white set of cards (#1 to ?) titled *U.S. Army and National Guard Series.* These pre–World War I cards (copyright 1905) illustrate various activities at camp, ranging from social- to training-related.

Donaldson. *American Heroes* set, 14 cards. These beautiful cards show inset vignettes of various heroes, with miniscenes of their heroics around each inset. At the bottom of each card is a description of the individuals pictured. Heroes include Robert E. Lee, Oliver Hazard Perry, Sam Houston, John Smith, Paul Revere, John Paul Jones, Winfield Scott, William Penn, George Washington, Abraham Lincoln, David Glasgow, and Philip Sheridan. This is a set worth possessing.

Elcelsior Fine Art (E. F. A.). A British company that produced a numbered series of colored cards of pre–World War I British regiments.

Enrique Muller. Published an unnumbered set of colored cards of U.S. battleships in 1908. A relatively common set, but desirable nonetheless.

Gale and Polden. A British company that issued a superb set of colored, artist-drawn, pre–World War I cards of British regiments.

George Falkner & Sons. Offered a set of artist-drawn (J. McNeil) colored cards of British regiments; historic; pre–World War.

Hampton's Magazine. Published a *North Pole Gravure* series in blue-tonė. Various illustrations related to Cook and Peary.

Harper. Published a set of real-photo (set of five) views of the New York State Soldier's and Sailor's Home. Post–World War I cards.

H. T. Cook. Published an unnumbered artist-drawn set of cards that humorously depict life at camp, soldiers in romantic situations, or soldiers while intoxicated. There are at least ten cards in this colored set.

Illustrated Postal Card Company. Published an unnumbered set of cards in 1908 titled *U.S. Sailors' Life.* Shown are a group of colored views of life aboard ship, including duties, equipment, and recreational activity. An interesting set.

I. M. Cline. An American firm that published a set of sepia cards titled *Anglo Life Series,* depicting a soldier with his sweetheart. Various scenes at the same setting. Cards are lettered and numbered (SL1–SL6).

Inter Art Company. Produced a set titled *The Language of Stamps.* Cards show a soldier or sailor inset in the center, surrounded with stamps. Interesting and illustrative.

International Art. Produced a #51000 series of artist-drawn (Chapman) patriotic colored cards of military personnel; set of six.

J. I. Austen. One of the more interesting and historically significant postcard sets printed in America was the series (#A-300s) of 24 cards devoted to *America's Famous Men.* A large inset of the individual is surrounded by patriotic motifs. This is another set worth obtaining.

J. Koehler. This early publisher offered a series (#A20s) of American patriotic symbols.

J. L. Maduro. This Panamanian firm produced an eight-card set on the trial and execution (and aftermath) of the Panamanian liberal General Victorianno Lorenzo in his country's internal war between the conservatives and the liberals. Captured by the victorious conservatives, he escaped and was recaptured. His unpredictable troublesomeness made his execution a certainty. The execution, in turn, made Lorenzo a sort of national hero to later generations of Panamanian nationalists. The eight black-and-white cards include:

#1:	A court-martial view.
#2:	Lorenzo being escorted to the execution site.
#3:	The execution.
#4:	The bullet-riddled body.

#5–#8: Related scenics and multiviews, including one of the later heroes, Ésteban Huertas, who was credited with leading the revolution separating Panama from Bogata.

Individual cards are relatively easy to locate, but the set is rarely seen.

Julius Bien. Issued a *National Flag Series* (#700). Patriotic orientation; color.

Kawin & Co. This American company published what is undoubtedly the best series of postcards ever published about the North Pole discovery. The 40 sepia cards are of two types: artist-drawn and phototypes. All have what looks like a border of snow. Titled *How Cook and Peary Discovered the North Pole*; many have captions, while all are numbered with descriptive writing on the back. Examples of some captions include:

- ☆ *Captain Bartlett and Crew of the Steamship* Roosevelt.
- ☆ *Doctor Frederick A. Cook in Arctic Dress*
- ☆ *Dr. Cook's Eskimo Bodyguard*
- ☆ *Dr. Cook Putting on His Dash to the Pole*
- ☆ *Peary's Ship the* Roosevelt *and Throng Bidding Him Farewell at Oyster Bay*
- ☆ *President Roosevelt Bidding Peary God Speed*
- ☆ *The Steamer* Bradley *Icebound*

A truly historic set of cards, these are usually found individually, but seldom as a group. Highly recommended.

Langsdorf. Produced a pre–World War I set of men in military uniforms in the various branches of the armed services. Nice set; colorful.

L.L. This producer offered a sepia series of numbered reproductions of paintings from the museum at Versailles. Many are of Napoleon.

L. R. Conwell. Published a beautifully colored unnumbered series of postcards relating to American soldiers with their sweethearts. Each card is titled; intent seems to be both humorous and romantic.

L. T. McDaniel. Published an unnumbered set of colored cards of various monuments in the Shiloh Military Park at Pittsburg Landing, Tennessee.

Millar and Lang. Produced a lettered and numbered set (X-1 to ?) of colored, real-photo-type cards of military uniforms in the British Army. Pre–World War I.

National Souvenir Company. Offered a set of eight cards with a patriotic, sentimental motif. Cards are in color and include a few related to American armed conflict.

N. D. Phot. Produced the following:

- ☆ A black-and-white numbered set of painting reproductions of Napoleon.
- ☆ A numbered series of sepia cards on famous persons (royal, military, social, political).
- ☆ Also, a real-photo-type numbered series similar to the series on famous persons, but from artifacts at the Louvre (stationery, paintings).

Paul Finkenrath (P. F. B.). This German publisher issued a #200 series of metamorphics of national and military leaders. Pre–World War I; some are most difficult to locate.

Penn Publishing Company. Issued two series (#1 and #2) about *Fun in the Navy.* Six cards in each set.

P. F. Volland & Company. Produced a #400 series of patriotics that includes people and symbols; more than ten cards.

P. J. Plant. Produced several numbered pre–World War I series (#1 to ?) of U.S. military cards. Published 1904–1910, the cards are a mixture of black-and-white and colored scenics relating to life at camp, romance, military duties, and recreational activities. Both soldiers and sailors are shown in these sometimes-humorous illustrations.

Post Fund (Soldier's Home, California). Issued an unnumbered set of cards related to the California Soldier's Home. These colored cards, believed to number at least 12, include pictures of the various buildings and overviews of the facility. This is a scarce set, as Soldier's and Sailor's cards are generally found individually rather than as a set.

Raphael Tuck. Various sets include:

- ☆ Educational series #404 of artist-drawn colored, embossed cards depicting pre-1920 representative ranks and organizations of the American Army; 12 cards; scarce.
- ☆ Empire #200 series dealing with pre–World War I Royal Navy ships; undivided backs.
- ☆ Oilette series #3041, *Military in London,* dealing primarily with king's guards; artist-drawn (Gerald Hudson).
- ☆ Oilette series #6412, *Military in London,* the London Guard; artist-drawn (Harry and Arthur Payne).
- ☆ Series #159 for Independence Day; 12 cards.
- ☆ Series #1076, *U.S. Navy,* about the Navy and its ships; 6 cards.
- ☆ Series #2323, *U.S. Navy Cruisers;* 6 cards.
- ☆ Series #2324, *U.S. Navy Battleships;* 6 cards.
- ☆ Series #2325, dealing with American naval vessels (one, for example, is of sailors on a revenue cutter, firing handguns, titled "Pistol Drill").
- ☆ Series #2326, *U.S. Navy;* 12 cards.
- ☆ Series #2435, *U.S. Navy Cruisers;* 6 cards.
- ☆ Series #2436, *U.S. Navy;* 6 cards.
- ☆ Series #2500, a pre–World War I group titled *U.S. Army Maneuvers;* colored.
- ☆ Series #2510, *Heroes of the South,* dealing with the American Civil War. Six artist-drawn, colored cards dedicated to pictures of Robert E. Lee and "Stonewall" Jackson; difficult to locate all 6.
- ☆ Series #3578 (Oilette), *Trooping the Colours.* British king involved with the army and his guards; 6 cards.
- ☆ Series #6600, which featured the "Nelson Centenary."

☆ Series #8800 (Oilette); 6 cards on military mascots.
☆ Series #9100, *The Rise of Our Empire Beyond the Seas*; scenes of British conquests and glory in bygone days; artist-drawn; color.
☆ Series #9132 (Oilette), *Deeds of British Heroism;* famous deeds pre–World War I.
☆ Series #9134 (Oilette), *British Battles.* Paintings of historic battles done by the famous artist R. Caton-Woodville.
☆ Series #9135 (Oilette), extension of the *British Battles* series.
☆ Series #9137 (Oilette), *Eventful Nelson Incidents;* scenes in the life of England's greatest sailor. Artist-drawn (Robert H. Smith).
☆ Series #9237 (Oilette), titled *Japanese Navy*; colored; 6 cards.
☆ Series #9624, *Our Ironclads,* English battleships; 6 cards.
☆ Unnumbered series for Confederate Memorial Day; Southern heros, scenes, and symbols; 12 cards.
☆ Unnumbered series, *Arlington National Cemetery;* colored.
☆ U.S. Naval series similar to American Army series.

Rose Company. Produced a patriotic set of at least six colored cards of famous Americans (George Washington through Theodore Roosevelt).

S. H. Kress & Co. Published a numbered (#217700–?) series of at least 50 cards of pre–World War I U.S. ships. Included are submarines, battleships, cruisers, and dreadnoughts; there are also action scenics. A very colorful group that has descriptive information on the back of each card. Nice artistic and educational series.

S. I. P. Published a numbered series on Emperor Napoleon, colored and tinted. All are reproductions of paintings in the museum at Versailles. Within this grouping are also postcards related to the French Revolution and other topics.

Taggart. Produced an embossed series, #602, for Memorial Day. Patriotic slogans and songs.

Also produced a #39000 series of cards relating to the North Pole discovery controversy. Included are cards on:

☆ Commander Peary
☆ Dr. Frederick A. Cook
☆ Encampments, exploits, and other things
☆ Eskimos
☆ North Pole terrain
☆ Ships used by these explorers

Valentine Souvenir Company. Produced a numbered (#217726) series of cards on U.S. naval vessels.

Washington's Birthday Series. The following are series, by various publishers, relating to Washington's birthday:

☆ *Anglo American.* A numbered series (#725/1–?).
☆ *International Art.* Series #51766, artist-drawn (R. Veenfleet); eight cards.
☆ *International Art.* Series #16209, set of artist-drawn (Ellen Clapsaddle) cards.
☆ *L & E.* Series #2200.
☆ *Nash.* Series #W7.
☆ *Nash.* Series #W19.
☆ *Raphael Tuck.* Series #124; six cards.
☆ *Raphael Tuck.* Series #156, set of six.
☆ *Santaway.* Series #152.
☆ *Taggart.* Series #605, set of six.

West Point Series. The following are series, by various publishers, relating to West Point:

☆ *A. C. Bosselman.* Published two sets (an #8000 and a #9000 series) of cards on West Point.
☆ *Albertype Company.* A group of numbered cards.
☆ *American News Company.* At least three sets of cards about West Point: a #5000 series, a *C* series, and an *M* series, and many individual cards on the same theme.
☆ *B. Rose.* #39000, #45000, and #48000 series.
☆ *Bryant Union Publishing Company.* Many cards (both numbered and unnumbered) on West Point.
☆ *Detroit Publishing Company.* A number of series relating to West Point (#5600, #9300, #9600, #70000, #71000).
☆ *Hudson Day Line.* Numbered series.
☆ *Hugh Leighton Company.* #1000, #5000, and #7000 series.
☆ *Raphael Tuck.* Series #2322.
☆ *Raphael Tuck.* Series #2502.
☆ *Rotograph.* Series #2000.
☆ *Ruben Publishing Company.* Various series.
☆ *Rotograph.* #2000, #A2000, and #G2000 series.
☆ *Valentines.* #202000–#207000 and #211000 series.

Wild and Kray. Published a set of numbered (#640s) artist-drawn (G.B. Rowlandson) cards of pre–World War I British regiments.

William Ritchie. Published a numbered series (#100) related to regiments in the British Army.

Woolstone Brothers. Produced a Milton 500 series of six cards about the *Life of Nelson.*

Anonymous. The following sets and series are by anonymous publishers. Origin is indicated when known.

☆ American. A lavish artist-drawn series titled *Historical Series.* Concerned with significant events in American history, beginning with the American Revolution. Cards are numbered and colored.
☆ A French set of artist-drawn sketches (Georges Henri Hautot) of French soldiers.
☆ A series (#104) on *Active Army Life.* Over two dozen cards with patriotic red-white-and-blue borders.
☆ A series (#593) titled *Sailor Lovers.* Colorful cards are pre–World War I and contain six in the series.

☆ A series (#596) of 12 color designs titled *Soldier Lovers.* Scenes show soldiers in obvious romantic situations. Whimsical, as are most of this type.

☆ A series (#2205) of ten artist-signed (Witt) cards titled *I Wish I Were a Soldier.*

☆ A series of card drawings by artist Maurice Milliere titled *Life at the Indian Camp.*

☆ A set of ten artist-drawn (Cenni) colored cards of Italian troops in action. The delicate coloration is a visual delight, while the cards themselves relate information about the pre–World War I Italian army (1901). The publisher and artist are both believed to be Italian. A highly recommended set.

☆ A set of 40 postcards of Colonial heroes. Included are battle scenes of the American Revolution, cameos of heroes, patriotic symbols, ceremonies, and other scenics and events. A good set for capturing the flavor of patriotic, sentimental America as it was before 1920.

Publishers

A	
A & G Black	British
A. C. Bosselman & Co.	American
Acacia Card Company	American
Adolph Selige	American
Albany News Company	American
Albertype	American
Alexander Manufacturing Company	American
Alexander Manufacturing	
Alfred Manzer	American
A. L. Jansson	Dutch
A. L. Simpson	American
American Art Publishing Company	American
American Art Works	American
American Greeting Publishers	American
American Historical	
American Post Card Company	American
A. M. P.	
A. N. Company, Inc.	American
Anglo American Post P. C. Company	
A. Pearson Company	
Army and Navy Novelty Company	American
Art Company	American
Arthur Livingston	American
A. S. B.	American
A. S. Company	American
Asheville Post Card Company	American
B	
Barton and Spooner	
Berger Brothers	American
Birn Brothers	British
B. K. W. I.	Austrian
Blum and Degen Ltd.	British
Braun Post Card Company	American
Bromley & Company	
Bryant Union Publishing Company	
B. S. Reynolds	American
Burn Brothers	British
Burnham News Agency	American
C	
C. A. Blocher	American
Capitol Souvenir Company	American
Carter's News Agency	American
Cassell	British
Cecil C. Nixon	American
Central Art Gallery	British
Chapin News Agency	American
Charleston News Company	American
Chessler Company	American
Chicago Sunday American	American
Cochran News Agency	American
Collotype	American
C. W. Hughes and Company	American
D	
Davidson Brothers	British
Detroit Photographic Company	American
Detroit Publishing Company	American
D. Goldberg	American
D. J. Voorhees	American
E	
Ebers-White	American
Edgar Schmidt	
Edward H. Mitchell	American
E. F. A.	British
E. F. Otis	American
Enrique Muller	American
E. P. Charlton	
F	
F. Chapeau	French
Forbes Lithograph Manufacturing Company	American
Forson Brothers	American
Frank D. Kelley	American
Franz Schneider	Austrian
G	
Gabriel	
Gale & Polden	British
Galveston Wholesale News Company	American
Garrison Toy and Novelty Company	American
George Falkner & Sons	British
George J. Davis	American
George W. Buohl	American
Gibson Merchandise Company	American
Golden Gift Shop	American
Graycraft	American
Guggenheim	
G. W. Morris	American
H	
Hamptons Magazine	
Hans Pernat	German
Henderson	American
Hennessy	American
H. H. Stratton	American
Hill Brothers	American
Hoke Drug Company	American
Hong Kong Pictorial Postcard Company	Hong Kong
H. T. Cook	American
Hudson River Day Lane	
Hugh C. Leighton and Valentine Company	American
Hungerford-Holbrook Company	American
I	
I. & M. Ottemheimer	American
I. L. Eno	
I. M. Cline	American
Imperial Cigar and Tobacco Company	American
Imperial Greeting Card Company	American
Inter City News Agency	American
International Art	American
The Interstate Company	American

J

James Hendrickson	American
J. I. Austen	American
J. Koehler	American
J. L. Maduro	Panamanian
J. Miesler	German
John J. Keyes	American
Johnston's Art Stores	
Joseph F. Morsello	
Jos. Schmidt	German
J. P. Walmer	American
Julius Bien	American
J. Winsch	American

K

Kawin & Company	American
Keliher	British
K. G. H.	German
K. H. G.	German
Koch News Company	American
Koelling & Klappenbach	American

L

L & E	American
Lange and Schwalback	American
L. H.	French
L. Klement	German
L.L.	French
Longshaw Card Company	American
Lounsbury	American
L. R. Conwell	American
L. T. McDaniel	American

M

Manhattan Post Card Publishing Company	American
Manson News Agency	American
Marken & Bielfeld	American
Martin Harpich	German
Mather Book Store	American
Mebane Greeting Card Company	American
M. Ettlinger and Company	
Millar and Lang	British
Minsky Brothers & Company	American
Misch	British
M. Mraschall	American
Mrs. Howard Grey Douglas	
M. Seeger	German
M. W. M.	American

N

Nach	American
National Art Views Company	American
National Color Company Inc.	American
National Council for Prevention of War	American
National Portrait Gallery, Trustees	British
N. D. Photo	French
Nestor Gianclis Ltd.	Indian
New York Central Lines	American
N. Ferrell	

O

O. T. Reilly	American

P

Penn Publishing Company	American
P. F. B., Paul Finkenrath	German
P. F. Volland & Company	
Photo Arts	American
Pictorial Newspaper Company	British
Picture Postcard Co., Ltd.	British
Picture Postcard Company	
P. J. Plant	American
Post Exchange, U.S. Soldier's Home, Washington, D.C.	American
Post Fund, Soldier's Home, California	American
Prudential Insurance Company	American
P. Sander	American

R

R & R News Company	American
Raphael Tuck and Sons	British
Red Cross	American and others
Reinhardt	Germany
Reuben Publishing Company	American
Rochester News Company	American
Rose Company	American
Rosin & Company	American
Rotary	British
Rotograph Company	American

S

Sabold-Herb Company	American
S. & S. News Agency	American
Santway Photo-Craft Company, Inc.	American
S. H. Knox & Co.	American
S. H. Knox & Company	American
S. H. Kress	American
Shrevesport News Agency	American
S. I. P.	French
S. Langsdorf	American
Souvenir Post Card Company	American
Spangenthal's Wholesale	American
Standard Printing Company	American
Stanley A. Piltz	American
Stengal and Company	German

T

Taggart	American
T. Brudmann	German
Teochrom	
Tichnor Brothers	American
Tom B. Johnson	American
Tomlin Art Company	American

U

Ullman	American
Underwood and Underwood	American
Union News Company	American

V

Valentine & Sons	British
Valentine Souvenir Company	American
Van Ornum Colorprint Company	American
V. O. Hammon Publishing Company	American

W

Washington News Company	American
Wayne Novelty and Publishing Company	American
Weiner News Agency	American
Western Publishing	American
Wezel & Naumann	German
W. H. Stockbridge	
Wild and Kray	British
Wilhelm Kleinschmidt	German
William Ritchie	British
Williamsburg Post Card Company	American
W. J. Harris	American
W. L. Erwin	
W. M. Cline Company	American
Wm. Weiss & Company	Bermudan
Woodcock Manufacturing Company	American
Woodgifts	American
Woolstone Brothers	
The World Post Card Company	American
W. T. Baker	
W. T. Lattig and Company	

Artists

Although there were a large number of artists at work during this lengthy period, most did not make their identity known. Of those who did, the following seemed to be the more prominent:

Lt. Robert Batey
C. Becker
N. Berand
Francis Brundage
C. Bunnell
W.F. Burger
Captain Ben Caldwell
Chapman
Ellen Clapsaddle
B. Conti
H. B. G.
E. A. Holloway
Gerald Hudson
J. McNeill
F. O'Beirne
Arthur Payne
Harry Payne
Robert H. Smith
R. Veenfliet
Alexander Wilke

U.S.M.A. Detachment acting as escort to secretary of war; Commencement Day, 1907, West Point. American News Company. R2

Cadet Chapel, U.S. Military Academy, West Point. Curt Teich. R2

Birthplace of Douglas MacArthur. Inter-City News Agency. R1

Brigata Pavia remembrance card. Italian card. Anonymous. R4

Soldier from German Cavalry Regiment #5, pre–World War I, in Düsseldorf. J. Miesler. R4

German kaiser parade, 1897; as was always the case in affairs involving Wilhelm II, the military was well represented. Jos. Schmid. R4

Chinese Soldiers, pre-1920. Kingshill. R3

Hundred-year defeat of Napoleon; insets are of Prussian rulers. N.P.G. R4

The new M-1 rifle being tested during 1st Army maneuvers at Plattsburg, New York, 1939. Anonymous. R2

"Major-General Leonard Wood at the Virginia Military Institute on Graduation Day"; pre-1920. McCrum Drug. R3

Chinese regulars protecting an arsenal; Chinese Civil War, 1911–1912. Anonymous. R4

Northern soldiers occupying a fort at Woosung; Chinese Civil War, 1911–1912. Anonymous. R4

"Major Marina Raskova, Hero of the Soviet Union." She was one of three Soviet women who flew nonstop from Moscow to the Far East in 1938. She later commanded an Air Regiment during World War II. Foreign Languages Publishing House. R4

Happy New Year from the German Army, 1901. Wilhelm Steinberg. R4

"A Daughter of the Regiment" (embossed). Decoration Day series #2. Anonymous. R3

"Killed during fighting at Hankow"; Chinese Civil War, 1911–1912. Anonymous. R4

"Service of Love," pre-1900. Bavarian Soldier's Postcard, 3rd Infantry. R4

"Christmas Greetings; Maurading Chunchuses" (the Chunchuses are a bandit people of noted ferocity); pre-World War I. Raphael Tuck. R3

Austrian crown prince Ferdinand with Austrian Admiral Anton Haus, pre-World War I. J. Deil. R5

Reichspresident von Hindenburg, 1930s. Anonymous. R3

Italian-Turkish peace treaty, 1912. Anonymous. R4

"Man Wanted." Anonymous. R2

General Charles "Chinese" Gordon monument in Chatmam. G. D. & D. R2

"Ship's Company, U.S. Training Ship Constellation *in Newport, R.I.," pre-World War I. C. D. Dadley. R3*

King George V shaking hands with "Shorty" Schirm aboard ship. Anonymous. R4

Austrian emperor and crown prince (Archduke Franz Ferdinand) at a military parade, pre-World War I. J. Deil. R4

Napoleon Bonaparte, metamorphic; note the military personnel composing his head. E.L.D. R4

A U.S. Navy trainee, pre-world War I. Anonymous. R2

"Present Arms," a new twist on an old theme, pre-1900. P. J. Plant. R3

Decoration Day series #107. Raphael Tuck. R2

U.S. Battleship Ohio, *1908. Enrique Muller. R2*

Japanese emperor with crown prince observing grand army maneuvers, 1919; special cancellation. Anonymous. R4

Surrender of Cornwallis at Yorktown, October 19, 1781. Historical Series, #1. R2

Bismarck and von Moltke in 1866. Anonymous. R4

A detailed and interesting pre-1900 sketch of Bismarck. Hildebrandt. R4

Bismarck, The Great Century *series, #132. R3*

"300 days left in the army," used in 1902. Henrich Worringen. R4

Greetings from German maneuver field, pre-1900. Anonymous. *R4*

Views of a German military base, pre-1900. Von Reinhardt. R4

American Legion Convention, October 6-9, 1930, Boston, Massachusetts; poster-type. Forbes Lithograph Manufacturing Company. R3

"Comrades in Arms." Series 593, Sailor Lovers. *R2*

"Decidedly Military," 1904. A. L. Jansson. R2

Hundredth anniversary of German Death's Head Hussars Regiment. Von Wilhelm Kleinschmidt. R4

"General Sam Houston's First Residence, Houston, Texas." Anonymous. R2

"Rest." P. J. Plant. R2

U.S. Naval instruction. Gold's Art Studio. R2

Lord Nelson's monument at St. Paul's Cathedral in London. Anonymous. R1

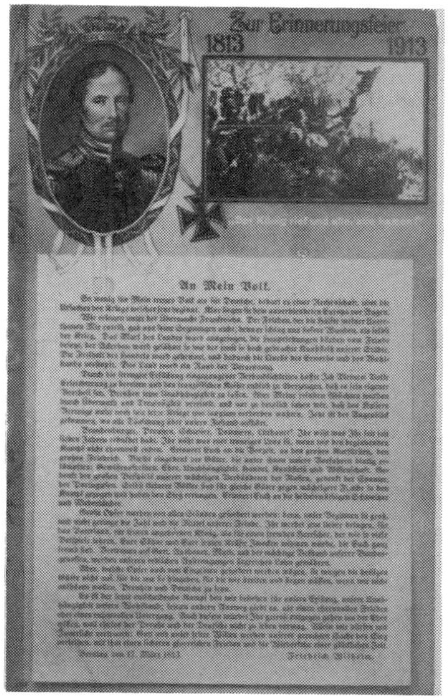

Hundredth anniversary commemorative of the defeat of Napoleon. Gustav Liersch. R3

Hundredth anniversary of birth of Bismarck. Gustav Liersch. R4

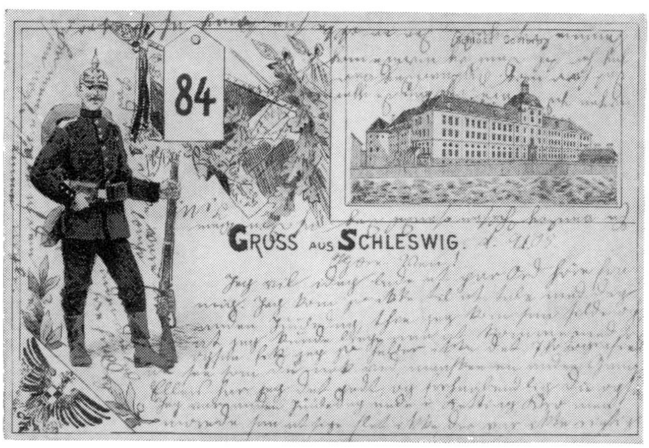

"Greetings from Schleswig," German. Anonymous. R3

The Alamo. Raphael Tuck. R2

Military Academy, Poughkeepsie, New York. Valentine & Sons. R1

"State, War and Navy Departments, Washington, D.C." Rosin and Company. R1

"Main Entrance to Bancroft Hall, U.S. Naval Academy, Annapolis, Md." Curt Teich. R1

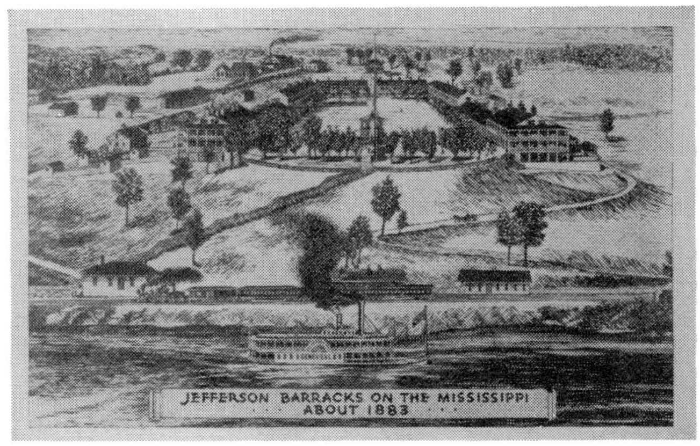

"Jefferson Barracks on the Mississippi—About 1833." Anonymous. R2

"Commanding Officer's Quarters—Jefferson Barracks, Mo." Anonymous. R2

"'On Parade', Jefferson Barracks, Mo.," circa 1915, St. Louis News Company. R2

"United States Naval Training Station, Newport, R.I." Albertype Company. R2

Napoleon viewing the battle. S.I.P. R2

Emperor Franz Joseph with his staff on maneuvers, 1907. Rotophot. R3

General Moses Cleveland, founder of Cleveland, Ohio. Cleveland News Company. R1

Napoleon the emperor. S.I.P. R2

Napoleon on his way to exile. Raphael Tuck. R2

An overweight ex-emperor on Elba. Giovanni Sassi. R2

Napoleon with his adoring army. Museum of Versailles. L.L. R2

Napoleon with his devoted followers, Museum at Versailles. S.I.P. R2

Marriage of Napoleon and Marie-Louise. Museum of Versailles. L.L. R2

Napoleon taking control. Museum of Versailles. L.L. R2

Napoleon playing the role of parent. B. K. W. I. R2

The classic pose. Museum of Versailles. L.L. R1

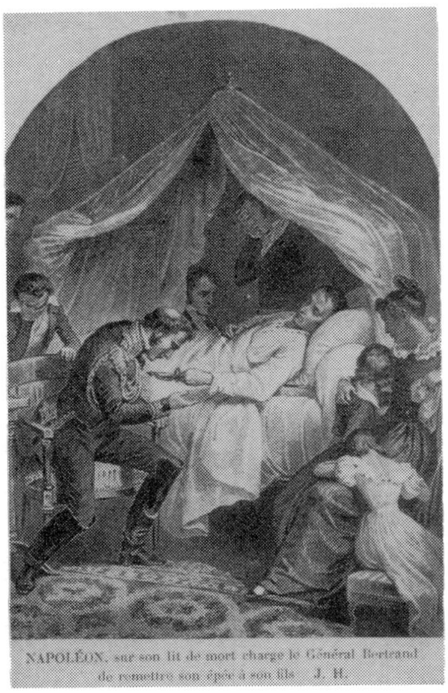

Death of Napoleon. Anonymous. R2

Captain Garcia Hernandez, pre-Spanish Civil War hero. R3

Captain Rodriguez, co-conspirator with Hernandez. R3

"U.S. Sailors Life 'Marines Drill,'" pre-World War I. International Post Card Company. R2

Representation of Joan of Arc. Anonymous. R3

Idealized statue of Joan of Arc. D. Saudinos-Ritouret. R2

Monument at Nantes to Joan of Arc. F. Chapeau. R1

Joan of Arc in warrior's armor. N.D. R1

Joan of Arc as the simple, pious maid. The Louvre. N.D. Phot. R1

Joan of Arc receiving her heavenly vision. Anonymous. R2

Insets of General Ulysses S. Grant, his cabin, and Grant's Tomb. Educational Series, Rose Company. R2

American Civil War general George Meade and corps commanders at Gettysburg, Pennsylvania. A. C. B. & Company. R2

Civil War general Hooker with staff, Lookout Mountain, Tennessee. L. M. Mullinix (Tichnor Brothers). R2

Civil War Union soldiers on the Petersburg front, massing for the final breakthrough. Mayer Post Card Company. R2

General Robert E. Lee and Traveler at Gettysburg. Blocher's (Tichnor Brothers). R1

Boyhood home of General Pershing, La Clede, Missouri. Woodgifts. R1

Colonel George Goethals, chief engineer of Isthmian Canal Commission; autographed. J.L. Maduro, Jr. R3

John H. Bliss, Civil War private; autographed on reverse. Anonymous. R3

Governor Hughes of New York and General Grant at Pine Camp, New York. Hungerford-Holbrook. R2

The famous engine General, *used against the U.S. Confederate army. W. M. Cline (Tichnor Brothers). R1*

"Old Bloody Lane, 1862; Antietam Battlefield Where the Dead Lay Two Deep." O. T. Reilly. R2

"Commodore Perry at the Battle of Lake Erie." Anonymous. R3

Officers Quarters, Ft. Sill, Oklahoma. S. H. Kress. R1

Soldiers and Sailors Monument, Madison, Indiana, with insets of sculptor and donor. W. W. Crozier. R3

Monument of Lord Nelson; souvenir of Trafalgar Day. Beagles. R2

"Statue of Lafayette, Donated by John Wanamaker—Lafayette College, Easton, Pa." Mebane Greeting Card Company. R1

Yeomanry *series; "Prepare to Mount." Davidson Brothers. R3*

Yeomanry *series; "Roll-Call. 5:45 A.M." Davidson Brothers. R3*

Yeomanry *series; "Action!" Davidson Brothers. R3*

Yeomanry *series, "Lemon Cutting." Davidson Brothers. R3*

Italian army series of 1901; painted by Cenni; 10 cards. Anonymous. R3

Italian army series of 1901; painted by Cenni. Anonymous. R3

"A scene at Fort Oglethorpe"; the last days of cavalry, pre–World War I. D. R. Weill. R2

Drum beaten at the Battle of Lexington. Anonymous. R1

"The Constitution (Old Ironside)." Reichner Brothers. R1

U.S. Army Military Tournament (the largest ever held up to 1908) at St. Joseph, Missouri; Hospital Corps contest. Samuel Stone. R4

"Church Parade, 4th Can. Engineers, Point St. Charles, Montreal." Valentine & Sons. R2

A group of Chinese soldiers, pre-World War I. Anonymous. R3

A 30-caliber machine gun in training action. Dexter Press. R2

Soldier's greeting, military souvenir. Anonymous. R3

Prussian defeat at Maxen by the Russians in 1759. Max Gläser. R4

Peace memorial in Toronto; Liberty is seen with the wings of an angel, but the swords of war seem to be executing man's judgment rather than that of God. Jack H. Bain. R1

Postscript

As the illustrations in this book aptly demonstrate, postcards are and always have been a mirror on the world, its peoples, and its events. Moreover, postcards illuminate and highlight, and they are both general and particular in their instant analyses of the world.

A subject of which authors and readers alike never seem to tire is that of *war.* Humankind is alternately delighted and anguished about war as it peers into the face of bravery and glimpses death as the sometimes backside of heroism. The marriage of postcard and war has been defined as uplifting when viewed from the angle of glamour, but it is equally valid at displaying carnage and casualty. Battle is what the postcard says it is: acquisition and destruction, homesickness and pride, courage and cowardice, politics and the military, filled with ideals, yet devoid of what they represent.

If you've reached this observation, the author will think his efforts worthwhile. Perhaps the day will arrive when we'll regard war as solely a topic of historical study and never again as an ever-coming event.

It is hoped that these pieces of pasteboard have been instrumental in demonstrating that the *result* of conflict is the *beginning* of conflict.

Bibliography

Bernhard, Willi. *German Picture Postcard Catalog, 1870–1945.* Hamburg: Willi Bernhard, 1972.

Blemenson, Martin. *Patton: The Man Behind the Legend, 1888–1945.* New York: William Morrow and Company, Inc., 1985.

Book of History, The. Vol. 7. Danbury, Connecticut: The Grolier Society, 1920.

Bowan, Ezra, et al. *The Epic of Flight.* Alexandria, Virginia: Time-Life Books, 1980.

Burdick, J. R. *Pioneer Postcards.* Franklin Square, New York: Nostalgia Press, 1956.

Carver, Sally. *American Postcard Guide to Tuck.* Brookline, Massachusetts: Carve Cards, 1977.

Chant, Christopher, et al. *Hitler's Generals and Their Battles.* Secaucus, New Jersey: Chartwell Books, Inc., 1976.

Claire, Israel Smith. *Library of Universal History, Volume XIV.* Union Book Company, 1908.

Coy, Harold. *The Mexicans.* Boston and Toronto: Little, Brown & Company, 1970.

Cram, George F. *Pictorial Atlas Illustrating the Spanish-American War.* Chicago: Robert Grainger Press, 1899.

Daniells, Arthur G. *A World in Perplexity.* Hagerstown, Md.: Review and Harold Publishing Assn., 1918.

Davis, Richard Harding. *Real Soldiers of Fortune.* New York: Charles Scribner's Sons, 1914.

Davis, Richard Harding, et al. *The Russo-Japanese War.* Peter Fenelon Collier & Son, 1904.

Duncan-Clark, S. J., et al. *History's Greatest War.* E. T. Townsend, 1919.

Duval, William, and Valerie Monahan. *Collecting Postcards in Color, 1894–1914.* Poole and Dorset, England: Blandford Press, 1980.

Fitzlyon, Kyril, and Tatania Browning. *Before the Revolution: Russia and Its People Under the Czar.* New York: The Overlook Press, 1978.

Gurney, Gene. *Flying Aces of World War I.* New York: Random House, 1965.

Halsey, Francis Whiting. *The Literary Digest History of the World War, Volume I.* New York: Funk and Wagnalls Company, 1920.

Hammerton, Sir John, and Harry Elmer Barnes, eds. *The Illustrated World History.* New York: William H. Wise and Company, 1938.

Hewlett, M. R. *Pictons Postcard Catalog.* 4th ed. U.K., 1972.

Holt, Tonie, and Valmai Holt. *Till the Boys Come Home.* Deltiologists of America, 1977.

Horne, Alistair. *The Terrible Year.* New York: Viking Press, Inc., 1971.

Johnson, Rossiter. *The Clash of Nations.* Nashville: Thomas Nelson and Sons, 1914.

Jones, Virgil Carrington. *Roosevelt's Rough Riders.* New York: Doubleday & Company, Inc., 1971.

Kandaouroff, Dimitry Prince. *Postmarks, Cards and Covers: Collecting Postal History.* London: Peter Lowe, 1973.

King, Lt. W. Nephew. *USN: The Story of the War of 1898.* New York: Peter Fenelon Collier & Son, 1900.

Klein, Henri F. *The Standard History of the World.* Standard Historical Society, 1929.

Kull, Irving S., and Nell Kull. *A Chronological Encyclopedia of American History.* New York: Eagle Books, 1952.

Langer, William L. *An Encyclopedia of World History.* Boston: Houghton Mifflin Company, 1972.

Lowe, James. *Standard Postcard Catalog.* 2d ed. Ridley Park, Pennsylvania: Deltiologists of America, 1982.

Lund, Brian. *Picture Postcard Annual.* Nottingham: Reflections of a Bygone Age, 1987.

Magruder, Frank Abbott. *National Governments and International Relations.* Rev. ed. Newton, Mass.: Allyn and Bacon, 1942.

Mahan, Captain A. T. *The War in South Africa.* New York: Peter Fenelon Collier & Son, 1902.

March, Francis A. *History of the World War.* The United Publishers of the United States and Canada, 1919.

Maxwell, Charles. *Causes and Battles of the Colossal War in Europe.* A. J. Humphrey, 1915.

Monahan, Valerie. *Collecting Postcards in Color, 1914–1930.* Poole and Dorset, England: Blandford Press, 1980.

O'Toole, G. J. A. *The Spanish War.* New York: W. W. Norton and Company, 1984.
Parkes, Henry Bamford. *A History of Mexico.* Boston: Houghton Mifflin Company, 1966.
Peck, Anne Merriman. *The Pageant of Middle American History.* New York: Longmans, Green and Company, 1970.
Putnam's Dictionary of Events. New York: G. P. Putnam's Sons, 1927.
Ruiz, Ramón Eduardo. *The Great Mexican Rebellion, 1905–24.*
Russell, Thomas H. *The Great War in Europe.* J. R. Peper, 1914.
Sladen, Douglas, ed. *Who's Who 1898.* London: Adam & Charles Black, 1898.
Source Book, The. Perpetual Encyclopedia Corporation, 1926.
Strode, Hudson. *Timeless Mexico.* New York: Harcourt, Brace and Company, 1944.
Wallis, John Abbot, et al. *The Nations at War.* Syndicate Publishing Company, 1917.
War of the Nation's Portfolio, The. New York: New York Times, 1919.
Whitehouse, Arch. *Heroes and Legends of World War I.* New York: Doubleday & Company, Inc., 1964.
Wilberforce, Archibald. *The Great Battles of All Nations.* New York: Peter Fenelon Collier, 1898.
Wistrich, Robert. *Who's Who in Nazi Germany.* New York: Bonanza Books, 1984.
Wolstenholm, G. *Over 900 Things to Know About Postcard Collecting.* West Yorkshire: West Yorkshire Postcard Centre.
——*Peeps into the Postcard Past.* Mirfield, England: Secretarial Services.
Woodward, David. *Armies of the World, 1854–1914.* New York: G. P. Putnam's Sons, 1978.

About the Author

Jack H. Smith's keen interest in world history led him to select that field of study in college, and his preoccupation with the exploits of governments and their rulers did not end when he received his bachelor's degree in secondary education.

He is now an avid collector of postcards as well as stamps, autographs, antique books, medals, coins, paper money, and historical documents.

Military Postcards, 1870 to 1945 is Jack's second book devoted to the subject of collectible postcards. His first title, *Royal Postcards,* is also available through Wallace-Homestead Book Company.

A third-generation Oklahoman, Jack currently resides in Cincinnati with his wife, Sherry, and their daughter, Shanna.